CRETE

N SEA

3 Bty's
1941

Seige of Tobruk.

2 Bty's
1941
Crete.

Alexandria

Sollum · Mersa Matruh   Galal
Fuka
EL Alamein
Himeimat Bir Ridge

CYRENAICA   EGYPT.

Sherwood Rangers.

in North AFRICA.

S·F·H '45

AN ENGLISHMAN AT WAR

With Best Wishes

David.

www.**transworldbooks**.co.uk

AN
ENGLISHMAN
AT WAR

The Wartime Diaries of
Stanley Christopherson DSO MC TD

1939–45

Edited by
James Holland

BANTAM PRESS

LONDON • TORONTO • SYDNEY • AUCKLAND • JOHANNESBURG

TRANSWORLD PUBLISHERS
61–63 Uxbridge Road, London W5 5SA
A Random House Group Company
www.transworldbooks.co.uk

First published in Great Britain
in 2014 by Bantam Press
an imprint of Transworld Publishers

A CIP catalogue record for this book
is available from the British Library.

ISBNs 9780593068373 (cased)
9780593068380 (tpb)

Addresses for Random House Group Ltd companies outside the UK
can be found at: www.randomhouse.co.uk
The Random House Group Ltd Reg. No. 954009

The Random House Group Limited supports the Forest Stewardship Council® (FSC®), the leading
international forest-certification organisation. Our books carrying the FSC label are printed on
FSC®-certified paper. FSC is the only forest-certification scheme supported by the leading
environmental organisations, including Greenpeace. Our paper procurement policy can
be found at www.randomhouse.co.uk/environment

Typeset in 11.75/15pt Minion by Falcon Oast Graphic Art Ltd.
Printed and bound in Great Britain by
Clays Ltd, Bungay, Suffolk

2 4 6 8 10 9 7 5 3 1

Contents

PART III: D-Day to Victory,
June 1944–May 1945

Introduction

IN EARLY JUNE 2004, I was in Normandy with a small group of friends, one of whom was David Christopherson; of our group, his was the only father who had both fought in the war and landed on D-Day, and David was understandably keen to see some of the places where his father, Stanley, had been in action. Knowing my particular interest in the war, he shared with me some of the passages of his father's wartime diaries, which he had brought along. It seemed the Sherwood Rangers Yeomanry had got through D-Day itself without suffering too many casualties, but then had been involved in a particularly tough fight near a village called Tilly-sur-Seules, to the south of Bayeux. By chance we were staying very close by so, together, David and I found our way to Point 103, a hill overlooking the village of St Pierre, where the Sherwood Rangers and Stanley had been sent on 8 June 1944.

They had moved into positions on this piece of high ground using trees as cover. Sixty years on, David and I found the spot easily: a thick line of trees ran off the road to St Pierre and Tilly along a slightly sunken track. From here, along that ridgeline, it required little imagination to picture the tanks and men of the Sherwood Rangers, positioned along there, the hulls of the Sherman tanks on the track, the barrels of their guns hidden by the foliage and branches of the beeches. And from between the trees, there was a clear view down to the villages and the rolling Normandy countryside beyond.

David was both excited and wistful about the discovery. He'd been to Normandy with his father, but only once, some years before, and he'd not asked enough questions. Stanley had passed away 14 years earlier, in 1990, and during his lifetime had not talked to his son much about his war. Now, as we walked the old battleground, it was too late to ask Stanley about his memories of what he'd experienced all those years before.

Walking along Point 103 fired our interest. David explained that his father had served throughout the war, and that he wished he now knew more. The pages of the diary he'd brought with him were just a fragment – there was a mass of it, from 1940 until the end, and mostly transcribed too: Palestine, Tobruk, Alamein, Tunisia, Normandy, Operation MARKET GARDEN, the crossing of the Rhine. David vowed to reread it; I urged him to send me a copy. He was as good as his word.

Together, the diaries amount to more than three hundred thousand words: one of the most astonishing war records I have ever read by a British soldier in the Second World War.

Stanley Christopherson was born in 1912 into a comfortable middle-class family. A large part of his childhood was spent in South Africa, where his father became managing director of Consolidated Goldfields. Father and son were close, and Stanley once wrote, 'I would rather be alone with my father for company than any other man.' From his father he inherited the charming, humorous and optimistic outlook that exudes from his diaries.

Like most boys of his age and class, he was educated in England, first at Locker's Park preparatory school, where one of his many uncles was headmaster, and then Winchester College. By this time, the Christophersons had returned from South Africa – Consolidated Goldfields had an office in London, although Stanley's father was often based in South Africa for long periods.

With the family in England, however, holidays were now spent at their home at Belmont Paddocks, near Faversham. Stanley adored it. Here he was surrounded by family and friends; they played golf, cricket and tennis; they had dogs and horses so there was hunting and shooting, and weekend parties with croquet, after-dinner cards and other games. The Christophersons were nothing if not sociable, and the impression from his early letters and diaries is of an idyllic time that offered no hint of what was to come in the war.

Although Stanley won a place at Oxford, he decided to sail to

South Africa instead, to be with his beloved father. He spent a year out there before returning to England, and in 1935, aged 23, he took up a post with Rowe Swann & Co, stockbrokers with links to South Africa. It was during this time that he joined the Inns of Court, a Territorial Army regiment that recruited not only barristers, but solicitors, stockbrokers and former public-school and Oxbridge men living and working in the City. A cavalry unit, it aimed to train these young men at weekends and at an annual summer camp so that, in the event of war, they should have some military experience.

With the outbreak of war in September 1939, all members of the Inns of Court were immediately called up, although there was never any question of this TA unit ever becoming a regular regiment. Instead, the three squadrons were split up for further training after which the former London professionals would be posted to various yeomanry regiments now mobilizing for war.

Stanley Christopherson began the war as 'acting lance-corporal unpaid' and ended it a lieutenant colonel, commanding the Sherwood Rangers Yeomanry. Almost no member of the Rangers managed to get through the war unscathed, and Stanley was no exception, although he was one of the very few to be still standing at the end. The Sherwood Rangers had an extraordinary war. They began as little more than amateurs – horse- and sport-loving country folk with little understanding of what was about to unfold. A picture of them taken at the 1939 Annual Summer Camp shows them lined up on their horses, Sam Browne belts and riding boots gleaming, looking as though they are heading off to the Boer War of forty years earlier. Six years later, they finished the war as the single unit of the British Army with more battle honours than any other, having fought in the Middle East and North Africa, landed on D-Day, then led the British charge through the Low Countries and into Belgium.

In many ways, the Sherwood Rangers can be seen as a leitmotif of the British Army in the Second World War. They began rooted in an earlier age with little understanding of what modern war had become, but gradually, often painfully, learned the lessons, and evolved into a highly efficient outfit. They were rarely complacent and the diaries repeatedly show the strong desire of officers and men to become a more effective and efficient fighting machine. The transformation over the course of nearly six long years is startling.

Guiding us through this time is Stanley Christopherson. He was 26 when the war began – still young, but old enough to have lost the callowness of youth; by the war's outbreak, he had seen something of the world, had the makings of a career, and was able to view his experiences with a degree of the objectivity that is often missing in the writings of those a few years younger than him. As with the very best diaries, his character shines through: charming, intelligent, thoughtful, and possessed of a great sense of humour.

There is also ambition. From the outset, Stanley wants to become a better soldier. When sent on courses, he is determined to do well and to achieve as high a mark as possible. He wants to move up the ranks and is never more thrilled than when given command of his own squadron. There is ambition for the regiment too. The Sherwood Rangers may have gone to war on horseback, but there is never any question of standing still. One of the most remarkable features of the diaries is the amount of training and analysis of combat that goes on, especially once they have become mechanized and are given a front-line role in 8th Armoured Brigade. The British Army in the Second World War has often been criticized for complacency, and for consisting largely of reluctant conscripts more interested in stopping to drink tea than getting on with the business of defeating the Axis. Stanley's diaries reveal a no less human bunch of soldiers, but an increasingly professional grouping that evolves into one of the finest armoured regiments in the entire British Army.

Yet the Sherwood Rangers never lost their informality – one that drew on their origins as a Yeomanry regiment. Even in north-west Europe, they were recognized by the number of pots and pans dangling from their tanks and the live chickens that often accompanied them – they were still countrymen at heart. Newcomers also commented on how friendly their men were and how easy it was to become accepted. There was little of the spit and polish of regular army units.

Few regiments can have provided as many wartime memoirs as the Sherwood Rangers. Hermione Ranfurly wrote about her husband, Dan, a member of the regiment, in *To War with Whitaker*. Myles Hildyard, another Sherwood Ranger, published his letters home, *It's Bliss Here*, while Stuart Hills gave an account of his time from D-Day to the war's end in *By Tank to Normandy*. Several others from the regiment self-published memoirs, including Padre Skinner, who would prove such a comfort to Stanley during the Regiment's time in north-west Europe. Keith Douglas, perhaps the finest British poet of the war, was another member of the Sherwood Rangers. He wrote a brilliant memoir of the Regiment's time in North Africa, *From Alamein to Zem Zem*.

None of these, however, can rival Stanley Christopherson's diaries for the completeness of the story or the immediacy and lack of self-consciousness. As such, they provide a remarkable record of one man's, and one regiment's, passage through almost the entire war.

Stanley (*left*) with his mother and brother Derrick. December 1919.

Stanley and his father in South Africa, after leaving Winchester.

Stanley (*middle row, second left*) with his friends Tony Farquhar (*top row, far right*) and Clive Priday (*front row, left*). Winchester 1930.

A Note on the Text

Stanley Christopherson was not the finest speller in the world, and particularly when it came to names. Many of those mentioned, including good friends, had their surnames misspelled, or spelled in several different ways. As far as possible, I have tried to give them the correct spelling, but admit I may not always have been entirely successful. The same goes for many of the encampments, stops and small villages, especially those dotted throughout North Africa and Palestine, that are mentioned in the diaries. To give Stanley his due, however, there is often a lack of consistency in the spelling of many such places. Please accept that every effort has been made to locate and provide the correct names, for people and places, and that any errors are entirely unintentional.

Stanley also uses a large number of acronyms: I have included a Glossary (page 519) in which their meanings can be found. Understandably, he mentions friends and family without explanation as to who they are. For the most part, they are referenced more fully in Personalities (page 522).

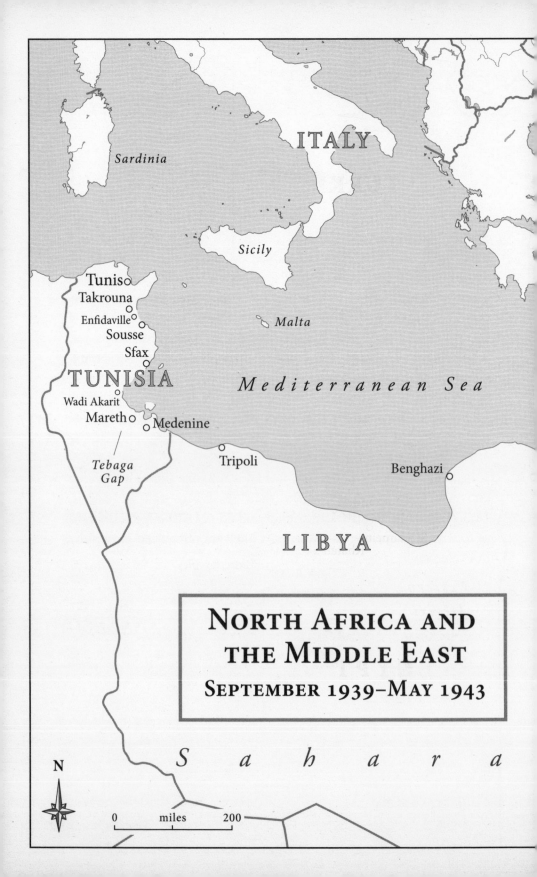

Sardinia

ITALY

Sicily

Tunis
Takrouna
Enfidaville
Sousse
Sfax

TUNISIA

Wadi Akarit
Mareth
Medenine

Tebaga Gap

Malta

Mediterranean Sea

Tripoli

Benghazi

LIBYA

NORTH AFRICA AND
THE MIDDLE EAST
SEPTEMBER 1939–MAY 1943

S a h a r a

N

0   miles   200

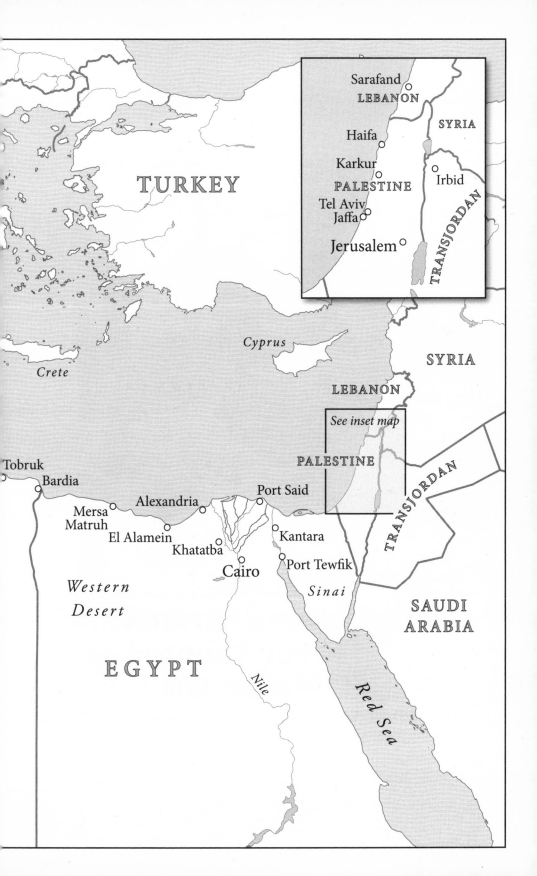

Stanley Christopherson in Tripoli for Churchill's Parade, 1943.

PART I

PALESTINE AND TOBRUK
September 1939–December 1941

1

To Palestine

A contemporary postcard from Palestine.

STANLEY BEGAN his diaries in 1940, but after the war he wrote a brief outline of his pre-1940 war experiences.

At the outbreak of war C Squadron of the Inns of Court was posted to Redford Barracks in Edinburgh. We were the horsed squadron. The two mechanized squadrons, A and B, were posted to Sandhurst.

After a few weeks we were given the choice of nominating the Yeomanry we wished to join. I chose the Scottish Horse because John Seymour-Darling, a very good friend from my time at Winchester College, had already joined. However, this was not to be as I was posted to the Nottingham (Sherwood Rangers) Yeomanry, better known as the Sherwood Rangers Yeomanry, together with Lawrence Biddle, a lawyer in civilian life (and a very bright one), and John Walters, an accountant.

We bade farewell to our friends in the Inns of Court and proceeded to London to purchase our uniform from the regimental tailor and boot-maker. Lawrence and I received orders to report to Malton in Yorkshire, where the Sherwood Rangers were stationed. We boarded a train to Malton, this time attired as second lieutenants, sporting riding breeches, boots and spurs, and tunics. We were slightly apprehensive as we had heard the Regiment boasted three Masters of Fox Hounds and that the pre-war officers were extremely wealthy and very insular.

On our arrival we were interviewed by the adjutant, Captain Gerald Grosvenor, who had been seconded to the Sherwood Rangers by the 9th Lancers. After a formal introduction he said, 'We generally select our own officers, and at present we have a full complement. I should like one of you to become signal officer, to be attached to RHQ.' After a long pause Lawrence Biddle eventually volunteered. One of Lawrence's many hobbies was wireless and any form of signalling, and I am quite certain that he knew more about it than any of the present serving officers. He then told John and me that we should be posted to one of the sabre squadrons.

We soon found that Gerald Grosvenor was a most charming and delightful person. He remained as our adjutant until he rejoined his regiment while we were in the Middle East. He eventually commanded the 9th Lancers and was wounded at the Battle of Alamein, as a result of which he died after the war. I remember so well that he used to say, after he had inherited the title, 'I used to worry about a hundred pounds, now I have to worry about a million pounds.'

At this stage I was very fortunate as a good friend of mine, Michael Gold, whom I knew in the City, heard that I had joined the Regiment and through his squadron leader applied for me to be posted to his squadron, C Squadron. I had simply no idea that he had joined the Regiment the year before.

Much to my delight I found another friend of mine in the squadron, Michael Parish. I knew him in London and we used to ride in Hyde Park before going to work. We had also attended various weekend house parties. I had no idea that he had joined the Regiment a couple of years before the war. Peter and Michael Laycock were also officers in the squadron. We had all been at the same preparatory school, Lockers Park, but I had never seen them since those days. Peter was second-in-command to the squadron and Michael a troop leader. All my fellow officers were very friendly and made me feel welcome.

The other troop leaders were Stephen Mitchell and Dan Ranfurly (The Lord Ranfurly), with whom, for a short time, I had to share 3 Troop.

My squadron leader was Major Donny Player, of the cigarette family. In spite of being very rich, he was friendly, charming, with a grand sense of humour, very fastidious about his dress and appearance, but at the same time an extremely efficient commander, admired and liked by both officers and men of his squadron.

I shared billets with Stephen Mitchell, two rooms in a farmhouse. Before the war he worked for Player's cigarette company. His father's tobacco firm amalgamated with Player's and used to manufacture Three Nuns Tobacco, the brand which I always used to smoke. Each tin had 'Stephen Mitchell' stamped on the outside. I had great pleasure in telling him that every one I smoked added to his family millions, which used to irritate him. Naturally, we became great friends. We discovered that our families had mutual friends, Jim and Rae Wilson from Invertrossachs in Scotland and Tommy [Tammy?] and Jim Hutchinson, also from Scotland. Stephen, too, hailed from 'the wild lands north of England'.

In order to reach the stairs I had to pass through Stephen's bedroom. I noticed that on his dressing table there was a bottle of most expensive hair lotion, which he ordered from Douglas, the Bond Street gents' hairdresser. I could not resist giving my hair an application each time I passed through his room. I justified my action because while I was at Lockers Park an assistant from the shop came down from London to cut the boys' hair, including mine. I did admit to him what I had done and he accepted my excuse with cynical resignation. Somehow he had never noticed.

Stanley is typically generous about the people he met when he joined the Nottingham (Sherwood Rangers) Yeomanry, but there was actually

considerable resentment at the arrival of these new men. John Semken,
who joined the Rangers from the Inns of Court a few months after
Stanley, says they were warned beforehand that they would not be
welcomed with open arms, and that Stanley, Lawrence Biddle and John
Walters had been received quite huffily by the Earl of Yarborough, who
believed it was still up to him to choose the officers for 'his' regiment.
'They worked for a living,' says John Semken, 'and didn't keep horses or
hunt twice a week. They hadn't been to Eton or Harrow, so they had
nothing to talk about and were pretty roughly treated.'

Friday 12 January 1940

C Squadron, Notts (SR) Yeomanry sent their Horse Party to Palestine.
This included all the horses, 21 men per troop, and five officers. Peter
Laycock in command of the squadron, and Michael Laycock, Michael
Gold, Michael Parish, and self.

We had a hearty send-off from Brocklesby – we were the last
squadron horse party to leave. Lady Yarborough and the two girls
came to see us off at the station, and all the remaining officers.

I have left my car at Brocklesby for Lady Diana to drive. She gave
me a copy of Kipling's poems before I left and inside rather a touching note, which said, 'Read this when you are weary. Take care of
Michael and *do*, do take care of yourself.' I do feel sorry for the girl. She
is so overshadowed by her mother, and not being a boy – and possess-
ing neither looks nor personality, her family find no interest in her
and neither father nor mother mind showing it.

We were most comfortable in the train. Michael Parish and I
shared a first-class cabin, and our servants were right next door. Our
first stop was Leicester where the men had tea, and our first casualty
came at 12 o'clock at night. One of Donny Player's chargers, having an
ill-tempered horse next door, was badly bitten, and fell with a very
badly cut head. We had the greatest difficulty in moving the other
chargers into another truck, so that the damaged horse could lie down
at full length. The wretched animal looked a dreadful sight, and the
groans it kept making were terrible to hear. Donny Player had given it

Loading the horses, England, January 1940.

to Michael Laycock as a charger – and Michael was all in favour of shooting it, but we decided against it in the end. We eventually got moving after an hour's delay.

We had another horse down at Redhill, which had kicked its way through the truck and had made a great hole in the wood. We almost had a tragedy there when a horse being led along the platform almost fell on the live electric rail. The fellow who was leading it just managed to pull it back again.

At this time, war had not broken out in the Middle East, but there were good reasons for maintaining a reserve of British troops in Palestine. Although the area had been stable in the 1920s, by the late 1930s it threatened to erupt into violence. The Italians were agitating Arab nationalism. A former ally, Italy, under the Fascist dictator Benito Mussolini, not only formed an alliance with Germany, but with ambitions in Africa and the Mediterranean, looked increasingly likely to enter the war against Britain. Not only was it necessary to suppress any Arab uprising, it was also British strategy to ensure there were enough forces in the Middle East to take on any Italian move against British possessions in the area, including Egypt, which was not officially British but a country on which Britain had a right to depend. In effect, it was a colony in all but name. Not only was Alexandria a vital port in the Mediterranean, the Suez Canal linked Britain to India and the East, while the area as a whole protected vital oilfields in Iran and Iraq. It was also recognized that Britain could mount operations from Egypt and Palestine throughout the Middle East and North Africa.

Monday, 15 January

At 2 o'clock during the night, or I should say early morning, the train stopped and one of the men came along the line and woke me up with the news that a horse in his truck was queer. I put on a pair of gum boots and returned with him, and found that one of the horses had lain down through pure exhaustion. After a little difficulty we got him up again, I returned to bed and the train went on. The horse in question actually belonged to Michael Gold's troop.

We had an excellent breakfast of eggs and bacon, which was most enjoyable. At Valence the train ran over a French soldier who was cut completely in two. Fortunately I did not see the accident. At about midday we were delayed for some considerable time by another train in front that had come off the rails. Michael Laycock and self went down to have a look at the horses. The train started off so hastily we had to clamber into a horse truck and travelled like that for quite a distance.

After one stop, Michael Gold, Michael Laycock and self travelled in the engine for about 50 miles. It really was great fun, and the French drivers were charming and most amusing. Michael Gold, who speaks French perfectly, got on very well with them. We stopped three times during the day, watered and fed the horses and also the men. The arrangements on the whole were very good. At 4.18 that afternoon we arrived at Marseilles; the train then took us on to the village of Au Bagne where we were met by the colonel and Dandy Wallace who is acting as adjutant. Carmichael, the doctor, was also there, all with very depressing news about the discomforts of the Château de la Reynarde, our alleged resting camp. The horses were watered and fed, and the men were given an excellent meal at the station. We slept that night on the train in a siding and very cold it was, as all the heating had been turned off, it having no engine.

Tuesday, 16 January

I was called at 5.45 a.m., being duty officer. The men had breakfast and started unloading immediately. I think that Peter Laycock, as squadron leader, has no idea of organization. The unloading was a dreadful muddle. His capacity for looking after himself is excellent, but not his troops.

At 7.30 I went off with Mike Parish and had breakfast at the Café de la Cours in Au Bagne, which I thoroughly enjoyed. I also had a very excellent wash. I had to return fairly soon to relieve the others who were waiting for breakfast. At 9.15 we started to lead the horses from the station to the Château de la Reynarde, where we are supposed to rest for a week. It was about a four-mile walk. We had heard a few rumours about the discomforts of this so-called château, and they were not the slightest bit exaggerated. The place had not been lived in since 1934. Naturally no kind of heating whatsoever, except a fire in one downstairs room, which was used as a mess. The only furniture in the whole house was a few chairs and tables. The bedrooms mostly had stone floors, and some had no glass in the windows, and each room had 15 or 16 officers. Even each colonel had to share a room with the squadron leaders. Most unfortunately the weather has suddenly turned terribly cold, almost as bad as Lincolnshire. The château holds all the officers of the Brigade, i.e. ourselves, the Yorkshire Dragoons, and the Yorkshire Hussars – that is, of course, the horse party of each regiment. The personnel party will arrive at Marseilles and go straight on to the personnel boat. It seemed a very long walk up to the château especially for the men, who were very weary after the long journey. My troop sergeant, Rodger, could hardly make it, as he had caught a very bad chill. When we eventually reached the camp, we tied up the horses on lines which were already up for us. The rest are in tents.

Wednesday, 17–Tuesday, 23 January, Château de la Reynarde

We had all been informed that the château would be a rest camp. Nothing could be further from it. We were working practically the whole day. Mostly, of course, it was the horses which caused all the work. Unfortunately Marseilles had the coldest spell for 50 years. Every single pipe froze, and we had the greatest difficulty in getting any water at all. All the watering of horses had to be done with buckets at a neighbouring stream and it took a great deal of time. However, they provided us with ample forage, as much bran and hay as we wanted.

Most of the officers complained that the food was quite dreadful, but personally I consider that it might have been very much worse. Unless orderly officer, I was never in for dinner: we all went down to Marseilles every evening for a bath and dinner.

When we arrived we thought that the château was far too full, and that we would try and find somewhere else to sleep. The colonel flatly refused to allow us to sleep either in the village or in Marseilles. Peter Laycock found a barn for himself, Michael Laycock and Michael Gold and told Michael Parish and self that there was not enough room for us, so we looked round for ourselves. With the greatest difficulty we managed to procure a tent, and pitched it on some ground overlooking an encampment of an Indian transport regiment. Both the Indians and their mules made most strange noises during the night, but it was the intense cold that kept us awake. The next night we moved our tent on to the terrace in front of the château. From there we had rather a beautiful view, and what is more we got the sun. However, that day, the camp commandant, a most repulsive major, came into the tent and said to Michael Parish in a cold stern voice, 'Who gave you leave to have a tent? Who gave you leave to pitch your tent here, you insolent young cub?' However, after a few words, Michael managed to smooth matters, and the major told him that the Indian officers were leaving and that we could have their room. So we moved again into a large room in the château with a stone floor and on the door written in chalk 'For the senior Indian officer'. The room possessed a large fireplace, and it wasn't long before our servants procured some coal (I think by stealing) and we had a roaring fire. It made Michael and me laugh to think of our senior officers shivering in the barn while we had a room with a fire. Naturally the place had no lights of any kind, except for a hurricane lamp. However, it's wartime, and it might have been very much worse. The intense cold weather added to our discomfort.

About 5 o'clock each evening we would go down to Marseilles to the Hôtel Louvre et Pays, have a bath and then some drinks, mostly champagne cocktails, and then go off to dinner at one of the very many restaurants. Some evenings we continued on to a nightclub and danced, but since the war, the whole place shut at midnight, and it was quite difficult to get a taxi back again even at that hour.

Mostly we went to a place called Dans. Pat McCraith had fallen very much for a girl who sang there. She really was rather sweet, with a very charming voice, and an excellent dancer. Pat was quite nuts about her. What is more as far as you can tell, her morals were distinctly high. Lovemaking, or anything like that, was quite out of the question, much to Pat's annoyance. I liked another very attractive dark girl there. She danced beautifully. She had large brown eyes and gave one the impression of being very cold. The band there was excellent, so too the cabarets. We always had great fun there, but it shut at 12 o'clock. The Domino was another place which we visited.

On 23 January we left the château, and marched 11 miles with the horses into Marseilles and embarked on the *Rajula* for Palestine. I think most of the Regiment were very pleased to leave the place. Six men out of 21 from my troop went down ill, which meant that most of those left had to lead three horses from the château and the docks. The roads were all ice, so riding was impossible. I had to collect the clearing certificate from the camp commandant, and actually left the château with the doctor in the last ambulance taking the sick to the boat. It was rather sad to see such a place, which not so long ago must have been very lovely.

Tuesday, 23 January, SS Rajula

To start with the sea was pretty rough, which increased the work below with the horses considerably as many of the men went sick. There are six troop ships in this convoy, and we are guarded by two destroyers – Australians, I think.

It is rather an impressive sight, all the six ships on the clear blue Mediterranean headed by the two destroyers – they look so small yet so tigerish!

It's the first time since I joined this Regiment I have got to know officers in the other squadrons. At Brocklesby and at Malton we lived entirely as a squadron and saw very little of the other squadrons. They are not a bad lot but rather inclined to be on the dull side.

Dandy Wallace is acting as ship's adjutant; he is not a bad person.

The doctor, Alex Carmichael, and two other officers have gone down with chills. Personally I think the officers have been very comfortable on this boat. The food has not been at all bad and we have not been really overworked, and for the last two days the weather has been quite perfect. George Hinds, the veterinary officer, has been rather tiresome. He is scared stiff of losing horses, and complained to the colonel that the officers had not been giving enough attention to the care of the horses, which is absolute tripe. We have actually lost two horses and that was through bad luck in each case. The Yorkshire Dragoons in this convoy have lost nine or ten. We have seen them throw them overboard.

Our programme for each day has been as follows: early morning stables at 7 o'clock; breakfast 8.30; stables, water and feed horses 10.30 – generally lasts for about 1½ hours; men's lunches at 12.30, our lunch at 1 o'clock; stables again at 3 o'clock; men's tea at 4 o'clock also ours; finally 'Hay-up' and water 9 o'clock. Rest days we had various parades. Michael Laycock has been in command of our squadron and on the whole has done it pretty well.

Monday, 29 January

This morning at 6 o'clock we arrived at Haifa. Last night we were told that our ship would be the first to unload, and that the horses would start going off at 8 o'clock. Accordingly the men were up at 4.45 clearing up and packing their things. I got up about 6 o'clock. As usual, all previous orders were cancelled and the ship carrying Yorkshire Hussars went in before us. That meant that we should do nothing until four o'clock in the afternoon. However, it is just about 9 o'clock now, and it is almost certain that fresh orders will come through again.

We have been told that we should arrive in the rainy season, and we have certainly done that – it has been pouring with rain ever since

5 o'clock. From here Haifa looks larger than I expected. It extends quite a distance on a side of the hill. First thing this morning, our squadron sergeant major, Heathershore, pointed out the hill where in the last war he went over the top 22 years ago. I told him that he would be doing the same in 22 years' time. He really is a grand little man. I told him that after the war he could come as our stud-groom.

My drink bill for the voyage was 30s. I made up my mind not to drink anything, and didn't do so until last night, when we celebrated Jos Abel-Smith's wedding anniversary. After dinner we went and drank with the sergeants. B Squadron has a grand SSM called Cassidy. A true Irishman with a beautiful voice. We made him sing, but he got very tight, and when he went to bed, he insisted on blowing the alarm with the result that most men turned out on deck. Fortunately the colonel didn't hear a thing. He wouldn't have taken a very good view.

Wilfrid Bennet, the second-in-command of the Regiment, who went before us, as advance party, has just come on board. He tells us that as soon as we leave the ship we go to a place called Rehovot to a rest camp for three weeks, where we shall be in huts. After that we go to a place called Gadeira, 90 miles from the coast and our nearest town is Jaffa. He also told us that our address will now be N (SR) Y Palestine, that we can send letters by airmail, which will take a week, as compared with a month, and that Barclays Bank at Jaffa will cash cheques for us.

When we arrive at our final destination we shall be under canvas. What is more we can send a cable home advising families about our address etc. I shall send one immediately I get on shore.

Tuesday, 30 January

I was baggage officer and was responsible for all the luggage, leaving the ship and being loaded on to the train. It was very wearying having to stand on my feet from 6 a.m. to 12.30 p.m.

I was unable to start unloading until all the horses were off, as there was only one gangway. That meant all the luggage had to be rushed off and reloaded without any kind of organization. We then had a long four-hour journey in a most uncomfortable train, from Haifa to Rehovot. We arrived about 6 o'clock in the evening. The Greys sent down lorries to meet us and brought us up to the camp here.

The Greys had prepared all the camp for us and had made the whole place most comfortable. We share the officers' mess with them. The food also is high class. We are billeted in bungalows.

The horse lines are not at all bad, although in the sand it's rather difficult to keep the posts in.

There is a bathroom with a geyser, but at this moment it is not working.

Thursday, 15 February

Today we left Rehovot, and came across country to the camp which has been prepared for us at Latrun by a squadron of the Greys. We left at 10.30 and C Squadron, my squadron, acted as advance to the Regiment.

Being advance guard, all my troop were armed and we led no extra horses; these were taken by the other troops. The first leg was about 15 miles and most enjoyable. Parts of the country were lovely, and reminded me in many ways of South Africa. We passed through one or two Arab villages, which were most quaint, and one quite large town. Their standard of living seems extremely low, and most of them seem to live in abject squalor. When we got on to high ground, it really was a most impressive sight to see the column, stretching for a long way, following on behind. We halted every hour to look round our horses, and lunched off rations at about 1.15. It was very hot as the colonel insisted we should ride with full marching order, including gas masks. We were not allowed to ride in shirt sleeves. After leaving Rehovot we first passed through a little village (Arab) called No-ar-ord. Horribly dirty and mostly consisting of mud huts.

Niara was the next place, also an Arab village but larger, followed by Abri-Thusha, which was considerably larger with very narrow streets and quaint houses. It really was most interesting. After that we left all roads and tracks and went across country. In spite of the heat I thoroughly enjoyed my ride.

We arrived at Latrun just about 4.15 p.m. and after watering and feeding the horses, grooming and shackling, we all went to bed at a very early hour.

Friday, 16 February

On the whole I think we shall be comfortable here – each officer has his own tent, and there is no sharing, thank goodness, as the tents are not too large. In my tent I have a camp bed, a chest-of-drawers, the top of which I use as a wash-hand stand, a folding table, facing the entrance as a desk, a folding chair, and a small stool. When the heavy luggage arrives I shall have my tin box.

The men sleep on palliasses, in large tents holding about 12 men in each. As for our mess, we have two wooden huts, one as a sitting room, and the other a dining room. The officers' tents have a lovely view from the side of a hill, which includes the ruins of Latrun. The site has never been built up except for a few mud huts round the out-skirts in which the Arabs live now.

We have the brigadier and the BHQ with us. They are situated in the monastery just outside Imros.

In the morning we led out the horses. They lasted out the journey very well, and have suffered hardly any ill effects. Their feet were in rather a bad state, and it was a difficult job to pick them out.

In the afternoon we spent our time at stables and cleaning up and getting the camp in order. I went to bed almost immediately after mess.

Saturday, 17 February

Half the squadron led the horses out for exercise, and what remained cleared up the lines. All the troops are expected to make gardens outside their tents, and a prize is to be given by the squadron leader for the best garden at the end of two months. In the afternoon we had a troop leader's conference with the colonel presiding. He gave us some details about our programme here, which I understand is going to be very intensive. On 23 February we start a month of intensive troop training; that means each troop leader will be responsible for the training of his men. The colonel pointed out that the brigadier insists that a troop leader should justify his position, and that if he does not come up to the required standard, there will be plenty to take his place, and that if his men are not trained sufficiently by the end of the period he can expect a 'bowler hat'. Actually I do hope that troop leaders, especially in my squadron, are given very much more independence and scope in the organization and the training of their troops.

The colonel ended by saying that if we did our best and made a success of our job, which was essential, he would be behind us and that we could either come to him or our squadron leader for advice; but all the same I think that he is a difficult man to approach.

At the moment we have done very little real training. None of the men, since the start of the war, have fired a single shot on the range. We have spent all our time moving from place to place. First Grove then Malton, Brocklesby, across France to Marseilles for 10 days, through the Mediterranean, via Haifa and Rehovot for two weeks, until finally we reached our camp here where we shall start our training in earnest. A very good thing. All our time so far has been spent in getting the horses fit.

Sunday, 18 February

After lunch I called a meeting of my section leaders and troop sergeant, gave them an outline of the training programme, and had a general discussion with them. Sergeant Rogers, our troop sergeant, was excellent, in fact the best in the Regiment. My section leaders consist of two reservists and two Yeomen. The two former are very much the better.

I was also informed that I had been made president officer of the Debating Society, and that I should have to organize debates every week. Some of us discussed the matter after dinner and came to the conclusion that if the debates were not too serious, we could have a deal of amusement.

Monday, 19 February

This morning we exercised before breakfast; parade was at 6.15. I told my servant Smith to call me half an hour before parade and, like a fool, he thought parade was at 6.30. I saw the squadron leader leave his tent while I was only half dressed. It needed some quick action and a flanking movement round through A Squadron tents, to enable me to get on parade before the squadron leader. I arrived thoroughly out of breath and it was somewhat of an effort to appear calm and collected to the squadron leader when he came round to my troop – old Mike Parish was in the same position and arrived on parade after me. He received something of a rocket as his troop had to act as advance troop and he had come on parade without a map.

After breakfast we had an hour's saddle cleaning and fixing up our saddle tents, then stables followed as usual. As we left for early-morning exercise old Stephen Mitchell's horse got his hind legs caught up in the guy ropes of his saddle tent. It really was a magnificent sight from where I was sitting on my horse. He just managed to save himself from crashing to the ground. The horses are gradually beginning to look better, and are getting full of life.

We have just come off stables. I must go and have a wash and get ready for lunch.

This afternoon from 2 until 3.15 all the squadron were on cleaning saddles and arranging our saddle tent. Stables at 3.15, after which all the men in the squadron had a hot bath. Water and feed at 4.30 and late feed again at 7.15.

We started Hotchkiss gun classes. Two officers from each squadron have to attend a class under Sydney Morse. Stephen and I represent our squadron.

Some mail arrived today. I received one letter from Mummy, dated 27 January, and one from both parents dated 8 February. I also had a letter from Barbara Congrave, Clive's VAD girlfriend [Clive Priday: Stanley's best friend from Winchester College].

After mess this evening Stephen and I walked over to the horse lines and had a look at our horses. We came to the conclusion that two horse-line guards for the squadron were quite inadequate, and that it would be the easiest thing in the world for the cunning Arab to take horses off the line.

Poor old Michael Parish has collected a few rockets today and is rather afraid that he might get a bowler hat. I gather that our move is a certainty, the date I believe 15 March – the Ides of March. It's bed time, 5.30 call tomorrow.

Thursday, 22 February

Troop feeding of horses starts tomorrow, so I put a fatigue, which included self, on making a cement stand for mixing feeds. Sly, a bricklayer in private life, did some good work but we did not get very far this evening. From 5.30 to 6.30 Hotchkiss gun lectures. Myles Hildyard is most amusing at these lectures. He always has the greatest difficulty in working the gun. Sydney Morse who takes the class is an excellent teacher especially as he only had a five-day course.

The Hotchkiss compared to the Bren is a most clumsy and out-of-date weapon. They have taken our Brens away, given them to the infantry and replaced them with the old Hotchkiss.

We really are very comfortable here. True, we work all day, but the work is interesting, the climate attractive, food excellent, and working out of doors makes all the difference to life.

Friday, 23 February

Last night Donny Player got instructions from Brigade that he should send one of his troops on a reconnaissance patrol to an Arab village about three miles off. He decided to send Dan Ranfurly and prepared the whole thing with him last night. A message came through this morning that Dan had to sit on a court of enquiry and so was unable to go on the patrol. So he told me that I should have to take 2 Troop in place of Dan. It only gave me about half an hour to prepare the whole thing. We paraded at 8.45 and the colonel, Donny and a fellow from Brigade came with us. We should have had an interpreter but he let us down.

The last part of the journey was across cultivated country, and the officer from Brigade told us that we had strict instructions from Brigade not to go over cultivated lands. In spite of that I made a very poor plan. Instead of sending each section round the flanks, I waited until I had arrived at the village before doing that and my line of approach was not very clever. The officer went into the village, and we were received very courteously. They gave us oranges and we gave them cigarettes. We found one Arab who spoke English.

The colonel was very decent and told me that we only learned by mistakes.

Saturday, 24 February–Sunday, 10 March

On Saturday, 25 February, we received instructions from Brigade HQ that no officer was to leave camp until the second-in-command Major Bennett, who is acting colonel while Lord Yarborough is away, had returned from a conference at Brigade HQ. There was much speculation about the reason, and this increased considerably when we had orders that the Regiment should leave at nine hours' notice for an unknown destination, taking the 18 best men and horses from each troop, leaving the remainder and HQ squadron in camp. These are the possibilities of our speculations:

(1) The brigadier was being bloody-minded and this was his idea of training (unlikely over a weekend).

(2) The Australians, who are now in this country, have been causing trouble: one has killed an Arab. We were going to get them out of Tel Aviv.

(3) Trouble between Arabs and Jews at Jaffa and Tel Aviv.

We started early Sunday morning. C Squadron advance squadron and 3 Troop – my troop advance troop (as usual). Our destination was Sarafand, which is about sixteen miles away and might be described as the 'Aldershot of the East'.

We put up our horse line, the men were billeted in some large garage sheds and the officers lived at the Brigade HQ for the Lyder area, which was most comfortable. There was even a fire in the mess after dinner. But still we were not told the object of our visit.

We spent our time doing some training, standing ready to move at a moment's notice. Two days later we were told the reason of our visit: it was in fact to help the civil power on the issue from the Foreign Office of the White Paper on Palestine. They anticipated trouble from the Jews in Tel Aviv and the authorities had us in reserve at Sarafand.

As a result of this White Paper, the Jews are prohibited from buying large tracts of land from the Arabs as a result of which they were gradually but certainly gaining control of the whole place. From this paper it was made quite clear that Palestine could no longer be considered the home of the Jews. On Wednesday, 28 February, much to my irritation, Donny Player decided to send me back to camp to look after the rest of the camp squadron, which we had left behind. Dan Ranfurly, who had been left, had gone sick, also the only remaining sergeant, and Corporal Bond was left in charge.

I left at 6 o'clock in the morning and really had the most enjoyable ride home across country. I took with me Smith, my servant, Gardner, my groom, and Davidson. It was a grand morning, the country looked lovely, and we made excellent time arriving home for breakfast.

Monday, 11–Wednesday, 27 March

Last weeks at Latrun Camp. At one time during this period I suffered from the most frightful toothache, but I was fortunate enough to get into Tel Aviv to be attended by a Professor Gottlich. He is world famous and before being turned out by Hitler he used to practise in Vienna. He certainly cured my toothache by removing three nerves from a back tooth. Before leaving I asked him why it was with his reputation he had not gone to England or America. He replied, 'I am a Jew, and am proud of it. I have been turned out of one country, which was my home. I do not wish that to happen again so I have come here, where I am most happy.' Rather pathetic but very true.

The fun had started while I was away. The Regiment was called out at a moment's notice from Sarafand. Riots had started over the weekend, mostly the students. Curfew was immediately brought in and we were called out to enforce it. Things looked rather bad at one time, and A Squadron under Basil Ringrose, had to make a mounted charge with drawn swords in order to clear the streets and rescue some police who had been cut off. We did not do much damage to any person and suffered not many injuries ourselves, except for a few broken heads and limbs caused through some stones and bricks. Fortunately no horses were damaged at all. Rioting still continued over the next few days, but to a lesser degree. We patrolled the streets mounted during the day, and each squadron took it in turns to patrol in lorries by night. In the end it was a very wearisome and dull job at nights. After a few days the curfew was lifted and we left Jaffa for camp at Latrun again.

In many ways, it is amazing to think that even in the Second World War the British Army were still carrying out mounted charges, with sabres drawn, and yet, of course, mounted police are still used today, albeit using batons rather than swords. Since the Sherwood Rangers were being used primarily as a colonial police force, perhaps it is not so extraordinary after all. This was, however, the last such charge in the Middle East, although mounted troops were still operating in Syria the following year. The last recorded British cavalry charge, with swords drawn, took place on 19 March 1942 when mounted cavalry of the Burma Frontier Force charged Japanese troops near Toungoo airfield in Burma. It ended badly, with most of the 60 men killed, including the commander, Captain Arthur Sandeman.

Easter weekend

Over Easter all the officers and men could take a night off. I went to Jerusalem with Michael Parish and Myles Hildyard. We left on Sunday midday in a hired taxi, which we kept the whole time. On Sunday afternoon we motored down to the Dead Sea with Araminta MacMichael, the governor general's daughter, and a girl called Marion Young. Both are friends of Michael Parish. The Dead Sea and surrounding country I found most attractive. There is a hotel there and a golf course and would be an excellent place to spend a weekend. We didn't bathe.

We went back for a drink at Government House, which is quite beautiful, with the most wonderful view over Jerusalem. Sir Harold and Lady MacMichael were away. Araminta is only 20. Quite attractive, amusing, sophisticated but definitely intelligent, she is engaged to a man called Benson from the Black Watch on the staff of General Wavell. Marion Young, the other girl, is the daughter of the leading chartered accountant in Jerusalem. She, too, is very young, but unlike the other is most unsophisticated. Michael thought her very attractive. Myles did not agree at all. I admitted that while she did not appeal to me personally she did possess quite a pretty face. Strangely enough, the MacMichaels live in Kent at Selling, only four miles from Belmont Paddocks, and are great friends of the Harrises. Araminta did ask me to stay some time. We all went to dine at the King David Hotel. It was not a very late night, and we were in bed by 1 o'clock.

After depositing the girls home we returned to the Eden Hotel which was most comfortable, and really quite reasonable.

Easter Monday – the following day – Myles and I spent wandering about in the old city of Jerusalem, which was really most terribly interesting. We saw the August Sanctuary sacred to the Moslems, the Mosque of Omar and the Dome Rock, where Abraham offered up his son Isaac. One of the most impressive sights was the Palace of Solomon and the vast substructures below the south-east corner of the area, which was later used by the Knights Templar for their horses. We also saw the Wailing Wall, which was most interesting. Quite a few Jews were wailing. We returned to lunch rather late at 2 o'clock to the Eden Hotel where we found that lazy dog Michael Parish still in bed. We excused him for his laziness as a few years ago he had been to Jerusalem. After lunch Myles and I visited the church of the Holy Sepulchre. The church is supposed to have been built on the Hill of Calvary or Golgotha. It is interesting to note that the door-keepers are Moslems, and the post of custodian is hereditary, in a Jerusalem Moslem family. Being Easter Monday we found a procession in the church. It was fascinating and rather stirring to watch. And finally we entered Christ's Tomb over which a priest always keeps watch. I had my St Christopher medal blessed by the priest and sprinkled with Holy Water and was also given a spray from the flowers, which are always kept in the tomb. I found it most impressive.

Arrived back in camp about 6.30. I enjoyed the two days. It was a change. I found some letters awaiting me, one from Ione telling me about her engagement [Ione Barclay was a close family friend]. I was amazed when I read about it.

Stanley mentions General Wavell, who was commander-in-chief of Middle East Command, created in 1939. This was a vast area that covered British interests in the Levant, Egypt and all the way to Persia. He was a highly cultured and competent man, although never quite saw eye to eye with Churchill, who was to become prime minister on 10 May. Incidentally, Myles Hildyard wrote a very detailed and informative letter home about this same weekend.

A few days later, the Regiment was on the move, leaving Latrun for Karkur. While two of the squadrons had stopped near a village to water the horses and get a hot lunch, the horses of C Squadron suddenly stampeded. The men had been eating at a long wooden table near a grove of gum trees when suddenly two hundred horses hurtled towards them. Two horses managed to jump and clear the table, but the rest charged on through, with men leaping out of the way. A number of men were injured – 12 were taken to hospital – several horses were lost for good, and the Regiment was left with a huge bill for damages and no small amount of humiliation.

Wednesday, 3–Tuesday, 23 April

After the stampede they decided that C Squadron horses should be separated from the Regiment. Actually I think it is just likely that the cause of the trouble originated in HQ. However, it was decided that C Squadron would leave. We were sent off to a village called Hadgia about four miles from camp, and occupied the billets and covered standing that the Royals had when they were here. We could not have been more comfortable. The horses were under cover, each troop had two saddle rooms and racks, and the men slept in a block of disused flats. The officers had their mess next door in another block. We had a large room each, and three bathrooms between six of us, also a mess room downstairs. At first we had to have our meals with Brigade at BHQ, which was in the village. We could not very well refuse their invitation to eat with them. Miller, our brigadier, was very much more human and amusing when you got to know him. Our breakfast was cooked by the café underneath and sent up to us, and very excellent it was too. After a time Brigade went on manoeuvre, and we cooked all our meals in our mess. We got Picirini from the camp officers' mess to come and cook. He really is excellent – but I rather dread our mess bill as we did a certain amount of entertainment, and a quantity of drink was consumed.

Parade was usually at 6.15 a.m. and generally we used the ground near the sea for training, which was very excellent for that purpose. At that time of the morning it was lovely and parts of the ground near the sea were simply covered with wild flowers. The birds, too, are quite exceptionally lovely, many of them passing through to other countries. Stables and cleaning parade took up the remainder of the morning. No work on Wednesday and Saturday afternoons except for stables, and on the other weekdays stables followed by a lecture in the evening.

The court of enquiry on the stampede was held at BHQ soon after we arrived there. Lord Grimthorpe was in the chair; Major Townsend from the veterinary hospital and another man were on the committee. I was one of the chief witnesses. We spent the whole day there from nine o'clock until six; while we were waiting we played bridge. The colonel was in much better form when we played bridge. In the end I was not called as a witness for the stampede, which rather annoyed me after having waited all that time. I feel quite certain that they will not be able to find the cause of the trouble. Townsend asked the most intelligent questions, and was quite the live wire of the enquiry.

Karkur Camp, June

During our stay here I have been most slack in keeping up this diary. In fact, except for my stay at the pumping station together with my troop, I have hardly written anything. On the whole it has been quite a pleasant time while we have been here. We finished troop training, squadron training, regimental training, and last week after a three days' scheme we finished brigade training. Next week we move to Acre, in Palestine. When we get there I suppose we go back again to troop training, that is, if we are not sent to some kind of active service.

Six of the officers have got their wives here; they managed to bring them out by the back door. They have all taken houses in the Jewish village across the field, which has been most convenient for them. They sleep out on Saturday night only and are supposed to dine in mess two nights a week. The wives are not recognized out here at all and therefore never appear in camp, which is quite right. In a way it is rather hard on the men when they see that officers have their wives out.

There have been one or two changes in the command. Wilfrid Bennet has left and gone to Division at Haifa. Flash Kellett has taken over command of the Regiment. Basil Ringrose is squadron leader of C and Gerald Grosvenor of A. Dan Ranfurly has left the squadron and has been made machine-gun officer in HQ Squadron, Henry Trotter second-in-command of B Squadron, and Michael Laycock second-in-command of A. Another new addition: each squadron has had two donkeys attached, which have proved most useful in cleaning up the lines. Jack Abdy was fast asleep in the mess the other evening, so Donny Player collected one of these donkeys and brought it into the mess and placed it opposite the chair in which Jack was sleeping. Jack woke up with a start to find himself face to face with a donkey. He immediately waved his hands in front of his face, as if to clear the dreadful vision from before him. It was really a most amusing sight. He has had his leg pulled unmercifully.

The officers' mess was burned down one morning at 3 o'clock. A great deal of wine and food was destroyed, and the cause of the fire will never be discovered. It will make the mess bills rather high. We have since discovered that the mess accounts were in a dreadful state. Joss Abel-Smith has no idea where all the money has gone, and the mess sergeant has turned out a wronger. Donny Player has now taken on the role of PMC [president of the mess committee], and Joss, self and John Walters are on the committee. We have now got another contractor in, and are messing at 4s per day, which is considerable, especially for junior subalterns who are endeavouring to live on their pay. But still at the moment the food is good.

The feeling among the men is not good. The food is rotten since we have been put on a wartime basis, and they are all getting very bored out here, doing comparatively nothing. Most of all, they miss their letters. We have had no mail for about three weeks.

It was Lady Yarborough, the colonel's wife, who led a group of the officers' wives out to the Middle East, which included Dan Ranfurly's wife, Hermione, and Henry Trotter's wife, Rona, among others. This, of course, was not only entirely irregular, but highly inappropriate. They had obtained the destination of the Regiment from the War Office and decided that they would follow their men to war, rather than sitting it out without them back home in Nottinghamshire. 'Rules were for the hoi-polloi,' says John Semken, 'but they weren't the hoi-polloi, so those rules did not apply!'

Tuesday, 11– Friday, 14 June, Power Station, Karkur

Last night we heard over the wireless that Italy had entered the war against the Allies. Mussolini has given as his reason that he had to look after his Mediterranean interests. Italy entering into the war might make all the difference to us out here, but still we shall have to wait and see.

Saturday, 22 June–Thursday, 4 July

The war has developed in a most amazing and unexpected way. Since war started, Germany has gradually annexed the whole of Europe: Czechoslovakia before war, then Poland, Denmark, Norway, Belgium, Holland and now finally we have just heard that France has accepted the crushing armistice terms imposed by Germany, which have been signed in the same railway carriage as the Versailles Treaty. She has done this without any consultation with England, her only ally. This wrong has been well commented on by Churchill. They had no right to accept without first consulting England, however desperate their plight might be. The Germans demand a complete domination of France and her colonies by Germany and Italy, and absolute disarmament. However the French navy and air force are still intact, especially the large French force in Syria. What will happen to them? Will they all come over to us or will they scuttle themselves before handing over all to Germany? Only time can tell. I understand that all British troops are out of France and that more Canadians and Australians have been landed in England to protect her. I do wish that we could see some activity out here but at the moment I don't see it. The gunners attached to the division have been sent to Egypt, and they keep on taking men from this regiment for various other jobs, and as Donny Player and Basil Ringrose are going on courses, and taking their sergeant majors, I don't see that they can call upon us to do anything very active.

Italy's entry into the war and France's surrender changed Britain's position dramatically. At the beginning of the month, the Mediterranean had still been open to the British. Suddenly the French and Italian shores on the northern Mediterranean were in enemy hands, and so, too, was much of the North African coastline to the south; Libya, for example, Egypt's western neighbour, was an Italian colony, while Tunisia and Algeria were French, as was French Morocco. In the eastern Mediterranean, both Lebanon and Syria were also under French control. Not only would this make supplying Egypt and the Middle East much harder for Britain, it also meant the short route to India and the Far East via the Suez Canal was now closed. Furthermore, with Britain still reeling from the loss of France, the last thing she needed was any attack by the Italians into Egypt. Britain's pre-war plans had relied heavily on France's large army, and British re-armament had focused on air power and the navy. With much of the army's equipment left on the beaches at Dunkirk, Britain in June 1940 found herself woefully short of guns, tanks, rifles and other equipment. Meanwhile, in Egypt, British troops amounted to just two divisions of some 36,000 men, and only 27,500 men in Palestine. On paper, at any rate, it seemed some way short of what was needed. In Libya, for example, the Italians already had some 215,500 men.

Tuesday, 25 June

Rather a dull day. Donny has gone for a fortnight's course to the cavalry school so Peter has taken over the squadron. We leave here next week for Acre, trekking all the way so we are giving the horses an easy time. In the evening I went to the camp cinema and saw quite an amusing show called *Five Ways into Tonn*.

Wednesday, 26 June

In the morning I took my section leaders out over the plain and we did some compass work. Renny, who at the moment is acting leader of 1 Troop, was quite easily the most intelligent. In the afternoon Lawrence

Biddle, Basil Ringrose and I went for a swim, which was really enjoyable. We really are most fortunate being so near the sea and able to bathe under such perfect conditions at the government's expense. When news comes through that England is being bombed one rather feels perturbed being here and so well out of the enemy's way. But I suppose in some way we are doing good here.

Thursday, 27 June

At lunch today Lawrence Biddle and I decided that as we had not seen Caesarea and we are due to leave this camp on Tuesday we would make an evening trip there. I took Corporals Brittain and Gardener from my troop and Lawrence brought some of his men. We took beer and sandwiches with us. Without hurrying it took us about 1¼ hrs. We didn't actually go across the desert but skirted the north side. There is no road to Caesarea and you can't get there by car, only on foot and horseback. We arrived just before dark and had a most interesting time looking around. Now it is nothing more than an Arab village but the remains of Herod's palace and St Paul's prison can easily be seen. The palace was right on the sea, which flows over the remains that have fallen to the ground. The wall that the Crusaders built is most fascinating.

We came back another way, i.e. along the seashore, until we struck the river and then turned eastwards. It was a longer way but more pleasant. The sand was hard and it was a lovely night so for the first mile we travelled at a split gallop, great fun. We had the beer and food on the way home and met a police patrol en route. The sergeant in charge told me that a strong current of bad feeling still existed underground between the Jews and Arabs.

We arrived back in camp about 11.15 and found the place a perfect hive of activity. Orders had come through from Brigade that the Regiment should supply a colonel, adjutant, doctor, RQMS, some corporals and I think 40 other ranks. The party had to be ready to move at 6 o'clock the next day for some unknown destination, dismounted. Each squadron had to supply so many men and they took all from my troop and, what is more, they took four of my best men, Corporal Hill, Renny, Lacey and Large. There is a great deal of speculation about the cause of all this. It is pretty certain that Syria or the frontier is their destination but most improbable that they are forming an advance for this Regiment as Flash Kellett has been promoted to acting lieutenant colonel and various other members have been promoted. Nobody seems to know whether they will come back to the Regiment.

Friday, 28 June

We have heard today that the French Army in Syria has had instructions from the Vichy government under Marshal Pétain to cease hostilities against Germany and Italy. This is very surprising after all the assurances we have seen in the press, that the French colonial empire, especially Syria, would fight on. Apparently this caused all the activity last night, and other regiments have done the same. They anticipated that there would be a great influx of French soldiers across the frontier to join up with us so the high command have founded these camps to receive them, taking a number of officers from the 5th Cavalry Brigade.

I went out to dinner with Sydney Morse and his wife. She is a most eccentric and nervy woman, and most anxious to get home, but at the moment she has not got a hope. All the wives out here might find themselves in rather a mess if we should suddenly have to go off to fight. After dinner we were all sitting round having our coffee when the colonel's car drew up driven by Michael Parish. We went to the door to meet him, and were told that the Regiment had to be ready to move at 4.30 next morning. That immediately sent Mrs Morse into a flat spin. I naturally wanted to get back to camp as soon as possible, but had to wait for Sydney to collect all his things and say goodbye to his wife. As it was he had had far too much to drink and our journey back to camp across the fields was most precarious.

I found Stephen Mitchell still in bed as he had not been warned and he was acting squadron leader as Donny is on a course and Peter has taken adjutancy since Tony Holden had gone the night before. We called a conference of troop sergeants, had the men warned, then packed up everything so that we should be ready to move at 4.30 next morning. Reveille was at 2.30 and in the end we managed to get a couple of hours' sleep. Orders then came through that we should not saddle up but that the Regiment, was on an hour's notice. We waited the whole day ready to move at a moment's notice, but of course nothing happened and we have not yet heard the cause of all the trouble, but I gather they wanted us to hold a line on the Syrian frontier. I hear that in order to prevent French soldiers from crossing the frontier, agents of the Vichy government have spread rumours that the British authorities would not receive any French soldiers or arms, and that some French soldiers who had crossed had been fired on. Personally I think there is a very good chance of us now walking into Syria, and I am quite certain that we should do that.

Saturday, 29 June

Today we stood ready to move at an hour's notice. All the men were very weary as they had had practically no sleep for the last two nights. We did absolutely nothing for the whole day except stand by.

Sunday, 30 June

The order came through that we no longer need to stand to, so we proceeded to unpack again. We exercised the horses in the morning and this was followed by stables. After lunch, Lawrence Biddle and I went for a bathe, which was most enjoyable. After such excellent bathing out here, bathing in England will be a very poor second.

2

Mounted Cavalry No More

Guarding the Pong Station.

Tuesday, 2 July 1940

WELL, TODAY WE have had quite the greatest day's shock of the war, for this regiment, anyhow. We were all told that we were going to lose our horses immediately. The colonel gave out this news at an early regimental parade. The reaction was quite extraordinary; our future at the moment is a mystery. The colonel informed us that we should most likely be nearer the enemy and the front line but our future role is quite obscure. This morning we had our usual squadron parade, and it seemed most strange and very sad that in all probability this was the last time that we should parade as a mounted squadron. The horses of A and B Squadron left camp today for the remount depot at Nathaniya HQ and we ourselves go tomorrow.

Wednesday, 3 July

We spent the whole of today packing. The horses went off to Remounts at Nathaniya under Stephen, one man to two horses. It was very sad seeing them all going away. I shall miss Bob terribly. I didn't ride over myself, but left Gardener to take my horses. Donny Player was perfectly miserable when he saw the squadron leave. Actually, he has arranged a home for both his chargers at the cavalry school. His sole interest in life is horses and now he says he feels like a ship without a rudder. He broke down, poor chap, as the last horse left camp. The whole thing happened so terribly suddenly that I cannot bring myself to understand the full significance. In the afternoon the brigadier came and addressed NCOs and officers. What he said wasn't too bad, but he was very ill at ease. He gave us no indication about our future job or destination.

The old pre-war county regiment was rapidly beginning to shed its skin. They might still have been a yeomanry regiment in name, but they were now professional soldiers and would remain so until the war's end. The British government and the Middle East command were being forced to adjust to rapidly changing circumstances. General de Gaulle, who had escaped France to London and assumed command of the Free French, had urged all French forces to continue the fight, a message that appeared to have been heard in Syria, but the new puppet Vichy government had sent General Weygand to Syria at the end of June to urge the army there to accept the terms of the armistice signed between Germany and France on 22 June. It was not clear whether British forces would soon be fighting Vichy French as well as Italian forces. One thing was for certain: that the Sherwood Rangers needed to be prepared for frontline duty rather than a colonial policing role. It was equally clear there could be no more highly damaging, not to mention expensive, stampedes: the horses had had to go. Even so, the Sherwood Rangers were left with a very uncertain future. With the collapse of France, there was an urgent need to rebuild the army, but this would take time – and especially as Britain's priority was to defend herself at home against the inevitable onslaught from the Luftwaffe.

Thursday, 4 July

This morning we made the final arrangements for our departure. After lunch we left Karkur Camp and marched down to the station. The brigadier came to see us off, but he didn't get a very enthusiastic farewell either from men or officers. Our first destination was Haifa to where we travelled in cattle trucks. We got out of the train just before Haifa. All except C Squadron were marched off to Peninsula Barracks, which are situated on the sea front and appear most comfortable with every form of modern convenience. My C Squadron have been put in a German convent. The nuns have been interned in Jerusalem. It is quite an attractive depot but has been left in a very dirty state by the troops who were billeted there before us, rather as if some alterations had been commenced and left off at a moment's notice, plaster and dust everywhere but we are putting the place in order. There is a lovely chapel attached.

The officers are all quartered in the barracks, about 10 minutes' walk from the convent. At the moment I am sharing a room with Derrick Warwick, but I hope to get a room of my own in the near future. It is all very comfortable and rather luxurious after tents. We have proper furniture in the rooms, bathroom next door, and a grand view out to sea. We also have a most comfortable mess, which we share with the Buffs – actually there are only three officers here. They have one battalion out here. I understand that they suffered very heavily at the retreat from Dunkirk. They have not had official figures yet.

Friday, 5 July

This morning we spent cleaning up our new billets. At 11.30 we had a troop leaders' conference and heard about our new fate. We are now to become gunners for Coastal Defence and the remainder Search Lights. I am afraid that the new organization will completely split up the old squadron. One officer plus his troop will have to go to HQ Squadron under Peter Laycock to form a battery of Search Lights. We were going to draw lots, but Mike Parish chose to go. The remainder of the squadron becomes three batteries of guns under Donny Player as battery commander, Stephen Mitchell second-in-command, and Dan Ranfurly and myself subalterns. The rest of the personnel consist of various HQ men, two teams of 20 men each for the guns, telephonists, signallers and electric-light personnel for each battery. Our total establishment: four officers and 113 men. Half our men have to be trained here, the other half at Kishon, which all makes the organization rather complicated.

Last night I went out to dinner with John Walters, Lawrence Biddle and George Luck in Haifa. We found George on 24 hours' leave in Haifa. At the moment he is an instructor at Bir Salem, the small-arms school. It is the first time I have seen him since Edinburgh. It was most interesting at dinner as all three of us are ex-Inns of Court. Apparently some of the snobs in the yeomanry regiments received some members of the Inns of Court very badly when they were commissioned to them. I understand the Leicestershire Yeomanry were worst.

A number of yeomanry regiments were permanently retrained as gunners, even though, as cavalry, they might more naturally have expected to become mechanized and be given tanks. However, at this stage of the war, numbers of tanks were very few and could not be built and transported to the Middle East overnight. Rather, they had to use what was available, and that meant often antiquated field guns.

Saturday, 6 July

Today we started our lectures in earnest. We are supposed to be able to fire the gun (6-inch) after two weeks' training, so it will have to be very intensive. All the officers including the colonel had three hours of lectures under a gunner major. A half-holiday in the afternoon. I went for a bathe with John Walters, Lawrence, Mike Parish. We went to a perfect stretch of sand just outside Haifa where we had some excellent surfing.

Now that France has fallen, an attack on England is expected at any moment. We have broken off diplomatic relations with the Pétain government.

Sunday, 7 July

Breakfast at 7 o'clock and our first lectures on the gun at 8 o'clock. It is all most interesting. We have been told that we shall fire the gun at a moving target after a week and ready to move and take up our duties at an unknown destination in a fortnight. Our instructor is the battery commander here, Major Ving. He is a most excellent and enthusiastic instructor and it is a pleasure to learn under him. In the morning we work continuously until 11.30, lunch 12.45 and lectures again from 4.15 until 6 o'clock in the evening. We have had no letters from home for ages. Air raids have been continuous over England but as far as we know they have not suffered many casualties and damage has been small. An invasion of England is anticipated and our defence of England has been increased by Australians and Canadians. At the moment the number of troops in Palestine is very small; in fact, there is not much more than the lst Cavalry Division.

Wednesday, 10 July

Lectures in the morning. The gun is really great fun in spite of being much out of date. It was made in 1902 and used in the Great War. A miniature range has been fixed up in a hut. The observation post is at the back of the room and the sea is represented by a raised stand covered with netting. Miniature ships are pulled across by cotton, a man stands underneath the frame with the netting above his head. With the help of the scale marked on the frame and powder spray, he is able to show the fall of the shell according to the fire order given by the battery commander in the observation post. It is a most ingenious piece of work and very good practice.

For dinner we had a guest-night. We asked our chief instructor,

Major Ving, Padre Hughes from Division, three officers from the Yorkshire Hussars, a couple from the Dragoons. I sat with Charles, Tony and the machine-gun officer from the Hussars, a fellow called Hudson. The latter has been to South Africa and has interests in mining machinery. His uncle is a great friend of Daddy's. The party got very rowdy at the end, and for some absolutely unknown reason Jack Abdy threw a butter dish at my head and cut my chin. The party became very hilarious. Mike Gold found his bed in the middle of the football field and Mike Parish, who had been out to dinner, found a donkey in his bedroom.

Next morning I was up early for regimental parade and had to turn the donkey off the parade ground. It was a very good evening.

Thursday, 11 July

We had a lecture in the morning, and then worked with our guns at Kishon. Instructions have now come through that all the Regiment is to be trained as gunners, which means complete reorganization. We have heard that the Wiltshires have been ordered to give up their horses. The supposition is that they will become Search Lights. We also heard that our horses stampeded again on the first night at Remounts, Nathaniya. Eight horses had to be shot. 20 were injured and 30 got away.

Friday, 12 July

Owing to the new organization, we have now had to form six batteries. Dan Ranfurly has now left our battery. Tony Holden has given up the adjutancy and become a battery commander, and Sydney Morse is the new adjutant. Michael and Peter Laycock are also battery commanders. Stephen is second-in-command to our battery. With the colonel and Flash Kellett I went to dinner with the Yorkshire Dragoons. They have a temporary camp just off the Plain of Israel, about 1½ miles away. None of us wanted to go as I understand that there is no love lost between the two regiments. Stephenson is there as their colonel and his brother a squadron leader. Flash put him under arrest at Marseilles as commander of the ship for being late on arrival. They are rather a rowdy mess, with a hard-drinking rowdy colonel, a great contrast to our colonel. Four Inns of Court fellows went to the Dragoons so I was well looked after at the junior end of the table. At dinner I sat between Francis Coppam and Pat Cox. They had heard a rumour that Geoffrey Rogers had been killed. I also heard that the Queen Victoria Rifles had been wiped out at Calais. I wonder whether Dennis Hamilton got through. I knew quite a lot of their fellows. One is quite cut off from news. We left about 10.30. John Gillies I hear is reported missing and believed killed, also Roger Bushell.

Stanley knew Roger Bushell from his time in South Africa and because he moved in similar circles in London, where the latter had been a barrister. Bushell was a fighter pilot in the RAF and commanding 92 Squadron, when, on 23 May, in their first engagement over Dunkirk, he had been shot down. In fact, he survived to become a serial escaper from German prison camps. He later went on to mastermind what became known as the Great Escape from Stalag Luft III, but was later recaptured and executed by the Gestapo.

Sunday, 14 July

A great event today: the first time for five weeks we had an airmail from England. I had three letters, one from Ione dated 11 June. From Ione, I learned that Dennis Hamilton is a prisoner and that Freddie Fitch is missing. I am still very worried about Clive.

Monday, 15 July

Today Palestine had its first air raid. Two waves each of five came over. Two bombers only for each flight, the remainder were fighters. They bombed Haifa port and the oil tanks at Kishon. It happened about

9.45 during a lecture at Carmel camp. This is the sequence of events:
1. Bombs were dropped. 2. The anti-aircraft opened fire. 3. Finally the
air-raid warning went off. From our position we could see the oil
tanks had been hit at Kishon and rather feared for the safety of battery
men who were training on the guns there. All our people were all right
and had a perfect view of the raid.

Tuesday, 16 July

During the lecture this morning the new commander-in-chief of
Palestine paid us a visit, Godwin-Austen. We were on the miniature
range at the time. He was very complimentary about us and told us
that he had been tremendously impressed by what he had heard and
seen. In fact, using his own words, he said we were a crashing success.
All the time he was speaking he had three fly buttons undone, which
made him lose some of his dignity. He has taken the place of Gifford,
who has gone to take over command in North Africa.

Wednesday, 17 July

Lectures in the morning and a half-holiday in the afternoons. Played
a game of cricket. Much talk in the papers about the forthcoming
invasion of England. We have been having many air raids, according
to the papers, but not much damage done.

Saturday, 20 July

My battery had its first shoot. We don't fire the 100-lb shells, but with
a rifle fixed fired a 1-lb shell. The target, consisting of three floats, is
towed along by a tug, with a very long tow-rope. I took one shoot as
battery commander and it went off well. It really was great fun.

Wednesday, 24 July

Another air raid on Haifa by Italian planes. They came over as Lawrence and I were on our way to the theatre. I heard the planes and said to Lawrence, 'Here the Italians are again,' and the next thing we heard was the anti-aircraft fire. Slight damage was done but they killed 40 people and injured 72. As usual, no kind of warning. Peter, Donny and I immediately went to Kishon to see whether our men were all right. There was a nasty mess outside the ordnance yard. A large crater had been blown in the centre of the road, and some dead and injured were lying about the place. Not a pleasant sight. The bombs had fallen very near the guns at Kishon. Ten had fallen in the sea immediately in port. One Arab fishing boat was hit directly and the two occupants killed. The anti-aircraft did no damage to any of the planes. Their opposition is practically nil. If they continue to bomb this place it will be essential to have some fighters here.

At 12 o'clock we had a regimental parade. A notice has come in asking for volunteers to form 'commando' to operate and harass the Italians along the frontier in Africa. The result was quite extraordinary: we expected the whole regiment to volunteer but only very few did. All officers did. I think they have become too keen on the guns.

One of the early proponents of the power of bombing was Giulio Douhet who, during the 1920s, predicted 'absolute air warfare' and was widely read both within and outside Italy. It was ironic, then, that by 1940, the Regia Aeronautica – the Italian air force – should have been so weak. Unfortunately for the Italians, they did not possess enough aircraft or sufficient modern types to make much impact. By June 1940, Italy had only 237 aircraft of all kinds available for operations in the Mediterranean, and of the bombers, most were tri-motor Savoia-Marchetti SM79s, which could only carry around 1000 kilograms of bombs. To put that in perspective, the RAF's twin-engine Vickers Wellington could carry more than double that load. Bombing tended to be carried out from high altitude and with little accuracy. All in all, however outraged the Sherwood Rangers might have been at the attacks on Haifa, such raids were not very effective.

Friday, 26 July

Arms drill before breakfast. Lecture in the morning from 9 till 12. After lecture Flash told me he had arranged a cricket match against HMS *Orion*, a cruiser of 8000 tons, which came into port last night. He told me also that 88 of the crew were coming to watch the match and that I should have to arrange transport and tea. So I had a very busy hour's work. I managed to get the IPC ground. I didn't intend to play myself but as four naval officers turned up I did play. We had a very good game and lost by 10 runs. I liked them all. It struck me how very young some of the officers were.

Saturday, 27 July

Lecture again in the morning. John Walters, Lawrence Biddle and I went sailing in the afternoon. For the race this afternoon we were allowed outside the harbour. They lifted up the boom for us. We had another collision and both boats flew the protest flag. After the race we had to attend a meeting and settle the protest. We won both cases. This was held in Spinney's restaurant. In the evening Michael Parish and I took out Sydney Morse and his wife to dinner and a cinema.

Monday, 29 July

The colonel and Donny got back from Egypt. They told us that our officers and men who are on the course there are being worked pretty hard and that after each week they have an examination paper, which is rather distressing to some of the officers. They are learning about naval guns, which are very much more up to date than those here, so what they learned here has not been much good to them. Usual routine.

Tuesday, 30 July

Lectures all through the morning. We always have a break at 11 o'clock. We then go to the back door of the NAAFI (all junior officers) and have a cup of coffee. This is all very much like university life. Lectures during the morning and exercise during the afternoon.

Saturday, 3 August

We heard today that Alasdair MacDonald, who joined the Regiment from the Inns of Court with Lawrence Biddle, John Walters and me, had been killed at Dunkirk. He became detached from his regiment before leaving England. He was an extraordinarily nice lad, only just married.

PT and a bathe before breakfast. The water was quite rough. I took the battery for an hour's drill on the square this morning. In the afternoon Lawrence Biddle, John Walters and I went for the usual Saturday afternoon sail. It really was a most perfect day for sailing. They lifted the boom, so we were able to go outside the harbour, where we found a good stiff breeze and quite choppy weather. We were all rather upset about MacDonald. It might so easily have been John, Lawrence or me, or John Walters. Such a lovely climate, and the easy time which we have been having, but hearing all about the fighting that has been in Europe and then again the pending invasion of England, makes us all wish that we could do something active and effective. News is so very scarce, and we don't know what friends we have lost. The C-in-C of Palestine made a broadcast to all the troops, pointing out that actually at the moment we are fulfilling a most important role and that he was quite convinced that our time would come.

In the evening Jack Abdy and I took Henry Trotter and his wife Rona out to dinner. Afterwards we went to the local nightclub. Henry refused to come but Rona was quite determined that we should go and that Henry should go home, so Henry was firmly pushed back into the taxi by Rona, and what surprised me was that he went with slight mutterings only. Jack went fast asleep in the nightclub, which suited

Myles Hildyard, Rona and Henry Trotter, with
Michael Parish.

very well, because Rona and I danced all the time. It was the first time
I have danced since being out here, and Rona really dances well. She
asked me to take her there again. I should like to very much, but on
the other hand, it's a very good policy to keep clear of all officers'
wives, especially such a young and attractive girl as Rona, and especially in a small community like this. However, I hope we shall go out
again. I saw Charles Eardley at the nightclub. He was with a certain
Lady Allin, who is known as the subaltern's benefit; she has been married four times, is aged about 35, and has just become engaged to a
young subaltern in the Staffords. It was good to see Charles again – we
had great fun at Edinburgh together. Tomorrow Rona goes off to
Egypt with Henry and the remaining officers who are going on this
gunnery course. She asked me to write. But it's a very debatable point
whether I shall. She is certainly attractive and dances well. But, still, I
have written enough about her.

Tuesday, 6 August

PT at 6.15. Gun practice at 9.15. A competition starts tomorrow for batteries, which is a very good thing as it will make the men keen again. After lunch Gerald Grosvenor, Jack Abdy, Derrick Warwick and I went bathing. After dinner Gerald, Jack, Jos and I went to a cinema in Haifa, which was very bad. While at dinner somebody went through all the rooms in this house. I was the only one who lost money, as I had left some in my drawer.

Wednesday, 7 August

Battery drew for second place in the battery competition. One team did an excellent shoot. We had half an hour arms drill during the morning. I have been very lazy arranging cricket for the Regiment. I must get a match for Saturday. There is going to be an athletics meeting in Jerusalem; Flash Kellett is very keen that the Regiment should enter. Myles Hildyard and Stephen have been given the job of training a regimental team. Some of the officers are going to enter. Both Stephen and Myles were record-holders at school. I should go in for the 100 metres and the two miles. It will mean very strict training for all the men, with special diet. All junior officers were on the square at 4.30 under the RSM. A damned bore. At 6 o'clock I had a single at tennis with Micky Gold at the Haifa Club. It was thoroughly enjoyable.

Still no letters from home. It's simply ages since any mail has come in.

During lunch we had an air-raid alarm, but it came to nothing. I heard that Tony Priestly in the Guards had got a bullet in the stomach, but he was all right. Robert his brother is out here with the Signals. This time last year I was with the Inns of Court at Camp Warminster, acting lance corporal. Tim Smallwood was in my section. He got a commission in the Sharpshooters. I wonder what he is doing now.

Saturday, 10 August

The usual PT in the morning. I must say I do enjoy it. At that time of the morning it is perfectly grand. After breakfast, arms drill on the square, followed by a lecture from Stephen on what he learned in Egypt. John and I spent some time in the officers' mess on accounts, which seem to be in a very healthy state. While I was playing tennis an urgent message came through from Sydney Morse, our adjutant, that I had to return to camp at once. I found when I got back that the colonel had cabled that I should go down and join him at Port Tewfik as Henry Trotter had gone sick to hospital. At first I was rather annoyed but Rona will be there! After work I can help entertain her. I had to be ready to leave Haifa at 7.30 next morning.

Sunday, 11 August

I caught the 8.15 train from Haifa East down to Kantara. I travelled down as far as Lydda with a captain from the Buffs, who was going on a course at Saratand. He was a Rhodesian who worked in Bulawayo. Not a bad fellow. From Lydda to Kantara I had a crowded train with two nurses returning to Cairo, and two officers who had just done a course at Bir Saline. We all lunched together. At Kantara we changed and had rather a long wait. I spent my time drinking beer with a colonel from the RASC. He lived in Guernsey, which has been taken over by the Germans, and is rather worried since reading in the papers that we have been bombing the place. At Ismailia I changed again, arriving at Port Tewfik at 11.15 where Jack Hall met me in his car. I found that I was to share a room with the colonel. He was asleep when I arrived but he woke up and greeted me heartily. He talked a lot, and I had the greatest difficulty in understanding what he said as he had no teeth in! At the best of times he speaks most indistinctly. On the way down, I caught a beastly cold. Most annoying.

Monday, 12 August

Port Tewfik is not at all a bad place in spite of what people say. We are situated in the old quarantine building overlooking the canal. Directly opposite we see Sinai, the desert, and the mountains behind. The canal opens into a large harbour, again with mountains in the distance. At night the colouring is quite beautiful. The officers have their mess on the first floor. The guns are immediately below us within 20 yards of each other. The mess is quite comfortable and I like the officers attached to this battery. In charge is Captain Hendry, a ranker but an excellent fellow. The colonel likes him awfully. Second-in-command is a fellow called Gummersall. He was master gunner to the battery before he got his commission. He knows his stuff from A to Z and is an excellent instructor. Heath and Jack Hall are the other two who make up the mess.

We get up at 7 o'clock. Breakfast at 8. We live off rations, which on the whole are not too bad. Lectures start at 8.30 and continue until 12.30 with half an hour's break. There is a great difference between the guns here and at Haifa. Here they have neither rocking bar nor auto-sight. All ranging is transmitted by means of the Vickers clock, which is a wonderful instrument. Everything is very concentrated, which is certainly convenient, but one well-placed bomb would blow up every-thing. We lunch at 12.30. The puddings are quite dreadful. The colonel never takes them. From 2 until 3 we generally sleep. At 3 the colonel insists on taking some exercise. We then walk to the French Club about a quarter of a mile away and play two or three sets of singles at tennis. The heat is pretty fierce and I endeavour tactfully to point out that perhaps 5 o'clock would be a better time to play, but that is quite out of the question. After tennis we walk up to the French Club proper about ¼ mile away and have tea. It's a very attractive spot overlooking the canal and in many ways reminded me of the Country Club in Johannesburg. You have tea on a very pleasant veranda overlooking the canal. We had to be back again by 6 o'clock for the manning parade, which lasted about an hour.

Captain Hendry asked us out to dinner. We all went to the local casino, except Jack Hall, who was duty officer. It was rather an amusing place, a good dinner and entertaining cabaret. There was one very attractive Hungarian girl there, who took part in the cabaret. Her name is Maria. She is a friend of Jack Hall. He goes there practically every evening. She is quite lovely and a good dancer. We made the colonel dance with her once or twice. I think Hendry is a bit of a lad, he was dancing round all the time.

Wednesday, 14 August

After the manning parade the colonel and I went to a cocktail party on board a destroyer, which is here in dry dock. She had a hole made in her side by an Italian plane in the Mediterranean, and she is having that put right. Her name is the *Havock* and her captain is a man called Courage. The whole thing was done very well and I thoroughly enjoyed it. I was amazed at the beauty of some of the lovelies from Tewfik. The colonel had a grand reception as he went on board. The captain met him on the deck, with the orderly officer standing behind, very smart in their white uniform. We had our drill uniform on, with tunics, and I think looked smart too. It made me think how very much I should have liked the navy as a career. Never have I met an unpleasant naval man. This destroyer took part in the second battle of Narvik; she also saw service at Rotterdam when the Dutch gave in. They showed us some excellent photographs which they had taken of an Italian ship sinking in the Mediterranean. The cocktail party was most enjoyable and thoroughly interesting. The colonel, Lady Yarborough and I dined afterwards at the French Club.

Thursday, 15 August

Tennis in the afternoon at 3. The colonel and I played Lady Yarborough and the pro. We just were beaten. A bathe afterwards. At 8.45 in the evening we had a practice shoot with the lights working in conjunction. Unfortunately, the navy failed to provide a target so it was all rather a flop. Dinner afterwards at the French Club.

Friday, 16 August

We finished work at 11 in the morning. In the afternoon the colonel and I caught the 3.20 train to Cairo. We had a very hot and dusty journey. I have never known anything like the dust. Lady Y joined us at Suez and we travelled together. We had the commander of the *Havock* and another naval officer in the carriage with us. We arrived in Cairo at about 5.30, went straight to the Continental Hotel, bathed and had tea. Rona Trotter arrived after tea from the Anglo-American hospital where she had been seeing Henry, her husband, looking as usual most attractive. She certainly dresses very well. The Continental Hotel is an enormous place. We have rooms overlooking one of the main streets. I have a room, quite comfortable, between the colonel and Lady Y on one side and Rona Trotter on the other side. Running water, but the noise is dreadful. Rona was out for dinner, which was disappointing. She didn't expect us to arrive until Saturday so had accepted an invitation. The colonel, Lady Y and I dined at a place called the St James. We sat out of doors and watched a cinema during dinner. We got back about 10.30. I heard Rona come in at about 2.30.

Cairo must have been a fascinating place to visit during the war. Unlike London, or most European cities, Cairo was not subject to blackouts, and both officers and other ranks could enjoy plenty of food, drink and female company; not only were there large numbers of English and other European ladies living and working in Cairo, with whom friendships might be formed, there were also plenty of brothels. Much of the heart of the city had been rebuilt in the second half of the nineteenth and early twentieth centuries with ornate mansions and villas, wide streets and electric tramways, and while the number of carts and animals were a constant reminder that it was, at heart, an old Middle Eastern city, anyone stepping inside Shepheard's Hotel or the Turf Club could be forgiven for thinking they were back at home. Cairo was rich in cinemas, bars, cafés, hotels, clubs, and manicured gardens as well as a belle-époque *area of curving boulevards called Garden City, in which GHQ, the British Embassy and other governmental bodies were based.*

There was the Gezira Sporting Club, with cricket ground, riding facilities and tennis courts, and there was also the older Islamic part of the city with its mosques, bazaars and other attractions. And as if that wasn't enough, there were Egypt's antiquities – its museums, the Pyramids and Sphinx. Despite the heat, flies and animal dung, Cairo was, during the wartime years, an exciting and vibrant place to live or spend one's leave.

Saturday, 17 August

At 8 I had some coffee, rolls, butter and marmalade in my bedroom, which I thoroughly enjoyed. At 9 I used Rona's bathroom to get dressed. At 1 o'clock we all left for the Anglo-American hospital to see Henry Trotter. He is going on slowly but will be there a longish time. The hospital is a most attractive spot with a lovely garden attached. The colonel, Lady Y and I left there for the Pyramids. I was most impressed when I saw them for the first time. The colonel and I climbed up both inside and out. From the top, you do get the most wonderful view over the desert. It took us about 20 minutes to climb to the top, and 15 minutes to get down again. When we got down we were very hot but a bathe in the pool at Mena House soon cooled us off again. Rona Trotter came there and joined us for lunch. She looked quite lovely today. Her complexion is her strong point. Lunch at Mena House was first class. In the afternoon the colonel, Lady Y and self went to the native bazaar. I can't think of the proper name. It was most interesting and we saw some lovely things. I would have loved to send some glass home to the family, but I don't suppose it would have ever arrived. I bought Lady Y a small present and also a tiny little box with a figure of Moses inside for Rona.

Mena House Hotel stood – and still stands – in the shadow of the Pyramids at Giza, and was open to officers who could either stay there or simply enjoy its bars and dining facilities. Beyond, on the edge of the desert, was the vast sprawl of Mena Camp.

That night we dined on the roof of the Continental Hotel. Our party consisted of the colonel, Lady Y, Rona, and Freddie Luck. We met Freddie in the hotel during the day. He is no longer brigade major to Milter, but has a staff job in Cairo. He was in great form. Unfortunately, Lady Y felt very seedy after dinner, so she retired to bed. The colonel followed soon after and Rona, Freddie and I stayed until the end. They had an excellent cabaret during the evening. Rona and I decided to go to a nightclub and went to a place called Jules. We demanded waltz after waltz and danced and danced until 4 o'clock. Rona dances the old waltz very well indeed. We got back to the hotel about 4.30 and crept to our rooms with shoes off so that we should not be heard by the colonel. Jules was highly respectable, with plenty of army people there. The floor was good, and the band consisted of one very excellent pianist. I am pleased to say that Freddie Luck did not come with us. We had an amusing time, and Rona danced well. Personally I think she is quite bored with Henry. I don't quite know whether she married him for his money. There is over 10 years between them in age. They have one child, a girl aged about two. She seemed to think that once a girl was married and had a child, the best of life was over. I endeavoured to persuade her to the contrary. On the way home I wondered whether I should make love to her and, bearing in mind that Henry was in my regiment (although I do think him the world's bloodiest fool) and that I was with the colonel, rather foolishly decided against. She is attractive, but rather cow-like about the eyes! The whole day was great fun, and a great change from the usual routine of life. I don't suppose such a situation will ever come again: to spend an evening with a lovely girl (married, of course), to stay in the same hotel, to have rooms adjoining by door, to get rid of the rest of the party and then say good night at the door.

Sunday, 18 August

In the morning we went to the hospital to see Henry Trotter, then proceeded to the Gezira Club where we bathed. The club is simply grand, with polo, tennis, squash, cricket and a magnificent swimming pool in which we had a swim. I ran into Boyd there. I have not seen him since I left Winchester.

The colonel and I then went to the station to catch the early train back to Port Tewfik. Very late we rushed to the station and by mistake we got into the wrong train, which took us 50 miles in the wrong direction. We then fortunately stopped at a tiny Arab station. The colonel's diarrhoea was in a bad state, but there was no lavatory on this extraordinary station. After great difficulty we managed to find an Arab car, which took us all the way back to Cairo. We went back to the hotel – Lady Y was amazed to see us again – had some tea, and caught the late train back to Tewfik. It was terribly crowded and we had the greatest difficulty in getting a seat. When we eventually did, we found ourselves next to two drunken Australians, who made a nuisance of themselves all the way down until one fell asleep on the shoulder of a fat woman next door. We couldn't find a taxi when we arrived at Tewfik so we walked to the French Club, not having had any dinner. But it was so late we could only get bread and cheese. So ended our weekend in Cairo, which I thoroughly enjoyed.

Monday, 19 August

The colonel's stomach is in a very bad way. During the morning he took some castor oil, which kept him running all through the day. He really has been rotten. After lunch he retired to bed until dinner-time. Usual lectures in the morning. In the afternoon I played cricket for the battery against the Royal Sussex Regiment, which is here at Port Tewfik. I didn't get an innings as we won before I was due to go in. We played on a very pleasant ground.

Tuesday, 20 August

We heard today that British Somaliland had been evacuated success-fully. I don't quite know at the present what that will mean. Before leaving for dinner I managed to dash off a note to Rona, which I sent up to Cairo via Nuttall, Henry's servant. The colonel would have been most inquisitive if he had found out to whom I was writing. His stomach is much better and he was in excellent form at dinner. He was really most amusing. The dinner at the Misv Hotel is good.

British Somaliland was one of her African colonies that Britain surrendered. Around 30,000 Italian troops had laid siege to the capital, Berbera, but on 19 August, Lieutenant General Godwin-Austen gave the order to the 6000-strong garrison to destroy the dock facilities and then withdraw.

Wednesday, 21 August

We are really having a very easy time here. We only work from 8.30 until 12.15 and today we had nothing to do in the afternoon. Not even a manning parade. And, what is more, I understand they are not giving us any kind of test papers, although they couldn't very well expect the colonel to sit down and do an examination paper on work he has done over the last three weeks. Today an RAOC officer arrived to test the guns before the practice shoot on Saturday. This battery was to have had its practice shoot on Friday but now it has been postponed until Saturday as a very large convoy is arriving here from British Somaliland, which was evacuated by the British the day before yesterday. I understand they got away with exceptionally few casualties, and that British Somaliland was evacuated entirely through Winston Churchill. He said to Wavell, when he was in London, that he absolutely refused to sacrifice another soldier's life endeavouring to hold land that would come back to us again in the near future. This statement, coupled with the fact that women with children over five are to be evacuated from Egypt to South Africa, points rather to possible activity here in the near future.

Thursday, 22 August

Usual routine in the morning. The practice shoot is going to take place on Saturday. Only once have they fired before, and that was at a drunken skipper of a merchantman who would not stop at the signal. They fired a shot across his bows to bring him to. It was a full charge, but a sand-filled shell, but the blast did £50 worth of damage to this building. So what will happen tomorrow the Lord only knows. Henry Trotter's servant, who went up to Cairo from here, returned today. He brought back a letter from Rona in answer to mine. She had actually written before she received mine. She said she loved our evening together, especially the waltzes. I must say we did have fun. Will it be a good thing to write back again? Don't quite know. I must think about it. But she is attractive.

I took the colonel and his wife out to dinner, as they really have been most kind to me. We had dinner at the Misv Hotel. Today I had some mail from England sent on from Haifa. A letter from Ione, one from Seymour. He has got a commission in the Greys. I do hope that he gets out here as I would greatly like to see him again. He really is a first-class person. I also had a letter from Martha.

Friday, 23 August

Today we had our last practice before the shoot tomorrow. The colonel will of course take the shoot from the BOP and I shall act as section commander. The colonel and I went into Suez after work.

We had a drink with Lady Y at the hotel and then came back here for lunch. During the morning this place was quite stiff with generals, Brigadier General Grant first, then Leslie, and then Pollard. The last is the real big man, the brigadier of this battery. He knows his stuff well, but I understand that he is not much liked. But he is clever. He came up and spoke to me while I was in the SC [staff captain] post and was very pleasant. He criticized the colonel a bit during his shoot. In the afternoon we played tennis at the golf club. Jack Hall took us there. I played with the colonel against Jack and Lady Y. The courts were excellent but the golf course looked pretty green.

Today an enormous convoy arrived here of 14 ships. Half went up the canal and the others disembarked here. Mostly Australians from Australia and some other troops from England. The troop ships going up the canal with troops lining the deck, passing the Indian war memorial, were really a most impressive sight. It reminded me very much of the similar scene from Noel Coward's play *Cavalcade*. They say that the convoy carries some mail. I hope so.

Saturday, 24 August

Today this battery, i.e. Y Battery of the 19th Heavy, shoot their practice series. We started the shoot at about 7.30 after various critics, representatives and observers had arrived. We had an Egyptian officer from the battery at Alexandria, two naval officers, and Brigadier Pollard and his staff. He appeared a very decent chap. They arranged for the Yeomen to have one shoot, and gave us eight shells per gun. The colonel took the shoot from the BOP and I acted section leader. The whole thing went off very well and the brig. appeared to be quite satisfied telling us that we had made history, i.e. a cavalry regiment manning and firing the guns after such a short period of training. The gun teams worked really well, especially No. 1 gun, which had a misfire. The No. 1 of that gun did very well. The blast and the noise was very considerable and broke all the glass in the quarantine building, also bringing down masses of plaster and cracking the walls. In the evening they had a shoot in conjunction with the lights. Unfortunately the tug drawing the target had great difficulty in navigating, so we didn't get started until 11.30. It was supposed to start at 9.30. Summersall and Hendry took the night shoots, and both did remarkably well after it was all over. We drank champagne in the mess. That concludes our training as gunners at Port Tewfik.

Tomorrow I go back to Haifa, and the colonel goes to Alexandria to see the battery, which is manned by Egyptians.

The colonel has been in excellent form during our time down here except for his tummy trouble. He has been very kind to me, also Lady Yarborough. They have had me to dinner practically every night. I have been with the colonel almost every moment for the last fortnight. I have also shared a room with him, and I have had every single meal with him. He is very restless, the most energetic man I have ever met. He has been a most amusing companion and we have laughed together a great deal.

Sunday, 25 August

Today I left Tewfik for Haifa, with the 22 men who have been training with us. We caught the 5.20 train in the evening. The colonel came to the station to see us off. Halfway between Tewfik and Ismailia the train was held up by an accident further up the line. We were stuck in this desolate spot for four hours. At about 12 o'clock lorries came from the prisoner-of-war camp at Geneifa and took us there for the night. The camp is guarded by a company of the Royal Sussex Regiment. Altogether we were a party of about 40 men, and eight officers, all consisting of specialists who had arrived from England by the last convoy, doctors and RASC. The Royal Sussex were most hospitable to us. We actually slept the night in a new section of the prison compound.

Monday, 26 August

We had barbed-wire fences all around us, and guards with Bren guns outside the wire. But we were very comfortable and the men well fed. The next day I sent a signal to Haifa advising Flash of our predicament. I went all round the camp. They had about 900 Italian prisoners, also some internees and a further 600 Libyans. They told me that quite literally they could not speak too sharply to the Italian officer prisoners otherwise they burst into tears. It was quite clear that all classes of prisoners were very content in the camp and much preferred being there to fighting in the desert for the Italian Army. In their present place they were safe, well fed and well housed. They all appeared very content. The company commander of the Sussex was a Captain Brown. A most charming person, who was very kind to all of us. They only had a small mess and we must have been rather an influx for them. They had one very amusing young officer, called Tom Warren, who had just become engaged to a French girl in Tewfik. He made us laugh a lot and he was continually getting into trouble. We all left at 6.15 on Monday evening and caught the train to Kantara.

Tuesday, 27 August

On my return to Peninsula Barracks I reported to the orderly room. I had a long talk with the adjutant, Sydney Morse, and Flash Kellett, who has been acting colonel, came in and joined us. Flash seems quite convinced that we shall not be gunners. All Hotchkiss guns and signalling equipment have been reissued to us. But personally I am not so sure. Brigadier Dunn did suggest that the colonel should visit the guns at Alexandria, and that Flash should follow him. I hear that one man per battery who volunteered for the commandos has gone, including Wilson from my troop in C Battery. So far they have not taken any officers from this regiment but they have done so from other regiments. I understand that they are forming a headquarters unit first as a nucleus. Since I have been away they have split up the Regiment, as we were far too concentrated from the point of view of air raids. A, B, C and X Batteries have gone to a camp at the top of Mount Carmel called Ahuza. The view from the camp is quite wonderful. One side you have a magnificent view of Haifa and the harbour, with Atlit Point in the distance. And from the other side you look over the plain and on a clear day we can see Afula. In peacetime one would have to spend a fortune to find a house with such a wonderful view. The air up here is quite amazing and there is always a cool breeze.

At about 2.30 this afternoon we had another air raid on Haifa. I was sitting in the mess with Donny and Stephen when we heard the planes. The next thing we heard was the whistle of the bombs. We moved pretty quickly and scattered in all directions. Ten planes came over but they did very little damage. A few casualties, one fatal, but no soldiers. We were a very small mess at dinner: Basil Ringrose, Stephen Mitchell, Lawrence Biddle and self. We had a most amusing evening. Donny Player returned from his course at Port Fuad, with the other officers. They don't appear to have enjoyed themselves at all, learned nothing, and spent a great deal of money, as they all lived in a hotel in Port Said. Apparently they didn't hit it off at all with the gunner officers. We had a very much better crowd.

Wednesday, 28 August

The colonel has returned from Alexandria. He spent a busy day on the guns there. It is still very uncertain about our future. I heard today that Bill Dawkins from the Inns of Court had been killed in France. He was with us in Edinburgh and was commissioned to the Yorkshire Hussars but, like MacDonald, was appointed liaison officer to a mechanized unit. I understand the colonel will be giving up the Regiment in September some time as he will be over the age limit. General opinion has it that Flash Kellett will then take command. Personally I think he would be an excellent person.

I found some letters waiting for me on my return from Egypt. Two from Ione, one from Martha, one from Ursula and one from Daddy dated 14 June. I sent him a cable yesterday asking whether any of my letters were getting through and whether all was well. It really is most worrying to hear about all the air raids they are having in England. A lot of damage must have been done.

Before leaving Tewfik I wrote a letter to Rona Trotter and asked the officer who had come from Ordnance for the shoot to take it with him to Cairo and drop it at the Continental Hotel. He gladly agreed to do it. Before he left he came and said goodbye to the colonel and me, and added that he would deliver the letter and left the room. The colonel asked what letter he was talking about. I pretended not to hear.

Thursday, 29 August

John Walters came and relieved me on the guns at 9 o'clock. I had quite a good night. I went and had breakfast at Carmel Camp and afterwards came up the hill with Gerald Grosvenor and Derrick Warwick, who had been away umpiring a battle training exercise between the Greys and Yorkshire Hussars. A rifle inspection in the afternoon. At the moment we don't seem to be doing much serious soldiering as the men have a tremendous lot of guards to do, having two camps, Division HQ at Stella Maris Monastery and also manning the guns each day. We all would very much like some definite job. There seems to be a lot of talk about getting our horses back and the guns seem to be dying a natural death. In the evening, John, Donny and I had a mess meeting. At the moment, the mess seems to be running pretty well, but we want some more money.

Friday, 30 August

Today the new C-in-C of Palestine came and visited the camp. He went first to Peninsula and then came here. He met all the officers and WOs. All the men carried on with their normal duties. His name is General Neame VC. He appeared quite pleased with what he saw and told the colonel before he left that he could tell us all that we were going to be mechanized but not in Palestine.

We were all very bricked on hearing this. I suppose it will be somewhere in the Western Desert. I expect we shall have to wait until all the staff come out from England, as at the moment they have not got anything to mechanize us with.

It has certainly been fun being gunners for a short time, and we have had a pretty slack time, except for the first fortnight. I also got on a trip to Port Tewfik, which I thoroughly enjoyed. But we would all like to get on with the job now.

Gerald told me that he had heard from Division that he is going to Cairo and leaving the Regiment. He does not know in what capacity. He can't join his own regiment, the IXth, as they are in England. He will be a great loss. To my mind he is quite the best soldier among us, and easily one of the most charming men I have ever met.

Saturday, 31 August

PT in the morning. It really is perfectly grand up at this camp in the early morning. It is quite a pleasure to get out of bed. I think I have enjoyed this camp more than anywhere else in Palestine, although I have only been here a few days. I have never felt better in my life. We have the advantage of being right out in the country yet within easy distance of Haifa.

Sunday, 1 September

Tent inspection at 10.30, no service. A message came through from orderly room at Peninsula Barracks that all men had to be called back from local leave, as we were moving on Wednesday, this time to Gedezeh. Also we heard that the 5th Cavalry Brigade was being re-formed: the Yorkshire Dragoons and Yorkshire Hussars are going to the same place. Charles Miller was giving up his post as governor of Jerusalem, and having the brigade again. This makes our future even more obscure as both the other regiments have their horses still. It may of course be the idea to have a mixed brigade, two regiments horsed and one mechanized. I shall be sorry to leave this camp, as it is such a grand slot, but it may be a step in the right direction. Personally, I don't want to see the horses back again. In modern warfare, against machine-guns, aeroplanes and tanks, horsed cavalry would not have a chance. For policing countries like Palestine, one couldn't get anything better.

Unfortunately we have to leave two batteries at Carmel Camp to man the guns there. I should have thought that the RA Battery could have managed without us, as they did before we came. I think X and Y are staying, but the batteries will be changed after a fortnight.

We really have had a most pleasant mess here. Donny Player has been in charge of the camp. His asthma has greatly improved since we left the horses, and he has been in excellent form. Gerald Grosvenor as usual his charming self. Stephen Mitchell, with whom I have a large tent, Basil Ringrose, Mike Riviere, Derrick Warwick, Peter Laycock and Lawrence Biddle comprise our mess.

Peter Laycock is very seldom here, as he always goes out to dinner. He certainly takes life very easily. I often wonder what he will be like under fire. Each time we have had an air raid here, I have noticed that he always pales. But that wasn't a very pleasant sight.

Tuesday, 3 September

We spent all the day packing and striking tents. It should be a very simple move as we are doing the whole thing by motor transport. I understand that we are taking over guard duties from a battalion of the Queens who are going to Egypt. Each squadron, or I should say battery, is taking over a different position all round about the Sarafand area. Gedezeh is to be RHQ. We are going to Tel Aviv. I think we shall have to guard the power station. By midday the tents were struck, and we all had to sleep in the open. There was no dinner in the officers' mess so we had dinner at Prosse's in Haifa. The party consisted of Peter Laycock, Michael Gold, Michael Riviere, Stephen Mitchell and Basil Ringrose.

As I was the only one with any money on me, I paid the bill. It seems extremely unlikely that I shall get any back from some members of the party.

I met Lady Yarborough, the colonel's wife, at Carmel Camp. She very kindly presented me with a little white ivory camel, in memory of our visit to Tewfik.

Wednesday, 4 September

Call out at 4.30, breakfast 5 o'clock, moved off from Ahuza Camp at 7.15. The convoy rendezvoused at the bottom of the hill.

Gerald Grosvenor was there, seeing the convoy off. It was very sad saying goodbye to him. He leaves the Regiment and goes to the armoured division in Egypt. He longs to get back to his own Regiment, the IXth Lancers, but at this moment, they are in England. They did get to France but got off very lightly. Their CO was wounded in the hand, and one young officer called Tew was run over and killed by his own tank.

At Petah Tikva, the convoy split. Our final destination was the Reading Power Station at Tel Aviv, on the outskirts of the town. When we arrived we took over from a company of Queens who are off to Egypt. At first it was arranged that I should take a detachment of 25 men, and guard a place 15 miles away; we were all packed up and ready to move when instructions came through that the post was to be taken over by another battery. At the moment Stephen Mitchell and I are the only officers present with the battery, as Donny is acting second-in-command, and Jack Abdy is away in Egypt on a course. The company commander of the outgoing Queens remained behind for one night. Quite a pleasant fellow called Captain Stobbs. He has been out here for two years and was just about to go home on leave when war was declared.

Thursday, 5 September

This is a most pleasantly situated place. The Reading Power Station is well out of the town, across the river and right by the sea. The building itself is most beautifully constructed, with magnificent proportions. Outside the buildings and within the wall they have constructed a most lovely garden, including large grass lawns bordered with flowerbeds. No end of money has been spent on the garden. They must use gallons of water each day for the grass to grow. It really is grand to walk again on a lawn.

The machinery inside appears most modern and up to date, and the control room reminds me of a scene from the H. G. Wells film. We are also responsible for the aeroplane hangar, and landing strip on the edge of the desert, which adjoins the power station. There are no planes here now: they have all been taken away by the government. We have been sleeping in the power station and also in the hangar.

The officers' mess is a small four-roomed hut, which used to be for Customs. It has a stove and also washing place. It faces onto the desert, with the concrete landing strip about 200 yards in front, and on one side there is the sea from which we always get a cool breeze. Twenty-two men have to go on guard, which is a lot. Our most important post is on the roof to watch for aircraft. We also keep a very close eye on the landing strip for fifth columnists, who might remove the obstructions that have been placed there. We had a busy morning organizing the place and various guards.

The guard was mounted at 18.00 hrs. They mounted in front of the power station. They were well turned out, and with the flower garden, the sea, and the lovely sunset, it made a perfect picture. For our dinner we had sausages and chips, bottled cherries, and sardines on toast, all prepared by Smith and Strachan our servants. They did it very well indeed. Stephen had a hamper of food sent him from Fortnum's, which helps our larder considerably. We had to buy a certain amount of cooking utensils and cutlery to start our mess, but we got them very cheaply. This very simple fare and way of living suits both Stephen and I, but I am afraid when Donny and Jack come back they will hardly be satisfied, and we shall be involved in rather a lot of expense.

At 12 o'clock midnight, I went round all the posts. The power station is rather an eerie place by night.

Friday, 6 September

A section of this entry is missing, but it seems the lady in question is his cousin, Pat, with whom he had fallen madly in love, much to the consternation of the family, who, according to Stanley, 'had visions of barmy grandchildren'.

I am not quite certain how I shall answer the cable. I thought I would cable first three words – 'I love you'. But after a great deal of thinking I could not make up my mind whether that was true. I shall think about it further later on. Anyhow one could have written and let me know that she had decided to leave for Canada.

Saturday, 7 September

Donny motored over to see us after lunch. We sat talking for a bit. He told us that Henry Trotter was back from Egypt but looked very ill. I suppose that means Rona will be back, and probably staying at Tel Aviv with Lady Yarborough.

All these wives are supposed to be evacuated from Palestine and Egypt on the 14th of this month. They are being sent to South Africa. If they do go there, I shall certainly give Rona some introductions.

It is now about 10.20. I am writing in the room which we use as a dining room. I have an oil lamp and it is rather hot on account of the blackout. Stephen has gone to bed and is breathing heavily, making rather a horrible noise. I shall be going round the guard posts at about midnight.

Stephen and I have been trying to place a most extraordinary noise. It's most difficult to describe but sounds as though somebody is polishing buttons on a belt with a hard brush. It varies in density, and appears to be very close indeed, somewhere around the side of the building, but we simply can't find anything. Probably some kind of insect, or even the wires making some kind of noise.

Sunday, 8 September

Today the King asked for a National Prayer Day, so we had a voluntary service here, taken by Stephen, and I read the lesson: II Romans:10. Not many came. I should have liked to see more.

In the afternoon we had a game of cricket. Power Station played against Hangar. Stephen played for Power Station and I played for

Hangar. We easily won, making 60, and getting them out for 10! Stephen came out first ball and so did I. We have an excellent pitch. I put the cricket mat down on the asphalt strip on which the planes used to land. It makes a wonderful level surface. There are no boundaries and you have to run everything. When the ball gets off the asphalt into the sand it stops dead. The hangar is about 400 yards from the power station.

In the middle of the match we had an air-raid warning, first from Tel Aviv and then the power station itself. We didn't think there was any chance of planes coming to Tel Aviv, and continued our cricket thinking possibly there was a raid on Haifa. However, we soon shot off to the trenches when we saw six Italian bombers coming in from over the sea! They flew right over the town, turned north, came back again and then flew off to sea. What they were up to I don't know – possibly reconnaissance over towards Sarafand. The guard right on top of the power station didn't like it at all. If a bomb should land on that power station, we all go to kingdom come! However, we finished our cricket match.

Today I had 12 letters from England – what a mail – and was I excited! I had quite a bunch from the family, some dated 18 June, and most extraordinary of all, two dated 19 August. They must have come through the Mediterranean, via the reinforcements and navy. I also had a letter from Diana Pelham, Nanny, Ursula Barclay and Bridget. I spent a most enjoyable ½ hour reading all my mail.

The family have spent a fortnight in Scotland with Rae Wilson, which they seem to have enjoyed. Brother Derrick has passed his cadet exam, which means that he will soon get his commission, which he thoroughly deserves. The family are very bucked.

Monday, 9 September

These dirty, yellow, bloody Italians raided Tel Aviv this afternoon. They dropped a ladder of bombs right through the centre of the town. No bombs were very near us as we are at the north end of the town.

Tel Aviv is a complete open town without any kind of protection, not even an anti-aircraft gun, and in the town itself they have not even air-raid shelters. I have not heard yet the extent of the damage but imagine fairly considerable. There was no warning and the first we heard was the exploding of the bombs. We saw the bombers at a terrific height. They turned north and then back out to sea. I can't understand why they raided Tel Aviv: there is nothing about in the military nature except 100 men under the charge of Stephen Mitchell and Stanley Christopherson guarding the power station, and disused aerodrome mostly against fifth columnists, and surprise landing. If they continue bombing here, they might make the power station itself their next object, and if they score a hit we shall go a long way up in the air.

The time is now 11 o'clock. The telephone has just rung and who should it be but Rona Trotter. I had no idea that she was here, and actually staying at the Gat Rayman Hotel. She had a very narrow escape, as a bomb fell almost 20 yards from the hotel. I am going to have dinner with HER tomorrow.

I saw in the paper today that John Graham had died of wounds. He was in the Black Watch. He was an exact contemporary of mine at Winchester. We started and went up the school together, leaving the same term. He went to the Varsity, and then on to the SE, and was on the reserve of the Black Watch. One could not meet a more charming man.

Tuesday, 10 September

Tel Aviv has suffered terribly as a result of this raid. Those dirty Italians certainly played their dirtiest trick of the war: 115 were killed including 55 children, and 130 were injured. One bomb fell on the Soldiers' Home, where tea had been laid for 150 soldiers' wives and children. Fortunately they were late by 10 minutes, and had not arrived. It was only a matter of 10 minutes.

There is no kind of anti-aircraft or fighters here. That is why I can't understand why they flew over at such a height. The only kind of gun is an old Hotchkiss on the roof of the town station. A tremendous quantity of buildings were brought down. Many bodies are still buried beneath the debris. There have been some frightful sights in the town.

Pamphlets were dropped in Jaffa, which said that Italy was already in Libya, would get Egypt very shortly, likewise Palestine, which would be handed over to the Arabs. That the Italians would exterminate the British and the Jews.

Donny Player has joined us here now, so there are three of us; we live simply but very comfortably. Our servants cook for us and look after us.

I went and had dinner with Rona and Henry Trotter. I had rather hoped that Henry wouldn't be there but he was. He was looking very seedy. Rona was looking lovely. Rona, with Dorothy Morse, is endeavouring to fly to Lagos and then take a cargo boat back to England. It will take a very long time.

After dinner we went to the local nightclub. Henry didn't stay long so Rona and I made the band play some old-fashioned waltzes and we waltzed around on a floor practically to ourselves. She looked lovely and danced well. I flirted outrageously!

Wednesday, 11 September

It is now 9.30 in the evening and we are listening to the news from London. The air raids there sound alarming. Buckingham Palace has been hit, a well-known museum, churches, buildings in the city – and a bomb fell close to St Paul's but no damage was actually done to the cathedral. The West End has also had its share. I only hope that No. 5 Lowndes Court is intact. Mother, I suppose, is working in London still, which is terribly worrying.

Churchill spoke on the wireless. Owing to the accumulation of boats down the coast from Norway to Spain, he anticipated an attack on the British Isles in the near future, and before the weather breaks. I wish I could be at home and help.

The news also had an account of the air raid on Tel Aviv. It pointed out that the Rome Radio had reported that Jaffa, which is entirely Arab and actually joining up with Tel Aviv, had been bombed. By so doing Mussolini openly breaks his promise that he would not wage war on the Arabs, whom he reckoned would turn against the British. Likewise this statement is an absolute contradiction of what he said in the pamphlets dropped over Jaffa. This has done more to cement the ties between the English and the Arabs, and even the Arabs and the Jews. The Jewish mayor of Tel Aviv has received condolences from many prominent Arab leaders and, even more, Arabs actually attended the funerals of the Jews killed in the raid which is absolutely unheard of.

One wonders where it will all end! It is also reported that the Italian armistice commission sitting in Syria has demanded the complete disarmament of all French forces there and control of all French air bases there. If they get these, Palestine is in for a bad time.

We had an air-raid warning early this morning but we saw no planes. We are getting some police reinforcements to help guard this power station.

No. 5 Lowndes Court was where the Christopherson family lived in London. His mother was working as a VAD nurse. The Blitz had begun on Saturday, 7 September, when the Luftwaffe deliberately targeted London for the first time.

Friday, 13 September

A good many nurses have arrived in Palestine and are stationed at Sarafand. After dinner in the mess they were discussing these nurses, who for the most part are advancing in years and very plain. Flash Kellett held the very definite view that they had no sexual desire, and he was backed up by the colonel, but John Walters, the doc, didn't agree at all. He declared that just because they were nurses, plain and advancing in years, that didn't exclude them from having sexual feelings towards the opposite sex. After dinner they all went to Sarafand cinema, where they saw that many subalterns, mostly in the RAMC or

RASC, had a nurse on his arm, for the most part plain and matronly! However, this did not impress Flash and he still held to his point of view, about which they all argued throughout the cinema. As they drove up to their mess after the show, Flash had his argument completely shattered, and admitted utter defeat, because in the bushes outside the mess, they beheld by the light of the moon, a plain matronly nurse, with a soldier, proving beyond any doubt, that sexual desire and sexual pleasure come to all manner of nurses!

Today is Mummy's birthday. I do so wonder where she is, and what she is doing now. I really am very worried because London has been raided both by day and night continually for the last few days, and I know that Mummy is doing work in London.

Fowler, who is in my troop, came and asked for my advice today. He has been married 3½ years, and has one child. He showed me a letter from his wife in which she wanted to leave him. It's not a question of another man, but simply through the influence of her people, who consider that she could have done better for herself. I have promised to draft him a letter on the lines that now is hardly the time to think of oneself, and of busting up marriages, especially from the children's point of view. A most difficult job.

I heard today that six more officers are on their way out to join this regiment, including Eric Jones. I shall certainly try to get him into C Squadron.

Sunday, 15 September

The papers and the wireless – in fact everybody – are all talking about the anticipated invasion of England. It is expected that preparations are going on all along the coast. If Germany does attack it's highly probable they will make some kind of offensive out here. It is rumoured that great preparations are going on in Egypt. (A slight interruption: an enormous rat has just run across the floor. Stephen and I had a terrific chase, but we lost him in the end. The place is stiff with rats; one evening we propose to have an organized rat hunt.)

In the *Palestine Post* today, it announced that Palestinians could now join the RASC and the RAMC, and that infantry battalions are to be formed both of Jews and Arabs under the control of the Buffs. This is a very excellent idea. They are very keen to fight, and feel very strongly that they can defend their land just as well as Australians and English. I am writing this sitting out on the balcony, by the light of a most beautiful full moon. How romantic this place could be, especially with this moon, if one could have with one the most beautiful girl in the world.

Monday, 16 September

This afternoon 3rd Troop, C Squadron challenged the rest at cricket. We had a very good game, but lost by 12 runs. Being able to get this cricket in the afternoon makes all the difference. Donny came back and joined the squadron again in the morning. I understand that the colonel will be going back on the same boat as all the wives, and Flash Kellett will then become colonel. The batteries will be reorganized into three original squadrons, which will be a very good thing. Peter Laycock will become our squadron leader, and the others will be Jack Abdy, Tony Holden and Basil Ringrose.

Tuesday, 17 September

As all the wives are leaving the country in the very near future Flash Kellett decided to give a farewell dinner party at RHQ. He telephoned Donny and told him to buy the necessary food in Tel Aviv. Stephen and I tossed up to decide who should go with Donny to this party. I won and went with him. All RHQ officers were there as all the other batteries like ourselves are at different posts. The party consisted of about 20. I sat next to Micky Gold and Lawrence Biddle. I had very much hoped I could have got next to Rona, who was looking very attractive but rather too made up. Anyhow I spoke to her for quite a long time after dinner. She gave me rather an attractive little animal made of ivory. I am not quite certain what kind of animal it is meant to represent, and it looks very much as if it is going to have a baby, but I appreciate the gift all the same.

After dinner I had a long talk with the adjutant (Sydney Morse). He was a bit tight. He told me that if the Italians attacked Egypt, and the Egyptians, manning the coastal guns, failed in any way, we should be responsible for those guns. The fact that the King of Egypt is so pro-Italian is causing the higher command a certain amount of uneasiness. We are the only regiment out here in the east who could attempt to take over the guns, and of course we are not really capable. We do not place a great deal of confidence in the Egyptian coastal gunners.

In fact, the Italians had already attacked Egypt, although in a decidedly lacklustre fashion. Marshal Graziani, commander-in-chief of Italian forces in North Africa, had no wish to attack, fearing his forces, no matter how numerically superior to the British, were ill-equipped for a march into the largely waterless Western Desert. However, under extreme pressure from Mussolini, he reluctantly did as ordered. On 13 September, the Italian Tenth Army invaded through Sollum and the Helfaya Pass, the British falling back in a leisurely fashion and hitting Italian targets hard with their artillery as they did so. Three days later, the Italians reached the insignificant village of Sidi Barrani, then halted. And, for the time being, that was the limit of the Italian advance into Egypt.

Wednesday, 18 September

At the dinner last night Donny asked Flash Kellett and his wife, Peter Laycock and Anne Feversham (Halifax's daughter) for lunch today. Of course he forgot all about the invitation. We, as usual, had our lunch at 12.30, eating up everything in the whole place, and they all arrived at 1.15 to find Donny naked on the veranda smoking a cigar! They all had to go off to Tel Aviv for their lunch! We all thought it a great joke!

Peter Laycock is an extraordinary person. He never greeted Stephen or me when he arrived here, and we haven't seen him for many weeks. His behaviour towards Anne Feversham is quite laughable. He may admire her, but there is no reason for him to sniff round her the whole time like a dog on heat, especially when she has a husband in the country. But between the reader of this diary and myself, I believe she also has another *amour* in the country.

Thursday, 19 September

Today a letter came round from our new brigadier (Keith Dunn) to be shown to all officers to the effect that we are to be mechanized and that we should not be kept on this security job for any longer than possible. We hear on the wireless and from the papers that air raids still continue over London. Bombs seem to have been dropped all around Lowndes Square, which is so worrying.

In the afternoon Doc Brooks brought over a team from the other squadron to play us here at cricket. We had a very exciting match and lost by 12 runs. Bob Knight played for them, and Donny played for us.

I went over to dinner with Henry and Rona Trotter at Rehovot. They have been lent a very pleasant house belonging to Henry's brother-in-law. For the present the colonel and Lady Yarborough are staying with them. The colonel wasn't there as he was dining in mess. Rona was looking very attractive. They have definite news now that they leave the country on Sunday. They go through the Red Sea, down the east coast of Africa and Cape Town, where they can either stay, or catch a Union Castle boat to England. The wives of this regiment, or the illegitimate wives, who came out on their own, against orders, have to pay their own way home, and will be the first to go. They are making a great fuss about it all, but to my mind it's quite right that they should pay as they came out against all orders and have had a wonderful time out here.

The family have sent me out an excellent portrait of each of them for which I asked. Three new officers have arrived from England to join the Regiment. I have not seen them yet, as they have been sent down to Haifa to join the battery, which are on the guns at the moment.

Saturday, 21 September

This morning the colonel came round and said goodbye to us all here. His time is now up after being colonel for four years, and he leaves for England tomorrow. We shall miss the little man: he has bags and bags full of guts. He said a few words, we gave him three cheers, he wished the officers good luck and then went off. He appeared very sad at leaving us. As he got in the car, he turned and wished me good luck. He is a grand person.

Flash Kellett will now become colonel and Donny Player second-in-command. It will be very sad to lose Donny as squadron leader. I have just about served one year under him. He is one of the most energetic people I have ever met, handicapped badly by asthma (which has improved since we gave up the horses). He has great charm, even for the lowest, and in spite of his wealth, is a most simple and generous person. But with all that he is also a driver and something of a task-master (sometimes unreasonably so), but no squadron was ever any the worse for that. I am very sorry indeed that he is leaving us.

I am now writing this diary with the gramophone playing. I shall go round the guard fairly early, and then to bed. During this afternoon we had a warning. No planes came over but soon after we saw clouds of smoke rising into the sky in the direction of Haifa.

3

Flash Kellett Takes Command

Lt-Col E. O. 'Flash' Kellett.

Sunday, 22 September 1940

THE HEAD PADRE from Sarafand came over and gave us a service. I had to be here to meet him. He gave us a very moderate sermon, and I didn't think he was much of a man. He gave us a sermon on brotherly love and, over a glass of lemonade afterwards, did nothing but slate and run down his junior chaplains. Donny instructed me not to ask him for lunch if I could avoid doing so.

Peter Laycock and Anne Feversham came over to lunch. Peter seems absolutely bats about the girl. I suppose in some ways you could call her attractive, but he really is nuts on her. It really is most amusing to watch. Jim Feversham, her husband, is a major in the Yorkshire Hussars. He came over and joined us after lunch. That, however, didn't stop Peter sniffing round. If I were Jim I wouldn't stand for it. But, still, it's no business of mine.

Monday, 23 September

Until we are reorganized into squadrons again Henry bloody Trotter has come to take over this battery. God help us!

Tuesday, 24 September

All officers' wives left today. I should like to have said goodbye to Rona. I wonder whether I shall see her again.

Thursday, 26 September

Dan Ranfurly is becoming ADC to Neame (OC Palestine), John Walters machine-gun officer, and Derrick Warwick gas officer.

I do enjoy my cricket. It brings back England more than anything else. Today I had a letter from Daddy dated 1 September, which was very recent. Both he and Mummy seem to be spending a lot of time in London, which is most worrying with all those raids. I also had a letter from Malcolm Christopherson, who was full of interest, but rather depressing. There is still no news of Nevill, which is bad. John Rowell, who was commissioned to the Xth from the Inns of Court, has been killed. It is most disturbing, as he was such a nice person. Malc told me that John Hanson-Lawson got back all right, so did David Steele, but his brother Dick is missing, believed prisoner.

We heard on the Italian propaganda news that the Italians were coming to bomb the power station at Tel Aviv, and raze it to the ground. This was going to happen today, according to the news, so when the alarm did go off, the men fairly bolted for the trenches.

Saturday, 28 September

Today we had a practice alarm. We telephoned a report that parachutists had landed at a certain point. Previously I had taken 16 men out to act as parachutists and take up offensive positions.

Stephen took charge of the defence of the hangar with the mobile patrol. The whole thing was kept from the troops, except, of course, my party. They were not very quick in turning out. We had quite a good battle. I dressed two men up as fifth columnists in civilian clothes, Lacy and Ellis. One of them managed to get right into the hangar. Lacy looked a dreadful tramp!

On the whole Henry Trotter is not too bad. Stephen and I are making him more human, and making it quite clear to him that there are many more important things in life, besides Henry Trotter and hunting.

On the news we heard that in the air battle over England yesterday the Germans lost 137 planes. The RAF certainly takes all honours. We also heard about the new agreement between Italy, Germany and Japan, by which Japan agrees to attack any other country that enters the war against Germany. This is all directed against the USA, who are not at all impressed.

At 6 o'clock I rushed down and had another bathe. The sun, a great red ball, was just about to disappear below the horizon, and sea was beautifully calm. The whole place looked lovely and I stayed in for about ½ an hour.

By late September 1940, the Battle of Britain was still raging over the skies of southern England, but the Luftwaffe were no closer to clearing the skies of the RAF. Hitler had already postponed any planned invasion and was shortly to postpone indefinitely. The very strong isolationist lobby in Washington was still pretty powerful and, with a presidential election coming up, Roosevelt seeking a third term, there was no way the USA was going to be drawn into the war just yet. Nonetheless, increasing numbers of American factories were now producing war matériel, not least for Britain, and the Tripartite Pact Stanley refers to certainly helped subtly shift the mood in the USA. Slowly but surely, the isolationists were beginning to lose ground . . .

Monday, 30 September

I gave a test paper to the NCOs on map reading and compass on which I have been lecturing for the last fortnight. The results were good. They all got about 70 per cent.

Henry Trotter came back from Sarafand with a rumour that officers were going to be allowed to have their chargers back. Stephen and I had a bathe in the afternoon.

Today the clocks go back to winter time. That will make the evenings very long especially with the blackout. I had a sea-mail letter from Mummy dated 10 July.

We had cricket here in the afternoon.

Tuesday, 1 October

Derrick Warwick came over and gave us all a lecture on gas. He had attended a course in Egypt. He spoke and knew his subject. The new gas, which the Germans have called Arsine, sounds rather deadly. At 11 o'clock I had to take the battery less NCOs at arms drill and marching.

In the afternoon we had a cricket match, officers and NCOs v the Rest. We lost. Both Henry Trotter and Stephen played. I don't suppose Henry has ever played cricket with the men before.

I believe that Henry Trotter is to be made a captain in the near future. The idea is quite fantastic. In civilian life he has never done a real day's work, except hunting hounds. He is quite illiterate. The sergeant major has to dictate orders, Stephen and I have to suggest the training programme for the men, and give the lectures. He had a letter from Rona, on her way home, she sent her love, which he passed on rather grudgingly.

Thursday, 3 October

Henry Trotter went off after tea to RHQ at Sarafand for dinner and to spend the night there so Stephen and I were left on our own once again, for which we were not sorry. I mounted the guard and wrote out orders. After supper Sergeant Sewell (now acting sergeant major) and SQM Tandy came in and had a drink with us. Sewell got on to relating his experiences of the last war. He certainly had a very rough time. He told us that the men who were in the Regiment with him during the last war seemed to be of a different type from the men in the Regiment today.

Friday, 4 October

I had a sea-mail letter from Bridget and also one from Daddy.

Usual routine during the day. Bathed before breakfast, and some men from the hangar came down with me. In the evening Henry Trotter and I went over to RHQ Sarafand to attend a lecture on Dunkirk from a Major Chap who was actually there. He belonged to the Royal Corps of Signals and was attached to Corps HQ of the 3rd Army Corps. He chiefly related his own personal experiences.

The three army corps were holding a line running east to west, just south of the France-Belgium frontier, ready to move into Belgium if the Bosch should break through. When the Bosch did break through there, they started marching in according to plan, but were rather disturbed to find that they had made a nasty gap in the French line, which was on their right flank. The extraordinary thing was that no effort was made on the part of the French to stop that gap, or even to liaise with the British on their left flank. After being surrounded the only course left to the BEF was to make for Dunkirk.

Major Chap actually spent six days on the mole supervising the embarkation of troops. At one time they were getting 3000 men off in the hour. All rifles had to be thrown into the sea to make more room, and save weight so great was the crush on the boats. He saw very little of what took place on the beach but the mole was continuously shelled and bombed. He was just about the last to leave, and came across the Channel to Dover on a destroyer, which, unfortunately, was sunk on its way back. He eventually ended up in Bristol, his home being in Salisbury!

Saturday, 5 October

I have a dreadful feeling that this war might last the hell of a time, and if we do invade Germany in the end, the war for us has not really begun. I see that Italy has sent 5000 pilots to Germany. This may be a result of the tremendous losses of pilots the Germans have sustained in the aerial battles over England.

Monday, 7 October

In the morning I set the NCOs a compass march over the desert. It took the form of a treasure hunt, and I made out three different routes. It took a hell of a time to make out and hide the clues. The winner got a bottle of beer but it ended up by all the NCOs having a glass. Sergeant Thompson easily won with his party.

Heard today that I am going on a rifle and machine-gun course at the Middle East Weapon Training School on the 22nd of this month for a month. It will be a change. Our address now is Middle East Force, and not Palestine.

Monday, 14 October

Exactly one year ago today I joined this regiment, at Malton in Yorkshire, as a second lieutenant, commissioned from the Inns of Court. At first, after an interview with Gerald Grosvenor, the adjutant, I was attached to B Squadron, but I ran into Micky Gold, in those dismal church dorms, which was RHQ and he asked for a transfer to C Squadron. I was very pleased to find that I knew Mike Parish as well in C Squadron.

It hardly seems a year ago. John Walters and Lawrence Biddle also joined with me from the Inns of Court. The third new officer was from the Cambridge OTC, a dreadful shit called Birch-White. When we came abroad he was left behind in England, and as far as I can gather, owing to his unpopularity, has been pushed round from station to station. It hardly seems a year ago. To celebrate the anniversary I went over to RHQ for dinner at Sarafand. Jack Abdy, John Walters, Lawrence Biddle, Doc Bob and Derrick Warwick were at dinner. Also Stephen Mitchell, who had gone over there to try and get rid of his earache.

He is going on a few days' leave to Egypt to stay with a cousin of his in the army who is billeted at Ismailia. I left here after guard mounting on a motorbike. It was a beautiful moonlit night, so the going was comparatively easy. I have never ridden at night before. After dinner we all went to the garrison cinema.

When I left I had rather trouble in starting the bike, and when eventually I got it to go, I heard a dreadful clattering noise behind, and on turning round found that two tins had been fixed on behind the motorbike. I ran over a heap of stones in Tel Aviv on my way home, and went A over T; neither the bike nor I was damaged and I got home safely.

I hear that Flash has put in for seniority for Lawrence Biddle, John Walters and self. Up the Inns of Court! The application will go to the secretary of state for war by the special government daily air service.

I only hope that it goes through.

Thursday, 17 October

The rains seem to have begun in earnest. We had a terrific downpour at lunchtime. In the afternoon Henry and I took a gun and went for a long walk out into the country. We saw quite a few quail but Henry missed them all. True to type he never let me have a shot. I don't think I could stand living with him alone for very much longer. What a life Rona must have with him.

The secretary of state for war, Anthony Eden, has arrived in this country. He arrived at Lydda airport by plane from Egypt. We gave him a guard of honour, which was commanded by Basil Ringrose, as at the moment he is guarding the airport with B Battery. We sent eight men from here. I chose the men with Sergeant Sewell.

Friday, 18 October

I understand that Flash Kellett had quite a long talk with Eden. He told him that quite definitely the 1st Cavalry Division would be mechanized, in all probability tanks, and we should be the first regiment to be mechanized, but not for a considerable time yet. It was, however, absolutely certain that we should never get our horses back again. All the stuff now is going out to Egypt. To Flash's question about the air raids in London, he answered that if you flew over London, you would never know that it had been touched but on the other hand if you walked from Marble Arch to Victoria via Berkeley Square, one would see extensive damage to some very familiar buildings. The morale of the people was good; they were more grimly annoyed than anything else. London was carrying on but under somewhat difficult circumstances.

The arrival of Anthony Eden, the foreign secretary, did much to reassure troops in the Middle East that they had not been forgotten at home. His visit, along with the recent arrival of a number of tanks, also showed that Britain intended to fight on in the theatre. In fact, General Wavell had already drawn up orders for the two British divisions in Egypt, the 7th Armoured and 4th Indian, to attack the Italian forces at Sidi Barrani. Even so, despite Eden's promises, the Sherwood Rangers were no closer to becoming mechanized. They were experiencing the reality of the vast mountain Britain had to climb to build up its army's strength.

Monday, 21 October

Stephen Mitchell arrived back early this morning from Egypt. He has been away for a few days' sick leave. He is not really fit yet, and is still having trouble with his ear. Frank Barley came over to tea from Bir Salim. He is in the Greys, and at the moment is adjutant of the Middle East Weapon Training School. I go there for a month's course tomorrow. I did some boxing in the evening with the men in the hangar.

George Luck told me yesterday that during the middle of

September the Germans had actually set sail across the Channel to invade England but the RAF had inflicted tremendous damage by pouring oil on the boats, then setting fire to them by machine-gun bullets. I don't know how much truth there is in this, it certainly never came out in the press.

There was no truth in it at all!

Tuesday, 22 October

Today I left the power station to start my month's course at the Middle East Weapon Training School at Bir Salim. I left the power station at about 9.30 with Smith, my batman.

I arrived at about 12.30. From outside it is rather an attractive place. Before the war it was an orphanage school, where they taught farming. The buildings are white with red-tiled roofs. Rather lovely gum trees surround the courtyard, in the middle of which there is an attractive well. The view over the countryside is also good. But inside it's not too hot. We are three to a room, without any kind of furniture. The mess is not really big enough, and there are not sufficient chairs to sit down even.

After lunch we had a lecture from the CO, telling us to be good boys and to work hard; we were then divided up into squads with a staff sergeant as instructor. I am squad No. 13, with one other officer, from the NSY (North Somerset Yeomanry), and the others are NCOs from various regiments. Two NCOs have come with me from my regiment.

Tuesday, 22–Friday, 25 October

I am working on the Hotchkiss gun, anti-tank rifle, rifle and pistol. There are about 30 other officers drawn from every kind of regiment, including Australians, NZs, Rhodesians, officers from the Western Desert, from the TJFF, Indian regiments, and from every branch of the army, cavalry, infantry, gunners, RASC. As well as the officers, NCOs also come. I brought one NCO from my regiment, Corporal Campbell from Y Battery.

In lectures we are divided up into squads of seven or eight. In my class we have two officers and six NCOs all from Yeomanry Cavalry units. Our instructor is a sergeant from the Warwick Yeomanry, a very nice person and an excellent instructor. The idea of the school is to produce instructors, so that we can instruct our units on what we have learned when we get back.

We have one period before breakfast from 7.15 to 8 o'clock; one hour for breakfast and off again until 1 o'clock with a twenty-minute break during the morning.

After lunch we have one other period and that finishes the lectures for the day. In the evening you have to do a certain amount of revision work.

Halfway through the course there is a practical exam, and at the end a written exam. If you do exceptionally well you get a D (for distinction) and that is what I am after. A full report on your work to your colonel follows when you leave. It's hard work here, but full of interest and quite fun.

I like all the other officers whom I have met so far, especially the Australians and NZs. I have not met the colonel, only seen him. The chief instructor is a Major Reeves from the Buffs. Strangely enough he married Cynthia Barrow, whom I have met quite a lot with the Burdens.

There is also Captain Court, an Australian, a grand person and a first-class instructor. George Luck is also here as an instructor. When war was declared we trained together at Edinburgh. We got our commissions at the same time and he went to the Warwickshire Yeomanry. I have not come across the other officer instructors yet.

I share a room with two other officers, Peter Seleri, just out from England, also Inns of Court, and commissioned to North Somerset Yeomanry, and a fellow called Downing. He started the war in HAC (anti-aircraft). Went to Norway where he had rather a rough time, had a few days' leave and then came out here. Life, in fact, is very similar to university or school. We work to a programme, sleep in dormitories, eat at long tables and work at 'prep' in the evenings. But I am enjoying it all.

Monday, 28 October

A long day and I worked most of the time. Rather startling news over the radio.

(1) Italy has waltzed into Greece.

(2) The *Empress of Britain* has been bombed and sunk two miles off the north coast of Ireland. Apparently there were 700 people on board, and about 46 have not been accounted for. They told us that the passengers mostly consisted of families evacuated from this part of the world; which is most disturbing news, as the colonel, Lady Yarborough, RSM Wallace, our squadron sergeant major, Heathershore, and various of the sergeants all left the east on the *Empress of Britain*. Also all the evacuated 'wives' of our regiment, which included Rona Trotter, Hermione Ranfurly, Sydney Morris's wife, and Toby Wallace were on the ship. Whether they were taken off at the Cape and did the rest of the journey on a Union Line steamer remains to be seen; likewise they may have been landed at a south port in England.

I shall have to ring up tomorrow and find out if Henry has heard anything. Captain Frank Bowler of the Greys, who is adjutant here, is Henry's brother-in-law. I didn't see him this evening but I did hear that he was very worried.

I sent all my photographs home via Heathershore. I shall be most annoyed if they have gone to the bottom of the sea.

Mussolini had not warned his Axis partner, Adolf Hitler, that he intended to invade Greece, but nonetheless this was what he did, giving the new theatre priority over North Africa. Hitler, who was with

Mussolini in Florence at the time, was furious. Of more immediate concern to many of the Sherwood Rangers, however, was the sinking of the Empress of Britain, *the 42,348-ton flagship of the Canadian Pacific Steamship Company. At around 9.20 a.m. on 26 October, as she was sailing some seventy miles north-west of Ireland, she was spotted and attacked by a German Focke-Wulf Condor, a big, six-engine long-range bomber. The* Empress *was struck twice by bombs, and although there were initially few casualties, fires started to spread and at 9.50 a.m., the captain gave the order to abandon ship.*

Tuesday, 29 October

It is certain that the colonel or (ex-colonel) and Lady Yarborough, Rona Trotter and Sydney Morris's wife were on board the *Empress of Britain.* But we have heard no news yet. A priority cable has been sent by the War Office. If our sergeants were on the boat, including Heathershore, those who were in this regiment during the last war will have been through it twice: going out to Gallipoli in the last war they were torpedoed and lost every single horse, and only one man. This time it's the *Empress of Britain* that has been bombed and sunk.

Usual programme of work during the day.

I wish there was more chance of getting exercise here. After dinner I went to a cinema in Sarafand. We saw Wallace Beery in a very good sea film. Sarafand seems to grow every day both in size and number of troops.

Wednesday, 30 October

During the morning we had a very excellent demonstration of concealment by Captain Court. We were taken onto an open field and within 50–80 yards nine Bren guns were so carefully concealed and cleverly that it was just impossible to spot their positions.

Thursday, 31 October

I went to dinner at HQ Sarafand, and both Mark and Donny were there. As I came into the mess I found two officers I had never seen before, one just out from England, by name Gunlan, another an SSM from the Greys commissioned to this regiment. I went and had a talk with Donny Player. He told me that Dandy Wallace had received a cable from the ex-colonel from Glasgow telling him that Toby, his wife, was missing from the *Empress*. He never mentioned anything about himself or the other wives.

Dandy has been struck off the strength of this regiment and works at the force HQ Jerusalem. Donny told me that they had sent him down to us for a change and to get him out of the office.

Both Donny and I are afraid that since the colonel didn't mention any of the other wives it would probably mean that he knew something had happened to her, and had cabled him in this manner to lighten the shock. It really is most dreadful to think about. I have never met a more kind or charming woman. She was quite the salt of the earth and had waiting for her in England two of the sweetest kids alive.

When I was in England, just before leaving Malton for Brocklesby, I got a bad kick in the stomach. Toby kindly had me to stay at their house, and made me terribly comfortable. I had never met her before and she could not have been kinder. The children are grand, especially the little girl, Jane.

We can only hope for the best. So far Henry has not had a word from Rona, or Sydney from his wife Dorothy. It's most disturbing for everybody.

I had a long talk to Mark about our future. We are now to be made into an armoured division. We are to be a brigade under Joe Kingston, with the North Somerset Yeomanry and Yorkshire Hussars. These two regiments will be cruiser tanks and our regiment will be a motorized infantry battalion in the brigade. One brigade of horsed cavalry will remain including the Greys, Yorkshire Dragoons and another regiment. They apparently will go immediately to the Syrian frontier. The Household Cavalry and Royals will be mechanized.

During the morning we had an excellent demonstration at the Jaffa ranges. We all fired the anti-tank rifle. We did some extra work during the afternoon.

Today is Daddy's birthday. How I wish we could have dined together at the Savoy.

Friday, 1 November

Usual routine during the morning. In the afternoon we had a rifle inspection followed by quite a good lecture on zeroing the rifle by Jack Finny.

I had a twelve-page letter from Jean Morris written from Canada. While she was staying at Fenton, Michael was there on embarkation leave hence no letters.

She had a terrible journey across the Atlantic all alone with the four children. The boat was terribly overcrowded and they ran into a full-scale hurricane. It was so bad that the children had to be on the floor on their backs all during the day.

Saturday, 2 November

After work in the morning I did some revision in preparation for the exam on Monday.

Today we had confirmation that Toby Wallace had been killed by machine-gun bullets while leaving the *Empress*. It's a terrible tragedy. Poor Dandy. What will he do without her? Why should it have been Toby? She was more like a saint than any other woman I have ever met. It's upset us all terribly.

The Empress *did not sink after the initial attack and most of the crew and passengers managed to take safely to the lifeboats. A day later, two ocean-going tugs arrived to try to tow her back to port, but despite a destroyer escort, the* Empress *was attacked and hit by U-boat U-32. At 2.05 a.m. on 28 October, she sank off the coast of Donegal.*

Sunday, 3 November

I left Tel Aviv early to return to Bir Salim as I wanted to do some work. The first part of the exam is on Monday: Hotchkiss gun and anti-tank rifle.

As I drove up this morning I saw lone figures wandering about the field talking to themselves or to the trees. Everybody saying their lessons to themselves for the exam tomorrow. It really is like school again.

Monday, 4 November

Today we had the first part of the exam. You have to get 65 per cent for a pass and 95 per cent for a D (i.e. Distinction). Two tests on the Hotchkiss gun and one on the A/T rifle. Unfortunately I did not bargain on getting stoppages as one of the questions on the Hotchkiss. I put all my money on 'Firing' Lesson Three! And learned the whole thing by heart! But still I got 80 per cent on the whole thing and was second in the class. The next half of the course is Rifle and Bayonet.

I sent a cable to the Yarboroughs and Rona Trotter congratulating them on their escape from the *Empress of Britain*. I also wrote to Dandy.

Tuesday, 5 November

The second half of the course started today and I have been moved to another squad, this time all officers and no NCOs. Quite an amusing collection.

One of the students, an officer from an Indian regiment, has been recalled to his regiment in Egypt. It looks as though they may be going off to Greece. The Greeks appear to be doing wonderful work, and pushing on into Albania with tremendous drive.

Guy Fawkes Day today, who would have thought it?

Today I sent off all my Christmas cards, 20 in all. I only hope they will all arrive in time.

Friday, 8 November

One of the instructor officers from the Rifle Brigade thought we were so bad at thrusting the bayonet that he gave us an extra parade this afternoon, much to our wrath and the wrath of our instructors as we all agreed that we were trying like hell!

Two letters today, one from Mummy and the other from Ione Barclay that was, now Ione Cassell. Both letters dated 20 September. Mother said that London was most uncomfortable with all these raids and that she had been without sleep for a week. She had now gone down to spend a few days with Daddy at Shaftesbury. Dad she told us was very much better, which was a great relief.

Ione answered three letters of mine written in May and June so it shows how long it takes to get an answer. Most extraordinary thing, Ione writes most regularly, and all her letters are most sentimental and loving. She told me in one that she has always been in love with me, and if I had asked her to marry me she certainly would have. Of course I have known her for simply years but I have never made love to her or even kissed her. That's probably the reason why. I am very fond of her and she is a sweet kid. I don't know this fellow Cassell, whom she has married.

In the evening I dined with Donny Player and George Massey-Smith at the Gat Rayman Hotel Tel Aviv. George was on this course having come up from the Western Desert. He is in the 7th Hussars. He has seen quite a lot of active service in Egypt, and I understand has done very well. His squadron leader was killed in the very next tank. Donny sent me back here in his car. It was beautiful, and the moon shining through the gum trees and over the buildings of Bir Salim made a beautiful picture. The peace and stillness made me think how wonderful this world of ours can be.

Saturday, 9 November

London still continues to be bombed. Chamberlain is gravely ill. Hitler made a speech in which he said Germany would fight to the end. Turin was bombed by the RAF from England. So was Munich. British troops have arrived in Crete and the Greeks are standing firm.

Sunday, 10 November

A very enjoyable day. Michael Laycock came over and picked me up and we went to the Jaffa club and had a game of squash. The first game since I left England. I beat Michael 4–1 and thoroughly enjoyed it. Afterwards we had a bathe. The Jaffa club is certainly a lovely spot; I have not been there since we were at Jaffa in about March or April quelling the riots.

In the afternoon and evening I did some work in preparation for the exam next week.

15,000 people have been killed through air raids in England since the war began. Not much news on the wireless this evening, except that Chamberlain passed away this morning. He must have died disappointed, but universally he was regarded as a most upright, sincere, hard-working man. I was at Winchester with his son Frank, a charming person. Winston Churchill is an old man. He is nearly 70 and one wonders what would happen if he suddenly went out.

Tuesday, 12 November

Three letters arrived from Daddy, one written on 16 September, another on the 20th, and finally the 27th. London is getting very scarred but the morale and spirits of the people are quite wonderful. Chelsea appears to have had it in the neck particularly badly.

I really am starting to work hard now for this damned exam.

Thursday, 14 November

Working all day. They certainly make us work here and there's plenty of it. But it's interesting. I am trying to get a D.

Saturday, 16 November

This morning we had an oral exam on rifle and bayonet. We were first required to give an introduction speech on the rifle. That went off all right, then two lessons on the rifle to criticize; one was all right, the other not so good and finally a lesson on the bayonet to criticize, which was not so hot. I would much rather give a lesson than criticize, like the Hotchkiss exam.

Jack Fany, officer instructor from the Rifle Brigade, told us that our results were disappointing and that we had all got about 70 per cent, one under. We don't know our individual percentages yet. I am disappointed – I thought I'd got about 80 per cent.

Sunday, 17 November

News came through on the wireless that Coventry had had one of the worst air raids of the war: 1000 casualties. London had also had a bad one.

Great surprise: I learned that I got 84 per cent for the practical exam on rifle and bayonet, which was top of the squad.

The bombing of Coventry particularly shocked Britain because it was the first time the centre of a British town had been so comprehensively destroyed, including the cathedral. In fact, 568 people were killed, but 4300 homes were reduced to rubble and two-thirds of the city's buildings damaged. Around one-third of Coventry's factories were also destroyed.

Monday, 18 November

Written exam for the first two hours during the morning. I liked the questions, of which there were five, except one, and I hope to get 80 per cent on that paper.

Tuesday, 19 November

We had a demonstration by two aircraft of planes attacking troops. They showed us high bombing, medium bombing and dive-bombing. The planes they used were old Lysanders and did not really give a true picture of the tremendous speed of the German dive-bombers.

We had our farewell speech from the CO, who expressed the hope that we had learned something and would pass on what we had learned to our units.

My total percentage was 86 per cent, which to my mind was very satisfactory. You have to get 90 per cent for a D.

Wednesday, 20 November

The course officially ended today. It's been great fun, but real hard work. I don't think I have worked so hard since leaving Winchester. I had a fond farewell with all my friends, especially Bill Ryder, the New Zealander, and 'Guns' Downing in the artillery. Both were charming persons. A lorry came to fetch me about 10 o'clock. I arrived at RHQ Sarafand just as Bob Knight was about to leave for Jaffa station to return to England, so with Donny and others I went to the station to see him off. I think he felt sad at going and we shall all miss him; he was a great quarter master, but at the end I am afraid the job was too much for him. Dandy Wallace was on the train. The shock of losing poor Toby seems to have knocked him up. He is only going home for the children's sake.

Thursday, 21 November

A very long day. Stephen and I went on the Jaffa ranges from 8 o'clock until 3.30 in the afternoon. An order has come from Brigade that all men who have not so far fired the Hotchkiss gun should do so. As a result we have had men coming on the range who have never seen the gun before. A huge waste of time and ammunition.

Stephen and I had our lunch out there. Actually it was a beautiful day and not too hot.

Monday, 25 November

Flash Kellett told me today that I was to be transferred to B Battery as second-in-command. That means I shall leave C, who I have been with since joining the Regiment. I shall simply hate leaving the men in my troop, they are such an excellent crowd, but I shall get back again when we are re-formed into mechanized squadrons. Basil Ringrose is my new battery commander. Flash was most decent, and said that he was transferring me because he wanted some greater drive in that battery, which I suppose was a compliment.

Tuesday, 26 November

I had a cable from Rona Trotter in answer to mine congratulating her on her escape after the *Empress of Britain* had been bombed and sunk.

Life at the moment is most hectic. Each morning I motor over to Bir Salim with Stephen and four NCOs to do a course on the Bren. In the afternoon we are lecturing to our cadre class.

At 6.30 I have to take another lecture on the anti-tank rifle. It is done by means of a cinema, which is rather a good idea.

Sunday, 1 December

Fancy, Christmas is almost here. The weather now is perfect. Sunshine all day but not too hot.

Today Donny Player, Lawrence Biddle, Stephen Mitchell, Jack Abdy and I went on a trip to Ashkelon. The ruins there are most interesting. In the evening I did some work on the Bren gun and prepared lectures for tomorrow.

Monday, 2 December

I have been made an acting, unpaid, first lieutenant and have been posted to B Battery as second-in-command. The same has happened to Lawrence while he is acting adjutant. So now we wear two pips. It is certainly a step in the right direction, as we have gone over the heads of about five other junior officers. I can't complain but I wish I could go back to C Battery now, especially the men in my troop, and even more so Corporal Lee, now Sergeant. It's rather annoying that I shall have to leave this cadre class of NCOs. Stephen will continue to run that now.

Thursday, 5 December

In the evening Stephen and I made out the examination paper, which they will get on Saturday afternoon. After dinner I discussed the paper with Sydney and the colonel.

Before leaving for Bir Salim this morning I inspected the cadre class before they went on the square under Sergeant London.

Before the inspection I put my lighted pipe in the pocket of my trousers. While inspecting I smelt a very funny smell, and looking down, much to my consternation, I found that my shorts were alight. I managed to hide the fact from the squad, which I considered a jolly good effort on my part and most noble.

Friday, 6 December

It has come out in regimental orders that we can send a letter home by airmail consisting of one thin page, free, which will arrive in time for Christmas. I wrote one off to the family.

Monday, 9 December

It really is great fun being battery commander, and being in sole charge here. The whole battery has to be trained in the Bren gun, so we have a busy time before us. I gave a lecture on fire orders in the morning and another on the Bren in the afternoon. The colonel paid a visit in the afternoon and stayed for tea.

I had a letter from Daddy, Seymour Pears and Ione. Ione asked me to be godfather to her first child. She told me one name it would have would be Stanley. Seymour has been commissioned to the Greys and expects to come out here. Daddy told me in his letter that Uncle Stanley's home in Regent's Park had been bombed, and that in spite of his age he had not left London. Derrick now has got a commission in the RASC. Clive, the old dog, has not written to me for simply months.

Wednesday, 11 December

Yesterday we made quite a large-scale attack in Egypt, but a fair amount of success.

The Greeks are still pushing the Italians out of their country.

Stanley's comments about the battle in Egypt are somewhat understated. In fact, Mussolini's plans were going very badly awry. The British Mediterranean Fleet had already won one victory against the Italian Navy at Calabria in July, and had then, on 11 November, inflicted a catastrophic strike against the Italian Fleet lying at harbour at Taranto. Using Fleet Air Arm Swordfish flying from an aircraft carrier, the British raid had put out of action three Italian battleships, halving their capital ships in just one strike. On land, the Greeks were unexpectedly pushing back the Italian invaders, a humiliation from which the Italian Army would never recover, while on 9 December, the British Western Desert Force launched an offensive in Egypt, Operation COMPASS. In two days, the 30,000-strong British force captured 38,000 Italians, 237 guns and 73 tanks, and recaptured Sidi Barrani.

Thursday, 12 December

There was a battery commanders' conference at HQ during the morning, which I attended.

The colonel leaves for the Western Desert to do an attachment with the Rifle Brigade. For our new formation and mechanization we are to be attached to the Rifle Brigade and I understand that each officer will get down there for a short time. It should be very good fun and most interesting. I stayed for lunch at HQ.

Friday, 13 December

During their advance, our forces have captured 20,000 Italians in the Western Desert. It appears that their tactics have been quite brilliant. The Greeks also seem to be pressing the Italians on all fronts. It makes one itch to join in and have a smack at them. But our time will come. Enemy activity over England has eased up for the last few days.

Stanley's estimation of the number of Italians captured is some way short of the reality, which was double the number cited. By 17 December, when Sollum and Fort Capuzzo were taken, the number of prisoners was more than 70,000.

There were, however, alarm bells ringing for Britain as, on 13 December, Hitler issued a directive for the occupation of the Balkans and the build-up of troops in southern Romania from which he planned the occupation of Thessalonika and, if necessary, all of Greece. This was on the back of the announcement made at the end of November that Hungary, Romania and Slovakia had joined the Axis.

For the British, it was one thing taking on the Italians in Africa, but quite another finding the troops to help the Greeks fight the Germans.

Saturday, 14 December

In the afternoon we had a cricket match. Roger Nelthorpe brought some of his men over to play against us. We easily won. B have got quite a good team, but it's not so good or so keen as C was. There is one very good player, a fellow called Knight. He was in the last war, and joined up again this time as a trooper. I think he played for Notts County.

Stephen Mitchell came over from RHQ for the weekend. He told me that our headquarters cadre class had been a great success. Derrick Warwick came over with 20 men from Lydda, as we had arranged a concert given by ENSA for the men, which was held in a hall at the Levant Fair. Before the concert we had a most amusing dinner party in the mess. We had a grand joke on old Roger. We arranged with the guard commander to telephone him up during dinner that he must return at once to Agir as there had been a fire. He came rushing back again into the mess falling over everything saying that he must go at once as Agir was on fire!

We then told him that we should arrange for our squadron lorry to take him back and let him go all the way up to the guard room, where the sergeant of the guard presented him with a note which said, 'We hope the fire is out – from the officers' mess.' The old boy took it very well!

We dressed up Smith, my batman, as an Egyptian waiter. He blackened his face, wore a fez and proper garments. When he first appeared, and started to hand round the dishes, the expressions of amazement were most amusing. The concert was quite good, and we entertained the artists on the stage afterwards. We sent some food and drink up from the mess. Derrick and Roger took their men back after the show. It was a most amusing evening and all went very well.

Stephen stayed the night. They took the main support away from my camp bed so that when I got in I crashed to the floor! Much to their delight.

Sunday, 15 December

I have just come in from going round the guard posts. The moon is full and it's a beautiful night. A pretty strong wind is blowing and the sea is rough. I do often wonder whether at some future date I shall read through this diary, or whether I shall not be there to do so and some other person will read it.

Thursday, 19 December

In the afternoon we played a rugger match against 2 Battery, Mike Laycock's, on the Stadium Ground. It was only the second game that we had played. Stuart Thompson, who has played a great deal, played and has really got the thing going. When he was with Michael in his battery he got him keen, and now he thinks about nothing else. He has gone crazy on the game. He has bought all his team very smart black rugger vests. Mike Gold played for them. We won 7–3. Which was a jolly good show. It certainly is a grand game. I should love to have gone to the Varsity and tried for a blue. I thoroughly enjoyed myself, but the whole time I was very nervous about my knee, and I felt it once badly. It really is a damned nuisance, because I think I am just as fast as I was at Winchester.

The bad knee Stanley refers to had plagued him since his schooldays at Winchester, when he badly damaged the cartilage while playing football. It had never properly healed.

Friday, 20 December

There have been unconfirmed reports that Germany has walked into Italy. We are still pushing on in the Western Desert, and I think we have captured about 30,000 prisoners.

I had a long letter from Mummy and Daddy, and three from Ione Barclay that was. She writes most regularly to me. Mummy's letter was most interesting. At last she has left London and taken a small house at Sunningdale, almost opposite Craigmyle. I am very relieved that she is out of London. That also means Daddy won't have to stay the night in town when he comes up to London. There seems to have been trouble with Derrick again. He had a row with Mummy before leaving to join his regiment, and neither of the family have heard of him for a long time. Daddy is rather worried and Derrick told his bank manager that his messing was costing him £5 per week!

Some of the officers have had letters from their wives with detailed accounts of their experiences when the *Empress of Britain* was sunk. Apparently the first bomb completely knocked out the anti-aircraft crew. The colonel went down to his cabin and had to escape through the porthole when his cabin fell in; he was almost knocked out. Rona Trotter was being let down the side when the boat into which she was being lowered was washed away and she had to drop into the sea. She was eventually picked up by a raft and machine-gunned by the enemy bomber. Apparently she behaved wonderfully well and had a wonderful write-up in the papers. I expect that I shall hear more details from Sydney, who has had a letter from his wife.

Saturday, 21 December

I woke up this morning with bad toothache, which lasted all day. A wisdom tooth coming up at the back is the cause of the trouble.

The colonel has got back from Egypt much earlier than expected. He went down to spend some time with the Rifle Brigade, but had to come back when they went up as reserve. He will go back, when they come back again. He and the adjutant, Sydney Morse, came and paid us a visit during the afternoon.

My toothache was bad so I went to bed very early.

Sunday, 22 December

Basil Ringrose came back from umpiring with the 6th Brigade, and assumes command of the battery. Personally, I like him and find him a most charming person. I have thoroughly enjoyed being in sole charge of the battery. Basil told me we should probably be equipped with Italian trucks, which have been captured in Egypt. It is almost certain that we shall be giving up these security duties in the very near future and start real training.

My toothache is still bad. I shall have to make a visit to the dentist.

In the afternoon we had a game of cricket. In the evening we played tennis and badminton in the hangar.

25 December, Christmas Day

We didn't get up very early. During the morning we had a rugger match against a team brought over by HQ. I was going to play but decided against it, as my bad knee has been giving me trouble. The game was a draw.

The men had their Christmas meal at lunchtime. The officers stood them some port and they all got very tight!

In the afternoon Geoffrey Brooks was going to bring a cricket team, but owing to the Christmas dinner, it did not materialize. There is no doubt about it, Basil is most popular with the men of his battery. The colonel and Sydney came over, and the colonel made rather a pompous speech. To my mind, he made a mistake not accepting a drink from the men. He refused because he was late on his rounds.

Basil Thompson and I drew lots as to who should go into RHQ for Christmas dinner and Basil stayed behind.

Dinner at RHQ was quite fun. I sat between Donny Player and John Walters. It all seemed rather forced. We went back in the open truck. It was a grand night, but cold. We dismissed the truck in Tel Aviv and Thompson and I went and had a drink at the Samakan. We taxied home, and got back to the power station at 3.30. Quite a pleasant Christmas Day, the weather perfect.

A cable arrived from Jean, which pleased me tremendously; also a letter from Bridget Wilkinson and one from Clive. Clive had no news at all. It was the first letter I had received for months, but he said he had been writing regularly.

4

A New Year

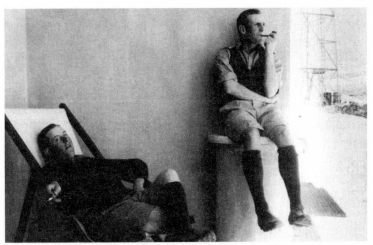

Stanley in Palestine, pensively smoking his pipe.

Wednesday, 1 January 1941

ANOTHER YEAR COMMENCES. I do so wonder what this year has in store for us. Where will we all be this time next year? At the moment I am at Port Said acting embarkation staff officer for the Armoured Division, which has just arrived from England. I came down from Palestine for this job with some others from various regiments, including Peter Ward from the Household Cavalry, Tony Bonham from the Greys, Richard Barber from the Cheshire Yeomanry, Hopkinson from the Beds & Herts. We have all had a most interesting and amusing time.

Yesterday I arranged and saw to the disembarkation of the *Duchess of Alloa* and slept on board. The Tower Hamlets were on board and I saw Mark Clayton who is now a major! Before returning to Palestine we are putting in for a couple of days' leave in Cairo. The KDG and Northumberland Hussars are in this convoy.

Friday, 3 January

Richard Barber, Charles Ward and I left early in the morning for Cairo. Paul Bestwood had to return to his regiment. It was a long and tiring journey and the train was very late. We met a gunner on the train, only a youngster, who had won the MC in France. We had a most interesting conversation with him, especially about Dunkirk. He eventually arrived in England with only a pair of blue shorts and one shirt.

We are staying at the Continental Hotel.

Saturday, 4 January

In the afternoon we went to the races at the Gezira Club. I ran into Jack Abdy, who has come down on leave. He lunched and came with us. It was tremendous fun, and I ran into heaps of people who have just arrived from England, including Christopher Taylor who is in the KDG. The whole setting and the weather were grand. The band played and I thoroughly enjoyed myself. I met Mrs Peyton, wife of Guy Peyton, who is now on the staff of the Armoured Division in the desert, and working with Gerald Grosvenor. She had a job in Cairo, and lives in a flat, which she shares with Hermione Ranfurly. The latter set off with all the other wives to England, got as far as Durban, then flew to Cairo, where she has now got a job. There has been a tremendous fuss about it all, but she has managed to stay. Dan, her husband, is now ADC to Neame, C-in-C in Palestine. I got one winner during the day.

Goddard has now got a commission and wears our badges. He is an Australian Jew, called Gobtlich, and joined this regiment as a trooper. Flash brought him in. Being a refugee he changed his name to Goddard. I didn't recognize him when I saw him on the racecourse. He has now got a job at HQ Cairo on the intelligence side as he knows many languages. Jack was furious about him wearing our badges.

Sunday, 5 January

I caught the wrong train back to Palestine after a most interesting and enjoyable time. The famous Lady Allen was on the train. She is a widow aged about 40, who has caught and become engaged to a young subaltern in the Staffordshire Yeomanry aged 23. She is a striking-looking woman, with rather an amazing mind.

Monday, 6 January

I arrived at Lydda early in the morning and drove back to Sarafand, and reported to the orderly room. I saw the adjutant and the colonel, also Donny Player. I find now that, since Basil Ringrose has gone, Michael Laycock has taken charge of the battery, and I have been transferred to Z Battery, which is now at Sarafand. I have also to start another cadre class next week for potential NCOs. Old Stephen has gone on a course at Bir Salim. At the moment, there is no other officer attached to Z Battery. I really shall be glad when we are re-formed again into squadrons.

Tuesday, 7 January

Sergeant Major Barker is the BSM of Z Battery. I always have liked him and get on well with him. We are still doing the damned security duties. This battery is in charge of Bir Salim and the wireless station. I went to the wireless station in the morning.

In the afternoon I walked over to Lydda with Sydney Morse to see Derrick Warwick. We had tea over there and came back by car. I have had a grand mail from England, including letters from Clive, a tremendous one from him, Ursula Barclay, Nanny, Rona Trotter and Martha Rodwell. Extraordinary the number of married women I seem to correspond with. Two letters from Bridget Wilkinson. Nothing whatsoever from the family, which is rather disturbing.

We have now taken 70,000 prisoners in the Western Desert. A great many are coming up to Palestine. Basra has fallen.

Wednesday, 8 January

A strong rumour went round today that we shall move up onto the frontier. Where will all this end? I often wonder whether I shall get through or not.

Monday, 13 January

The cadre class started today. Gave lectures during the morning and afternoon. Had an excellent airmail. Letters from Daddy, Pat, Rona, Ione and Diana Pelham. Pat writes an excellent letter. I hear that she is growing into such an attractive girl. She has the sweetest nature of any person I have met.

X Battery leave here tomorrow for our new camp at Banjaimara. Y Battery are returning from Cyprus. It will be an excellent thing when we are all structured as a regiment again.

Tuesday, 14 January

I inspected the cadre class at 8.15 and gave them various lectures during the day. No news from the Libya front. London got another bad raid. It's so very difficult to see the end of the war, even if we knock Italy out. I think personally that Germany will be beaten economically; if she is not, the worst is still to come, as it will take a very long and bloody battle to beat the German Army. At the moment the war is entirely a war of the air, each side endeavouring to find some new invention to combat the night air raids.

After dinner Mike Riviere and I went to a cinema in Sarafand. I am just listening to the news from England. They tell us that our air force is sweeping the Italian air force from the skies.

Wednesday, 15 January

I had a long discussion with Stuart Thompson as to whether the officers of this regiment lack the *joie de vivre* and companionship which a Yeomanry regiment should have. I am certainly looking forward to the Regiment being together again when we can really get down to training, and can take an interest in our own men, instead of being switched about from battery to battery.

Thursday, 23 January

Tobruk has fallen, and we have taken another 20,000 Italian prisoners. The Australians actually entered the town. We captured four more Italian generals and an Italian admiral off a destroyer which was in the harbour.

I wish we could be taking part, or doing something more than just sitting at Sarafand. I had quite a full day, three lectures in the morning and one in the afternoon.

Saturday, 25 January

I came in to lunch to news that Mark and Donny should report to Force HQ at Jerusalem to receive instructions for us to fulfil our role of last August – i.e., heavy gunners for coastal defence.

Great speculation as to where we should go. The colonel got back with the news that we were going to man the guns along the Libyan coast at the ports which have just been captured from the Italians and also in Crete. Consternation everywhere! On the first appearance, it looked pretty grim, especially after all the training we have done here, preparing ourselves for the formation of an armoured division; but on the other hand, we could not have done anything definite for about six months and certainly not have got any vehicles on which to train. Now we shall probably go to Benghazi and Tobruk, which will be very much nearer the scene of the action and, hang it all, it's experience. It will certainly be better than sitting in Palestine doing various guards.

After lunch I went for a walk with Henry, Myles Hildyard and

Whiting. We went up into the hills behind Ben Shemen. The country was beautifully green, and it was a most perfect day. We took guns and got a couple of pigeon.

The climate of this country is simply grand. I had a cable from Jean. She has broken her ankle. Donny Player, Henry Trotter and I went to dinner in Tel Aviv. We spent too much money, drank too much and got back too late. But it was a change. The first time that I have had a party since getting back from Egypt.

Henry is adopting a most foolish attitude about our becoming gunners again. He has made up his mind, which is so childish, but the poor chap hasn't got the brains of a child of 10, and you can't really blame him for that.

Sunday, 26 January

All the batteries are concentrating at Sarafand. The detachment came in from Jaffa Ranges. I went over there during the morning, as they are attached to my battery, and I met rather a nice major, who has been out in this country for 17 years in the Civil Service. He was connected with intelligence on the Syrian frontier. He told me that never at any time had there been any real concern and sympathy to us by the French in Syria. And after Syria had agreed to the armistice our military mission under Salisbury Jones, who was directly responsible to Wavell, was given only two hours to get out of the country, and had complained to the French authorities that they had treated him and spoken to him as if he were an Italian!

There was a conference for battery commanders in the CO's office at 11.30. He spoke very well and put the whole situation most clearly, pointing out that we had received a very good chit from the divisional commander when he came down here and that we had to do our very best in this new role. At the moment I shall be second-in-command to Z Battery with Michael Laycock as battery commander. We don't know when we leave, but when we do there will be two batteries in Crete and four on the Libyan coast.

During the afternoon I went for a walk with Geoff Brooks, our doctor. In many respects I am looking forward to getting up nearer the front. I think we have been long enough in Palestine, and living too comfortably at Sarafand – and feeding too well.

Monday, 27 January

Today Lawrence Biddle was made an acting – unpaid – captain and became adjutant in place of Sydney Morse who now takes over a battery. Lawrence will make an excellent adjutant. He has an excellent clear-thinking brain. Gradually the Regiment is collecting at Sarafand.

Stephen Mitchell now becomes a battery commander and has been made a captain. I could not be more pleased. Actually, at the moment he is not quite behaving like a captain, as he is doing a solo dance to a Gilbert and Sullivan record, which I have got on the gramophone, dressed up in his pyjamas and an absurd hat, in slightly an intoxicated condition. It's rather fun being together again. In this bungalow we have got Stephen, Doc Lawrence and self.

Mike Laycock came back and took over Z Battery; Thompson is the other officer. Actually, I was to be second-in-command to Sydney Morse but Mike Laycock asked for me to be changed. I would rather have liked to get back to C Battery. Henry is in command there, with Mike Gold as his second-in-command. My battery together with three others and RHQ are going to Tobruk, and the other two are going to Crete.

Nobody seems to know exactly when we will go. Tonight we sat down 13 to dinner, but I don't think many noticed it. The colonel was the first to get up from the table. He is a terribly superstitious man but I don't think he realized that we were 13.

Tuesday, 28 January

The colonel passed the cadre class off the square, and I gave them a practical Bren exam and a written exam. I have not collected all the papers yet.

Z battery includes Mike Laycock, as battery commander, Dan Ranfurly – who gives up being ADC to General Neame and returns in a month – Stuart Thompson and self. Flash, the colonel, told me the other day that I should be a captain in a month, but I don't see it. I really should be pleased to get a captaincy. Everybody is making frantic arrangements for this move. Nobody seems to know exactly when we will go, though.

We are limited to 200lbs of luggage so a good deal of storing will have to be done. I understand that Z Battery will fire two-pounders to deal with swift-moving motor torpedo boats of which Italy has a great many. We are still pushing on all fronts. It is reported that many German troops are now in southern Italy. There has been a fall in German air activity over England.

Had an early dinner and then went to a Spot Lights Concert in Sarafand, with Myles Hildyard, Mike Riviere, Jack Whiting and Roger Nelthorpe. It was really a most excellent show.

Thursday, 30 January

Roger Nelthorpe, Derrick Warwick, Micky Gold and I, plus four batmen and two NCOs left Sarafand for Lydda station to proceed to Tobruk as an advance party for the Regiment. We are going there for coastal defence work and when we arrive we have to report to HMS *Terror*.

We had a fond farewell with Sydney Morse and Mike Riviere as they are going to Crete with their battery, and Heaven knows when we shall see them again. We had a five-hour wait at Kantara as there had been an accident on the line, and we had to change at Benha at 1.30 in the morning. It was a most tiring journey. There was an air raid at Ismailia the day before. From Alexandria, I understand we are going to proceed by sea along the north coast of Africa.

That the Sherwood Rangers should be split up was not so unusual at this stage of the war, even if it was never ideal to do so. Britain was still rebuilding and enlarging her army, but while the Regiment had been earmarked for mechanization they needed to be put to use until such time as there were enough tanks with which to equip them. In North Africa, the Italians were still being driven back, but the build-up of German troops in southern Romania pointed to an imminent invasion of northern Greece. Should Greece fall, the situation in the Middle East and the Mediterranean would once again prove threatening to Britain. On 6 January, Churchill told Wavell to release troops for Greece. Five days later, on 11 January, Hitler ordered German troops to North Africa too. German intervention in the Mediterranean looked sure to alter the landscape dramatically. The trouble was, while Wavell had enough troops to defeat the Italians, he did not have enough to be assured of victory against the Germans in Greece and North Africa.

In the meantime, the Western Desert Force, renamed XIII Corps on 1 January, was continuing to throw back the Italians. Tobruk was surrounded on 7 January, while in East Africa, British forces were also pushing back the Italians. On 20 January, Emperor Haile Selassie re-entered Abyssinia, in Italian hands since 1936, and four days later, British troops entered Italian Somaliland from Kenya. In Libya, Tobruk fell on 22 January with 25,000 troops, 208 guns and 87 tanks.

Tobruk was another important port, albeit a small one, on the Libyan coast. If the British were to drive the Italians out of Libya, they needed all the ports they could capture and, once captured, needed to protect them. After the best part of a year in Palestine training but otherwise doing little, it made sense that the Rangers should finally be put to use. With the Germans entering the fray, the British were going to need every man they could get their hands on.

Friday, 31 January

At about 6 o'clock we arrived at a station just outside Alexandria where we decided to get out, which was fortunate as the RTO had some instructions for us. We had to proceed to the Waifa Palace Hotel, Alexandria, and await orders, while the two corporals had to go to the transit camp. We were fortunate enough to find an Australian lorry, which gave us a lift to our hotel. We then had a bath, shave and breakfast but as I was in the middle of having a bath orders came through that we had to report to the docks at 10.30, which made it all the hell of a rush. Just as we were leaving the hotel I ran into Bill May in great form. He has got the job of liaison officer. His regiment got rather a bad time.

At the docks we met the two NCOs and proceeded to board the *Ulster Prince* bound for Tobruk. There are about 600 on board. She only holds 400. Mostly AMPC and RAOC. I have got a cabin to myself. Should very much like to have had a couple of nights in Alexandria. We have an escort of one destroyer. Exactly a year ago we arrived in Palestine, and today we leave Palestine also via the Mediterranean.

I wonder where we will be this time next year.

5

Gunners at Tobruk

Stephen Mitchell, Stanley with cine camera, and Scottie.

Saturday, 1 February 1941

WE ARRIVED AT Tobruk at 12.30. It really was most interesting. It actually fell about a week ago, and in the harbour itself there are about 14 or 15 sunken craft, including an Italian cruiser, the *Georgia*, and a seaplane. The town itself from the ship does not appear to have been badly damaged, but that remains to be seen. When we landed we heard that there had been two air raids during the last 24 hours but no damage done.

On arrival here we had instructions to report to the HMS *Terror*, a monitor for orders. We left the others on the quay, and Roger and I took a launch and set forth. We met a charming officer but he knew nothing about us, and both the captain and the gunnery officer were ashore, but he gave us some tea and told us to report to Navy House and Base Area, but we could get no help from either.

We all met again on the quayside, having been in different directions, but without success. Nobody knew a thing about us. We were just giving up when fortunately the captain of the *Terror*, plus the gunnery officer and two other officers, arrived on the quayside from a tour of inspection. We made ourselves known to him, and he told us all to come aboard with him, and send the luggage up to the observation post. Having done this, all of us, i.e., four officers, two NCOs and our batmen, spent the night on the town.

Her job at the moment is coastal defence with her 15-inch guns, until they get some shore batteries working. They bombarded Sollum, Bardia and Tobruk, and gained for themselves a fine reputation against enemy planes. They made us all most comfortable, and could not have been more hospitable, to both ourselves and the men. The doctor on board is a man called McDowall. His father was a science master at Winchester, and I was there with his two brothers.

I had a long talk with McDowall about Winchester, then went to bed in a most comfortable cabin, which I had entirely to myself, and slept like a log. They could not have been more kind to us, and we all admired the quiet and efficient way the whole ship ran. I should have loved to be in the navy. It's a grand life with grand people.

Tobruk was a small port, even though it was a natural harbour. A long finger of headland extended east, protecting the port itself, which lay at the western end of a deep-water inlet a little over two miles long and, at its mouth, not quite a mile wide. Because it was so obviously a natural harbour, both the Greeks and later the Romans built fortresses there and it was also an important stop along the ancient coastal caravan route. When the Italians built a military post in 1911, it was little used, not much more than a village. In the following years, the Italians added a number of buildings, including offices, barracks and a hospital, as well as underground stores.

HMS Terror *was a monitor – that is, a small gunship – built during the First World War, which had seen plenty of action in the Channel and off the Dutch coast. In fact, in October 1917, she was torpedoed and beached at Dunkirk, although later towed back to*

Portsmouth and repaired. At the outbreak of war in 1939, she was
serving in Singapore, but was sent to join the Mediterranean Fleet.

Sunday, 2 February

We had a conference with the gunnery officer about our future. He is
a captain in the Royal Marines called Hoare. He told us that the *Terror*
had instructions to defend Tobruk with her 15-inch guns until shore
batteries had come into force, but they had not got sufficient personnel for the observation post on shore. That was why they had sent for
us, and it was our job to take over the OP.

We then explained to him that our gunnery experience consisted
of a three-week course six months ago, and we did not remember
much about it! But naturally we would do our very best. We were then
taken round the whole ship, into the gun turrets, which were most
impressive, and down into the shell rooms.

At 11 o'clock we came ashore after bidding farewell to the *Terror*,
and thanking them for all their hospitality. We then arrived at the OP,
which is behind the town and commands an excellent view out to sea,
and took it over from one officer from the *Terror*. The place is in a
dreadful mess: before they left, the Italians blew up a magazine.
However, the OP still stands, and also some barrack rooms, which
really is quite astounding. There are five 7½-foot guns, but their locks
have gone. Still, we may be able to get them going. One has been
blown completely out of the ground by the explosion. There are
masses of shells and ammunition and also rifles, but mostly with their
bolts gone.

The litter of clothing, boots and letters left behind by the Italians
is quite amazing. We have set up our mess in a barrack room
immediately below the OP, which strangely enough was not damaged
by the explosion. We are most fortunate because in the next room we
have a perfectly good stove. Our great difficulty is cooking utensils,
and those will have to be obtained by scrounging.

Another problem is water. All water has to be brought up from the
town, and the only transport up here belongs to the Yeoman signallers

next door, who occupy the other half of this building. After lunch, Micky Gold and I went out on a scrounging party. Our friend the Yeoman signaller took us in his transport, which is an Italian lorry. He is a grand person, and was a tremendous help. We soon saw that the Australians had made a mess of the whole town. They had got in first and wrecked the place. However, we set out with the main object of getting some transport, either Italian or otherwise. We were not successful but there may be hope tomorrow. We managed to bring back:

2 × beds Italian
1 × chest of drawers

At 6 o'clock we had a stand to, communicated with the *Terror*, and had a practice shoot, which was quite successful.

After supper the wind got up and it turned very cold. Our barrack room is terribly draughty and the mosquitoes are frightful. Fortunately I brought a net with me but none of the others did. We were all very weary, and slept pretty well, in spite of the most absurd noises, which continued throughout the night.

Monday, 3 February

As a result of scrounging today we have the following:

1 × cook (Italian prisoner, named Miguel)
1 × cask of wine
6 × chairs from the cinema
4 more beds
various pots and pans
1 × fatigue party of Italian prisoners, who removed a dead donkey from the front door which was beginning to smell.

The Italian prison camp is practically next door; also the cemetery – they are burying almost throughout the day.

Micky Gold and Derrick Warwick went off during the afternoon with our friend the Yeoman signaller. Micky Gold is first class at scrounging. Roger and I were in the OP for most of the day. During the afternoon, the captain of the *Terror* walked up to see us, had a look round the OP and seemed quite satisfied. He had tea with us afterwards. His name is Hayne, and he is a most charming person. At 6 o'clock we had two practice shoots. We all went up on the OP for that, and when we saw the 15-inch guns on the *Terror* turning according to our directions, we all got a big kick and felt very important. Just to think that we only had to give a different bearing, angle of inclination, for the guns to start changing direction!

We sent a signal off to the Regiment to say that all was well and to tell them to bring mosquito nets. It is now about 9.30 p.m. There is a hell of a sand storm, and the room is absolutely filled with sand and mosquitoes! We had an air raid during the afternoon. We didn't see much, but we heard that they were after an aerodrome opposite, and one of our Hurricanes brought down two planes. We saw the Hurricane: she came over and did her normal victory dive three times. I had a most interesting talk with an Australian who had been one of the first to enter this place.

Tuesday, 4 February

There was an air raid early this morning, about 5 o'clock, and lasted until 6. Quite a lot of bombs were dropped, also magnetic mines in the harbour. Some fell quite close to us and we felt the blast.

Every kind of gun opened fire, including the AA, plus captured Italian Bredas, machine-guns, and even rifles, and all fire seemed to meet over our heads. The searchlights were also working. The Wiltshire Yeomanry are here now working the lights. We are gradually getting settled, and today we managed to scrounge the following:

1 × Italian solid-tyred captured truck
150 gallons of petrol!
4 × mosquito nets

10 × blankets, Italian
1 × ice chest
10 × chairs from the cinema
4 × iron bedsteads
4 × mattresses, Italian

In the afternoon Micky Gold and I went to see about the truck. We first had to get written leave from Area HQ. We saw the DAQMG, an Australian called Major Gibson. After a bad start, and much persuasion we got the necessary leave, and off we went to an ordnance section that had arrived about two miles outside Tobruk right next door to a large Italian dump. Most of the lorries (there were every kind there) had been rendered U/S, but then came the question of petrol. We were told by the ordnance section that there was a dump about a mile away, so off we went in our new lorry over the most incredibly rough ground to the dump, which was being looked after by an NCO and two men. They asked us how much we wanted, and at first we asked for a fill-up, i.e., 9 to 10 gallons. The NCO in charge told us that we had better take a 50-gallon drum. Make it two, we suggested; he agreed. We then asked him how much the dump contained and he replied, 'Two million gallons of buried Italian petrol!' We took three drums, i.e., 150 gallons. Not bad! We have heard a rumour that the main dump has not been found, and that it may have a home bomb underneath it! I hope it's nowhere near the OP!

We got a great reception when we arrived back here with our new car. She looks like an old-fashioned bus with solid tyres. We took the Yeoman signaller with us to get the car. He really is a great chap and has been an enormous help to us in every way. Some naval people came in to dinner, one petty officer and three officers. They are all engaged in diving operations, trying to clear the harbour. The petty officer amazed us all by telling us his experiences in Norway, Holland and Dunkirk. We had an air-raid alarm during the evening and I think they dropped some bombs on the aerodrome the other side of the harbour.

Wednesday, 5 February

Some wretched RASC private picked up a fountain pen, unscrewed the top and was blown to pieces. It had been dropped during the raid the other night. A magnetic mine went up in the harbour, and just missed a merchant ship, but I am afraid she has been damaged. A small schooner also blew up, and the harbourmaster, who was aboard, is missing. They don't know the cause yet.

We ran out of bread – none was issued with the rations – so Micky and I went off to scrounge. We came back with five loaves. Micky is an absolute champion at the game. The town of Tobruk is rather a sad sight. We came across one Blenheim bomber, which had crashed into a house. God knows what happened to the British pilot. It had made a dreadful mess of the house.

For dinner we had with us two Australian officers, called Cohen and Dunlop. They had been in the attack on Capuzzo, Bardia and Tobruk, and they were both most interesting. In the attack on Bardia their battalion had lost 13 out of 14 platoon commanders, and two company commanders. Total casualties, I think, were 105. Tobruk casualties were very small. At the moment their battalion is staying here, and not going on to Benghazi. Major Cohen is in charge of the large prisoner concentration here. He told us that our organization for prisoners was quite appalling: 25,000 have had no food, water or blankets for 48 hours. But we had hardly expected such tremendous numbers. The small concentration which we have next door have been billeted in quarters under which I gather there are considerable quantities of cordite and high explosives.

I went down to the underground magazine right next door to the 6-inch gun near the OP. There are still a tremendous amount of charges and rounds. That part all escaped damage when the main magazine was exploded. We have christened our new lorry Anne. When we get her started she goes pretty well.

We are gradually settled in, and making ourselves comfortable. A NAAFI arrived in the town today from which we got a large supply of drink. Our duties up in the OP as regards the *Terror* are not very arduous. Her Captain Hoare came up and visited us. He asked us to go aboard some time, and have a meal with them. We get very little news about the rest of the war. I gather that they are still advancing on Benghazi, and that there have only been two raids over England during the last 14 days. It might be the lull before the storm. A most unpleasant sand storm is pelting up.

When visiting the petrol dump, about three miles outside the town, I ran into Ian Downing. He has an anti-aircraft section quite close to Bardia. He and I shared a room in Bir Salim.

Thursday, 6 February

It has been most unpleasant. A sand storm has raged throughout the whole day. It is quite impossible to keep the sand out of our room. The whole place is covered. When I woke up this morning my pillow and head were a mass of it. Visibility was nil, so it was not much good being up in the OP. You couldn't see more than 20 yards ahead.

I have never been so bitten in my life. I don't know whether it is mosquitoes, fleas or bed bugs but I itch all over the whole time!

British forces were continuing to push back the Italians. It was on this day that Benghazi surrendered to the British along with six Italian generals.

Friday, 7 February

Donny Player arrived today, having motored up from Alexandria with four new 15-cwt trucks and 10 men. We have billeted the men in the town. Jack Whiting, one of the new officers, came up with him.

Some of our guns have arrived, but there seems certain doubt as to who will put them in position. It's no good us doing it as we don't know the first thing about siting guns!

I understand quite unofficially that we shall be on this coastal defence work until June at the latest, then return to Palestine to train as an armoured division. In that case it will be a very long time before we see any real active service. We shall need at least eight or nine months' training.

Saturday, 8 February

Much to my amazement, the colonel turned up today. He had motored all the way up here from Alexandria. He stayed for lunch and then drove straight on to Benghazi, which fell yesterday. He said that he would take one of us on with him. We tossed for it, and Micky Gold, the lucky dog, won! He told us that X Battery under Peter Laycock will probably go to Benghazi, and that was his reason for going. He will also liaise with the Armoured Division and find out all he can in preparation for our becoming mechanized. I understand that the Armoured Division entered Benghazi first, and have pushed on for 40 miles. The question now is whether we shall push on to Tripoli.

At 5.15 Donny and I went on board the *Terror* for the evening shoot, and stayed for dinner. As usual they were all most charming. An oil tanker struck a magnetic mine in the harbour and went up: 18 people were killed. The flames were terrific.

Sunday, 9 February

Arranged for 30 prisoners to clean out the billets, which our men will occupy when they arrive, also to clean out some Italian gun pits, which we might use for the three-pounders when they arrive. After lunch Donny Player and I took a truck and went out on the Bardia road to have a look at the defences, both the inner and the outer perimeter. We saw the tanks, which they had dug in, and from which the Italians fired. They offered a wonderful form of protection, and if they had stuck there they should have been impregnable. Likewise the wire and the tank traps were formidable. The guns and the ammunition left behind were still a mess. There were hand-grenades in the thousand.

We went pretty carefully, as there must be a good many mines and booby traps about. We collected quite a few souvenirs on our journey.

We got back about 5.45 in time for the manning parade, but the *Terror* did not wish to have a practice shoot. It's been a beastly day, rained practically the whole time and very cold. The visibility has been bad all day. But our billets are pretty comfortable. We occupy one large room, part of the Italian naval barracks for those who used to man the guns. Three sleep one side and three the other. We eat in the same room off a long table running down the centre. We were most fortunate to find a kitchen with stove here.

At the moment Donny occupies a small room adjoining, which really belongs to the port war signallers. He has gone to bed with a rotten cold tonight. His asthma has been giving him trouble.

The colonel told me yesterday that a mail had come in, and that there were two letters for me, which he had left with Lawrence Biddle, our new adjutant. It's now about 11.30, and all the others have gone to bed. The only light which we have, of course, is an oil lamp, and as the oil is running out, I too, must hit the hay. Never have I seen such utter waste as I have in the last few days. The time, money and energy the Italians must have spent in this country is astounding, and all in vain; and what a place it is. There is absolutely nothing here but desert and, to my mind, it's not worth one single Italian life. It will ever be a source of amazement how we broke through their defences so easily. They must have been preparing for years.

The Italians had been preparing for years, but this preparation had been marked by ineptitude at almost every turn. Mussolini was not as absolute a leader as Hitler, still answerable to both the King and the Grand Council, and many of his senior commanders were ageing and out of touch. Red tape and an ineffective bureaucracy hampered every move, while Italy was simply not rich enough, economically advanced enough or blessed with enough natural resources to fulfil Mussolini's military aims. The navy was the most advanced and modern part of the armed services but lacked experience, while within the army, too much emphasis had been placed on infantry – most of whom were poorly trained and equipped. The successes in East Africa in the 1930s against what were largely tribesmen had flattered to deceive. In truth, Italy was simply not ready to fight a modern war; her string of defeats was ample testimony to that.

Monday, 10 February

C Battery and B Battery arrived today by sea from Alexandria. Henry Trotter is still in charge of C Battery, with Lovett as a subaltern. The latter was a squadron quarter master sergeant in the Regiment and has recently been commissioned. He is a very able and most charming person, in spite of the fact that many people considered it a mistake that he should get a commission in his own regiment.

We have still got the same mess but we shall have to get another bigger place when the other batteries arrive. It's pretty cold up here in Tobruk, especially at night. The men's billets in the town are not very good, and water is quite a problem.

The First World War had done much to break down the rigid class structures within the army, although matters had reverted somewhat during the 20 years that had followed. However, with the onset of war once more, commissioning from the ranks became more common once again, and increasingly so as junior subalterns, especially, had proportionally the highest casualty rates.

Tuesday, 11 February

I was on duty in the OP during the morning. A great deal of shipping came into the harbour. I can't understand why we have not had more raids, especially with all the shipping coming in.

In the afternoon Donny and I managed to procure a Breda gun from the navy. Actually Captain Hoare, the gunnery officer from the *Terror*, handed one over to us. They are excellent guns both for AA and A/T. We had an interesting conversation with a gunner today who is in charge of salvage operations. He told us that a systematic combing of the outer perimeter begins tomorrow. They anticipate finding a tremendous quantity of guns and ammunition. Donny and I are endeavouring to get hold of all the Bredas we can lay hands on, and unofficially form ourselves into light AA batteries because our chances of popping off our naval guns at the moment seem very remote indeed.

A and Z Batteries arrived this evening; RHQ was with them. The colonel and Micky Gold are still at Benghazi. The three-pounder and 4-inch guns have arrived, but nobody seems to know who will mount them. We hardly know how to fire the guns, let alone mount them.

I hear tonight that we have broken off diplomatic relations with Romania. That may mean that Germany will walk in there, and also endeavour to march into Greece. Turkey's attitude will be interesting. There is a rumour that the Free French will attack Tripoli from the west and take it; also that we have landed at Dunkirk and advanced 60 miles. But there is no confirmation at all.

The officers who arrived today, including Stephen, Jack Abdy, Lawrence Biddle and Michael Laycock, decided to stay the night on board. The men, of course, came off. Donny and I had tea at Navy House. Some officers off the *Terror* were there. They expect to move quite soon and suggested that their BOP staff should move with them. It would be grand if she went off to Benghazi or any other place for coastal defence work and demanded that we should go with her! Too good to be true!

Breda was an Italian armaments manufacturer and produced a number of guns. The one Stanley refers to here was the Model 35 20/65 20mm dual-purpose anti-aircraft and anti-tank gun. It had a range of around 2500m, a practical rate of fire of some 150 rounds per minute, and a velocity of about 850 metres per second. All in all, it was a pretty good and reliable weapon.

Wednesday, 12 February

Those who arrived yesterday were busy all day getting into their new billets. The town is really in a dreadful mess: no water, no light, no latrines, and the billets need a great deal of cleaning.

Donny and I spent most of the morning inspecting possible positions for our guns. The two-pounders we are firing were made in 1897! We had an advance officer with us who was most helpful. In the afternoon the officers and NCOs watched a demonstration of firing the Breda guns by an ack-ack battery. An urgent message came from Captain Hoare, the gunnery officer of the *Terror*, for Donny Player to go on board to see him and the captain; and later in the afternoon we saw two other officers from the *Terror* who told us the ship would be leaving tomorrow, and the BOP staff had to leave with her. That would mean that Roger, Derrick and I plus two NCOs would all sail in the *Terror* for the unknown destination, to man the observation posts in any port to which she went. That would be very much more exciting and interesting than sitting in Tobruk behind coastal defence guns.

Now that all the others have arrived we have started another officers' mess. We still have ours just below the OP, but now we have Geoffrey Brooks and Stephen, which could not be better. Good old Stephen is in tremendous form, and it's grand to see the old chap again. He is now a captain and battery commander of A Battery.

No official news about the war elsewhere. I gather that the Free French have walked into Tripoli from the west, and that the Armoured Division have gone well out forwards from Benghazi towards Tripoli.

News might not have reached the Sherwood Rangers at Tobruk, but the Italian Tenth Army had by now been destroyed by a stunning outflanking manoeuvre at the Battle of Beda Fomm in the western edge of Cyrenaica. On hearing the news, the British commander, General Richard O'Connor, signalled to Wavell, 'Fox killed in the open.'

That day, a further 20,000 men, 200 guns and 120 tanks were captured, prompting Anthony Eden, the foreign secretary, to ape Churchill's famous speech about the Few and say, 'Never has so much been surrendered by so many to so few.' Since the launch of Operation COMPASS in December, O'Connor's troops had captured more than 130,000 prisoners, 400 tanks and nearly 2000 guns, as well as twenty-two generals.

However, on the same day, Generalleutnant Erwin Rommel arrived in Tripoli. The Germans had reached North African shores.

Thursday, 13 February

Today I boarded HMS *Terror* and set sail westwards, with Roger Nelthorpe, Jack Whiting, Jack Abdy, two NCOs and our four batmen. Donny Player was to have come, but as the colonel is away, and he is in command of the Regiment, Jack came in his place. I understand that we shall be OP staff for the *Terror*. I am very excited to be one of the four! They have made us very comfortable on board, and made us members of the wardroom. Commander Haines is the captain of the ship. I have a cabin up on deck.

After dinner I played bridge with the first officer, doctor and paymaster and won! It was about the first time that I have played since leaving England. Smith, my batman, is most thrilled about his trip, and tells me that forward is very good, and that they are well looked after.

We set sail tomorrow at about 6 o'clock. Before coming on board we had a talk with the harbourmaster, Commander Drift. He is an enormous fellow, about six foot, with a terrific stomach and red beard. He is most entertaining. He told us that during the last week in Tobruk they had buried eight naval officers and 30 other ranks as a result of magnetic mines in the harbour and air raids.

Friday, 14 February

We had an escort of one destroyer against submarines. The gunnery officer, Captain Hood of the Royal Marines, has mounted six Italian Breda guns on the deck, which were captured at Tobruk and Bardia. We have offered to man one of these guns. So, in the event of an alarm,

Roger, Jack Whiting and I will man one on the port side. They are excellent guns, and can be used either against aircraft or against ground troops. All the ammunition are tracer, and very excellent.

Life is most pleasant on board, and all the members of the wardroom could not be more kind to us. I feel more than ever now that I made a mistake in not joining the navy. We spend our time going round various parts of the ship, eating, drinking and sleeping. During stand to at 18.00 hours we climbed up into the directing tower and watched the shore.

Saturday, 15 February

At last we arrived at Derna. As far as we can see from the ship, the town has not been damaged. It looked a much more pleasant place than Tobruk. There were actually some green trees. I understand there is an excellent water supply. We were going ashore but as there was a strong wind and the sea was rather rough, they did not let down a boat, which was rather disappointing.

At 11.30 we set sail again westwards. During the afternoon we went all over the engine rooms with the chief engineer. At 4.30 in the afternoon we fired the Italian Breda gun, which we are manning. Now we have three destroyers as escorts; we signalled them that we were going to fire for practice; and they all joined in, which was rather fun.

Again bridge after dinner; same four and again I won. The last four days have been for me about the best so far of the war.

Sunday, 16 February

Today we arrived at Benghazi, which we captured from the Italians nine days ago. We tied up alongside at 11.30 approx., and full marks go to the captain, Commander Haines, for the way in which he brought the old *Terror* into the harbour because he had not got an inch to spare. Last night there was an air raid on Benghazi – we could see the flashes as we approached. They dropped a good many magnetic mines in the harbour itself, and outside, and also bombed the town. The minesweepers escorted us into the harbour, and some of us saw two mines go off in front of us as we approached.

It was all rather tricky.

After lunch we went ashore to look for an OP and also billets. The first one we looked at was a lighthouse right in the Arab quarter and next to the prison. We actually found ourselves inside the prison, and met the commander in charge, who was an Italian sergeant, as usual covered with ribbons, which probably meant nothing. We certainly had a lovely view from the top, but finding billets there was out of the question.

We then called at Area HQ, which was a most impressive building adorned with marble and marble staircases and columns inside. We found the billeting officer, who was also staff captain. He was not at all helpful and seemed to know nothing. We asked him to take us to the bank, which possessed a high tower and might do as an OP.

We had a look at some flats opposite for our billets. They had been knocked about a good deal, but were most elaborate inside, and one or two of them half furnished. In one flat we found what remained of a nursery, with a child's cot, and toys all over the place. It was a pathetic sight. At Area HQ we asked about the colonel and Micky Gold who had left Tobruk for Benghazi about a week ago. They had seen them, but could find no information as to their whereabouts now. However we saw his sergeant major, who showed us a wonderful collection of rifles, guns (shooting and otherwise), automatics, swords, rapiers, etc., which had been handed in as a result of a proclamation. I have got my eye on a magnificent pair of German sporting guns. He gave me a firing .22 and two boxes of ammunition, which was most decent of him. *The Times* naval correspondent came on board for lunch. He has travelled a bit with this ship.

As far as we knew the Armoured Division was about 100 miles south-west of Benghazi. During the afternoon an unidentified aeroplane flew over the harbour and was fired on, but no bombs were dropped. Everybody is expecting an air raid again tonight, and I am afraid that the town is a rather obvious target. We shall have to man our Breda gun. There have been raids here for the last four nights. But still they may not come. Most of the civilian population have left now, and the place is quite dead. At the moment there are very few troops in the town, and I can't see why the Italians would want to bomb it. They scored a direct hit on the hospital last night, and killed the Australian colonel in charge.

We played bridge again after dinner, and again I won. The doctor and the paymaster had quite a heated argument over a bid!

Monday, 17 February

There was an air raid very early this morning. The alarm went about 5.15, and the all clear at 6.45. I manned the Breda gun on the port side. We actually fired about 12 rounds at a plane, which got in the searchlight but it was miles out of range.

We went on shore pretty early and lunched at the hotel with the naval officers from this ship, and a naval commander from Navy House. It wasn't a very good lunch, and only service people were lunching there, a very representative crowd from the army, navy and air force. We have fixed up an observation post on the top of the port war signal station; we have also found some excellent billets in the shape of a flat in a block almost next door to the observation post. The block has been pretty badly damaged by a land mine, which landed practically next door a few days ago. We have collected some furniture from some of the other flats, and have made it really quite comfortable. These were the luxury flats of the town, and are beautifully built with marble, which must have been brought all the way from Italy.

On the whole, not a great deal of damage has been done. It's quite clear that the better class Italians evacuated this place in a great hurry.

After dinner we played bridge. Again I played with the paymaster against the first officer and the doctor, and we won for the sixth night in succession.

Tuesday, 18 February

While we were ashore this afternoon there was another air raid, mostly on the harbour. Their target was the convoy, which arrived in from Alexandria. There were about nine planes, all German, and they dive-bombed on the harbour. We saw the beginning of the dive, then took cover. No damage was done. I heard that two were brought down and three damaged. A pretty formidable barrage was put up.

We got on board about 4.30, and then at 6 o'clock, or just as it was getting dark, they came over again. This time high bombing; which is most unpleasant, as you can hear the planes but can't see a thing until the bomb falls. I have an idea that some magnetic mines were dropped; also quite a lot of stuff fell on land.

Wednesday, 19 February

We have had five air raids in the last 24 hours but no damage has been done. They almost hit a man-of-war as she was leaving harbour. I was on shore for most of them, and had an excellent view of the one in the afternoon when they did some dive-bombing on the harbour. During the morning we were busy making preparations for the arrival of X Battery, and choosing the position for their guns. During our tour, we came across the old barracks and found the QM and medical store, also the armoury. Never have I seen such equipment, especially the medical stuff. Unfortunately most of it had been opened and also instruments looted. I never thought that I should see such utter waste. The Italians must have been preparing for years before war.

We called at Ordnance and found a most pleasant colonel in charge. He told us that he had a very lucky find during the morning. Locked in a drawer he discovered a map showing the positions of all the petrol dumps in the district. One was practically next door to his ordnance depot, and a great many bombs had fallen round them. That's what they are probably after.

We keep on bringing their planes down. Yesterday when we went ashore we saw two German pilots who had been brought down by A/A fire; two others had been killed. They looked typical Germans.

Thursday, 20 February

Donny Player, Jack Abdy and I left Benghazi for the front line with a view to collecting some captured Breda guns for our air defence. We took Corporal Matthews and one driver, and set off in a 15-cwt Ford truck.

We didn't go very far the first day and camped for the night in the desert a few hundred yards off the road. The road was excellent except where it had been blown up by the retreating Italians but it had been quickly repaired. It turned very cold at night, but we made ourselves quite comfortable.

By the noise there appeared to be quite a bit of bombing further up the line. The sunset was lovely – it all rather reminded me of the trip Daddy, Derrick and I made in the South African game reserve.

Friday, 21 February

We made an early start and went forward a further few miles and found HQ of the Armoured Division.

Gerald Grosvenor, our ex-adjutant, was there, and in excellent form, also Guy Peyton, who was chief instructor at the Inns of Court. We all lunched together. They really are a most charming crowd. One could not find two nicer people than Guy and Gerald. They are very similar types.

After lunch Donny and Jack went further on to a salvage dump to try to pick up some Breda guns and ammunition, and I went back to prepare the camp for the night. Just outside a village 12 German bombers came out of the sky and machine-gunned the village, road and a camp at the side. We kept well off the road and flat on our noses.

Jack and Donny were also machine-gunned at the camp. We camped at the same spot.

Saturday, 22 February

We travelled all day and arrived back at Benghazi in the afternoon. We brought back with us two Italian lorries and four Breda guns plus ammunition. Quite an extensive air raid during the evening, and some damage was done to the harbour.

Benghazi is certainly quite an extensive place. Graziani had his palace there, and there is also a Roman Catholic cathedral, which the priest told us was damaged when we raided the place endeavouring to hit the Fiat works next door.

Sunday, 23 February

At midday after lunch at the hotel, Donny Player, Jack Abdy and I left Benghazi to return to Tobruk. We left in three trucks.

Monday, 24 February

We motored all day – about 300 miles from Benghazi. It's an excellent road. We certainly have a long line of communication, and there is only one road.

On our arrival outside Tobruk we saw there was an air raid in progress so we stopped and watched. It looked like a display of fireworks from where we were with all the Breda tracer bullets. After the raid was over we continued, and arrived at our HQ in Tobruk at about 8.30 p.m. On our way down we stopped once or twice to make a fire and cook some food.

Tuesday, 25 February

Woken up at 6 o'clock by the air-raid siren. We all went round to the shelter, but nothing was dropped. The colonel came round after breakfast and told me that I should not go back to C with Henry Trotter, but I should go to A Battery as second-in-command under

Stephen Mitchell, and also that I should be promoted acting, unpaid, captain. A Battery are at the moment on the north point of the harbour together with Z Battery.

I was most pleased to be made a captain although it is only acting and unpaid, and it will be grand to be with old Stephen again.

I'm afraid we have lost rather a lot lately. First, the old *Terror* was sunk the day after we left here, but no lives were lost, and in the raid here at Tobruk they got a direct hit on a destroyer – the *Dainty*, which blew up immediately. I understand very few were saved. And finally a minesweeper struck a magnetic mine in the harbour and was a complete loss.

In the raid last night we brought down one German plane and possibly two others. The town got a direct hit, four were killed and 80 went to hospital. One tanker was hit in the harbour, one bomber cut off its engines and dived within 50 feet before letting go its bombs.

The Terror *had been attacked by German Junkers 88s on 22 February soon after leaving Benghazi. She was badly damaged, but still afloat. The crew had abandoned ship and then she had been towed back towards Alexandria. Sadly, she never made it, and finally sank off the coast near Derna. The Mediterranean Fleet had had a desperately busy time since the Italians declared war, battling the Italian Fleet, supporting the ground forces in North Africa, and providing escort work for convoys heading to Malta. The Fleet had a mixture of ageing capital ships and more modern destroyers, as well as aircraft carriers like the* Illustrious *(badly damaged by the Luftwaffe in early January). The indefatigable and hugely experienced Admiral Andrew Cunningham, known as ABC, was commanding the Mediterranean Fleet. He was equally well served by a number of skilled and experienced commanders. At this stage of the war, much of the fleet was still manned by pre-war regular members of the navy, and this level of seamanship counted for a great deal.*

Wednesday, 26 February

Now I am a captain (acting and unpaid!) in A Battery and second-in-command to Stephen. Our battery is situated on the north side of the harbour, or I should say the north point.

We spent a very busy day pitching tents, and cleaning old Italian gun pits in which to place our three-pounder gun. We also man an Italian gun, in perfect working order, to protect the boom, a captured Breda gun, and two Hotchkiss guns. There is also a proper ack-ack battery on this point plus searchlights worked by the Wiltshire Yeomanry. I understand that we are going to get a couple of lights for our coastal defence guns. At stand to during the evening, the harbour-master and another naval officer came and took up a position on the point with a view to seeing from which direction the bombers dive onto the harbour. In the last raid one came down to 50 feet and hit an oil tanker. It must have come down with its engines cut off. Nothing happened this evening, and the two naval officers stayed for dinner. The Rome radio announced that two German Armoured Divisions had clashed with our troops west of Benghazi.

Thursday, 27 February

Another long day working on the gun pits, pitching tents and digging slit trenches. We had three alerts but nothing was dropped. Derrick Warwick left here and joined C Battery. Jack Whiting came back from Benghazi and has joined A Battery; he told us that since he left raids have practically ceased at Benghazi since we have no shipping there now.

X Battery have gone up there under Peter Laycock. I had a cable from the family wishing me a Happy New Year. It's taken over two months! It was confirmed on the wireless that our troops had clashed with German troops west of Benghazi. I suppose they got there by sea, or possibly by air.

Friday, 28 February

Flash Kellett, the colonel, came round today and told us that the Greys were handing in their horses on 28 March and becoming cruiser tanks in a brigade with us and the Warwicks. We hope to be relieved of this job by June latest.

Saturday, 1 March

Another air raid last night. As I was duty officer I went up to our Breda gun. The weather has been absolutely foul. A gale has been blowing, which has created a perpetual sand storm, and it's been as cold as hell. Last night three of our tents were blown down, Michael's observation post under the cliffs was swamped and became quite useless, and his boat for going across the harbour broke away, and is now half full of water in the middle of the harbour. So it's not been a very good day.

After dinner we played strip poker, which was great fun. Poor old Jack Whiting eventually had to stand on the chair without socks or shoes, and only a shirt and trousers, and it was a very cold night! In the middle of it all, the air-raid siren went off.

Sunday, 2 March

At last a mail. Letters from Pat, Ione, Bridget and Diana Pelham. I loved hearing from Pat all about the Christmas holidays, and how they spent Xmas Day. Pat told me in her letter that poor Lady Mickey had died on Xmas Eve. She was a most generous person, and had always been terribly kind to Derrick and myself, especially when the family were away. Holme Park was always a second home to us. It made me feel very sad. I shall have to write to Sir Archie. I now feel a longing to get home and see all the family, and my friends.

On the news tonight we heard that German troops had definitely entered Bulgaria. Apparently Bulgaria has not declared war, but she can no longer be considered as a neutral party. Turkey hopes for peace but has quite plainly made it clear that she won't stand for any infringement of her independence.

It's now about 10.30; I am writing this by candlelight, and am just about to turn in. We had some enemy planes over about 7.30, and we have had three warnings altogether. I don't know what damage has been done, if any.

Wednesday, 5 March

We don't get any news here, but we gather that German troops have fully established themselves in Bulgaria. There was also a very scary rumour that Germany had sent an ultimatum to Turkey but we have heard no detail or confirmation. The colonel got back from Benghazi where he had been visiting X Battery under Peter Laycock. He told us that they were all most comfortable, and free from air raids. Our fighters had brought one German plane down; the pilot had just arrived out from Germany, and had done a raid on our front line. He flew over Benghazi, and tried to land, thinking that he had got back to Tripoli.

The colonel brought some eggs back with him. Tobruk does not possess a single egg or chicken. We really are most comfortable in our mess, consisting of A and Z Battery officers. We all get on very well and have a most amusing time.

Thursday, 6 March

Today I helped in the calibration of the 6-inch Italian guns, which C Battery have taken over. We have got some gunners to do the thing for us with the help of Ordnance. I had to observe the fall of shot from an OP on the left wing.

Friday, 7 March

Four German pilots have been brought down from Benghazi to an officers' prison camp here. The harbourmaster, who came in for a drink today, had an interview with them. They could all speak English, all were polite, and very confident that Germany will win the war. Ordnance are gradually getting our 4-inch guns into position. But it's a very slow job.

The British Expeditionary Force began landing in Greece on 7 March 1941. In all, some 100,000 troops – a mixture of British, New Zealanders, Australians and Poles – would be sent to help the Greeks.

Saturday, 8 March

Daddy told me in his last letter that Uncle Kenneth had died on Xmas Day, which was very sad. He was a grand person.

The men were on fatigues during the morning. After lunch I went into Tobruk with Michael to do some scrounging. In a yard we found a small sideboard, ideally suited for our mess, so we quickly had it in the truck, feeling rather guilty, as we heard somebody round the corner. We subsequently heard that the Ordnance sergeants had just left it there five minutes ago for their mess.

Monday, 10 March

We have definitely been registered as a tank regiment: it came out in regimental orders. Also, all officers have to learn, read and send messages in Morse code in a week's time.

Wednesday, 12 March

The colonel is going on a visit to Crete where we have B and Y Batteries manning coastal guns. We gave him a list of things to bring back from Cairo, as the NAAFI is practically empty, these days, and we almost live entirely on rations.

Friday, 14 March

We had a very big raid last night, which lasted from 2.30 until 5.15. They dropped about 84 bombs on the aerodrome a few miles away, but no damage.

Jack Whiting was duty officer and on the guns. He came rushing down here in the middle of it to tell us that they suspected gas had been dropped. There was certainly a stony, acrid smell but we concluded that it was caused by so much HE. It gave us all rather a nasty shock.

One German plane came very low over the harbour, and appeared to drop mines. Unfortunately our Breda got a stoppage at the critical period and only fired one shot. The patrol boat reported that he flew out to sea at a very low height and appeared to be in difficulties.

Saturday, 15 March

We had a football match against the navy in the afternoon, which we won. After tea I boxed with Mike Laycock and as usual my nose bled. Good exercise.

A young naval officer stayed to dinner as his motorbike broke down. 'Scottie' Myles and I spent half an hour trying to start the damned thing.

Sunday, 16 March

At the moment I can't see the end of the war. Germany, I hear, has concentrated all her latest bombers and fighters on the Bulgarian and Greek frontier. America has just passed the Lend Lease Bill, which is one in the eye for Germany. One feels that there has been so much preparation for destruction by both sides that before it all ends there will be a tremendous amount of bloodshed. Of course, it may end in stalemate but I do not think so. I have a feeling that Germany may make a landing by air in Syria. She landed 20,000 troops in Holland all from the air, and that was with opposition.

According to the wireless, our shipping losses lately have been considerable. Germany is certainly concentrating on our shipping both in the Atlantic and out here.

The Lend Lease Bill signed by Congress on 11 March meant that the United States could now provide Britain and other Allied nations with goods and war matériel without contravening its own neutrality laws. These had been set up in the 1930s as part of an effort to keep America out of any future European wars and, in a nutshell, forbade the selling of any arms to foreign powers on credit or lending belligerent nations money. Britain had got around this by buying with hard cash, but by the beginning of 1941, having largely stopped exporting goods once war had begun, was suffering from a lack of foreign exchange and running out of cash. The United States was not only sympathetic towards Britain but also concerned that Germany, if allowed to dominate all of Europe, posed a threat to her own sovereignty. The trouble was, even though Roosevelt had been re-elected for an historic third term the previous November, the isolationist lobby was still a powerful body and a proportion of the American public felt very strongly that America should keep out of the war. Lend Lease meant that the US could continue to help Britain without actually becoming directly embroiled in the war. However, not only was rising American economic might now being channelled towards the Allied war effort, many believed it signalled an important step towards the United States' eventual entry into the war. Certainly, Lend Lease nailed America's colours even more firmly to the mast.

Stanley was echoing the concerns of Britain's war leaders about the rate of shipping losses, which were admittedly considerable. However, Germany was still not achieving the monthly targets of Allied shipping sunk that was believed to be necessary to force Britain out of the war and, as it happened, March 1941 was to see a change in Allied fortunes in the Battle of the Atlantic – for the time being, at any rate. The Germans lost three leading U-boat aces that month, while the announcement of Lend Lease showed that an early decisive strategic result in the shipping war was out of their reach.

Tuesday, 18 March

Today the *Barona* was blown up by a mine in the harbour, dropped by enemy aircraft the other day. She sank in about 10 minutes. Stuart Thompson arrived on her yesterday and she was on her way back to Alexandria with prisoners. The prisoners panicked, and the shouts could be heard at the BOP. I saw the whole thing. It was a most depressing sight. I have had no confirmation about loss of life. I understand she used to be the Lord Mayor's yacht, and used by the Duke of Windsor for his cruise in the Mediterranean when he took Mrs Simpson.

Thursday, 20 March

We are still at Tobruk. That is RHQ, C Battery under Henry Trotter, A Battery under Stephen Mitchell, and Z Battery under Michael Laycock. X Battery is at Benghazi under Peter Laycock and B and Y are in Crete under Tony and Sydney.

Tony and I have had a letter from Mike Parish who is now in Crete. He appeared in very good form. I must write to him.

The colonel came back today from Cairo and Alexandria. He set off from here with the intention of visiting our batteries in Crete, but was quite unable to get further than Cairo, owing to transport. He came back with a very strong rumour that ourselves and the 1st Cavalry Division are all getting horses back again, and will go to Greece as horsed cavalry!

Apparently there are a good many Greeks in Cairo, and we are supplying horses to them. The prospect of fighting with horses is not very alluring – suicidal, actually.

Saturday, 22 March

All the morning I worked in the gun pits, which have to be enlarged. We have put these 4-inch guns in Italian gun pits, which are really too small for them. I got hold of the REs and they lent us a compressor to work a drill for blasting. An Australian came up and worked the engine for us. He was a typical tough Aussie, aged 47! When I asked him where he came from he immediately showed me about a dozen photos of his wife and family in Sydney, also two photographs of the public executions of Arabs, which the Italians used to have annually in Benghazi.

My stomach is not at the present in very good working order, and I have got toothache. Otherwise I am keeping very fit, and taking plenty of exercise, in the form of manual labour. In the last 10 days, two more mails have come in, but not a single letter for me. The doc has received 20 this month!!

Monday, 24 March

I have got toothache, a boil coming on my face, and a stomach out of order – otherwise in perfect health.

Jack Whiting is quite out of control these days. Last night he insisted on bringing into the room we share a stale old goat cheese that stank like the deepest drain in Jerusalem. He is always in great form and is a most amusing person.

I fear that we are losing a lot of shipping in the Atlantic through German submarines. Having established bases on the French coast, it makes the position very difficult for us. Our need for destroyers for escorting convoys is very great.

The 4-inch guns are not ready yet, and we are still converting the pits, and making sleeping quarters for the men. I have never done so much manual labour before, and as a result have grown blisters on my hands.

Wednesday, 26 March

In the afternoon I went to the dentist at the CCS. The place was run by the Australians and was all rather primitive. I almost gave up, but decided to face it. He was a most charming Australian who actually didn't hurt me at all – but he didn't cure my toothache! It's still just as bad.

There was a great deal of blood about the place, and he had to work his drill by foot. But I suppose we are lucky to have a dentist here at all.

Saturday, 29 March

We had a regimental cricket match against the Wiltshire Yeomanry. We got beaten badly. I did not play as I was on duty. They had a very good team, including Charles Awdry. Jack Whiting played, also Thompson. He had to hitch-hike all the way from the south side. Doc Brooks, our best player, could not play.

We heard news tonight that there had been a big naval action in the eastern Mediterranean, but we have heard no details. We heard a rumour yesterday that the Italian fleet had been seen off Benghazi and that C Battery had stood to.

I had a grand mail. Letters from Daddy, Mummy, Clive, John Hanson-Lawson, Ione, Bridget, and Diana Pelham.

As I was duty officer I had to sleep the night in the BOP. It was a good chance to write some letters. Poor old Stephen has a touch of pleurisy and is in bed so I am in charge of the battery.

Sunday, 30 March

A large-scale naval battle has taken place in the eastern Mediterranean, and so far we have heard three Italian cruisers and two destroyers have been sunk, and one battleship damaged, without any harm at all to our fleet.

One of our small craft reported that she had sighted Italian cruisers. We sent out a reconnaissance plane, which confirmed that the Italian fleet was 40 miles off Derna. Cunningham, C-in-C Mediterranean Fleet, decided to turn out everything that we had got and as a result our fleet was waiting for them. The news tomorrow will be most interesting.

Two naval officers from Navy House came to dinner. One fellow called Drew was a South African, and is harbourmaster here. He has lived in Johannesburg for 10 years, so I had a most interesting conversation with him. We had a great many mutual friends, and strangely enough his sister is engaged to Bill Ward-Jackson. I must write and ask Daddy whether he knows the name at all. The other naval officer was a grand person. I can't get his name. He was on the *Southampton* when she sank. One could not meet two more delightful men. They came up on a motorbike, and we have just seen them off. We had great fun in getting the thing started.

It seems most strange that there has been so little air activity over England, and we have not had a raid here for over a fortnight, touch wood. The colonel leaves tomorrow for the front line to have a look at the Armoured Division and learn a bit about how tanks operate.

Fifty Australian nurses have just arrived in Tobruk! I have not seen one yet! It will be the first woman I have seen for many a day.

Admiral Cunningham had been trying to draw out the Italian Fleet ever since the Battle of Calabria the previous July, but had finally picked up signs that the Italians were planning a big operation towards the end of March. Ordering his second-in-command, Vice Admiral Pridham-Wippell to sail four cruisers and a number of destroyers from Piraeus in Greece, Cunningham then arranged to rendezvous west of Crete with his own part of the fleet from Alexandria. On the afternoon of 27 March, Pridham-Wippell neared an Italian cruiser squadron and, after an exchange of fire, managed to push the Italians towards Cunningham's advancing force. It was now clear that unless Cunningham attacked that night, the chance to strike the Italians would be gone. However, night actions were fraught with risk because of the confusion involved. Unknown to Cunningham, one of the Italian cruisers, the Pola, *had been damaged by British aircraft that afternoon and two of the enemy's heavy cruisers had been ordered to slow and help the listing vessel, unaware that the main British Battle Fleet was near and preparing to attack. One of his gunnery officers that night was Philip Mountbatten, later Prince Philip, Duke of Edinburgh, and he and his fellow sailors made short work of the Italians. Opening fire at just 4000 yards – effectively point-blank range – all three Italian cruisers were destroyed in short order. The only British loss during the entire battle was one two-man aircraft. It was an emphatic victory and, after Taranto the previous November, ensured the Italian Fleet never posed a significant threat ever again.*

Tuesday, 1–Friday, 11 April

I have sent all this year's diary back to Alexandria by sea.

Michael Gold sent a suitcase back, and I sent my diary and cine films in the case to be stored at HMS *Nile*, Alexandria. It is not a ship but a kind of transit camp for the navy.

Life has been so hectic for the last few days that I have got rather behind with the diary so I shall give a brief description of events from 1 April to 11 April.

The Regiment is still at Tobruk, and we are manning the coastal defence guns. We have evacuated Benghazi and X Battery are back here with us. We have also evacuated Barce and Derna and the Huns and the Italians are now around Tobruk. Troops have been rushed up and we are now manning both the inner and outer perimeter. We are urgently in need of tanks, which I hope are coming up from Alexandria.

I hear also that they have cut the Bardia road, which, if they have, means that we are cut off from Egypt, except by sea. Air activity has been intense, especially on this point here. We have had a couple of 1000-lb bombs within a few hundred yards of us. Old Stephen was making for a shelter, which was hit by a 1000-lb bomb. A lucky escape. It rather shook the old boy! They hit both hospitals here, the one on the shore and the other in the town, killing about 20 in all.

Soon after, X Battery arrived back from Benghazi, 60 of them, under Jack Abdy. Roger Nelthorpe and De La Rue went back to Mersa with 5000 prisoners. They have not been able to get back by road and I suppose eventually they will return by sea. After X Battery came back from Benghazi, they had no guns to man so we formed a mobile striking force to go out to the perimeter to any vulnerable point. The force was under Peter Laycock, and officers from this unit were Scott, Derrick Warwick and myself.

We received the code-word to turn out about 4.30 p.m. on Sunday afternoon. When it came through we were halfway through calibrating our 4-inch naval guns. One of the artillery majors was in charge of the proceedings but in the early morning a captain and subaltern arrived with the news that the major was ill so couldn't attend. We all expressed sympathies but just as we were going to commence a car drove up and out of it jumped the major himself. His landing from the car was not too good and it didn't take us long to realize that he was as tight as a lord! He made rather a precarious journey from his car to the guns, just managed the steps of the gun pit and finally crashed into No. 1 gun, much to the amazement of the gun crew and Jack Whiting. He was most rude to Jack, who had never said a word, and told him that after being with guns all his life there was nothing he didn't know about them. He then endeavoured to conduct the shoot.

The young subaltern from the gunners was most worried about it all and said to us, 'I do apologize about the major, but we locked him in his room before we left and thought that he was secure there but he has got out.'

We then went out on patrol in most decrepit old trucks supplied by Ordnance and rendezvoused at the El Adem crossroads about six miles out and there formed up with the remainder of the mobile force, which consisted of ourselves, a party of gunners with Breda guns, and 50 of the navy from Navy House with two naval officers! We then proceeded on to El Adem, which we had to take over from the 18th Lancers who were going to patrol further out. We also had six Bren carriers attached to our force, all under Peter Laycock.

That night our troop was in reserve and we made our HQ with the 18th Lancers. They were a grand crowd and couldn't have been kinder to us. They supplied us with a first-class dinner under most difficult circumstances, and plenty to drink. They have not long arrived from India and have been operating out in the desert, Indian troops officered by British. A Major Fowler was in charge.

That night I slept in the back of a lorry, and spent a most

uncomfortable night as I had no blankets, it was very cold, and we had a sand storm most of the night.

At dawn the next day I had to go on a patrol, and with me I took three Bren carriers, one 8-cwt truck and one 15-cwt truck with eight men. I had naturally never operated with Bren carriers before but I worked on the basis of cavalry tactics and sent two carriers out as advance points with the other acting as point commander. The other two trucks followed behind. I went in the 8-cwt truck. We were in touch with HQ by wireless most of the day.

When we arrived at El Gubi, I remained there with one Bren carrier, which had the wireless, and sent the other two carriers and the 15-cwt truck off on single patrols in different directions. We saw nothing except some Arabs on camels, whom we rushed across to inspect, thinking they might be parachutists in disguise. We also sighted a 15-cwt truck, which we stalked and found was one of ours which had gone over a Thermos bomb.

The 15-cwt truck shot a buck, which we brought back with us. It must have been an excellent shot as they were travelling at 50 m.p.h. when they fired. Those Bren carriers move like the wind. The three on patrol with me belonged to the KRRC. They had been in a good deal of fighting during this campaign. Each carrier has an NCO in charge.

On our way home we had some trouble with the 8-cwt truck but we got her back all right. When we eventually arrived we found Peter Laycock rather worried about us as news had come through that another patrol had sighted some German tanks about seven miles from where we were. But we had seen nothing hostile. At 6 o'clock the rest of the striking force had been recalled and others had taken over.

It certainly was an amazing force that Peter had to command. I thoroughly enjoyed my patrol and we certainly went like the wind across that desert!

It was no wonder that Stanley had been busy because much had happened in the North African campaign during that time. The Sherwood Rangers in Tobruk had been formed into an ad hoc mobile strike force of some

125 men and a further 100 Royal Navy personnel, who would be expected to plug any gap in the perimeter defences of Tobruk, should it be needed, and at 15 minutes' notice. It looked as though they might well end up being flung into action.

General Rommel had been sent to North Africa with just two divisions and told to stop any further British advance but not to take the offensive himself. However, he recognized that the British forces were now vulnerable. Not only were they still only two divisions strong, they were also fresh to combat as the 7th Armoured and 4th Indian had been replaced by the 2nd Armoured and 9th Australian Divisions. Moreover, their lines of communication were at least a thousand miles from Alexandria, and the British were distracted by events in Greece. Ignoring his orders to hold fast, Rommel began a limited advance on 24 March to capture El Agheila, and so began a rapid and startling advance that was to push the British back across Cyrenaica in just a fortnight.

Having captured El Agheila with ease, on 2 April, Rommel split his force into three columns: two raced across Cyrenaica, while the third headed along the coast to Benghazi, which it captured, unopposed, on 4 April. Three days later, Derna fell, too. It was a bad day for the British because General Richard O'Connor, the XIII Corps commander, and General Philip Neame, the military C-in-C of Cyrenaica, were both captured, stripping the British of their commanders in one strike. Both were outstanding soldiers: O'Connor had done brilliantly with Operation COMPASS, while Neame was a hugely talented and respected VC winner and Olympic gold medallist. Also captured that day was Neame's ADC, Dan Ranfurly, formerly of the Sherwood Rangers.

Two days later, on 9 April, Rommel captured Bardia and the following day, the 9th Australian Division withdrew into Tobruk. The events Stanley describes were the first German attacks on the garrison. On 12 April, the encirclement of Tobruk was complete. The siege had begun.

6

The Siege of Tobruk

Still smiling. Standing by during an air raid on Tobruk.

Saturday, 12 April 1941

THE BATTLE STILL goes on around Tobruk. There has been a considerable amount of artillery fire all day and I gather that we are holding them on all sides. I understand that we are using both the inner and the outer perimeter used by the Italians. It's very difficult to get any accurate news and we live on rumours. Last input, I gather we repulsed five tank attacks. News also came through that the German and the Italian columns engaged each other! I am not surprised as we, the Germans and the Italians are all using Italian tanks!

We had a series of air alarms during the morning and five German planes came over just before lunch. The AA on our point brought down one bomber, which landed very close to our HQ. Both pilots were taken into the orderly room and both were unhurt. I gather they came from Derna. The Australians got to the plane first and stripped the pilots of their revolvers and watches until they were stopped by some of our RA. They were very confident that our army would be cut off in Greece, that more German forces were arriving, which would take Egypt, and the war would be over by November. Mike Gold, who saw them, told us that both pilots stank of scent! One was a corporal and the other an operator. I understand that a couple of Italian fighters were escorting.

Tomorrow is Easter Day. How I wish that I could be at home.

Sunday, 13 April: Easter Day

At 06.45 I went up to HQ for Holy Communion, which was held in an enormous cave. It was an ideal place and forms an excellent air-raid shelter.

During the day we had three air raids, the worst in the evening about five o'clock. We heard that 12 planes were brought down. On the news tonight from England the Germans claim to have captured Bardia and surrounded Tobruk. The BBC didn't confirm this. If this is true it means the road to Egypt is cut and our only outlet is by sea.

The news from Greece is not encouraging. Russia and Japan have signed a pact, which says, I gather, that in the event of either party being attacked the other would remain neutral. Not so good.

Stanley was right about the situation in Greece, which had been attacked on 6 April through Bulgaria. Three days later, the key port of Salonika had been captured, while German troops from Austria, Hungary, Romania and Bulgaria also poured into Yugoslavia. In the face of this onslaught, it was clear the Yugoslavians were crumbling, while in Greece British forces began falling back towards Mount Olympus. To add to British woes, there was also an Axis-led revolt in Iraq.

The only cause for British joy was in East Africa, where their forces continued to trounce the Italians. Addis Ababa, the capital of Ethiopia was captured on 6 April and two days later Massawa, the last Italian stronghold in Eritrea.

Monday, 14 April

At about 9 o'clock in the morning we had the code-word down from RHQ that some German tanks had broken through the perimeter, which meant that there was a formal stand to. Later we heard that 12 tanks had broken through and later still we heard that we had scuppered 10 of these tanks and we had taken 200 German prisoners.

During the stand to we had a nasty air raid. I should think at least 30 planes came over, dropped bombs on the harbour and on the town. Later during the day I heard that we had brought down 12 planes. Fortunately their bombs did little damage. The colonel lost his private car at HQ and Laurence's bedroom was destroyed.

On the news tonight we hear that Bardia and Sollum have both been captured by the Huns. But, still, he has a hell of a line of communication to maintain.

Stanley is as perceptive as ever. Yes, Rommel's lines of communication were certainly now overstretched and, having reached Sollum on the Egyptian border, he ordered his troops to halt their advance. The ability of each side to manage its lines of supply in the vast open stretches of desert was to prove the key feature of the war in North Africa.

Wednesday, 16 April

On the news tonight we heard that Yugoslavia had fallen. Churchill gave us to understand that the position in Greece and Libya was serious.

Last night the Huns made two attacks but were repulsed each time. We heard that Jerry pushed the Italians forward on the point of the bayonet to lead the attack, and we gave them stick.

On 14 April, the Germans had destroyed the Yugoslavian Army in the south and then poured through the Monastir Gap, so cutting off much of the Greek Army in Albania.

Thursday, 17 April

A most hectic day, possibly a little too exciting. After lunch, at a time when I was hoping for a quiet afternoon in the BOP, the code-word came that 12 German tanks had broken through the perimeter defences so we had to stand to for a couple of hours. During the morning we had a dive-bombing attack by German planes but nothing fell close to us. I should think at least 20 came over.

To cap it all, later in the afternoon some enemy artillery started shelling the harbour from the south side. It was most difficult to see what was firing, but we could clearly make out the flash. Their ranging was very accurate and they almost scored a hit on a minesweeper, destroyer and gunboat in the harbour. Some of the shells came unpleasantly near our shore. The destroyer and the gunboat dashed out of the harbour and started a bombardment, after which we got no more shelling. Certainly an exciting day.

Saturday, 19 April

I slept in the billets last night and Stephen was in the BOP.

The raid started early this morning, at 4.30, and continued until dawn. They dropped a good many mines in the harbour and all around the coast. Not many bombs were dropped.

During the morning a large convoy came into the harbour so all day we were expecting a raid, and sure enough, it came about 3 o'clock in the afternoon when 17 German dive-bombers came and attacked the harbour and the town. At the time I was in Navy House with Scott. We went down to the shelters, which were quite amazing, extending miles underground and absolutely safe from any direct hit. While down there I had a long talk with the skipper of a merchant boat in harbour, which had been dive-bombed here the other day, and damaged. He only lost one man, the gunner, who had his leg shattered. In the last war he was torpedoed off the north coast of Ireland and spent one hour in the water in November. But the Merchant Navy take it all in their day's work. They are amazingly brave and don't really get all the credit due to them.

A terrific barrage went up over the harbour, especially the escort vessel to the convoy, which let them have it. Seventeen planes came over and six were brought down, four by AA and two by fighters. Two crashed into the harbour, two out to sea and the fighters got theirs over land. All the pilots who came down into the sea must have been killed instantaneously.

As we were leaving Navy House with a couple of naval officers an Australian came up and asked us to have a look at a bomb that had landed about 300 yards away and practically next door to the NAAFI. We followed him and found the largest bomb I have ever seen, which had gone straight through a house and broken in two. The nose of the shell stood about 4 foot high with a diameter of 2 feet. Fortunately, especially for the Australian, the bomb had failed to go off. The plane that had dropped it, so the Aussie told us, had come very low over the town, machine-gunning, and had finally dropped this contraption.

Another bomb fell right in the middle of the courtyard of Area Headquarters, making a crater 15 feet deep, but again no damage to personnel.

Tuesday, 22 April

Today was Stephen Mitchell's birthday. He is 28. I wished him birthday greetings at stand to, i.e., 3.30 in the morning.

I spent last night in the BOP. A most disturbed night as one gun kept on maintaining that a motor-boat was somewhere outside the harbour.

As a matter of interest, the colonel told us that since arriving here we have had 100 air-raid alerts and 80 raids.

Wednesday, 23 April

During the morning, the colonel, Derrick Warwick and I went out towards El Adem to look for possible observation posts in the event of a breakthrough and our having to shoot our guns across the land.

On our way back a tremendous air raid started: almost 30 German bombers escorted by fighters came over. The fighters had their battle right over our heads but it was most difficult to distinguish what exactly was happening. It was a distressing sight to see one of our Hurricane fighters crash in and burst into flames. I am afraid that we lost three but six enemy planes were brought down.

On the road we passed one Hurricane brought down on Easter Monday. The pilot had been buried beside the wreckage of his plane and on the simple white cross there was his name, 'Pilot Sergeant Webster, killed in action 4.4.41'. On the cross lay his flying helmet and stuck in the grave the blade of the propeller.

April 23 had been a day of heavy air activity. Some 70 enemy aircraft had attacked Tobruk, mostly Stuka dive-bombers and Messerschmitt 110 twin-engine fighters. In the mêlée, Sergeant Webster shot down a German Hesche 126, then, having suffered some damage to his Hurricane, force-landed. As he did so he was shot up by an Me110 and killed. It was a bad day for 73 Squadron, who also lost their hugely popular and highly experienced Canadian flight commander, Flight Lieutenant 'Smudger' Smith, a veteran of France and the Battle of Britain. Both men now lie in Tobruk War Cemetery.

One of the failings of the RAF in the first part of the war was the lack of Spitfires sent to the Mediterranean and Middle East. In 1940 the Hurricane had been under-performing against the latest German Messerschmitt 109E fighter aircraft, and most certainly so by 1941, when 109Fs were entering theatre. Although it was a solid gun platform, most Hurricanes were equipped only with machine-guns rather than cannons and lacked the kind of rate of climb needed, which meant it was invariably vulnerable to attack from above. It was also slower than both the Spitfire and the Me109. Spitfires were far more plentiful than Hurricanes and new cannon-armed Spitfire Mk Vs were now running off the production line, yet RAF Fighter Command insisted they should be kept in the UK. It was a poor decision.

Thursday, 24 April

During the raid this morning it looked as though Tobruk had been completely blotted out, but after the dust had blown away, from here it looked exactly as before.

Friday, 25 April

Last night I was on duty in the BOP. During stand to in the early morning we had a raid and about six bombs were dropped among our tanks. A slit trench with 10 men inside was straddled and the sentry on duty had one bomb bursting five yards away from where he was lying and never had a scratch. It was certainly his lucky day. A sergeant major had one 20 yards in front of his tank.

The men are bearing up wonderfully well to all this bombing.

During the morning we had a battery commanders' conference and as Stephen is still sick I had to attend. We organized a scheme to deal with an attempted landing on our piece of coastline, which quite likely may be attempted, especially as we have made landing parties on Bardia and Sollum with considerable success. There is no reason why the other side shouldn't try the same.

I went into Tobruk afterwards to get the pay for the men. The place is in a dreadful mess. Every house appears to have been damaged. I have never seen such a desolate sight. They scored a hit on Navy House, causing considerable damage but no casualties. The NAAFI also had a hit and has moved out of the town.

At 5 o'clock I paid out the battery. There is absolutely nothing to spend money on here for the men.

I had a grand mail today, letters from the family – Dosai [?], Mother, Pat, Ione, Ursula and Clive. How wonderful it is to receive letters from home. It's also fun writing them.

News from Greece is not good and I am afraid that we shall have to consider the campaign as a magnificent withdrawal.

Saturday, 26 April

A sand storm blew all day, visibility nil, hence we were free from any raids for 24 hours. What a change.

We are rather expecting to hear at any moment that Greece has capitulated. She has made a most gallant fight and we couldn't do anything else but send troops and material to her aid.

The colonel came down from HQ and had dinner in our mess.

The campaign in Greece was now all but over. On 19 April, the Germans had captured Olympus and Larissa, and the Waffen-SS troops of the Leibstandarte Adolf Hitler cut off the retreating Greek troops. There was now very little defence left, with the British now in full retreat. The next day, Alexander Korizis, the Greek prime minister, committed suicide and on the twenty-third the King and government fled to Crete. The evacuation of British troops began that day, while Athens fell on 27 April. The last British troops were lifted on 30 April, and although some 50,000 men escaped, the Greek campaign had cost Britain dear in terms of men, equipment and shipping.

Sunday, 27 April

I saw a copy of the signal sent by Cunningham to Navy House here. 'Congratulations to mine spotters. Keep your tails up.' SNOIC's answer to this was, 'Roof down but tail well up.' Navy House scored a direct hit yesterday.

Churchill made a speech on the wireless at 11 o'clock at night. I didn't hear it as I was up in the BOP, but Mike got it on his wireless. It was quite up to his usual standard. He made it quite clear an invasion of England would be impossible, which was most encouraging. He was very rude about Mussolini.

This was Churchill's first speech since February and one in which, despite all the terrible setbacks that had occurred in the interim, he tried, as ever, to be positive. 'Tobruk – the fortress of Tobruk – which flanks any German advance on Egypt, we hold strongly.' He ended by pointing out

*that there were many more British – and American – people in the world
than Germans and that together the British Empire and the United
States 'possess the unchallengeable command of the oceans, and will soon
obtain decisive superiority in the air. They have more wealth, more
technical resources, and they make more steel, than the whole of the rest
of the world put together.' Churchill's point about resources and shipping
was undeniable.*

Monday, 28 April

German planes started coming over here at 5.30 in the morning and
continued periodically throughout the day. We have no fighters here
at all now and for some reason our AA fire seems quite ineffective. In
consequence, the Hun does more or less what he likes. One
Messerschmitt flew over us only a few hundred feet up. There are none
of our fighters to engage them so they come along and machine-gun
the ground.

Wednesday, 30 April

Run-through on gun drill during the morning.

At 12.30 I left with a wireless truck, signaller and Sergeant Kettner
for my forward OP. On arrival I established communication with
Stephen, who would control the shoot from 2 Battery BOP for our
landward firing. Derrick Warwick did the same for C Battery.
Communications were excellent. I found some tanks had taken up a
position around our OP. They were charming fellows, showed me over
their tanks and gave me some tea.

When I got back I found the two Cocks (alias Mike and Peter
Laycock) reinforcing our air-raid shelter. After tea we all worked on that.

The colonel rang up and wanted to discuss our proceedings
during the afternoon and I went up to HQ. After the conference the
air-raid alarm went. I went up to C Battery BOP from where one had
the most amazing view over Tobruk, the harbour and the perimeter
defences. And they are in communication with FOP who put through

all details, e.g., 40 planes from south bearing one hundred, height 8000, eight miles away. Their information is amazingly accurate.

The attack this evening was on the perimeter and we saw the explosions all the way along, and the planes diving. Two planes attacked and machine-gunned a minesweeper, about four miles out to sea, but they missed. Fortunately they left the convoy of small tankers, which had just left harbour. After the raid we put up a tremendous artillery barrage on the perimeter. It's still going on now. Whether we are preparing for a push, or being pushed, remains to be seen.

We hear that the evacuation of Greece still continues. Up to the present, 40,000 have got out; 3000 casualties killed and wounded.

Turkey has made a trade agreement with Germany, which is rather distressing news. I should think the Germans would endeavour to take this place before we get reorganized in Egypt after the evacuation of Greece.

Today Tobruk had its 154th raid since we took the place and I should think that I have been here for ¾ of them. I am most weary this evening. The barrage still goes on but I shall go to bed.

How I wish all this would end.

I have not gone to bed yet. I am still talking in the mess. The conversation has turned to public schools. Five of us are sitting here, Peter Laycock, Mike Laycock, Stephen Mitchell and Mike Gold and self, and all were at Eton except myself, who was at Winchester. We were discussing which school we should send our sons to if not either Winchester or Eton. How different the Etonian is from the Wykehamist.

Thursday, 1 May

Rather a hectic day. The Germans launched their largest attack so far against Tobruk and penetrated the outer perimeter. At 8.30 this morning the code-word came through for us to stand to, followed very shortly by the code-word for us to be prepared to shoot landwards. So Derrick and I each got into our wireless truck and proceeded to Division HQ. Mike Gold came with me, as we had to produce a liaison officer. We had to be prepared to occupy our OPs at a moment's notice.

Nothing happened during the morning. There was a great deal of artillery fire. We saw a large variety of people at Division HQ, including the interpreter and some war correspondents.

The interpreter was quite interesting. He had just finished interviewing some German prisoners. He told us that you could get nothing out of German artillery or tank personnel, but the mechanized infantry always volunteered something.

The perimeter has come in for some very formidable dive-bombing and machine-gunning from the air. We get a very clear view from our position and it is certainly a grim spectacle to see 40 or 50 dive-bombers hurtling down, dropping up to six bombs and machine-gunning.

I saw three German prisoners outside HQ. They looked very fatigued but appeared well fed. I saw the Australian sentry give each of them a drink of water from his own water bottle.

Friday, 2 May

I reported at dawn with my wireless truck at Division HQ. Derrick Warwick of C Battery also reported with his.

A very severe sand storm has been blowing for the last 24 hours and visibility is practically nil. We were given the state of the battle. The counter-attack we made last night was held up by machine-gun fire.

I had a postcard from Daddy, which took just over a month to arrive. A new special postcard airmail service has been started for ME Forces. One also came from Ione and Bridget.

Another heavy air raid on the harbour in the evening.

Sunday, 4 May

Usual routine during the morning and also the usual raids.

A plane came over while we were having lunch. We heard the

whistle of a bomb, which landed not very far from our mess. The individual actions of those having lunch were quite amusing to watch. For some reason I ran rather hastily to my bedroom, a very foolish place to make for. Jack Whiting went under the table, which actually I think was the right thing to do. Mike Gold threw himself on the floor and Scottie ran for the shelter.

In the evening 20 planes, escorted by fighters, first dive-bombed the inner perimeter, aiming at our artillery. Twelve more then flew over the harbour and each one deliberately dive-bombed the hospital ship, which came in during the morning. Bombs fell all round her (at least 40) but not one hit her. But I am afraid that some fell so close to her that her plates were damaged and she had to be towed out of harbour after dark. That is the second deliberate attack on a hospital ship during a month. They are all painted white with enormous red crosses.

Two more planes came in from the north and dropped about 12 bombs right from the old POW camp to the ordnance depot. They were only about 800 yards from us. The raid lasted about ¾ of an hour. We saw one plane crash into the sea through the rangefinder about 12 miles out to sea.

Scottie and I both hinted to Henry Trotter that a drink would be most acceptable before returning home but the old Scotchman didn't play. Both Scottie and I were wild.

Mike Gold told us a good tale at dinner. At RHQ we have a few Australian Ordnance attached, including one officer. One of them went to the field hospital and our colonel went to see him. He wrote and told a pal that the colonel had visited him and described him as being 'stonking lovely'. Flash Kellett, our colonel, is always beautifully turned out under any conditions, and does use a certain amount of eau de Cologne. The same Australians have made up a most clever song about the Yeomanry.

However nerve-racking it was to be on a ship when under attack from the air, it was still very difficult for aircraft to hit a moving vessel. At any kind of height of more than, say, a couple of thousand feet, ships often looked like little more than narrow pencils, while swooping in low was extremely dangerous: not only did the aircraft become a bigger target in turn, there was less room for manoeuvre should anything go wrong.

Monday, 5 May

In spite of raids, we are arranging to have a gun team competition for our two guns in this battery. Stephen Mitchell, Peter and Mike Laycock will be judges. I can't judge as I am in charge of one of the teams.

Tuesday, 6 May

One of the worst sand storms today that I have ever seen. Visibility absolutely nil. You can't keep the sand out. It gets into your eyes, hair, food and ears. It's quite hopeless trying to compete until the damn thing is over. It lasted all day. As a result there was no activity either from air or land, which was some compensation.

Wednesday, 7 May

We had five air attacks today, two really bad ones and each of those two were directed on the distillery the other side of the harbour. The large minesweeper had two direct hits and sank immediately. Only one person was killed on board, which is absolutely amazing. The captain was blown off the bridge into the water, and so were many of the crew. The harbour was shelled again during the afternoon and some of the small craft had lucky escapes. Some of the shells landed in the water not far from us.

Rather a hectic day. Despite it all we had the first round of the gun team competition. Our team under Sergeant McCann just managed to beat Jack's team under Sergeant Hunt. There was terrific enthusiasm among the men. The shelling started just as we had finished.

Thursday, 8 May

Air activity not so bad today. During the evening the Germans dropped one shell very close to our magazine. It made the hell of a noise but we found the nose cap, which showed it to be an AA shell. It appeared to be made of poor stuff and had hardly any effect on the ground.

During the afternoon we carried on with the gun team competition and the other two teams contested. I am afraid that our team lost to Jack's by three marks. That leaves Sergeant McCann's team and Sergeant Kettner's team in the final.

After dinner we played 'Little Old Man' – a great success as I caused much amusement. This was followed by a kind of acting charade game. To see Mike Laycock endeavouring to convey 'The Boy Stood on the Burning Deck' to the rest of his side by acting without words was a sight for the gods. This was followed by a game of Mike's in which each person had to draw a plan of a part of London and put in the name of the streets and important buildings. It really was rather a good game.

As usual, Mike Gold was in terrific form, kept us roaring with laughter and the war topic was kept off most of the evening. We eventually went to bed at 1.15, to the boom of artillery, which continued throughout most of the night.

Saturday, 10 May

My turn for duty in the BOP. Only one raid, bombs dropped on the other side of the harbour.

Mike Gold and Sergeant Stockton are going on a mechanical course to Palestine, the lucky dogs. The colonel and Henry Trotter came and had some food with us this evening and we gathered from the colonel that an 'all arms force' was due to come up from Egypt and that the road from here to Egypt should be open again in the not too far future. Let's hope there is truth in that.

I had a look at the harbour this evening as I was walking back to the mess. There was no shipping in at all but I counted 20 wrecks, of all shapes and sizes, protruding out of the water. On the other side of the harbour, beached and burned out, were two Italian troop ships. In the middle of the harbour the mast of *Lord Magnus* yacht, which had been converted into an armed merchantman, and which I saw sunk full of Italian prisoners. Tobruk harbour has been the grave for many craft of all nationalities and kinds, and we have witnessed the destruction of many of them since we have been here.

Sunday, 11 May

We had the final of the team competition, Sergeant McCann v. Sergeant Kelfrian.

The colonel also came down and watched the competition. We lost by two marks. We gave the winning team a bottle of beer and a packet of cigarettes each, and a bottle of whisky for the sergeant.

After dinner we had a most hectic time. It started off by Jack Whiting endeavouring in vain to be initiated as a cardinal by Scottie

Scottie and Jack Whiting, May 1941.

by drinking the health of Cardinal Puff in whisky. Of course, old Jack got hopelessly tight. Highly amusing.

Monday, 12 May

Two very bad air attacks during the day, both concentrated on the south-west corner of the harbour and, sad to relate, they secured two direct hits on the *Ladybird*, which came all the way from China at the beginning of the war where she was a river gunboat, and has been in Tobruk ever since we occupied the place. Our people here made particular friends with the crew, especially the first mate, who came ashore and helped us a lot with our 4-inch guns.

Wednesday, 14 May

At 5 o'clock in the afternoon the colonel made an address to all officers, WOs and sergeants. He started off by saying that he felt some of us had lost the spirit of aggression that was essential to win this war. It is quite clear that this pep talk was caused through Henry Trotter being most averse to firing his naval gun across land to silence the German gun that has been shelling the harbour and shelled us yesterday when we opened fire. As usual, he spoke very well and what he said in principle was quite right. But, as Peter pointed out, one must fight with one's head as well as one's heart.

The colonel went on to say that the experience we had had out here had been most valuable both to us and to him. He had been able to see how officers and men behaved under shellfire and dive-bombing, and on these pictures he would build up the construction of the Regiment when it re-formed to train with the new 1st Cavalry Division.

He read us all one passage from a book he had been reading about the fall of France: 'Prosperity in France had undermined her capacity for aggression.'

He ended up by reading a telegram received informing him that two batteries of coastal defence would be ready to relieve us at Tobruk at 24 hours' notice from 16 May. On being relieved the Notts Yeomanry would report back to Palestine to train with the 1st Cavalry Division. This was received with great enthusiasm.

But on the other hand, in spite of all the bombing and shelling, the men have been more content here than doing nothing in Palestine.

Sunday, 18 May

Again some bombers came over before dawn. They hang around for about an hour. It's rather a bad time because the lights can't pick them up and the AA can't see them.

During the morning we spent an hour or two on signalling. The Morse procedure takes a lot of learning but it's quite interesting.

I was on duty in the BOP during the day. News came through that we had captured Fort Capuzzo again and also Sollum, where we had captured 400 German prisoners and put 200 tanks out of action.

In the evening I had a bathe. At the moment the climate here is absolutely perfect – sunshine throughout the day with a slight breeze coming off the sea. It is much more pleasant than Palestine and everybody feels so well.

At the moment I am reading *Gone With the Wind*, which I find a most depressing book.

Tuesday, 20 May

After lunch I went down to the docks with Donny Player to collect some food and drink which had been sent up by Jack Abdy on a small vessel that arrived last night. An Australian called Captain Palmer runs the ship and he has no other officer with him. We found that our stuff took up most of his vessel. It included whisky, gin, soda water, lime, eggs, oranges and some fine cooking stuff for the men. It could not have come at a more appropriate time, as there is not a spot of drink in the place and the NAAFI is completely out of everything. We have had no ships in at all for the last week.

The water question was also getting rather bad. We only drink sea water which has been distilled. Each battery has made its own distillery. But all the water has a strong taste of either salt, rust or both.

We asked Captain Palmer to come and have a drink with us before going to dinner at HQ. We asked about his various trips up here. Last time he said that a submarine had fired five torpedoes at him but missed each time. The time before, a Heinkel bomber nosed around him for a long time but he didn't fire, neither did the bomber, which, to use his own words, 'tickled' him somewhat, 'as I had several tons of high explosives on board'.

Among the things he brought up for us were some baking powder and blancmange for the men. When one of his crew saw these packages clearly marked with their contents he turned to him and said, 'God, sir, look at this. No wonder the bloody army is always retreating!' He really was a most charming person and highly amusing.

We heard today that the Germans have made a large-scale attack on Crete, using airborne troops – parachute troops and troops landed from gliders. The prime minister had made the announcement and told us that the position was in hand. He also added that the troops had landed in New Zealand uniform.

Half of the Regiment are there manning coastal defence guns, one battery under Tony Holden and the other under Sydney Morse. Mike Parish is there as well. All this trouble will probably mean there will be a delay in both ourselves and the batteries on Crete being relieved. It really will be great fun when the Regiment all gets together again. I have not seen Mike Parish for almost seven months.

I understand that we shall re-form at Allenby Barracks, Jerusalem. But there is absolutely no telling when we will be relieved, and when we are, and if we do go to Jerusalem, I anticipate that our real job will be patrolling the pipeline in trucks. I simply can't see our getting tanks.

This was the day the Italians in East Africa formally surrendered after a 94-day campaign. However, that piece of good news was severely dampened by the German attack on Crete the same day, in which some 8000 paratroopers were dropped on and around the key airfields of Maleme in the west and Heraklion in the centre north of the island. Defending Crete were some 32,000 British and imperial troops and 10,000 Greeks under command of the New Zealand general Bernard Freyberg, a First World War winner of the Victoria Cross, and a soldier much admired by Churchill. Although poorly equipped in terms of artillery, armour and air support, Creforce, as Freyberg's defenders were called, should have been strong enough to see off the initial assault.

Wednesday, 21 May

Henry Trotter and Sergeant Major Sayers left Tobruk in the evening as advance party to Allenby Barracks, Jerusalem. He went on the schooner, which left harbour at stand to in the evening. I bet he hopes he has seen Tobruk for the last time!

Another small mail came in, which brought me a letter from Mummy and from Ione.

I hear that the Germans are continuing their attack on Crete by parachutists and airborne troops. I gather that they attempted to land a division. I feel quite certain that when they try and attack this place again they will drop parachute troops in the back areas and try and get control of the harbour. It remains to be seen whether we will have been relieved by then.

Ione in her letter told me that she had heard from Dennis Hamilton, now a prisoner of war in Germany. The letter only took a month and he said he had Kenneth Crockett with him. Her letter was very cheerful.

Thursday, 22 May

Three air raids, nothing very personal. The colonel told me today that he might send me on a signalling course at Cairo in place of Mike

Riviere, who at the moment might not be able to go as he must be rather busy in Crete. It would be a good break, especially in getting away from here. If I did go it would probably mean a trip in a destroyer.

Friday, 23 May

A cable arrived from Daddy, sent off on 30 April, so it took just over three weeks to reach me. It was addressed to Captain Christopherson. First time!

Saturday, 24 May

We heard the most distressing news that the battleship *Hood* has been sunk by the new German battleship, *Bismarck*. A lucky shot penetrated the magazine.

There is still no sign of our being relieved. It is now almost 10 days since the colonel told us that some coastal defence gunners were at 24 hours' notice to come and relieve us. Events in Crete, I suppose, won't help the other half of the Regiment being relieved from there.

They still continue to land parachute troops and airborne troops. The navy, however, laid hell into a convoy of 30 ships, sinking one destroyer and sending all the other ships back that were carrying troops to Crete. Our forces there are without any air support.

Sunday, 25 May

We had a service in the gun pit in the morning. The padre is rather good at these short services. He gave us a short sermon, his text was 'endurance' and 'the ability to carry on'. Just as he had completed his talk with the words, 'you must always carry on', the AA opened up and he turned to Peter and said, 'Shall I carry on?' After taking cover for a short time he completed his service by saying a special prayer for our families, wives and sweethearts. I was standing next to Peter and when he paused for us all to say a silent prayer for our sweethearts I kept on wondering which of his many sweethearts Peter was praying for. He couldn't decently have prayed for more than one at a time.

During the morning German bombers attacked three ships entering harbour, a couple of minesweepers and a schooner. They had some very narrow misses, which made us hold our breath, but they all got back into harbour. I am afraid, however, they sank our oil tanker about 70 miles out to sea on its way here.

Monday, 26 May

Today, 29 years ago, Stanley Douglas Christopherson was born to Alma Christopherson, wife of Douglas Christopherson. On that night, previous to the great day 29 years ago, the said Alma Christopherson went to a theatre called *Autumn Manoeuvres*. She only just got home in time. On the same day 70-odd years ago, Queen Mary was also born.

I have just had breakfast, having been relieved by Stephen in the BOP where I had a disturbed night. The telephone kept ringing and I couldn't sleep on my right side as I have a boil on my right hip, which is most painful. It's a most glorious morning, beautiful sunshine with quite a fresh sea breeze, the sea looks bluer than I have ever seen it before, and there's not a ripple on the water. The beauty of the whole situation is spoiled by this damned war.

During the morning, usual routine, including one hour's signalling. In the afternoon we had a swimming competition against the ack-ack next door. It was great fun and our fellows won most of the events. We had to take cover two or three times on account of air attacks.

Jack Whiting and the doc came to dinner. Stephen fortunately got a parcel today from home filled with luxurious food so we had a most excellent dinner, consisting of pâté de foie gras, tinned fish, bully beef, tinned apricots and coffee. Peter Laycock and I unpacked Stephen's parcel before he came in, hid the contents and food, for which we substituted stones. Old Stephen was furious when he undid his parcel and found the stones, and swore that he wouldn't let anybody eat his new supplies. But we refused to give up the food until we had extracted a promise from him that we should have the best of it for dinner. After dinner we played frivolous games but great fun. Old Jack was in great form.

Tuesday, 27 May

The *Bismarck*, new German battleship, has been sunk by the *Ark Royal* and *Prince of Wales*, our new battleship. Fighting in Crete still goes on.

Wednesday , 28 May

Usual routine during the morning. In the afternoon I had a bathe at the point. I don't think that it would be possible to improve the bathing here in any other part of the world. You can dive in off rocks into 30 feet of water, so clear and blue that you can see the silver sand

The one consolation of being in Tobruk: swimming in the sea.

glistening on the sea bottom, and very often fish swimming about, which we kill and eat by using Italian hand grenades.

Thursday, 29 May

Stephen and Mike Laycock were bathing down at the point today when suddenly the ack-ack opened fire and two shells, failing to explode in the air, fell into the water not many yards from where they were bathing and exploded. 'They are on us,' shouted Scottie, who was also there, and they all three dived into a hole in the rocks. All were quite naked except for tin hats. Stephen told us afterwards that he had never felt so undignified in all his life, hurling himself into a hole wearing only a tin hat and a pair of Italian Army boots, and running away from one of our own shells.

News from Crete is not good: we are withdrawing east of Suvla Bay. That means that Notts Yeomanry in Crete must have spiked their guns and withdrawn in the hand-to-hand fighting. Very heavy casualties on both sides.

On paper, Crete should never have fallen. There were only 8000 German paratroopers in the assault, while there were more than 40,000 defenders. The key was their successful capture of Maleme airfield in the west. Even so, German airborne troops, armed mostly with short-range submachine-guns, should have been successfully repelled at this key airfield, where the defenders were armed with much longer-range Brens and rifles. However, fearing a seaborne assault, Freyberg had been slow to divert troops to the mounting crisis at Maleme, and once German aircraft began landing on the island, the build-up of enemy troops was rapid – and decisive, despite the high casualties among the German paratroopers.

The subsequent evacuation from the south of the island was also putting increasing strain on the overstretched Mediterranean Fleet. The triumphant victory at Cape Matapan must have seemed like a distant memory, as Cunningham struggled to support the besieged garrison at Tobruk, ensure convoys safely reached the equally besieged island fortress of Malta, and now carried out the second major evacuation in a month.

Despite the fillip of the sinking of the Bismarck, *it had been another tough 10 days for the British.*

Friday, 30 May

Captain Palmer and his schooner came into harbour today. On his way up he shot down a Heinkel bomber. Peter Laycock went back to Alexandria with him. I have never seen anybody more pleased to leave the place and I don't really blame him. He was due to leave the harbour at 7.15 in the evening but as the minesweeper got out of the boom the shelling started. The second shell landed 100 yards from our mess right in the corner of our little bay. Scottie and I were playing a game of chess outside. When we heard the whistle of the shell we moved like shit out of a shovel! C Battery immediately opened up with Tilly and Tolly. They make a hell of a noise. All this delayed Peter's departure from the harbour because as soon as the shelling started the schooner put back again. I bet he had wind-up as we had a red warning and a German bomber flew across the harbour. He eventually left just as it was getting dark.

Our mess has grown very small now that Peter Laycock and Mike Gold have gone and Henry Trotter from RHQ. It's now almost a fortnight since the colonel told me that some gunners were standing at 24 hours' notice to come and relieve us. According to the record we are keeping, we have now had 200 air raids during the last three months or so.

Saturday, 31 May

I am not feeling too hot today. The pains in my neck are most painful.

Sunday, 1 June

In the evening we had a very heavy dive-bombing and machine-gunning attack by low-flying German aircraft. Some of our gun pits were well sprayed with machine-gun bullets. We all stood behind the mess firing our rifles as fast as we could. One German plane flew over no more than 100 feet high. Hardly any damage was done at all and I gather we brought five planes down.

We heard this morning that we were evacuating Crete and that up to the present 15,000 had been got away, but we admitted heavy casualties. We have heard no news about our other batteries, which are in Crete under Sydney Morse and Tony Holden. I expect that now we have left Crete and given the Hun an excellent air base he will make life even hotter for us here.

It will be interesting to see his next move – possibly Cyprus? Or even an attempt at Malta, but more probably an attack into Palestine via Syria, where he continues to land troops.

Stanley was not far off the mark with his figures for those who escaped Crete. In all, some 16,000 were successfully evacuated, although around 5000 had to be left behind. Some were picked up by submarine much later, others joined the Cretan resistance, and most were captured, along with around 12,000 who were captured during the battle. The Royal Navy suffered particularly, losing 1800 dead and nine ships, including three cruisers and Lord Louis Mountbatten's destroyer, HMS Kelly. To lose nine ships in one operation was a bad blow, made worse by the damage caused to a further 17 vessels, three of which were battleships.

Monday, 2 June

About 7 o'clock in the evening we had one of the largest dive-bombing attacks and machine-gunning which I have seen. A good many bombs were dropped between here and HQ. Then about six bombers came and machine-gunned our area. Officers and men all have rifles now and blazed away at any low-flying aircraft. We took up our position behind the officers' mess as usual, five officers, five batmen and Woods, the officers' mess cook. I was actually standing in front of our mess behind the sand bags when suddenly four Heinkels flew over, no more than 100 feet high. These were followed by another, which had been hit by the Beauforts and had one wing completely shot away. I was so excited that I threw my tin hat in the air, let forth a series of victorious shouts, dashed out of the mess towards the guns because I felt absolutely certain that the plane had fallen near our guns. When I reached our BOP I found that the plane had crashed into the sea about 100 yards from the shore and furthermore two other planes had shared a similar fate, having been hit by the Beauforts and ended up in the sea.

I suppose there must have been 20 or 30 planes escorted by fighters and, as far as I know, we suffered no casualties and no damage was done, so on the rubber we are well up. We found plenty of machine-gun bullets from the planes. One had actually hit our rangefinder but no damage. All the men are in terrific order and the colonel's idea that all men should retaliate with their rifles during these air attacks (especially low-flying), instead of diving for shelter, has proved a great success.

Donny Player is endeavouring to get us some Bren guns – he hopes to get about 12. That will make a great difference. The old Hotchkiss is somewhat cumbersome.

The evacuation of Crete seems to be complete. So far we have had no word about B Battery and Y Battery under Tony Holden and Sydney Morse, who were manning coastal guns in Crete. I only hope that they got away safely. I understand that the dive-bombing attacks by German aircraft of our men-of-war as they were evacuating our troops have been quite incredible. I am longing to see old Mike Parish again. Pray God they are all safe.

Wednesday, 4 June

The colonel had a letter from Mikey Gold who left here a few weeks ago by sea for a mechanical course at Sarafand. In Cairo he called on ME and even saw Wavell. Old Mikey would see anyone if he set his mind to it. Apparently all the mechanized squadrons of the 1st Cavalry Division have gone to Iraq. Heaven only knows when the division will all get together again.

We still have heard no news from the batteries who were in Crete.

Thursday, 5 June

We have had a pamphlet sent us by the War Office on the 'extermination of rats'. With it I had a letter from the colonel appointing me RRO (regimental ratting officer), result of which has been a great deal of leg-pulling.

Two destroyers are coming into harbour tonight. We have great hopes that they may bring our reliefs.

Friday, 6 June

The colonel came down during the morning and told Stephen and myself the very distressing news that only 34 men from our two batteries in Crete had so far reached Egypt. Up to present no officers had appeared. It's all most disturbing and we must hope for the best – and that if they did manage to get a ship it was not sunk by all these dive-bombers. We can only hope that they are alive, but it is a great blow to the Regiment if all these officers are lost, i.e., Tony Holden, a major, Sydney Morse, captain, Mike Parish, Mike Riviere and Myles Hildyard, let alone all the men.

It's almost a month now since the colonel told us that some gunners were waiting in Alexandria at 24 hours' notice to come and relieve us. The lack of shipping is the trouble. The Wiltshire Yeomanry are in the same position. It seems more unlikely than ever that the 1st Cavalry Division will ever re-form again into an armoured division. They seem to be all over the place.

Saturday, 7 June

Today I met a most remarkable man. I came out of our BOP during the morning and I saw Brown from Navy House walking about with an army officer, and also with what appeared to be an Italian admiral! I went over to them and Brown introduced me to Admiral Cowan. He has joined up again this war as a commander and is attached to the Naval Commandos force under Bob Laycock at Mersa. He is 73 years old and was an admiral in the last war and fought in the Boer War with old Joe Laycock (Mike's father). He is also secretary of the Warwickshire Hunt. He and the other officer (Life Guards, I think) came up from Mersa on the tanker that arrived today to man the AA guns on board and also to have a look round here. It really is a most amazing effort. I had a long talk with him and found him most charming. He particularly wanted to see Mike Laycock as he knew his father so well. I found Mike doing some signalling in his BOP and told him that an admiral wanted to see him. He told me to '— off' as he was busy. However, with difficulty I managed to persuade him that an admiral did wish to see him and he came out and had a long talk with Cowan. He asked me whether I was related to the famous cricket family.

Mike and I went to dinner at Navy House and had a most enjoyable and interesting time. I sat next to Commander Perry and Lieutenant Brown. Perry is a grand person and is a survivor off the *Southampton*. We had a very excellent dinner, including some melon, which had been sent up from Alexandria. They also gave us far too many cocktails, which they made out of Italian brandy and gin: most intoxicating. We found Admiral Cowan staying at Navy House. He told us all about his experience on the gunboat *Gnat*.

Navy House, which looks over the harbour, was never finished by the Italians but all the same it's quite an imposing building despite the end wing having been knocked down by two direct hits by German bombers. The damaged wing presents an extraordinary sight from the rather imposing corridors on the first floor.

After dinner we went out on the balcony overlooking the harbour. The almost full moon made it as light as day, and lit up the numerous wrecks. This place is certainly a veritable grave for shipping, both Italian and English. Immediately below us alongside the quayside we could see the pathetic burned-out remains of one of our merchant ships. On the other side of the harbour, also burned out and beached, one Italian liner and merchant ship, and further up the harbour still the outline of an Italian cruiser.

It's all very inspiring and I only wish that I had the literary ability to describe it all. Mike and I left Navy House, both rather tight – and I had a headache!

Admiral Sir Walter 'Titch' Cowan was every bit as extraordinary as Stanley makes out, having first gone to sea as a midshipman in 1886. Before the century had ended he was commanding his own gunboat and serving on the cruiser HMS Barrosa. *He also took part in the Battle of Omdurman and later commanded the Nile gunboat flotilla during the Fashoda Incident. Steadily climbing the ranks, he commanded the battleship HMS* Princess Royal *at the Battle of Jutland. After the First World War he went on to command HMS* Hood, *and later was naval ADC to King George V. Although retired before the war, he rejoined the navy with the lower rank of commander and became one of Bob Laycock's Commandos. Although Layforce, as it was called, was disbanded, he remained in the Middle East and fought at Bir Hacheim during the Gazala battles and was eventually captured while singlehandedly manning a tank and armed with only a revolver. In 1943, he was lucky enough to be repatriated, so rejoined the Commandos and fought with them in Italy, winning a bar to an earlier DSO. Britain can have had few more tenacious and enduring warriors.*

Sunday, 8 June

Eight bombs fell in our camp area. One of our tents plus all the kit inside was completely destroyed. Most fortunately all the occupants of the tent were out at the time.

I heard today that we had marched into Syria where the Germans have been infiltrating. They have already occupied the main aerodrome at Damascus, Aleppo, and it is reported that German tank personnel have arrived disguised as tourists to take over the French tanks.

Alderson, one of the occupants of the demolished tent, happened to have gone to a Catholic service in the town. When he returned and saw his pullover riddled with holes on the ground, he said, 'Is that my bloody pullover? This is far too personal for my liking.'

We still have no fresh news about our lost men in Crete.

The Middle East command was vast and Wavell had an enormous task on his hands trying to firefight all the various crises that seemed to be arising across this massive territory. By the end of May, the Axis-backed revolt in Iraq had been quelled but had required the diversion of more troops: on 31 May, British forces entered Baghdad, and on 3 June, a new Iraqi government was formed. Then, on 8 June, Wavell launched Operation EXPLORER, an invasion of Vichy-controlled Syria and Lebanon from Palestine, using both British and Free French forces. By 9 June, they had advanced 90 miles and taken the key city of Tyre.

Wednesday, 11 June

About 20 planes came over in the early morning and attacked the inner perimeter. The only damage they did was to kill 12 donkeys.

In other parts of the world we have advanced to within 15 miles of Damascus. Opposition in Syria has been patchy.

There is talk of our Imperial War Cabinet. It will be interesting to see whether WC will last as PM for the duration.

I understand two destroyers and five other ships are due in tonight. Let's hope there may be signs of our relief.

Still no news of our losses in Crete as regards the Regiment. I think the colonel should warn the men that we have heard nothing, especially those who have brothers and great friends in the lost batteries. He argues that one shouldn't worry them until we know the worst.

Friday, 13 June

Spent the night in our BOP, which was disturbed from 1 o'clock onwards owing to enemy aircraft overhead. During the morning we had a couple of high-level bombing attacks, one on the harbour and the other on the heavy AA. One Bren gun post next door to the heavy AA got a direct hit. I have not heard the casualties yet.

Lieutenant Commander Giles, the mine expert from Navy House, came round this evening and brought Mike Laycock a tin of naval tobacco, which he asked us to give him. Jokingly he told us to tell Mike that the tobacco had been dropped during the last raid. We took him at his word and played a most amusing joke on old Mike.

We took all the paper off the tin and dropped it in the sand. When Mike came back we told him that Navy House had rung us through with information that booby traps had been dropped during the last raid in the form of tins, and that we had found one just outside the mess. Would he make a report on it to Giles at Navy House?

Mike got very thrilled about this, rushed to examine the tin, which was just exposed above the sand, approached it most gingerly and then ordered all the area to be cleared. Donny Player and Lawrence Biddle appeared on the scene and we managed to let them into the joke and we all played up.

Mike then decided he would shoot at it and try to explode it in that way. He fetched his tin hat and rifle and took cover behind some sand bags, ordered all of us to do the same, which we did, having the greatest difficulty in controlling our mirth. He fired five shots, missed with three and scored two hits. Nothing happened, of course, so we all got up and stalked the wretched tin of tobacco, and found bits of tobacco sticking out of the tin, which certainly rather resembled an explosive substance. Mike was most intrigued and fired another two shots, this time practically bursting the tin and loosening all the tobacco. Scottie then went forward with a great show of bravery and gingerly lifted up the tin, bringing it back with him.

Mike then realized that the tin contained nothing else but tobacco and that the whole thing was a leg-pull. He hurled the tin at Stephen, who ducked, but it hit him on the back and bounced off to a spot 15 yards away. He took the whole affair terribly well and rang up Giles at Navy House to thank him and told him all about the joke.

The colonel came down and had dinner with us. Afterwards we had a most interesting discussion, trying to determine in our minds exactly what the war aims of Germany were now, and we concluded that at the moment she would welcome any reasonable peace terms.

Above: The annual summer camp was the highlight of the Yeomanry regiment's year. With their polished riding boots and Sam Brown belts, the Sherwood Rangers Yeomanry, here at Welbeck in August 1939, belonged to an earlier era. In a world of landed estates, hunting and playing cricket, they were enthusiastic amateur soldiers totally ill-prepared for war.

Above: The Sherwood Rangers began their war by being posted to Palestine along with their horses. They were soon involved in a cavalry charge, sabres drawn, against Arab insurrectionists.

Above: Arthur Cranley (*left*) and Roger Sutton-Nelthorpe (*right*) in Palestine, where the SRY were based throughout 1940. Arthur Cranley was later captured at Villers-Bocage in Normandy in June 1944

Left: Emerging after a dip in the sea. There was not much to enjoy during their time in Tobruk, but the cool waters of the Mediterranean were a small consolation, particularly with the lack of sanitation and the gradually rising temperatures.

Below: Near their gun position, sandbagged behind. From left to right: unknown, Mike Laycock, Jack Whiting and Scottie Myles.

Above: Tobruk. Stanley sits in the centre.

Right: Stanley with just a towel and a tin hat. No matter how awful it was at Tobruk, at least they could swim in the sea.

Below: Sergeant Hutchinson and Trooper Butler.

Above: Some of A Battery at Tobruk. Stanley is on the far left at the back, holding his cine camera.

Left: Stephen Mitchell – Stanley's greatest and most enduring friend in the Sherwood Rangers.

Below: Scottie Myles in a towel with Stanley saluting. Tobruk was a brutal posting. Repeatedly bombed and shelled and cut off entirely except from the sea, they lived in harsh conditions under constant danger. Keeping a sense of humour and optimism was essential.

Above: In the spring of 1942 the Sherwood Rangers were, at long last, mechanized, and Stanley took over command of A Squadron, about which he was thrilled. Stanley is seated in front of one of the squadron's fast, light Crusader tanks.

Right: General Montgomery (*right*) arrived to take command of Eighth Army in August, just as the Sherwood Rangers were deployed for action for the first time as an armoured regiment.

Below: Britain invested much in wheeled tank transporters, which not only saved wear and tear but also enabled many broken-down tanks to be removed quickly from the battlefield and repaired.

Above: A wrecked Junkers 88 bomber. During the Alamein battles, large numbers of Luftwaffe and Italian aircraft were destroyed by a resurgent Desert Air Force and bombers from RAF Middle East.

Above: A destroyed Italian M11/39 tank and the much-feared German 88mm anti-tank gun.

Left: Sherwood Rangers pause to look at a damaged 50mm anti-tank gun in the aftermath of the victory at Alamein.

Below: A knocked-out Italian M11/39 tank. Italian tanks were more numerous than German models in North Africa, and for the most part were inferior to those used in the Eighth Army.

Above: A long column of German and Italian prisoners captured at Alamein.

Right: One of the most significant prisoners taken at Alamein, as witnessed by Stanley, was General Ritter von Thoma, commander of the Deutsches Afrika Korps, here jumping down from a scout car.

Below: Sherwood Rangers clamber over a destroyed Panzer Mk III. It was understandably fascinating to have a good look at captured enemy war materiel.

Colonel Flash Kellett (*left*) and Major Donny Player. These two men were the beating heart of the Sherwood Rangers in the first half of the war. In many ways they belonged to a different era and yet both were forward-thinking, dynamic and strove to make the regiment as fine a fighting force as any in the Eighth Army. The affection for these fearless warriors ran deep among the men.

Playing a trick on Mike Laycock (13 June 1941).

1. Close examination.

2. Taking aim.

3. Scottie being brave.

She must realize that she can never completely conquer England, the Empire and America, even after many years of struggle.

It's a strange war, becoming more complex every day, and more difficult to see an end. When we do beat the Germans again, we can't make the same mistake as last time. They are a highly intelligent people and in many ways similar to us, and must be given a position in the world. It somehow seems strange that this can't be arranged without the loss of millions of lives (including women and children) especially when 90 per cent of both races don't want war.

The Higher Command told the colonel last week that we and the Wilts might expect to be relieved here in a week's time, and that brings us to tonight. We have had information that two destroyers are due in here. Will they bring our reliefs? They are due in any time after 11 o'clock and it's half past eleven now.

Sunday, 15–Wednesday, 18 June

There has been very little to write about these last few days, the main point of interest being the Commando officers whom we have billeted on us. HQ have also got five billeted on them. Peter Beatty and Randolph Churchill are also with us.

Flash Kellett asked Randolph Churchill to give all available officers, NCOs, and men a talk about conditions in England. He spoke very well and what appeared to be a great deal of sense, pointing out, although we are rather inclined to think so, that ours is not the most important battle front. The Home Front is the most important, followed by the Battle of the Atlantic. He spoke a bit about America, pointing out that although they were giving us all the help that they could, it would all take time as factories had to be built first. He gave the war another 18 months to two years. They do say there will be no further need for these Commando forces. I don't quite know what they will do if the force is disbanded as most of their regiments are in England. I have an idea that the colonel will try and put Bill McGowan into this regiment if they are disbanded. He asked me all about him.

In the early morning of 16 June we made a big push up from

Mersa and captured Fort Capuzzo. The Commando force are up here in connection with that push. Today we heard that they withdrew again in the face of superior numbers back to their original line, which is most disappointing as we had great hopes that Tobruk would be relieved and we should go back to Alex by road.

Randolph Churchill was the prime minister's son and, although also a Conservative MP, was a serving officer with his father's old regiment, the Queen's Own Hussars. In light of the string of defeats, his father had recently been forced to defend himself in Parliament; Churchill's premiership came under considerable scrutiny at this time, his rallying cries and defiance of the previous summer seemingly forgotten.

Meanwhile, more than 200 tanks had arrived in Egypt in recent weeks so, in conjunction with the operations going on in Syria, and with Rommel seemingly run out of steam, Wavell launched Operation BATTLEAXE, in an attempt to push the Axis back out of Egypt and relieve Tobruk. Unfortunately, within a day of fighting, the British had lost large numbers of tanks, which had rumbled straight into Rommel's waiting screens of anti-tank guns. On 17 June, BATTLEAXE was called off. The British had taken more than a thousand casualties and lost some 91 tanks.

There was, however, brighter news from Syria, where Free French forces captured Damascus.

Thursday, 19 June

We heard a rumour tonight brought back from the area commander by Randolph Churchill that we have withdrawn to Sidi Barrani. We don't seem to be able to give these Germans a crack. It really is most disappointing. It's amazing what stuff the Germans must have got here. Our information is three panzer divisions. It's true that their lines of communication must be getting very long but I don't like having the Hun so very near Egypt. We are not making very much progress on the Syrian frontier. The Vichy forces are putting up a strong resistance outside Damascus. There is also talk of a Treaty of

Friendship between Turkey and Germany, which is bad, and what with our shipping losses, the outlook this evening is somewhat sorry.

I have very bad flea bites. Two bites on my hip and the glands in my thigh have swollen up.

The general opinion is that we can't win this war in under 18 months or two years.

Friday, 20–Sunday, 22 June

Our push up to this place has been held up at Sollum and we have withdrawn to our original line back there, which is so disappointing. I understand that they hoped to relieve this place. When eventually Tobruk is relieved it will be interesting to see whether we evacuate by road and hold a line further back. In the mean time we continue to be bombed each day: 286 raids up to the present in the harbour area and we still have no air force here. The heavy AA on the north point do damned well as, during practically every raid, they have been the object of the attack.

On Saturday we sent about 40 of our men back to Jerusalem under the RSM. Our battery sent 20. That leaves us with just one team per gun. A good idea, as that means less people to feed and less to get out if we have to evacuate the place by sea, which I hope will not be the case as the navy declare it will be a most unpleasant job.

At the end of June we will have been here five months.

Still no news from Crete, except that only 50 men got out, including Sergeant Rodger, our old troop sergeant, and Corporal Vickers, one of our troop corporals, in the days when we had horses. All the officers are still missing.

No mail has come through from the family for a great many weeks.

Life goes on much the same each day. We are living on rations completely. For the last few weeks there has been no NAAFI at all, so that means no drink. Personally it does not worry me, although it does some. Things could be very much worse and we can't grumble. The climate is grand and personally I never find it hot. The fleas and the flies are bloody awful.

Monday, 23 June

We have just heard that Germany has walked into Russia without any declaration of war. So Germany and Russia are at war. Nobody knows Russia's strength, but this may make all the difference and shorten the war by at least six months or a year.

Obviously, Germany is after the wheat and oil in the Ukraine. Up to the present she has been sure of success before attacking, having well prepared the way by fifth-column activity – let's hope she has made a very great mistake this time.

Hitler had been planning Operation BARBAROSSA since the previous autumn when he realized Britain would neither come to the peace table nor could be defeated that year. Instead, he decided to bring forward his intended assault on the Soviet Union, hoping to win another rapid victory as he had in the west the previous year. Then, with manpower and resources a-plenty, he could turn back to deal with Britain – and, he hoped, before the United States and her increasing economic clout had intervened more fully. It was an enormous undertaking not least because of the sheer size of the country, the huge logistical difficulties, and the ferociousness of the Russian winter, should victory not be as rapid as hoped. And history, of course, was against Hitler. As Stanley appreciated, Germany's invasion of the Soviet Union was a huge gamble.

Tuesday, 24 June

The Hun had the nerve to drop leaflets during the afternoon. These were addressed to the Aussies, calling on them to surrender. I must try and get hold of one of these pamphlets. I would not care to be in the shoes of any German sitting outside Tobruk, or for that matter in Egypt or Libya at all. I am afraid that it might be difficult to get hold of one of these pamphlets as they will be eagerly sought after as souvenirs.

At 6 o'clock this evening we had a debate among the battery in the magazine. We made it voluntary and it really was quite a success.

The motion was whether, in the opinion of the house, a horse was a higher animal than the dog. Sergeant Ketchum spoke for the motion and Corporal Darnie opposed. It was then thrown open to the house and we had some very funny remarks. Stephen then summed up and decided the result by a showing of hands. The dog was found to be more intelligent than the horse by one vote only.

The colonel came in during the debate. Somehow he didn't appear to be in very good form. He wants to get back very badly to find out more news about our troops lost in Crete, and what those who got out are doing now.

We have still got the Commando officers staying with us – Bill McGowan, Captain Dr Sellar and Vivian Berry. They were due to leave Thursday but their departure has been cancelled. No doubt I shall hear the reason in the morning. It's great fun having them with us. Sellar, the doctor, went out on an expedition last night, about which I can write a lot more after the war. He got in again very early this morning. It was not very successful.

I have a boil on my bottom, which is very painful.

The Commandos spent a lot of time cooling their heels in North Africa after Layforce; the Commando detachment led by Colonel Bob Laycock was deployed to the Middle East in early 1941. One of the outlets that Laycock found for them was as additions to the garrison at Tobruk during the siege. Small detachments were sent on rotation, in order to give them experience of being on the front line. There was a fair amount of raiding too, and this entry probably refers to some such expedition.

Wednesday, 25 June

We had three raids during the day, single bombers coming over and dropping stuff from a high level. After tea I walked with Mike Laycock to see Thompson, who is in hospital here with malaria. He is in the old Italian hospital, which is a pretty grim spot. In the next bed to him there was an Australian with whom we had an interesting talk. He has been on the perimeter and told us that since we started our big push from Sollum there has been a great decrease in the number of German troops round Tobruk and, in spite of our push being somewhat of a failure, we should have made a push from here, as he had been out on patrol practically every night and met absolutely nothing in the way of enemy armoured forces.

We walked back via RHQ. We had to take cover twice when a Heinkel bomber came over and dropped some shit, but nothing very close.

I never knew before that the Italians had built enormous reserve water tanks underground, just close to the old Prison Café. They are at least 60 feet below ground and contain at least 30,000 gallons of reserve water. We found some Aussies in charge, who took us down into the control room, which is also almost 60 feet below ground. We had to climb down a ladder and eventually came into a good-sized hall, which was a kind of control room. Pipes ran all the way down to the harbour from these tanks (concrete) so that the water could be pumped up into them from ships. The sergeant in charge promised to let us have some on the quiet, and added, of course, that he could always do with some whisky if we had any to spare! However, good fresh water can be far more valuable than whisky in these parts.

Smith, my batman, told me today that his wife has given up her job in a factory and has become manageress of a men's canteen. He is most disturbed about this.

Thursday, 26 June

My day for duty in the BOP. Usual routine during the morning and we had a long hour of signalling. I think I can read Morse code pretty efficiently at 10 words a minute now. I am not so hot at lamp. I had a practice shoot during the morning.

One feels in a way that, after having been here for so long we should really still be here, as part of the original garrison of Tobruk, when the whole place is relieved by a force from Egypt. But who knows? We may yet be here. However, I understand that A Battery will be the last to leave.

Our Commando friends, Bill McGowan, Bill Sellar and Vivian

Berry, left last night by destroyer for Alexandria. It has been great fun having them with us.

Friday, 27 June

Last night 40 men and one officer arrived by destroyer to relieve us and take over the coastal defence of Tobruk. They have been sitting in Egypt waiting to come up here for about a month. A certain Major Dockrell was the officer in charge. In spite of having made it quite clear to him that we had absolutely no instruments, that we'd had to improvise for everything, that we'd had to build our own gun pits and put the guns in the pit, he kept asking questions about wind and tide, etc., and then had the nerve to call our BOP very 'Mickey Mouse-ish' and the shooting of our guns 'bow-and-arrow shooting'. However, he knows his job.

He asked Lawrence what we did about wind gauges, to which he replied that we had two methods to gauge the wind, first sucking your finger and putting it in the air and second by feeling the wind on the back of your neck.

Sunday, 29 June

The padre gave us a short service in one of the gun pits. He made quite a good address. We also sang some quite good hymns.

As this might have been our last service here, I could not help feeling that it was rather like the last Sunday at school, and thought that the hymn 'Now Thank We All Our God' would have been most appropriate. I mentioned this afterwards to the padre, who said, 'Let's get out of the place fast!'

Never in all my life will I experience again that wonderful sensation and happiness of the 'last Sunday before the holidays'. I don't care what anyone says, the school days are the happiest, especially the day before and the first day of your holidays. Of course, that all depends whether you have a happy home.

Some bombs fell unpleasantly near the mess.

Monday, 30 June

We had it confirmed that one of the destroyers bringing up our reliefs was dive-bombed and sunk last night. That was the reason why they didn't arrive. Fortunately they managed to transfer all personnel on to the other destroyer. She sank after they had her in tow. That means we won't get away as soon as we anticipated.

Tuesday, 1 July

Rather an unpleasant day and quite the most hectic we have had for a long time, from an air point of view. At daybreak we had some ships in the harbour. They were shelled as they came in, which was followed very quickly by some high-level stuff, some of which fell on our point and quite close to our mess. At lunchtime we had about the biggest dive-bombing attack that the place has had, mostly on the harbour. Some estimate that 70 planes were in the attack. The harbour barrage was very effective. Our Hotchkiss gun just behind the mess let off over 400 rounds.

Later in the afternoon we had some shelling. Their guns appeared to be much closer and shells were landing right opposite Navy House and all around the ships.

Finally, in the evening, we had another German high-level bombing attack. In spite of all these attacks, as far as I know, we suffered no casualties and no damage was caused, to the shipping at any rate. At least three enemy planes were brought down.

We have heard that three destroyers are coming in tonight so there is every chance that some more of our relief may be arriving.

I do feel now that I should like to get away from this place, and away from all the war. Steve and I talked about leave together when we do eventually go. What fun it was and what fun it will be.

It's quite difficult to decide where to go. Alex is not much of a catch with all this bombing they are having there. Cairo is so desperately hot and I don't particularly want to go to Palestine. We even considered waiting until Syria is ours but then again we have found that if you don't take leave when you get the chance the chance does not often come again. But, still, we have to get out of the place first.

Wednesday, 2 July

Last night on the destroyers 34 men and two officers of our relief arrived. They were different from the last lot and will relieve either A Battery or Z Battery on this point. Scottie went down to the docks to meet them and had rather a long wait, which must have been unpleasant when some Hun planes came over.

Thursday, 3 July

When he left here, Bill McGowan promised to send us some whisky up from Mersa. He did this via an air-force officer. In fact he sent two cases. Donny Player went across by truck to the south side of the harbour and broke down. An air-force officer gave him a lift back. They got into conversation and asking the name of Donny's unit he asked whether there was a certain major called Player. 'I'm your man,' replied Donny. The air-force officer then broke the dreadful news about the whisky. Bill McGowan had given him the whisky to bring up and on the boat his batman got somewhat suspicious about the contents as there was such a rattle in the package. They decided to open the cases and found one filled with stones and the other with bully beef. Donny then had almost eight fits of combined rage and disappointment. The whisky will have to be paid for. The question is, do we charge the air force?

We had hopes that more of our reliefs would arrive but no luck.

This shelling from the Huns is becoming rather uncomfortable. Their shells are landing all over the place. It appears that they have got a gun in position near the harbour and of great calibre. I heard that an unexploded shell had been found as large as 5.9 inches. We have replied with Tilly, but without much effect.

I had dinner at HQ and sat next to the colonel and opposite Major Dockrell, who will be in charge when we all leave. The colonel is tremendously pleased that Wavell has just got the push and also that Oliver Lyttelton is coming out here with full Cabinet powers to preside over army, navy and air force. The lack of co-operation has been bad and I think this might have had some bearing on our failures just lately. Daddy will be very pleased when he hears about Oliver Lyttelton's new job. He is a capable man and I hope the new scheme, and Lyttelton himself, will prove a success.

We had two or three raids during the day, mostly high-level stuff.

When I got back a new sentry was on duty, one of the new relief. He, of course, didn't know me when he challenged me and as I had no identification card on me he insisted that I should have to be identified before he would let me go on!

Wavell was much admired and had handled the pressures of such a giant command with unfailing calmness, yet Churchill had never really warmed to him and had been looking to move him on for some time. The failure of BATTLEAXE had given him the excuse he needed, so he had been sacked on 21 June and immediately sent to be C-in-C India. His replacement, General Claude Auchinleck, known to all as 'The Auk', had arrived to take over on 1 July.

Friday, 4 July

We had rather a heavy dive-bombing attack about 6 o'clock. Some of the planes attacked our point while we were teaching the new gunners on the 4-inch guns. Two bombs fell about 20 yards from our battery office and mess room.

The new gunners were very scared and our men in the gun pits set a very good example by calmly shooting at the planes with their rifles. Some of the planes came down within 20 feet of the water to avoid Beaufort and small-arms fire. The Beauforts on the north point had some wonderful targets but unfortunately the dust and muck caused by the bombs obscured their view. I think we might have got two down but that has yet to be confirmed.

Incidentally, the new so-called gunners don't know the first thing about the 4-inch guns, in spite of having a three-month course. It's quite funny that we have to teach the gunners.

Saturday, 5 July

It's now about 9.30 in the evening and I am writing this in the BOP. I am on duty again tonight. Stephen and Scottie have just been up to say goodbye. They leave by the destroyers that are coming in tonight, with the colonel, Donny, Derrick Warwick and about 60 men. We expect a good many more of our reliefs to arrive by the destroyers, which are due in about 11.30. They are all terribly excited about going. The prospect of a week's leave after six months in Tobruk, without seeing a civilian, let alone a woman, is enough to excite anyone.

I shall be the last to leave. The colonel came down this afternoon and said he wanted me to stay and bring the last of the men away. Lawrence goes tomorrow, and Mike Laycock will follow him, and I shall bring up the rear. I was the first here and will be the last to leave. It really is rather like the last week at school, but I won't think about it until I step ashore at Mersa or Alexandria.

During the morning I went up to RHQ, then on to Navy House where they gave us a drink. I had a most interesting talk with a naval officer who has just joined the staff there, having arrived from Crete. He actually lived for a time with Tony Holden, Mike Parish and Jon Abel-Smith, our officers from Y Battery whom we sent to Crete. It's very sad to think that when we all meet again at Allenby Barracks, Jerusalem, all the officers of B and Y Batteries will be missing, and practically all the men too. Little did we realize this would happen when they went to Cyprus and on to Crete – and Sydney Morse, Mike Riviere and Myles Hildyard took B Battery to Crete, and we came to Tobruk. I only hope that our people have a safe journey back to Alex. Unfortunately the moon is almost full. We had some planes over and they started that damned shelling in the harbour, just after the second destroyer crossed the boom. As they passed through the boom I made our trumpeter blow the cavalry call for 'Trot', followed by 'Canter', 'Gallop' and, finally, 'Good Night'. I feel certain that they heard it as the wind was blowing in the right direction.

Sunday, 6 July

Today I think has been the worst we have had since we have been here – continual high-level and dive-bombing, also shelling from the other side. They are using a pretty big gun. We can see the flash and worked out that it's about 20,000 yards away.

During the afternoon we had some unpleasant shelling. One landed over at X Battery, knocking out their home-made distillery and injuring two of our men, Corporal Smith and Trooper Smith, and one lance bombardier from our reliefs. He got it the worst.

Mike and I went to see them in hospital in the town. We had some difficulty in finding them at first, and had to walk through the serious wounded ward, which was quite one of the most depressing sights that I have ever seen, and only brought home too clearly the horrors of war, and the utter futility.

Monday, 7 July

Spent most of the day showing the two new officers around the place. Major Howell is really rather gloomy and dismal. He never speaks a word and the young lieutenant who came up with him tells me that he never does, unless he is well oiled either with gin or whisky. What a hope he has got here! What is more, he has not changed his shirt since he arrived.

Tuesday, 8 July

I came down to breakfast after spending the night on duty in the BOP and Mike greeted me with the news that all the remainder of our relief had arrived last night in the destroyers. I spent the most hectic day handing over all guns, stores, ammunition, etc. I had to do A, Z, and X Batteries. It is now about 10 o'clock in the evening.

Mike Laycock has just gone off to the docks as he and Lawrence leave tonight by the destroyers, with all our remaining men except about 30 across on the south side. So that only leaves the doc at HQ (thank God for him), my batman, Smith, his medical orderly and the men on the south side.

It's full moon tonight, bombs have been dropped twice and also the harbour has been shelled. Mike does not like the idea of the journey at all. It really is as bright as day outside. Once they are out of the harbour they will be all right. I shall be damned glad to get out of this place. Almost six months of constant bombing and shelling. With any luck I should be away by Thursday evening.

Wednesday, 9 July

Today I was busy handing over to our reliefs all the posts on the south side of the harbour. It was not made easier by the lack of co-operation between the two batteries and the stubbornness of Howell, who would not detail the correct number from his battery. There appears to be no discipline and the NCOs have no control over their men. I had to do most of the work myself. Eventually we got off but not until 3.30 in the afternoon. I had very rarely visited the south side as all the posts were manned by Michael's men, so we experienced the greatest difficulty in finding the way, especially to the outlying posts. The truck broke down at one point, we had a series of bombing attacks on the south side and saw a dive-bombing attack on our position on the other side of the harbour. It was quite fun to watch it from a distance. We eventually got back at midnight to find that no food had been left for us, so we made ourselves some tea and ate some bread and marmalade.

Thursday, 10 July

Today was my last day in Tobruk and I took great care not to get damaged in any way in air raids. I made up my mind not to get killed on my last day and in this I was successful! I am immensely pleased to leave the place, especially as all the others from the Regiment have gone and I shall be the last to leave with 30 men.

Two destroyers come in every other evening, stay just long enough to unload and then dash out again. That is the only way that they can supply Tobruk now. Shipping during the day is quite out of the question, in the harbour or off the Sollum coast. The destroyers must be out of the danger area before daybreak as they don't get a fighter escort until then.

In the morning I made arrangements for Geoffrey Brooks, myself and 34 men to be down on the docks by 11 o'clock to catch the destroyers.

I wasn't sorry to say goodbye to our reliefs. What a bum lot they appear to be. I have discovered that Howell has five bottles of whisky hidden in his room. It's been bad enough in Tobruk with a grand lot of companions: I simply can't imagine what it will be like with these chaps.

On my way to the docks I called in at Navy House to bid them farewell. What a grand crowd they are and what a hectic time they have had.

The destroyer, *Defender*, and the Australian *Vendetta* arrived in harbour about 11 o'clock, hastily unloaded and we then embarked. It didn't take us long to get out of the harbour and we all said a very happy goodbye to Tobruk. Unfortunately, it was a bright moonlit night and we were shelled as we left, but we made very good speed and were damned glad to see the last of the place.

Stanley's relief at leaving Tobruk is all too evident, but with his usual understatement, his diaries do rather skate over just how relentlessly grim it was for those besieged there. Even those in the trenches in the First World War were regularly rotated out of the line, but those at Tobruk had to withstand the aerial and artillery bombardments without any respite. The conditions were appalling: during the early months, freezing cold at night and uncomfortably warm by day, and by the summer, blisteringly hot during daylight hours and with little water, almost no sanitation, millions upon millions of flies, and virtually no creature comforts. The smell and sight of death and decay were unavoidable, and there was not a man there who did not find the experience horrendously grim, to put it mildly. The stoicism of Stanley and his fellows was, frankly, quite astonishing.

7

Mechanized at Last

A new American-built Sherman surges across the desert.

Friday, 11 July 1941

WE HAD QUITE a few troops on board who had left Tobruk with us, as well as our own unit. I went down into the wardroom and it wasn't long before I was fast asleep in a chair. I was woken up at dawn by an alarm bell ringing and guns firing on deck. On reaching the deck I found that a damned high-level bomber had dropped a stick across us and likewise the same on the other destroyer. Unfortunately one had scored a very near miss and broke the *Defender*'s back. We went alongside and took all personnel off, except a skeleton navy crew. We then spent about three hours trying to tow the crippled destroyer back to Alexandria, first with a wire rope, then a hawser and finally with the anchor chain, but to no avail. Both ropes broke and we failed with the anchor chain. It was rather an uncomfortable time as we were not far off the Sollum coast and the Hun air bases. However, all was well, and it was not long before we found our fighter escort, which was a most encouraging sight. All the crew was taken off the *Defender* and we had to sink her. We fired a torpedo, which was a remarkable sight and caused a terrific explosion, but that didn't sink her and we had to sink her by shelling. It took at least 12 shells. When eventually she finally disappeared under the water both crews took off their hats and cheered her as she went down. And so we proceeded to Alexandria. We had at least 1000 troops on board so we were very crowded as well as the two naval crews.

Soon two other of our destroyers appeared, which had been sent out from Alexandria to escort us back. We eventually arrived at about 7 o'clock in the evening, where we were met by RASC transport and taken to Amariya staging camp, all very hungry and weary. We didn't actually get to the camp until midnight. But the men were given a meal. Geoffrey Brooks and I had a whisky and soda and some bacon and eggs, the first drink and a meal of that kind for many a day. It didn't take us long to get to bed and sleep the sleep of the very weary and relieved.

Sunday, 13–Saturday, 19 July

A week's leave in Cairo after six months in Tobruk is certainly a grand change. I stayed at Shepheard's Hotel, ate too much, and spent far too much money. I didn't really enjoy myself: it was far too hot, quite unbearable at times, and there were far too many army about. On the other hand, I saw a great many friends. I wanted to spend my leave with Stephen but he was sent off on a course. Mike Laycock was there some of the time with me but had stomach trouble all the while. He left for Palestine before me.

I spent most of my time shopping. I sent a present out to my god-child in Canada. I also bought a new silk suit, which is quite smart. It cost me £6. I spent quite a good deal of time at the Gezira Club, and played some tennis.

On my last Saturday I ran into the colonel, Flash Kellett, who had flown down from Palestine to Cairo for a conference about our future role. He told me that the Regiment, having re-formed at Jerusalem

(Allenby Barracks), would stay there for about five weeks and do all the training possible. Another armoured division was going to be formed and we were going to be brigaded with the Greys and the Staffordshire Yeomanry.

We ourselves, the Notts Yeomanry, were going to be equipped with American tanks, the first of which might arrive in about six weeks' time. The colonel told me all this when I met him on the steps of the Continental. He is most thrilled at the idea of becoming a tank regiment.

As we are so short of officers he asked me to go back immediately to Allenby Barracks to look after A Squadron.

Sunday, 20–Sunday, 27 July

I left Egypt for Palestine with Patrick Ness from the Queens Bays. He was with Layforce (Commandos) when they were disbanded. Flash got him into this regiment. He has had a certain amount of experience with tanks. I find him rather a bore, but no doubt I may be wrong.

The Regiment has now re-formed at Allenby Barracks, Jerusalem, where I arrived on Sunday afternoon. At this time of year the climate here is simply lovely, and a tremendous contrast to Cairo, which is quite unbearably hot. The barracks are most comfortable and I have got a very decent room, and I am quite looking forward to some peacetime soldiering again for a time. When I arrived the colonel told me that I was to have command of A Squadron until Stephen returned from his course. The squadron is made up from nearly all the old A Battery and personnel from X Battery.

For the present I find that Mike Laycock has command of B Squadron, Henry Trotter C Squadron, and Stephen A Squadron. I understand that Henry Trotter will be boarded home on account of his bad leg.

I had a long talk with the colonel about Peter Laycock. He was most dissatisfied with his efforts at Benghazi and Tobruk. The bombing and raids completely broke his nerve and in this case he does not think that he is a fit person to lead a squadron of tanks into battle.

When the colonel makes up his mind about an officer or man, he acts. So, unknown to Peter, he applied for a staff job for him and it has just come through that he will report to Oliver Lyttelton as military political secretary, which I understand is nothing but a glorified ADC's job. Michael, his brother, is absolutely furious and terribly upset. The whole thing has been most sudden. However, I think on the whole that the colonel adopted the correct policy. His one aim is to produce a first-class regiment so that we can win the war, and to achieve this he has no scruples. Mike Gold is also most upset about this as he and Peter were terrific friends. But there is no doubt that Peter's morale at Tobruk was at a very low ebb.

I had a long talk with the colonel about the whole position and he was most frank with me and actually told me that he would prefer to give Peter a staff job than let him have a squadron. He has now gone, and went at very short notice.

Monday, 21– Sunday, 27 July

I have been a week at Allenby Barracks now, which is a most comfortable existence, but plenty of work. The Regiment is now to be trained as a tank regiment, equipped with American cruiser tanks, which are now arriving from America with satisfactory regularity. I am acting squadron leader of A Squadron with Bill McGowan as my second-in-command and Jack Whitney and Stuart Thompson as subalterns.

Bill has just joined us. He left the Scottish Horse for the Commandos, but Layforce has now been disbanded. It's rather strange that we should now be in the same regiment. He is a grand person. I understand that we shall be here for almost six weeks.

Monday, 28 July

We had a full day's work. Stuart Thompson is now back with the Regiment so we have our full quota of officers. No, I am wrong – we should have six.

I had a game of cricket in the afternoon. We played C Squadron. We play on the parade ground. Of course, the ball only lasts one game.

I had a long talk with the colonel about future officers. I told him that as Sergeant Kettner from my squadron is due for a commission I considered it a good thing to have him back here. We know him and like him, and realize his great capabilities, and he would fit in well in the mess. We are short of officers and we might so easily get some absolute dud. He had considered the possibility before, and liked the idea. We then discussed the whole question of officers from the ranks and even at the present time we have a good few, i.e., Jim Lovett, Scottie and Jack Whiting. To my mind, the colonel has got the right idea, he always looks ahead. His great aim is to win the war, and to do that efficiently is essential, both with officers and men, and no matter how unpleasant it may be, you must be ruthless in order to safeguard the future, not the present or the past; while he is endeavouring to maintain the cavalry-officer spirit, he does not wish our mess to get the atmosphere of the sergeants' mess, which might result by having a majority of commissioned NCOs. On the other hand, in war an efficient 'Scottie' commissioned from the Greys is essentially preferable to a charming and pleasant but thoroughly inadequate Peter. We can only win this war by training our regiments and armies more efficiently than the Hun, who has had such a start on us. Flash Kellett, our colonel, is well on the way to do that.

Stanley reveals here a steely determination that lay at the core of his character. Once again, there is evidence that the Sherwood Rangers were gradually shedding their old, amateur, pre-war skin. Stanley was among a core of officers who were resolved to transform the regiment into a highly trained and efficient unit, no matter what role they were given.

Tuesday, 29 July

I think there is a very good chance that I may get A Squadron, as Stephen may go to HQ Squadron when he returns from his course. If that does come off it will be rather hard on Stephen as HQ Squadron is a very poor command. That also might mean being made a major, but that is looking rather far ahead.

In the evening a lot of us went down to see my movie films. I had them developed in Cairo.

These films have survived and, although amateur and unedited, show many of the characters and places Stanley writes about in the diaries.

Thursday, 31 July–Wednesday, 13 August

In the past week I have been so busy that I have not been able to find the time to write each day. Life at Allenby Barracks has been extraordinarily pleasant, especially after Tobruk. In spite of being midsummer the climate is extraordinarily pleasant. We work very hard all through the day, training on gunnery, signalling, D&M in preparation for becoming tanks. I understand that our first vehicles arrive about 21 August, when we shall move from here and proceed to Karkur Camp where we spent a few months last year.

I am now a major; the colonel has given me command of A Squadron. I am most thrilled as it has been my one ambition to have a squadron and I am most attached to A Squadron. I think my promotion has been pretty rapid because I was a second lieutenant a year ago, but my pay is still that of a second lieutenant! But before long I hope to get a packet of back-pay. Of course, promotion has been due to casualties in Crete, but I suppose that is natural. It certainly will be an interesting time now that we are to get tanks. We shall all be starting from scratch.

Life here continues to be quite gay in spite of hard work. I went to one very good open-air dance at the Jerusalem Country Club. It was full moon and most delightful. We went in a large party of about 10, dining first at a restaurant in Jerusalem. I sat next to a girl called Ruth. She has a job out here and her husband is in the army in Syria. She was quite the nicest girl in the party and I danced most of the evening with her. It really was rather pleasant as it was full moon.

Another evening I dined at Government House and we all went on and danced at the King David. At dinner I sat next to Araminta MacMichael, the high commissioner's daughter.

Hermione Ranfurly, wife of Dan, who is now a prisoner of war, has got a job as private secretary to Lady MacMichael. I asked her about Dan but she has heard nothing.

I played a good deal of cricket and one day made 50 not out. Haven't enjoyed myself so much for a long time. There were also excellent hard tennis courts at the club of which we made full use, and the barracks had a squash court, so life at Jerusalem was altogether very pleasant.

Thursday, 14 August, Karkur Road Camp

At 9 o'clock we left Allenby Barracks, Jerusalem, and proceeded by bus to Karkur Road Camp. A Squadron and HQ Squadron were the first to leave; the remainder of the Regiment will follow tomorrow. It proved a very easy move and we covered the journey in 2½ hours. We take over the camp from two squadrons of the Yorkshire Hussars and they go to Jerusalem.

How strange it is to be back here again. We left here almost 14 months ago after handing in our horses at 24 hours' notice, and what a lot has happened since then.

Friday, 15 August

The remainder of the Regiment arrived today. We spent the day in cleaning up the camp, which is in an absolutely filthy condition. It is a disgrace that the YH should have left the place in such a condition.

In spite of not being the senior Yeomanry regiment (actually, I think we are No. 4), it is rather creditable that we, with the Greys and Staffordshire Yeomanry should be the first brigade to be mechanized, and to be known as the 8th Armoured Brigade. The Staffs are now at

Karkur Sea Camp, which, according to its name, is on the sea and most pleasantly situated.

We spent the day clearing up the camp. At five o'clock in the evening we had a squadron leaders' conference. Training will start in earnest on Monday.

We heard today that Sydney Morris was a prisoner in Germany. We have also heard the same about Jon Abel-Smith.

The camp now possesses a new garrison cinema, which will hold 700 people. After dinner we went to see Grace Moore in a film, which was quite good.

Saturday, 16 August

We are gradually getting settled in. Geoffrey Brooks, our doctor, one of the best men in the world, is running the officers' mess. We have dispensed with the contractor and we are cooking and buying our own food. John Walters is doing the financial side, but he is due to go away on a course.

Some Dragoons arrived today for training purposes, also some 3-ton tanks, and each squadron has been issued with two 15-cwt trucks for training purposes. In the near future each squadron leader will have a car of his own, and we expect to get our first tank in a few days, which will be named Robin Hood. One officer and six NCOs have arrived to be attached to the Regiment for instructional purposes on the tanks when they arrive.

It really is most thrilling having a squadron of my own, especially now we are all starting from scratch and training on something new. I am making my squadron office pretty smart.

Sunday, 17 August

Old Stephen (Mitchell) arrived back from his course in Egypt. It was good to see him again. When he arrived he hadn't heard that I had taken over A Squadron and he was taking over HQ Squadron. I was afraid the old chap would be terribly disappointed as he was attached to A Squadron and HQ Squadron is not much of a job. I simply had not the courage to tell him when he started talking about A Squadron and declaring that he wouldn't part with me as second-in-command, even though we both were majors. I dashed down to Lawrence Biddle, the adjutant, and told him to break the news to Stephen.

I can't get over having a squadron. It seems all too good to be true. I dread that something will turn up and spoil it all.

I read in the paper that Tobruk has had 1000 raids in the last four months. I am glad to be out of that place.

Monday, 18 August

Donny Player arrived back yesterday. He has been on a senior officers' tactical course in Cairo. He had some very interesting lectures, one from Freyberg on Crete, and here are some interesting points about that campaign.

1. The Germans expected Crete to fall in two days and if that had been the case the whole force of the German attack would have been through against Turkey, and then on to Syria and Palestine. For this attack they relied mainly on their airborne troops.

2. The fact that Crete held out so long and inflicted such severe losses on their air troops and troop-carrying planes, frustrated this plan.

3. Cyprus would also have been attacked had Crete fallen.

4. The Germans expected the Russian campaign to be over in a fortnight. If Russia holds out until the end of this month, this will prevent Germany starting another campaign against the Middle East owing to weather conditions.

5. If things had gone according to plan, Germany would have simultaneously made a drive through Spain and Portugal with the object of capturing Gibraltar and so completely cutting off the Middle East.

6. I gather the Turks at the moment are hopelessly unprepared.

It was true that, despite their victory on Crete, the Germans had suffered high numbers of casualties – out of 22,000 airborne and mountain troops used, some 6500 were casualties and 3352 were missing or killed. Also, more than a third of the transport aircraft used had been lost too. The British, in contrast, suffered 3500 casualties, of which 1700 were killed – fewer than the German invaders. It is also true that, after Crete, Hitler vowed never to use his paratroopers in a major airborne operation again. Even so, it sounds as though Freyberg was attempting to put a good spin on what had happened.

By mid-August, Germany had conquered vast swathes of the Ukraine and was closing in on Leningrad in the north and Odessa in the south on the Black Sea. Among the German High Command, confidence was high at this stage, even though there were signs that Russian resistance was not as broken as they thought. There was no German plan, however, to drive through Spain and Portugal.

It wasn't going entirely awry for the British. A mutual assistance pact had been signed with the Soviet Union, and the last Vichy French troops in the Middle East had surrendered; British troops had entered Beirut on 15 July.

Wednesday, 20 August

Three tanks arrived today, the first to reach the Regiment. Tanks all the way from America. They will be called Robin Hood, Friar Tuck and Little John. The colonel, Donny and the adjutant went across to Tulkarm and drove them back. They arrived this evening while my squadron was playing a football match against C Squadron. Flash drove his tank right across the ground, much to the excitement of the players. The officers will start training tomorrow.

Thursday, 21 August

We spent the day training and had our first drive, under RTR instructors, on the new American tanks. They are a wonderful bit of work and certainly most thrilling to drive. What a difference it is spending ½ hour on maintenance instead of possibly 2½ hours grooming, feeding, etc., in the case of a horse.

Friday, 22 August

One gets a great thrill driving these tanks, which can travel up to 40 m.p.h. It will be even more so when a complete crew is trained. It is so strange training now with tanks over the same ground on which we trained before with horses.

Saturday, 23 August

After lunch I motored up to Jerusalem with the colonel. Each squadron leader now has a staff car allocated to him and they have just been issued to the Regiment, brand new from Canada. Of course, they have not been run in yet. I went in the colonel's car and mine followed. He is spending four days in Cairo, staying with Oliver Lyttelton. We had quite a long talk about Peter. He told me that in getting rid of Peter he and Donny had made an enemy for life. And I am afraid he has. Personally I think he has had the courage of his convictions and taken the dead right course.

As it is, Peter and Michael are making out that the colonel got rid of Peter because Peter always stood out against him, and he (the colonel) wanted squadron leaders under his thumb, so that he could completely run the Regiment without interference from squadron leaders. Which, of course, is completely untrue and a rotten thing to say.

Sunday, 24 August

I didn't get up very early after spending a most comfortable night on the couch in the sitting room. An excellent breakfast – two fried eggs and bacon.

At 11 o'clock, after writing some letters, I went out. Jerusalem looked lovely bathed in sunlight, especially the garden of the YMCA where I spent quite a time. I then made my way to the 60th General Hospital and saw Henry Trotter, who is there with a bad leg. He didn't look too happy and expects to be boarded home in the near future. I ran into Charley Eardley in the hospital. He has almost recovered from a face wound received in Syria from a piece of bomb. He was commissioned into the Staffordshire Yeomanry from the Inns of Court at the same time as I was commissioned. We were at Edinburgh together. He is such a nice person.

I walked back to the King David Hotel and dropped in for a drink, which I had with Reggie Bush. He was struck off the strength of the Regiment many months ago (in fact, almost as soon as we arrived in this country) to become billeting officer. We compared the amazing changes which have taken place in the Regiment since we were last at Karkur Camp. We have another colonel, we have lost our horses, become gunners and now have tanks. Poor Toby Wallace is dead, six officers are missing and 150 men. It would have been absolutely un-believable had we been told that all this would happen to us within 14 months.

Monday, 25 August

A very busy day. During the morning the officers are on a D&M course from 9 o'clock until 12 o'clock. From 4 o'clock in the afternoon until 6 we have wireless instruction. We had rather fun this afternoon and practised the new R/T over the wireless set, which had been placed out over a large area. Donny was control and we had six out stations. We stuck strictly to procedure but the conversation was most amusing.

Friday, 29 August

Squadron leaders' conference at 09.00 hours. Nothing very important discussed. Lectures for the rest of the morning. At 4.30 in the afternoon we had R/T practice on the wireless sets. Lawrence Biddle, the adjutant, made up a small scheme, which went off very well.

Most difficult on the news today. Tehran has ceased all opposition. The Vichy prime minister, Laval, was shot yesterday in France. Don't quite know how bad he is. Russia still continues to hold out, is counter-attacking at several points, but is also being pressed at several parts of the front.

Would like to have some more mail.

There had been a large number of German nationals in Iran, many of whom were working in government services, and which the Tehran government refused to expel. This made it a hot-bed for both espionage and potential incitement against Britain, and threatened the crucial supply line from the Persian Gulf to the Caspian Sea, through which Britain hoped to send aid to the Russians. A joint Anglo-Russian demand was sent to the Persian government on 17 August, which was rejected. Persia actually fell under Wavell's remit as new C-in-C India, and with co-operation from Moscow, a joint Anglo-Russian invasion was launched on 25 August. It was entirely successful and by the end of the month the Persian Gulf was secured.

Sunday, 7 September

I did think about going to Jerusalem for this weekend. Michael Morris is leaving for Alexandria and was having a farewell party, but both the colonel and Donny were away and the other squadron leaders so the colonel asked me to remain behind in charge of the Regiment.

We had a service in the cinema. The padre gave us a most excellent sermon. He tried to explain why it was that we had so much to suffer in this world, especially now that we are entering the third year of war, by reminding us that Christ's teaching always showed us the difficult and long way round, and that he refused to perform miracles, especially when he had the power to save himself from all that suffering. As he refused to perform miracles to save himself, could we expect him to do the same for us? Which to me was a pretty conclusive argument.

A mail from England. Letters from Daddy, Bridget and Daisy Akers-Douglas.

Monday, 8 September

Training as usual during the day. At 11.30 I gave a lecture on map reading to our squadron signalling class. In the evening the colonel gave us our first lecture on tank tactics.

Tuesday, 9 September

We had a lecture from the divisional signals officer on regimental and Brigade signals organization. Haifa had a raid last night, or I should say early this morning. We could see the flashes of AA guns from here.

At the mess tonight we heard that the Russians had destroyed eight German divisions in the Smolensk area, and driven them well back, killing thousands of men and capturing a great deal of matériel. The Germans claim that Leningrad has been surrounded but the Russians are holding out well.

The Germans have sunk two American ships, one in the Red Sea and the other just off Ireland. Top this with the fact that a German submarine fired at an American destroyer: this might bring her into the war.

Whether we actually want them to come in at this moment is a questionable point because if they do the tremendous supplies that we and Russia are getting from America would be cut down and, furthermore, Japan would immediately enter the war and would direct her attention against America and Australia. On the other hand, Japan is still very occupied with China.

The colonel also told me that Turkey would probably come in against us as it appears that she is receiving more war matériel from Germany than she is from us.

He also passed a remark that we shouldn't be too surprised if old Mike Parish suddenly turned up again! That, of course, would be terrific. He wouldn't say any more than that but he has obviously heard something.

We have had confirmation from their families that Sydney Morse, Tony Holden and Mike Riviere are prisoners, and probably in Germany.

Stuart Thompson came back today from his intelligence course in Cairo. He had met one of our officers captured in Syria by the Vichy French and handed over to the Germans. When the armistice was signed in Syria we kept General Dentz and certain other French officers as hostages until our officers were returned. Paul Boswood in the Warwickshire Yeomanry was among our officers who went to Germany. They had a most interesting time, travelling right across Europe into Germany, and then, when they were released, coming all the way through France, both occupied and unoccupied. He said that throughout the whole journey their German guards were most courteous and that they were never really short of food. But the Germans took very great care that they should see nothing. They never entered an industrial centre by day, always by night. On the way through some places they had a chance to talk to some of our prisoners who were working on the fields and found that they were rather short of food. I understand that Paul is still rather cut up about having lost most of his troop when he was captured. They were surrounded and had to surrender and when they came out with a white flag they were fired on and shot up.

In the evening we had a lecture from the Brigade signals officer on the wireless layout for a regiment and brigade.

Friday, 12 September

Jim Lovett, Jack and I did an hour's Morse reading during the morning. It's quite extraordinary how it goes if you don't practise regularly.

There is quite a strong rumour going round that now America is giving so much help to Russia we may not get our tanks at the end of this month.

Saturday, 13 September

In the afternoon I went out with Lawrence Biddle and Geoffrey Brooks riding. We left at four in the afternoon and decided to ride to Caesarea but on the way we found the old Roman viaduct, which ran to Caesarea. Lawrence, who is a great expert on these matters, spent such a long time examining it that we never got to Caesarea. On the way there I fell into a ditch. I was trying to cross what appeared to be a small wadi but the mud was very soft and my horse sank up to its belly and I fell in.

It was a most lovely evening and we had a thoroughly enjoyable ride. Today is Mummy's birthday.

Wednesday, 17 September

The most wonderful bit of news. This evening Myles Hildyard, last heard of as a prisoner-of-war (captured in Crete), rang up from Jerusalem, I think Government House. And what is more, old Mike Parish is with him. Everybody is terrifically thrilled and longing to see them. I hope they will come to lunch tomorrow and then expect that they will go on leave again. Mike's cheerful madness and amazing originality and Myles's delightful vagueness is exactly what the Regiment wants as a contrast to the rather serious soldiering we have been doing. I am longing to see old Mike.

We had a Brigade TEWT today from 9.15 until five in the evening. Five officers from each regiment. It was a most interesting and well laid-out programme. It struck me that the Staffs gave the most intelligent answers. Our Brigadier Lloyd I thought most sound in all his answers.

Although the survivors of B and Y Batteries, which had been posted to Crete, had reached the evacuation beaches, the lift of men had ended before they could be picked up – the last ships had left on 31 May, when a number of B Battery had been just 20 yards from the embarkation point. At 4 a.m. on 1 June, the Rangers left on Crete had been told it was each man for himself. Most of the men surrendered, but Captains Myles Hildyard and Mike Parish managed to escape, eventually bought a small 20-foot caïque, a traditional Greek fishing boat, and island-hopped their way to Turkey, then, via Smyrna, Damascus and Jerusalem, eventually reached Cairo. The adventure is recounted in Myles Hildyard's colourful book of letters.

Thursday, 18 September

We have five new officers now, mostly Tank Corps out from England. A couple of them have been in the 1st Cavalry Division and then to an OCTU in India. A fellow called Lang has joined this squadron. He has been to France, flown an aeroplane in the RAF, driven many different types of tank and also was at Wellington. He seems very pleasant and seems to simply live for tanks. He appears to be a most intelligent person and owing to his enthusiasm we have nicknamed him 'Sparking Plug'. It's most descriptive.

Friday, 19 September

Great excitement today. Myles Hildyard came to lunch from Jerusalem. Poor old Mike Parish is ill in hospital with sand-fly fever. Also an injury to his eye is rather serious and there is danger he might lose it. He is deaf in one ear and broke his arm in two places as a result of falling down rather a steep cliff in the dark. Myles looked very well, in spite of his ordeal, and told us his truly amazing tale.

It will be great fun having them both back again with the Regiment.

Sunday, 21 September

We had a whole-day match (cricket) against the Greys. They came over and played us here. We had great fun and lost by 20 runs. Their colonel played. He is a very keen cricketer. Knows Winchester well, and also Kent. I had a long talk with him. I told him I knew Seymour, whom he said he liked. Thoroughly enjoyed the day.

We heard today that Kiev had fallen.

Tuesday, 23–Friday, 26 September

Each day this week has been much the same. No more tanks have arrived yet. They might have gone to Russia.

Most evenings I have been for a ride, which has been most pleasant.

Donny, Roger and two NCOs have gone up to Syria to make going maps.

Saturday, 27–Sunday, 28 September

I went to Jerusalem for the weekend. A great change and most enjoyable.

I had to take one of my corporals to see the advocate general at Area HQ in connection with a divorce. His wife has been put in a family way by a guardsman.

I then went to Kodak Ltd and saw a movie film I had taken at Jerusalem and had had developed in Cairo.

I lunched with Stephen Mitchell, who had been on a camouflage course, spending half his time at Jerusalem and half in Transjordan.

After lunch Stephen and I went to see Mike Parish in hospital. It was great to see him again, and to hear his description of the escape was most interesting. He can't open his damaged eye and at the moment he has lost the sight of that eye and I only hope that he gets it back again, which I am afraid is doubtful.

October

Life has been so very busy here that I have not had the time to keep up my diary.

At the moment we are in camp training to become part of the 8th Armoured Brigade, consisting of the Greys, the Staffordshire Yeomanry and ourselves as the armoured regiments and the Household Cavalry as the support group. Together with the 9th Armoured Brigade, we shall become the 10th Armoured Division, under General Sir George Clark. Our brigade is the first to be formed, and each regiment has got three American cruiser tanks, with the promise of more in the very near future.

Flash Kellett is still our colonel, and most efficient, so much so, I am afraid we shall lose him. Donny Player is second-in-command and now the squadron leaders are as follows: A Squadron, self; B Squadron, Mike Laycock; C Squadron, Stephen Mitchell; and HQ Squadron, Lawrence Biddle.

In my squadron the officers are as follows: Roger Nelthorpe, second-in-command; Mike Parish when he gets back, Jack Whiting, and two new officers called Hepton, commissioned from the Household Cavalry, and Ganalt, commissioned from the Warwickshire Yeomanry.

Life continues much in the same way each day. I am going to start writing daily again from Thursday, 13 November.

Thursday, 13 November

A regimental TEWT during the morning, which was organized by the colonel. We worked in squadron syndicates. My whole day has been spoilt by toothache. I went to the dentist last Tuesday in Haifa, and he is endeavouring to kill a nerve in a tooth, but ever since I left his chair, I have had toothache.

The TEWT was held at Point 78, along the Haifa road, where we had done many exercises in horsed-cavalry days. We really are getting to know all this country extremely well.

In the evening I watched a troop of my squadron play a troop of C Squadron in the league competition, which we lost. Each squadron was due to get three more tanks, but I hear not until some future date.

Friday, 14 November

I was called at 6 o'clock in the morning and went for a ride with John Walters. It was absolutely dark, and both moon and stars were up. We were back again by 7 o'clock – hardly time, but great fun.

Douglas, a new officer who has just joined the squadron, took his troop away to Syria for the weekend. It really is an excellent idea, leaving Friday morning and returning Sunday night. They take rations, bedding, etc., and go where the spirit moves them, camping where they like. This time they are going to Haifa, Beirut, Damascus, Baalbek. It's a great change for them to get away from camp, and a good chance of driving instruction.

I got the intelligence officer to give a lecture to my squadron on the present war situation. He is a most knowledgeable person and what he said was most interesting, especially as regards the Caucasus. I understand that we have got troops up there now. In the afternoon we had an inter-squadron tank commander competition, including D&M, gunnery, gas, first aid and general knowledge questions. In the evening my squadron HQ played C Squadron HQ at football. All officers played, and we lost 4–1. HQ Squadron and B did the same thing, and both Donny and the colonel played!

I heard on the wireless tonight the old *Ark Royal* aircraft carrier has been sunk in the Med, which is very sad especially after such magnificent work. She was torpedoed, and being towed back to Gib, then contracted a bad list and sank. I don't know the casualties yet.

I had an air-graph today from Betty Bailey, my cousin. I hear that she is going to leave Charles.

The new officer Stanley mentions was Keith Douglas, the poet. Douglas arrived with a number of others, including Kit Graves and Ollie Hutton,

which helped further to distance the Regiment from the old pre-war
outfit of privileged country landowners it had been during the
Yarborough era.

Sunday, 16 November

It's actually Sunday night, 10 o'clock, and I am just about to go to bed
with a headache, toothache and a pain in my lower abdomen. I went
out to Haifa for the weekend, and had a very late night on Saturday.

I left on Saturday afternoon about 4 o'clock, with Mike Laycock,
Scottie and Arthur Lang, our technical adjutant, with the idea of going
to the dentist, but I decided to stay the night. Before leaving, I rang up
Margaret Blieby who is in the air force at Haifa with a commission,
and asked her to come out to dinner. She said that she could, but that
she had arranged to go out with Pip Somebody, her boss, who is also
in the air force with a commission. So I told her that I would bring
along another officer and make up a four, and persuaded Scottie to do
the honours. Since Mike Laycock also came up to Haifa with us, we
couldn't very well let him dine alone so we asked him if he minded if
we brought two air-force officers along to dinner – not mentioning, of
course, that the officers were female.

When we arrived at Haifa, I paid a visit to the dentist, who didn't
stop my toothache, then met the others at the Lev-Carmel Hotel. After
changing, Scottie and I went to pick up Margaret Blieby and this other
girl called Pip Somebody – they both looked most attractive in their
uniforms. Then we all found Mike at the Piecadith restaurant. His face
was an absolute study when we introduced them! He had expected to
meet two huge, beefy, air-force officers, but instead there were two
attractive, slim girls in air-force uniform. As Pip had only just got out
of bed, we took them home early, then continued to another nightclub, where we found David Webb (of the Warwickshire Yeomanry),
very tight and dancing around with some girl.

All Haifa shuts down at midnight, but Mike Laycock said that he
knew of a place where we could get a drink. We arrived at some low-
down place, which was nothing else but an officers' brothel – we

honestly went there to get a drink. We were all in very good form and started opening doors along the passage, but opposite one door, the old madam barred the way, saying that the room had been booked privately by an officer. However, Scottie pushed past her and with a yell of delight came face to face with a subaltern in my squadron, waiting for his girlfriend! We roared with laughter, and pulled his leg unmercifully! Two minutes later, from another room came another officer from our regiment! I have not laughed so much since I have been out here!

We had a drink and then left them; and after two taxis breaking down, we eventually got back to our hotel.

The Lev-Carmel Hotel is actually right on top of the Carmel Range with a wonderful view over Haifa. Mike and I had a long walk, which was most pleasant, discussing the problem of marriage. He told me that to marry your cousin is a very bad thing. I had meant to get back to camp before lunch and play hockey for the squadron, but I was persuaded to stay up and lunch at Prosse's with all the others.

Tuesday, 18 November

I heard at dinner that our big push in the desert had started. The Russians are holding all along the line except in the Crimea. According to the news the *Ark Royal* only had one casualty when she sank.

Thursday, 20 November

The push in the Western Desert has started, and according to the news we have advanced 50 miles along a 150-mile front! All the opposition has been German and, according to reports, they were very much unprepared for the advance of our forces.

The push that Stanley mentions was Operation CRUSADER, the first major offensive by General Auchinleck since taking over as C-in-C Middle East in July; he now believed he had sufficient forces to retake

Tobruk and push Rommel's troops back across Cyrenaica. The Western Desert Force had been transformed into Eighth Army, made up from XIII and XXX Corps and commanded by Lieutenant General Sir Alan Cunningham, younger brother of Admiral Cunningham. Launched on 18 November, it caught Rommel, who was just returning from Rome, off-guard, and Eighth Army pushed 50 miles and captured the important airfield at Sidi Rezegh.

Monday, 24 November

Training continues as usual. We still only have three tanks in the Regiment. One is on Jaffa Ranges, and the other two are off the road. We have had no fresh news about the battle in the desert. According to the news, Hitler is making fresh demands from Pétain, including use of the French Fleet for convoy in the Mediterranean, and the use of French territory in North Africa.

After dinner I went to the camp cinema, and saw a rotten film. Afterwards I showed some of my own films on my new projector. Some were quite good.

Tuesday, 25 November

A good mail today, letters from Mummy, Daddy, David, Aunt Mabel, Bridget and Jack Yarborough, our ex-colonel. But nothing from Pat. Before break I went for my usual early-morning ride with John Walters, which was very pleasant.

Training as usual during the morning. Lawrence Biddle gave my officers a lecture on star navigation, which as usual was absolutely excellent. He really has the most remarkable brain. In the afternoon Paul Boswood gave his lecture on his experiences as a prisoner-of-war, after being captured in Syria, then taken to Greece and right across Europe to Germany. It was all most interesting and very well told by him. It was so typical Paul, as he was in the old Inns of Court days. He stressed the absolute amazing discipline he noticed in the German

Army whenever he came across German soldiers, the incredible pluck of the Greeks, and the great shortage of food there. His interview with the Gestapo officer before leaving for Germany was most interesting. At times they were very short of food, and most uncomfortable, and their party consisted of about 37 officers from all three services, including three Indian officers, all under a British colonel.

After dinner I had a talk with Stephen in his tent, and then returned to my own to read my mail and write letters. I also had a long and most amusing letter from Clive, all about his hectic love affairs. When last he wrote, he almost broke his heart, because Peggy Marriott wouldn't marry him, and now is having a violent love affair with one of his old flames, who is married with three children. At the same time having another hectic love affair with another married girl – who is a girlfriend of Roger Winlaw!

Wednesday, 26 November

The battle is still raging in the desert. Both sides have brought up reinforcements. I am afraid we may have underestimated the number of German tanks in Libya. Casualties have been very heavy on both sides. If we thoroughly beat up the Germans in this battle it will make all the difference in the world to our morale.

On the Russian front news is not too good. The fight for Moscow still continues.

The battle was certainly raging fiercely. On 22 November Sidi Omar and Fort Capuzzo, to the east and south-east of Tobruk, had been captured and the main coast road, via Balbia, had been cut. Rommel counter-attacked hard the following day and the 5th South African Brigade was encircled and destroyed by his Deutsches Afrika Korps. Thinking the British were in complete disarray, he then ordered a 'dash to the wire' to the Egyptian border, which became known by the Eighth Army men as the 'Matruh Stakes'. In fact, the British were not as disorganized as Rommel had thought, even though General Cunningham wanted to call off the offensive. The Auk refused this request, and on 27 November, as

Rommel's armour sped over the Egyptian border well to the south of Sollum, the Tobruk garrison linked up with the New Zealand Division. With large formations of both sides still loose and fighting to the east, Tobruk was still not safe, but the Auk's decision to fight on appeared to have been justified.

Sunday, 30 November

After lunch I produced a hockey team, consisting mostly of officers to play against my squadron. We lost 4–3.

The news on the wireless is much better. The desert campaign seems to be going as well as can be expected. We have captured one German general, who commanded a German panzer division. The Russians have retaken Vladivostok.

Saturday, 6 December

After lunch Donny, Lawrence and I went shooting at Wadi Faluk. As a result of the rains we had great sport in these swamps, and saw plenty of birds in the form of duck, snipe and quail. We all had a most enjoyable afternoon. We took the Bantam scout car, which is absolutely ideal, and will get you over any kind of ground. We got a very good bag.

Sunday, 7 December

Church parade followed by a service in the cinema, which I attended. Did some work in the office, and then Lawrence and I rode to Caesarea. It took us about 1½ hours. For the last few miles we followed along the beach, which was perfectly delightful. We had our lunch, which we brought with us, sitting on the old medieval wall overlooking the sea.

Afterwards we rode out and followed the old Roman viaducts, which brought water to the towns. All most interesting. We got back to camp about 4 o'clock. A most enjoyable day. In the evening I worked on the court-martial of which I am president on Tuesday.

Bridge in the evening with Jeffrey and Derrick. Papers arrived from England from the family, which were most acceptable.

Monday, 8 December

Japan today declared war on USA and Great Britain, by attacking Pearl Harbor by air, and other American islands in the Pacific! There are also reports that landings have been made on the Malayan coast, and Singapore was raided. The Japs are reported to have sunk one American battleship and one destroyer. Russia is still counter-attacking at Vladivostok. Not much news from the desert.

This was a more momentous day than Stanley realized. Because of the Tripartite Pact between Germany, Italy and Japan, the Japanese attack on Pearl Harbor led Germany to declare war on the United States, bringing America into the war not just in the Far East but in the West too. December 8 was also the day Tobruk began to be properly relieved after its long nine-month siege. At one point, General Freyberg, commanding the New Zealand Division, had thought he would have to pull back and leave Tobruk to its fate, but Rommel's situation was now more parlous than he had realized after the ill-judged 'dash for the wire' and 18 days' hard fighting. Consequently, on 7 December, he pulled back to Gazala, to the west of Tobruk.

Meanwhile in Russia, the Red Army was counter-attacking from the edge of Moscow. The Germans had got to within reach of the capital, but the bitter winter conditions, overextended lines of supply, and desperate defence by the Russians had ensured their goal had evaded them.

Tuesday, 9 December

During the morning I attended a court-martial of which I was president. It was the first that I have attended. Fortunately I had John Semken as a member: he is a solicitor in private life, and was a great help. James Hanburg from the Greys was the other member. It all went off very well. We convicted the accused, but I felt very sorry for him, and consider that he should never have been court-martialled. Pat Allistan prosecuted and Hitchin defended. I thought his defence was poor.

In the evening we had an ENSA concert, which I thought very good. The brigadier (Constance) came to dinner and to the show. A Christmas present arrived from Mummy in the shape of a Dunhill pipe and a shaving brush. I had my usual early-morning ride.

John Semken had received his commission in April 1940, and was then sent on a signals course while he waited to be sent to join the Regiment in Palestine. During the Rangers' time in Crete and Tobruk, John had been training Palestinian Arabs and Jews and had then rejoined the Regiment as signals officer.

Wednesday, 10 December

Bad news today. We have lost two capital ships off Singapore, one our newest, the *Prince of Wales*, and the *Repulse*. The Japs sank them by aerial torpedo. A nasty crack after three days' war with the Japs. The CO also told us the battleship *Barham* had been sunk in the Mediterranean. Apparently the navy received orders direct from England to deal with the convoy bringing reinforcements to Rommel in the Western Desert. This they did very effectively, sinking every single ship, but it cost us the *Barham*. I have an idea that Bungy Christopherson was on her.

The Russians claim the initiative along the whole of the front, and I believe that they have it. No fresh news from the desert. To me the end of this war seems to be just as far away as ever.

Bungy Christopherson was a cousin, but he was not among those killed on the Barham, *Admiral Cunningham's old flagship.*

Thursday, 11 December

General Cunningham has got the sack from the Western Desert, and a fellow called Ritchie has taken his place. The latter is very junior. Flash, our colonel, knew about this when he was in Cairo. Apparently Cunningham completely lost his nerve when the German column broke through into Egypt. He has flown back to England with the name of Jones.

I had an air-graph from Pat, number 14 and dated 16 November: the last letter I had from her was number 7. Outside the family, I look forward to her letters more than any others. I wish that she wrote more. I sometimes wonder whether I shall ever see her again. I shall read her letter through again before going to bed.

The new Eighth Army commander had been a major general and Auchinleck's deputy in Cairo before being hastily promoted to lieutenant general and sent to take command at the front. An undoubtedly very able staff officer, he had, however, little experience of command in the field. His appointment, when he had never commanded either a brigade or a division, let alone a corps, was a surprising choice, to say the least.

Saturday, 13 December

B Squadron, under Pat McCraith, made some 'Molotov Cocktails', which they threw and caused a very good explosion. I took our gunners to see the demonstration.

I asked Stuart Thompson to give a lecture on the American attitude to the war, which was very good, and following this Kurt Gottlieb gave a lecture to both A and B Squadrons on the present war situation, with special regard to Japan's entry into the war. That, too, was very good. Kurt has certainly got a very good brain, and is an excellent IO, especially as he speaks German, French, Italian and English. He is an Austrian and a Jew, and joined the Regiment as a trooper. Flash Kellett got him in.

Thursday, 18 December

This morning we had an intensive lecture from John Todd, colonel of the Greys who are brigaded with us. He went down to the desert as a 'recorder' for this latest campaign against the Hun, which is still going on. It's not often that one gets a first-hand lecture on a battle that is still in progress. Some things that he said were none too pleasant, especially about the 50mm and 75mm guns, the latter of which penetrates our general tanks. At one point out of 50 general tanks, only two were left.

Reports on the American M3, which we are to get, are good, especially from a mechanical point of view. Their speed and lack of mechanical defects were excellent. The defects we already know about. The Hun recovery tank organization was absolutely excellent.

During various battles in this enormous desert, the most amazing situations arose, especially when Rommel made his diversion thrust with two columns. On one occasion, a Hun recovery lorry drove into a Corps HQ leaguering area. On another, while Todd was attached to a certain divisional HQ, they came under shellfire, just as Cunningham arrived by aeroplane. They actually got onto the aeroplane in which he had come but fortunately it managed to get into the air with him in it. They decided to move their position 20 miles southeast, and when they halted they found two German trucks had tacked on in the rear, thinking they were a German column.

On another occasion one of our liaison officers drove into a German leaguer area by mistake and, on realizing (fortunately it was dark), took off his hat and asked for a fill of petrol, which he got! After saying, 'Dankeschön,' he made off!

It was quite the most outstanding lecture that I have heard.

Wednesday, 24 December

In the evening I took all my sergeants to dinner at the Edan Hotel, Nathaniya. The squadron officers also came, and I asked Stephen Mitchell, Bill Kepner, who was a Sergeant in A Squadron, and Derrick Warwick who was an officer in A Squadron for a long time. It was a great success, and great fun. We had soup, fish, turkey and plum pudding, and beer and whisky to drink. It cost me about £20, which consumed practically all my back pay.

Thursday, 25 December

Christmas Day again. Two years ago I spent it at Lindsay Lodge, Sunningdale, Surrey, with the family, Ann and Pat. How extraordinary that I have not seen them for all that time. Well, I wonder where we shall be next Christmas Day.

Sunday, 28 December

My squadron has now been given four tanks. I have made up Ronnie Hepton's troop, and have given the other troop to Squadron HQ and put my own personal crew in it.

Tuesday, 30 December

I am wearing an old shooting coat while I am writing this diary. I have just looked at the date and found that I bought it eight years ago from Billings & Edmonds.

Wednesday, 31 December

So ends 1941, and one can't help wondering what 1942 has in store for us. I heard today that John Wrangham and Sergeant Harper, both from the Tank Corps and who were attached to us as instructors for a few months, are casualties. Wrangham is reported missing, and Sergeant Harper killed. They were grand fellows, and excellent instructors.

Stephen, John Walters, Bob Brothero, Andy Lang and a few other officers drank in the New Year with the sergeants in their mess. RSM Cassidy was in formidable form, and we had an exceedingly good party, which finished about 1.30 a.m.

One of Keith Douglas's sketches, given to Stanley.

PART II

FROM ALAMEIN TO TUNIS

January 1942–May 1943

8

Tank Training

Stanley training in Haifa, January 1942.

1941 HAD ENDED *with the British back across Cyrenaica, having recaptured Benghazi on Christmas Day. While things might have been looking up in North Africa, however, the new war in the Far East was going disastrously. The Japanese had followed up their attack on Pearl Harbor with major strikes against British territories in Burma and the American-held Philippines. The Wake Islands and Guam had also fallen and Borneo had been invaded, while over Britain's key port of Hong Kong, the Japanese flag now fluttered.*

However, the first formal conference between British and American chiefs of staff had taken place in Washington. At the Arcadia Conference, the Allied war leaders had agreed to a 'Germany first' strategy. Despite the rampage of Japanese troops in the Far East, the priority of the war effort would be directed against Germany and ridding the world of Nazism.

Thursday, 1 January 1942

The colonel gave a most excellent talk to the Regiment during the morning, reviewing the whole war up to the present date, at the same time bringing in a certain amount of religion. He can speak exceedingly well. He finished up with some lines of Kipling, 'What stands if Freedom fall? Who dies if England live?'

After lunch John, Stephen and I had a conference with the CO about crew commanders training as a result of our brigade course. We then took a tank out, and tried out some crew drill, crew control and fire orders. Unless some kind of communication is established between crew commanders and drivers, conditions in the tanks will be chaotic. Mike Laycock's brother Bob, in charge of the Commandos, and reported missing, has now turned up again.

Friday, 2 January

The weather is quite frightful. It has rained constantly for the last two weeks and has turned incredibly cold with a wind almost gale force. Last night, it was so strong every officer's tent was blown down, except for three including the colonel's. We all moved into the mess – in fact there was a constant stream of officers coming into the mess with bits of bedding from 11 o'clock until 5 in the morning.

Squadron leaders' (from the brigade) course under the brigadier finished this afternoon. To my mind, it really has been most useful.

In the evening, saw a most excellent film called *All This and Heaven Too*.

Saturday, 3 January

The weather still grows colder. What must it be like in Russia? Badia has been taken and we have released 1000 prisoners. Manila has been captured by the Japs, and the position in the Philippines looks serious. It's essential that we hang on to Singapore.

So much damage was done to the bell tents in the gale the other evening, the officers have had to make shift in the best places they can. I have gone to my squadron office. Rather cramped but comfortable. I went for a good run this afternoon and felt much better for it.

At the moment I have five tanks in my squadron. One complete troop under Ronnie Hepton and I have our own tank, which I have placed under Sergeant Leinster.

My own crew is Lance Corporal Rush, Lance Corporal Dean and Trooper Brewster, my driver.

Wednesday, 7 January

General Martell, inspector general of the RAC, came and visited the unit with the divisional general and our brigadier: I was directing a sand table scheme between A Squadron and C Squadron. He watched for a time, and then Flash Kellett, our colonel said, 'Would you like to come and see the tanks?' to which he replied, 'I would rather watch this rather exciting battle for a time!' I am glad that he went when he did as the battle was becoming rather complicated to direct. As a result of his visit, I gather that a delivery of American tanks will not be quite so quick as we anticipated, as America rather wants most of the tanks she is making. That is one of the reasons why Churchill went to America.

I moved from my office back into a tent again. Jack Whiting returned from hospital, and Sam Garrett from a gunnery course, so I am getting some officers back again.

Monday, 12 January

Spent the day arranging all the training for the coming week as tomorrow I leave with Lawrence Biddle, Kurt Gottlieb, and Harry Fulton of Brigade for a week's skiing in Syria about which I am very thrilled. Roger Nelthorpe, my second-in-command, will be in command of the squadron in my absence. Letters from Anne Christopherson and Ursula Barclay – both ATS.

Tuesday, 13 January

Lawrence Biddle, Kurt Gottlieb and I left for a week's skiing in the Hebron Mountains. Harry Fulton, the staff captain, made up the fourth. We left camp at six in the morning in a staff car, which we managed to wangle, and picked up Harry at Brigade HQ. We had lunch at Beirut where we hired skis and boots. Actually I couldn't find a pair large enough so I had to buy a pair. I might sell them again. We arrived at our destination, Les Cèdres, at about 5 in the evening, after a rather tiring and hair-raising journey. Never have I been on such a precipitous road. We had the greatest difficulty in getting up the last few miles, as only with difficulty were they able to keep the road free from snow. Last week they were completely cut off owing to a very heavy fall – about eight feet. Outside the hotel there are four cars, completely covered, over which they have been skiing.

Les Cèdres consists of two hotels: Les Cèdres Hotel, which has been taken over by the Australians for the purpose of running a skiing school for the army. The chief instructor is Jimmy Riddle. The other hotel is Mon Repos where we are staying. The place is very crowded, and the four of us have to share one room, which is distinctly a bore, as Kurt Gottlieb is hopelessly untidy, and his bottles alone almost cover the room. There are about 20 other officers in the hotel, including Figanes and Cazatte from the Greys and John Cunliffe-Lister and two other officers from the Staffordshire Yeomanry, so the 8th Armoured Brigade is well represented plus the staff captain. We had the greatest difficulty in turning the staff car round on the narrow road, which had only just been cleared of snow and in the end we had to get about 20 Arabs to lift the front of the car and turn it round bodily!

Wednesday, 14–Tuesday, 20 January

We all had the most enjoyable time skiing during the holiday. I have never enjoyed myself more, or felt better since leaving England. We have skied every single day, including one day when the visibility was so bad that we had to go out on a compass bearing! Every day we have climbed for two or three hours and skied down on excellent runs. We climbed up as far as 10,000 feet, and looked down on Baalbek on the other side. That run was called 'Sans Soners' and probably the best run of the lot. In the evening we played a certain amount of bridge and retired to bed early each night.

Friday, 23 January

The news from the Far East is not good. The Japs have got within 60 miles of Singapore, and not far off Rangoon. Our advance light forces have withdrawn 60 miles eastwards. It looks as if Rommel is getting some kind of supplies. The Russians are still doing excellent work along the whole front.

A wonderful mail today, letters from the family, Pat, Bridget, Dycie[?]. Training as usual. Went to garrison cinema in the evening.

Allied fortunes in the Far East were certainly going from bad to worse. Kuala Lumpur had fallen on 12 January, while Japanese troops were also pressing into Burma. Fierce battles continued to rage in the Philippines and Borneo, and Australian New Guinea had been overrun. Meanwhile, in North Africa, Rommel had once again acted without consulting either his Italian allies or Field Marshal Kesselring, his theatre superior, and had launched a new offensive to reclaim Cyrenaica on 21 January. The following day, the German and Italian forces under his command had been formed into the Panzer Armee Afrika.

That day, the Italian General Cavallero, with Field Marshal Kesselring, had flown to see Rommel to ask him to stop this latest offensive, believing he had not given himself enough time to rebuild strength and fearing an overextension of his lines of supply once more. Rommel, however, was determined to keep going, encouraged by the first day of battle in which Mersa Brega had easily fallen. Although Cavallero refused to allow Italian troops to take further part, Rommel decided to push on with his Deutsches Afrika Korps.

Saturday, 24 January

The divisional general was to have inspected us on Monday but owing to illness it has been postponed.

While I was away I heard that a certain major from the 5th Tanks was attached to us. One evening he and certain other officers from the mess took a staff car under false pretences and went to Tel Aviv. This major got so tight that he was not capable of getting on parade the next morning. The CO put him under open arrest and packed him back to his regiment. He had to take a personal note from our brigadier who is from the Tank Corps back to his CO.

Last night I had an injection in both arms and as a result have felt pretty rotten today.

Sunday, 25 January

In the morning I went to the padre's service which he had in the men's reading room. In the evening I went for a ride with the officers from my squadron, Jack Whiting and Sam Garrett. They are a grand couple, both actually commissioned from the Warwickshire Yeomanry, both connected with horses in private life. Old Sam is a really dependable soul, and most energetic and enthusiastic.

Wednesday, 28 January

It's amazing to think that we have been in this camp for almost six months! The CO and I went out to the training ground and watched the troop from my squadron and C Squadron practise their demonstration for the divisional general on Monday. After lunch we had a practice march past with all the tanks. It was quite impressive. At 6 o'clock squadron leaders had a practice and demonstration on the No. 14 set. Again I almost lost Sergeant Leinster to HQ Squadron, but in the end Sergeant Franell went. Old Steve was livid as it was all done without reference to him.

Thursday, 29 January

All the tanks went out on a night scheme. We harboured for the night in the open ground a couple of miles from Hadera. Stephen was in command until midnight and then I took over. Reveille was at 6.30, and I had orders to move the squadron at 07.15. Rather a rush to pack up, cook breakfast, warm up and make a getaway but we did it.

We moved off to a place called Tel-a-dura, from where orders came over the wireless that we should attack enemy transport bogged in the area of our harbour, protected by A/T guns. My force consisted of a composite squadron, 1 Troop A Squadron, 1 Troop C Squadron, and 1 Troop B Squadron. The wireless was most distorted and I had the greatest difficulty in keeping control. Colonel Corney, second-in-command of the brigade, watched the whole thing, and spoke for 80 minutes at the end. I personally didn't think that the attack had gone too well but he appeared quite pleased.

We got back to lunch on Friday. I gave a lecture to the rest of the squadron on the exercise after lunch. At five o'clock, Donny Player, John Walters and I went up to Haifa, and I paid a visit to the dentist. I had a tooth out. It gave a little trouble in coming out. John and Donny came in the room while I was having it done. One tooth made quite a noise when it broke.

We dined at the Piccadilly with Vera Sharp, Margaret Blieby, and one other girl they got hold of for Donny. I didn't feel too well after my injection[?].

Saturday, 31 January

A bad day in every way. The war news is not encouraging. The Hun have re-taken Benghazi, the Japs have advanced to within 18 miles of Singapore. However, the Russians are still pushing the Germans back.

We had a full dress rehearsal for the divisional general's inspection on Monday. The wireless broke down during the demonstration, which Ronnie Hepton was giving, which resulted in a rocket for Hepton, the signals officer, and myself. And then I forgot to tell Sam Garrett to be on the range for his demonstration at 11 o'clock. We had to do the whole thing again in the afternoon, and it went off better that time.

Sunday, 1 February

The delivery of tanks is not so good. Since the Japs came into the war, America is rather keen on keeping her tanks and all that are coming into the country are going up to the desert.

The CO has now decided to hand over the tanks in the Regiment to another troop in each squadron. His policy is to have four troops partly trained, instead of one fully trained, in the event of having 16 tanks suddenly given to the squadron. The individual tank crews will be very disappointed, as they have all worked terribly hard and have taken great interest in their tanks. But I think this policy is the lesser of two evils.

Monday, 2 February

The Imperial Forces have now withdrawn to the island of Singapore from the mainland in Malaya. The Russians are still pressing the Hun on all fronts; the Hun is still advancing eastwards. Rommel has been substantially reinforced. General Clark, our divisional commander, inspected the regiment. We had a regimental parade and march past, which went off very well. He congratulated me on the turnout of my squadron, and asked me for how long I had had it.

After the inspection he spent a long time in my squadron office asking all kinds of questions and finding great interest in my crime book. But he appeared quite pleased in what he saw.

Tuesday, 3 February

Two air-graphs, one from Cousin Betty and another from Dorothy Walters. Usual busy day's training. Training is getting more difficult especially to keep it from getting monotonous. It's quite time we had a move.

Wednesday, 4 February

I played hockey for my squadron against the Indians camped quite close to us. They had a couple of British officers playing. They are a fine-looking set of men, and most enthusiastic, especially the onlookers. We beat them 3–2. Mike Parish's old servant, Bowles, lost his arm in a motor smash coming back from Haraih.

Kurt Gottlieb gave my squadron a very good lecture on recognition of German uniforms. He showed us some German pay books and epaulettes, etc., representing various units of the German Army.

My tank driver, Brewster, who has only one eye, had to go before the CO with other B3 men to see whether they were prepared to go into action. I was most disappointed to hear from the CO that Brewster demanded to be sent home. I fear that he was disappointed that his tank had been taken away from him. It would do us all good to get into action, and I only wish that we could get equipped.

Rommel halted his offensive on 7 February, having reached the Gazala Line, a short way to the west of Tobruk. This setback was as nothing, however, compared with the terrible defeat in Singapore. On 15 February, General Percival surrendered 130,000 British, Australian and Indian troops to General Yamashita's force of a mere 30,000. It was to be the worst defeat in British history.

Saturday, 21 February, Khatatba Camp

We are still getting settled in. Things are rather uncomfortable at the moment, and the food is inadequate, especially for the men. They make a balls of the indenting, so the men are going short.

I share a tent with Lawrence Biddle. There is nothing else but desert, and desert again. When the hot weather comes it will be rather unbearable, especially the flies.

Sunday, 22 February

This is a most enormous camp area – large enough to hold 40,000 men. All our brigade are here, the Staffs Yeomanry and the Greys practically next door. After lunch Donny Player, Pat McCraith and I went out in the Banbaur[?] and did some navigation in the desert. We tried to pinpoint the exact position on the map of our camp. The colonel and others spent the weekend in Cairo. The colonel told me at supper that, owing to the extremely active anti-British activities on the part of the King of Egypt, we demanded his abdication, and even surrounded his palace with tanks, and with cadets from the OCTU with Tommy guns, but he refused to abdicate, although agreed that his prime minister should be turned out of office, and one of our choice should take his place – named Nahas Pasha, who is pro-British. Oliver Lyttelton is going home to become a member of the Cabinet. I don't quite know who will take his place, and I don't quite know what will happen to Peter Laycock. I can't see him coming back to the Regiment, not with Flash Kellett as colonel. But I'm afraid that the Regiment will lose Flash. He is bound to get promotion. His place will be difficult to fill. We may even get a regular colonel. Flash has done a great deal for this regiment.

Monday, 23 February

In the morning we had a troop v troop competition against B squadron and then ended up in a general-knowledge competition. After lunch our luggage arrived as a result of which we are all much more comfortable. Stephen Mitchell, Myles Hildyard and Geoffrey Brooks, our doctor, arrived in camp tonight. Old Stephen has been on a senior officers' course at Karkur. I go on the same course at the end of the month. It will be strange going back to Palestine again. Myles has been ill. He is my second-in-command, I don't quite know how we will all get on. He is not a natural soldier. I am reading such a good book called *The Blind Man's House* by Hugh Walpole.

Tuesday, 24 February

I find it most difficult to train the squadron with no equipment, and at the same time to keep the training from becoming monotonous. It really was a most beautiful day, not too hot, and we have had no more sand storms. The whole Regiment did PT before breakfast, which was quite a good thing.

Wednesday, 25 February

Myles Hildyard, our second captain in the squadron, gave the squadron a most excellent lecture about what the Regiment did in Crete, how he and Mike Parish were captured, their escape and eventual arrival back to the Regiment after spending three months in the mountains.

Sam Garrett arrived with his troop and the tanks. They have had a long journey but enjoyed it on the whole. Sam is a most excellent man and a first-class troop leader. After lunch I went out with Pat McCraith (who was for a time in the Long Range Desert Patrol) and Stephen Mitchell and did some desert navigation with a sun compass.

Friday, 27 February

I heard today that the Cheshire Yeomanry and the North Somerset Yeomanry are going to cease to exist as regiments and are becoming members of the Royal Corps of Signals. This must be a dreadful blow to them. This will also apply to the Middlesex Yeomanry. We may get some of their officers.

I spent most of the day clearing up and handing over to Roger Nelthorpe, my second-in-command, as tomorrow I go to Palestine on a senior officers' technical course at the Middle East Armoured Fighting Vehicle Tactical School. They used to run the cavalry course and are next door to our old camp.

Saturday, 28 February

I left for Cairo in a staff car, with Donny Player, Myles Hildyard and Pat McCraith. I went to the bank and did some shopping, had lunch at Shepheard's Hotel, caught the 2.55 train to Kantara, and so on to Palestine. We had some German prisoners on the train with us. How I hate the journey from Egypt to Palestine.

I saw quite a lot of people whom I know in Cairo, including Basil Ringrose, whom I have not seen since he won his DSO.

Sunday, 1 March

Arrived at Hadera at about 10.30 in the morning after rather a wearying journey. I did have a sleeper but I had to share it with an officer in the Argyll and Sutherlands. I found I know one or two people on this course including Meynell from the Staffs, Roxborough from the Greys, Stephen D. Morgan from the Middlesex Yeomanry.

We are housed in bungalows with baths and electric light, and I have a room to myself. I am the boss! The mess appears quite comfortable and the food is good. I had a sleep in the afternoon, a walk with Meynell over to our old camp, which looks very forlorn now with all the tents down. The country looks very lovely at this time of year.

Tuesday, 3 March

This morning we had our syndicate discussion at 10.45, which was most interesting. I had to speak quite a lot. This was followed by a lecture on the German Armoured Division. In the afternoon new syndicates were formed to prepare a discussion on the German Armoured Division, comparing it with the British Armoured Division, and tactical handling of both. The trouble is that the final decision about the Armoured Brigade Group, and the division has not yet been taken. At six o'clock in the evening I went for a walk with Bill Weymouth. He is in the Wiltshire Yeomanry. At dinner I sat next to David Steele and John Walters.

Afterwards I had long talk with David about desert warfare. What he said was all most interesting as he has had plenty of experience. It's great fun seeing him again, and we had a long talk about our last Inns of Court camp at Warminster. I want to ask him some time how he won his DSO in France, and also about his brother Dick, who was killed almost on the same day.

Wednesday, 4 March

Another interesting day. I was very pleasantly surprised to hear a lecture from Guy Peyton who came down from the staff college at Haifa and lectured on armoured cars. I had a long talk with him afterwards. We had lectures on the REs and the Motorized Infantry Brigade.

After dinner I had a long talk with David Steele. He told me all about his sojourns in France, how his brother Dick got killed, and also Jonnie Roul in the Xth, and I made him tell me how he won the DSO. I like him so much. Margaret Blieby rang me up from Haifa. I wrote and told her that I would be coming up. John and I may go up tomorrow night.

Saturday, 7 March

Another whole day TEWT, which was a continuation of the same battle.

As soon as we got back in the evening John Walters, David Steele and I motored up to Haifa in John's car. We had dinner at the Piccadilly. Margaret Blieby, and another girl in the WAAFs made up the party. The other girl was called Peg. She was fat, aged eighteen, dull, and had a very bad cold, but I suppose a good sort. Guy Peyton and his wife were there. We all stayed at the Mount Carmel Hotel.

Sunday, 8 March

We didn't get up very early. Went for a walk along the Carmel Range. As Margaret was off duty, we took her and the dog Pat (bull terrier). We had a drink at Shimmey's and lunch at Prosse's. After lunch David and I did some shopping. I bought a fountain pen, with which I am writing now, costing 25s, a new pipe, which I am smoking now, and pouch.

We had dinner at the Astoria, which was very good. David and I then went to a film, called *Turnabout*, which was most amusing. I sat next to Pat Cox at the cinema. She is quite easily the most attractive girl I have seen in the Middle East. A typical English beauty – fair, blue eyes, turned-up nose, very young, and they say quite unspoilt and unsophisticated.

Monday, 9 March

Our forces have evacuated Rangoon, which is not too hot. Until America can really get going in production we will continue to have loss out there. The invasion of Australia is extremely likely, and the threat to India very ominous.

We had another all-day TEWT. I was a leader of a syndicate with Delmar Magan, Middlesex Yeomanry, McCraig, Scot's Guards, a most amusing person with a DSO. It's been a most glorious spring day, and the wild flowers in some places form a complete carpet.

The Middlesex Yeomanry has now been transferred into the Royal Corps of Signals and Magan said this evening that his colonel had phoned him to tell him that he was coming to our regiment as second-in-command to a squadron. I was most surprised when I heard it. If Pat McCraith has taken this special liaison job, I expect he will go to Mephon. If the colonel continues to take on new officers of captain and above, it becomes rather disheartening to the subalterns who look forward to promotion.

Tuesday, 10 March

Quite an entertaining day. John Walters went off to Haifa in the evening. After dinner I had a long talk with Pearson in the HAC. There were a few points that I wanted to clear up about the 25-pounder. The Japs are still advancing past Rangoon. They have committed great atrocities both in Hong Kong and Malaya, according to Anthony Eden.

British troops had evacuated Rangoon on 7 March, having destroyed the port facilities first. Stories of Japanese atrocities were quick to spread and often all too true. British troops had been savagely treated in Singapore and Hong Kong, and reports had emerged of prisoners being bayoneted and of horrendous overcrowding at Changi, the huge ex-British base on Singapore and now a POW camp. News also got out that around 200 Indian and Australian troops had been decapitated on the Muar river, while a further 600 were rumoured to have been bayoneted to death on Amboina Island in the Dutch East Indies.

Wednesday, 11 March

In the evening I wrote some letters. Two for Pat, one for Diana Pelham, who still writes rather sentimental letters to me, and one to Bridget Wilkinson. The country at this time of year looks simply lovely, especially the green crops, the violet flowers and the orange blossom. I am thoroughly enjoying this course and Khatatba will be a dismal place, but on the other hand, I am looking forward to getting back to the squadron.

Saturday, 14 March

Our course ended today. It has been most enjoyable, and most instructive, and in many ways I am sorry that it has come to an end.

We worked until midday, then John and I motored to Jerusalem in his small car. We sent our heavy luggage with our batmen by train.

We ran into Hermione Ranfurly in the King David Hotel, and she promised to come and join us after dinner at the hotel, with Araminta MacMichael and Michael and another couple. In the hotel we met Diana McConnell with whom we had tea. David Steele was also with us. I like Diana and think her most attractive. We spoke quite a lot about Seymour who was ADC to her father. They all liked him very much. I am very much looking forward to seeing him again.

After dinner John, David and I were found by Hermione, Araminta, another girl (dull, plain but nice) and Dick Scarswall, from Government House. One lady is a cousin of the high commissioner. We danced to the very excellent band of the King David. I also met Margot Williams. She married a man in the Buffs and they have been out here for about three years. I knew that I had seen them before. She is such a charming person and so good-looking. She and her husband were dining with a party which included a most attractive Australian VAD. We stayed that night at the King David Hotel, which was most comfortable.

Sunday, 15 March

After lunch with five other officers from the course, I went round the old city with a dear old lady who has been out east for 14 years and is the official guide for the KD Hotel. We met John and a very attractive Australian VAD at tea at the sports club. As John had to see about his car and David had to do some shopping I was landed with this girl, not that I minded at all as she was very attractive and most pleasant. Her name is Sue Otherson. As she had some shopping to do, we went to a little shop run by Austrian refugees. I saw a most lovely gold necklace with which I have heavily fallen in love. They are asking lb15. I am very seriously considering buying it in the form of an investment. If anything should happen to me I shall leave it to Pat.

Afterwards we went back to the hotel and had some tea. The attractive VAD had to go back to Rehovot. We expressed the hope that we shall meet again in Cairo when she has some leave.

Monday, 16 March

John Walters and I left the King David at 6.30 in the morning to motor back to Egypt to join the Regiment. It was a glorious day and we had a most enjoyable run down, arriving at the Continental Hotel 5.30 in the evening.

Tuesday, 17 March

Cairo is hot, full of troops and remarkably smelly. I saw one of my cine films which I had had developed at Kodak and which was jolly good. David Steele had come down from Jerusalem by train. We lunched together at the Tart Club with Pearson, the HAC gunner who was on the course.

After lunch I said goodbye to David, it was quite fun having him on the course with me and returned to Khatatba camp. Instead of taking the Delta road we came across the desert and got stuck. Fortunately we had only just left the road and an ambulance happened to be going along the same road.

Wednesday, 18 March

I started the day catching up and finding out what has been going on during the time I have been away. Roger has been in charge and everything seems to be in good order.

Thursday, 19–Friday, 20 March

No more tanks have arrived. The CO is doing an attachment up in the desert. Donny Player is in command. Training is becoming more difficult. Troop leaders are training their own troops.

Saturday, 21 March

We had a whole day indoor TEWT at Brigade HQ, colonel, second-in-command and squadron leaders from each regiment of the brigade. Each syndicate had a gunner attached. The brigadier and Colonel Corney ran the show. It lasted until four o'clock in the afternoon.

Sunday, 22 March

Pat now informs me that the King of Greece, whom he saw at the Gezira Club, has 25 medals (estimated). Man Soor, the sixth son of Ibram Faud, the Saud of Arabia, was at the ambassador's garden party, and although they tried to interest him in many things, he could not keep his eyes from a hedge. Eventually, he said, 'Oh, I see, it's a wall made of little trees.' This was because he had never seen a hedge before. Laughter from the rest of the mess who couldn't see the point of the story until supplied by Pat.

Note: Ibn Saud has had more wives than any living man. He has 60 registered sons and about 100 others unregistered. How many daughters, he has not been able to estimate. Pat has given me so much to write that I won't write any more.

Monday, 30 March–Friday, 3 April

I am getting very slack in writing this diary. But I don't seem to have the time. Training has gone on the same during this week. A Grant tank has arrived. It really is most impressive and makes the Stuart look quite small when they stand side by side. B and C Squadrons are going to have the heavies and my squadron for the moment will have the lights. As far as I can see, we shall be used entirely for reconnaissance and as a protective screen.

We had another brigade scheme during this week. We moved as a brigade, and the Regiment's navigator got 40° off the bearing and as a result we crossed over the brigade front. The colonel had the new

Grant tank out as his headquarters. Sam Garrett was acting as protective troop and when answering a signal from the CO to come towards him, owing to a misunderstanding between Sam and his driver, Sam crashed into the CO's tank and broke a sprocket! So the CO had to change chargers! It was a dreadful thing to happen to the new tank, but all the same rather humorous that the light tank should put the heavy out of action!

The CO continued on with a regimental scheme that went off quite well. Price McCowan has returned to the Regiment after an interesting time in the desert. He is going to C Squadron. Stephen Mitchell has gone off up the desert.

Friday, 3–Wednesday, 15 April

We are still at Khatatba, and we still have no more tanks. Each squadron has three lights and B and C Squadrons have one Grant tank each. As soon as B and C Squadrons get another Grant tank the CO is going to hand over all the lights to my squadron and our role will be reconnaissance and not to get heavily engaged. It should be rather fun, very similar to armoured cars.

Stephen Mitchell has done an attachment for a week with the 10th Hussars in the desert. He found everything very static and had quite an interesting time and had some bombing on his way home.

The CO asked me tonight whether I wished to go to the staff college and told me that if I did he was willing to put my name in, in which case I had to fill in a pro-forma. It's most difficult to decide whether to accept the offer or not. If I do have my name accepted it would mean a six-month course and some kind of staff job at the end and a very good chance of not coming back to the Regiment, which I would hate, more especially as we shall be getting all the tanks in the near future.

But on the other hand if I want to stay in the army after the war a staff college course would be a great asset. General Clark has left the division and Gatehouse has taken his place. All squadron leaders met him today.

Wednesday, 15 April

In the afternoon Lawrence Biddle, John Walters, Geoffrey Brooks and I went into Cairo. We went in my staff car. Tea at Gezira, which was most delightful especially as there was a cricket match on. I ran into Kim Semlies. I have not seen him since war began. He was with a very deadbeat-looking dame. I am going to have dinner with him one evening and hear all his news. The Gezira Club is certainly a most attractive spot, especially after Khatatba camp.

At 7 o'clock we all met at the Continental for a drink and then went to the St James restaurant for dinner, which was most excellent. We then went to the opera house and saw an American show of *The Gondoliers*, which I thoroughly enjoyed. It was the first time I had been in a theatre since leaving England.

Friday, 17 April

Stephen Mitchell is at the moment reading what I am writing and has added his comment. [You cheeky old devil! Stph] It's been a busy day. I lectured for an hour in the morning and took a Bren-gun class in the afternoon.

Two air-graphs from Martin Rosewell, also a letter from Bridget.

Squadron leaders' conference in the evening. I am reading such a good book, called *Invitation to the Waltz*. In a way there is something to be said for being killed off in this war. Only to have known joy and happiness and gained a certain position and some popularity and not to have known misery, poverty and sadness. I am writing this in the mess after dinner. The wireless is playing a most attractive waltz. Music is really very lovely and at this moment I somehow feel that I would rather lose our signet than our capacity for . . . music.

9

Into Action

Shermans moving forward.

STANLEY TOOK A BREAK *from writing his diary between April and June. The Sherwood Rangers were continuing to train on tanks in Palestine, and throughout the rest of April and much of May a lull had continued in the Western Desert. General Ritchie, the Eighth Army commander, had decided to make a stand along the so-called Gazala Line, with the intention of building up his forces, then striking back across Cyrenaica and, with luck, into Tripolitania. His line, however, despite extending some forty miles south, was not a continuous defensive position but, rather, strung out into a series of defensive 'boxes' each surrounded by wire and mines and in which various brigades were positioned. They were often so far apart that they could not be mutually supported. Realizing this, Rommel decided to strike first and did so on 26 May, both outflanking the line to the south and severing it in two.*

Furious fighting followed, in which the British lost large numbers of tanks, the line crumbled and, by 14 June, Ritchie had been forced to order his remaining brigades to fall back towards Tobruk.

Sunday, 14 June

In the last few weeks my diary writing has been very bad indeed. The war has not been going too well up in the Western Desert and as a result the Grant tanks have been taken away from us. This was followed by six of the light tanks being taken from our squadron. All very disappointing, but they have to have tanks up there. I have been up to Cairo once or twice and one weekend I stopped with Vera Philips and Hope Avery in their flat. I went out on the dicky and got tight with Vera. She is a girlfriend of John Walters and I met her through him. John has been away; he came back for a short time before going up to Haifa on a staff-college course. It was quite obvious to me that he objected and was most suspicious of my having taken his girlfriend out. But considering the fact that both he and Vera are married, he really has no cause to worry.

On Sunday night, 14 June, things began to happen. We had an order from Brigade that the Regiment had to be at ¼ hour's notice to move. All the light tanks of the Regiment, 28 in all, and all vehicles, were ordered to travel separately by train, to form a composite force of lights with the Greys and the Staffs under Lord Fiennes, the colonel of the Greys. The remainder of the Regiment were to follow under Donny Player, as Flash Kellett had left for a course. In the end our train party left on Tuesday morning, 16 June. I was OC that train.

We loaded the tanks onto the train flats and travelled with our crews on the same flat, as there was not a great deal of room. But I had my camp canvas chair and with the help of my tank crew, Corporal Bacon, Corporal Cash and Brentson, we were all most comfortable. A hot meal was supplied at Amaya and we continued on for a couple of days until we came to Machiefa, which is west of Sidi Barrani. There we formed up with the remainder of the tank force from the Greys and the Staffs.

We spent a couple of days there, waiting to be called out in the event of an emergency but we were not required. It was really just as well as we had with us no B Echelon at all, which, incidentally, had been thrown at us at the very last moment and were coming up behind on the road. After a couple of days, we then retreated back to Charing Cross, about ten miles south of Mersa Matruh, where we formed our respective regiments as a brigade group under Gatehouse, our divisional general.

After about a week we had orders to return east once again and finish off brigade training in the Alexandria area. I was to take the Notts tanks back first. Stripped, we loaded up the tanks onto the flats once more. Most of our loading and unloading had been done by night and the drivers had done very well. In the meantime, we have heard that the Huns have reached Sidi Barrani. While we were loading at Mersa, we had some bombing but no damage. After about four hours we reached Simla, only three miles from Mersa, and there I was informed by the RTO that the train was to return at once to Mersa! So back we went again, unloading the tanks again in the dark, but with a full moon and during an air raid. We spent the rest of the night on the perimeter. There was not much left of the night after we had filled up with petrol.

Early next morning we received the astounding order that we should hand over all the tanks to the County of London Yeomanry and 1st RTR. This really came as rather a cruel blow as we really considered ourselves a trained squadron now and, having been brought right up to the front line, fully expected to have a crack. We all hated having to hand over those tanks, which all the NCOs had looked after so well and had had for practically six months. However, we had to take the long view. The higher command had decided, and I think rightly, that it would be much better to keep our regiment intact and not split squadrons or troops to make up other units, and instead send us back up without our tanks to be re-equipped. My squadron handed over to the 1st Tanks, which have had a good deal of fighting and have been badly knocked about. They have now been made up to strength with a miscellaneous bunch of men and it was very galling to our men having to hand over to some crews who had never been in a Honey tank, never worked on a No. 14 set, and some of the gunners had never even seen a 37mm or Browning gun. A chap called Cruikshank was the squadron leader to whom I handed over. He told me the position and admitted that he only knew half his men by sight and that the majority of his crews had been formed on paper only. However, they all admitted that they had never taken over tanks in cleaner or better condition or better stocked with rations, which incidentally we handed over complete with all water cans, etc., which we had made on the way up.

However disappointing it may have been to lose their tanks, Stanley and the Sherwood Rangers had done well to avoid the front at this time. After nearly four weeks of battle, Eighth Army was being routed. On 21 June, Tobruk fell – a stunning blow, which had far-reaching effects. For Churchill, who was in Washington at the time and learned the news from President Roosevelt, it was a particularly bitter and humiliating loss – the latest in a string of devastating defeats that year. Eighth Army was now falling back in disarray to a new defensive position only 60 miles west of Alexandria. Known as the 'Alamein Line', after the tiny railway stop near the coast, it was, despite its alarming proximity to Alexandria and the Suez Canal, the best defensive position along the entire Western Desert because it was 40 miles long and ended with the vast Qattara Depression. This was impassable to vehicles, which meant it could not be outflanked. However, the defences had only been hastily prepared and whether they were strong enough to prevent the Panzer Armee Afrika sweeping on to Cairo and the Canal Zone remained to be seen.

During this time, Rommel's pursuit was being greatly hampered by the efforts of the RAF's Desert Air Force, which was operating round the clock and close to the front by using squadrons to leapfrog backwards from one landing ground to another. Their performance at this critical time probably saved Eighth Army from annihilation.

Thursday, 25–Tuesday, 30 June

After handing over our tanks we were supposed to leave Mersa Matruh at midnight 25 June but, owing to confusion, we did not leave until 4 o'clock next morning. The train was terribly crowded, consisting entirely of goods trucks and they were mostly open. I travelled in an open together with Major Le Grand, the Belgian major, Jack Whiting and John Bethell-Fox. We had also about 15 Indian troops and four other officers, so we were very crowded. The Staffs were also on the train under Bill Lewisham, who is a most charming person. Altogether we were 66 hours on that train and we were all very pleased when we arrived at Amariya.

Just after Derba there was a hold-up on the rail, which involved a two-hour delay. Bill and I decided to evacuate the train, which was just as well, as a German plane then came over and bombed and machine-gunned it. The Staffs had some narrow escapes. At almost midnight, we got going again and shortly after another plane came over and this time concentrated on the road, which ran parallel to and about 400 yards from the railway. It was a remarkable sight to see the plane going backwards and forwards along the road shooting from both ends. We expected any moment that it would turn its attention on us. Some of the coloured troops on our truck tried to jump the train (not the Indians) and we had some difficulty preventing them. We eventually arrived at Amariya and went to Maricopets Camp where we joined the rest of the Regiment.

In the meantime the Hun has been pushing on. Mersa Matruh, Fuka and Derba have fallen and we have taken up a position along the Alamein Line, about 40 miles from Alexandria.

There are no more diary entries until October 1942. It is possible that Stanley stopped writing for a while, but it seems more likely that these entries have simply gone missing. At any rate, it is a great shame because the period coincided with great changes in Eighth Army and also the Sherwood Rangers' first battle in their new role as an armoured tank regiment.

Throughout July, Rommel's forces tried to bludgeon their way through the Alamein position, but were held at bay. At the beginning of August, Churchill visited Egypt and sacked Auchinleck, the second Middle East C-in-C to lose his job in little more than a year. He was replaced by the imperturbable and hugely experienced General Sir

*Harold Alexander. General 'Strafer' Gott, formerly commander of XIII
Corps, took over Eighth Army. Tragically, he was shot down and killed
when his transport plane was attacked en route to Cairo in what was
almost certainly a deliberate assassination. His replacement was General
Bernard Montgomery. By this time, both sides had fought to a standstill
and during the remainder of August tried to build up strength once more.
For Rommel, now with horribly extended supply lines, this was no easy
task, and one made worse by the incessant assault on his supply convoys
from both submarines and air operating from Egypt and Malta. For
Eighth Army, conversely, the lines of supply were now very small, and
were being reinforced with weapons and matériel from the United States.*

*Rommel struck at the end of the month, desperately hoping for a
decisive breakthrough, but at the Battle of Alam Halfa, the line held once
more. On 1 September, the Sherwood Rangers went into action,
getting to within 800 yards of 15th Panzer Division's positions. After
losing a number of B and C Squadron tanks – and Stanley's friend, Jack
Whiting, who was killed by shellfire earlier in the morning – they were
ordered to withdraw. When Stanley's A Squadron pushed forward again
on 3 September, they discovered the Germans had withdrawn. The*

General Montgomery, the commander of the Eighth Army from 1942.

following day, Stanley pushed on further with one of his troops and captured three 50mm anti-tank guns and a number of prisoners.

Alam Halfa was a victory for Montgomery and for Eighth Army, but had been something of a rude awakening for the Rangers, who had charged forward and walked straight into a screen of anti-tank guns – the same error British tanks had been making since the Deutsches Afrika Korps had first arrived in North Africa. 'We made every mistake in the book,' says John Semken, 'but fortunately the battle only lasted a few days and we then had six weeks in which to sort ourselves out, reorganize and train, and learn from our mistakes.'

10

The Battle of El Alamein

General Montgomery talking to Lt-Col Jim Eadie on the latter's regimental command tank.

ON 14 SEPTEMBER, the Sherwood Rangers, along with the rest of 8th Armoured Brigade, had moved back thirty miles to a new training area, where they relentlessly practised moving through dummy minefields by night. New tanks arrived, including a number of the latest American M4 Shermans. The first four were handed over to the regimental HQ Squadron and named Robin Hood, Little John, Maid Marion and Friar Tuck; so began a tradition that the commanding officer's tank would always be called 'Robin Hood'. Stanley's A Squadron, however, was the reconnaissance squadron and so kept its Crusader tanks – lightly protected, armed only with a six-pounder gun, but fast. They were not known for their reliability, however, and especially not in the desert where the sand soon found its way into every working part. 'It was a miracle,' commented the Regiment's official history, 'if a Crusader engine functioned for more than about 36 hours without some strange and terrible trouble developing.'

The Regiment had been impressed by Montgomery, who, largely through Flash Kellett's influence, had visited them personally several times since arriving to take over Eighth Army. John Semken was certainly impressed by the new army commander. 'The effect of Monty was dramatic,' he says. 'He really was beyond all phrases.' What struck him most was the sense of complete control and Montgomery's statement that there would be no more retreats.

Montgomery was determined not to be rushed into launching an assault until he was certain of winning a decisive victory. Part of this process was building up sufficient strength, but another aspect was retraining, which was, as the Sherwood Rangers discovered, intensive. Every man, Montgomery insisted, was to know exactly what was expected of him and how to do it.

The basic plan was to punch two holes through the Axis defences, one in the north and one in the south, although it would be through the northern one that Monty would make his main breach. This was also the strongest part of the enemy line, but the army commander believed that any attack in the south would still have to wheel north at some point, and therefore believed it was best to hit the strongest point head-on first. This main breach would be over a ten-mile front. A combination of infantry, engineers and tanks would follow an artillery barrage, passing along two narrow cleared lanes through minefields. Once through, the armour would contain and hold off the enemy tanks, while the rest of the forces isolated and destroyed the enemy infantry, in a process Montgomery called 'crumbling'. This would be followed by the 'break-out' and 'pursuit'.

Montgomery reckoned the battle would last about ten days and it was planned for the third week in October. It was important it was no later, because the Allies were planning a second attack in north-west Africa, with a joint Anglo-US force landing in Algeria and French Morocco, called Operation TORCH. The aim was to crush French Vichy forces, then strike towards Tunisia. A victorious Eighth Army would also push the Axis forces back and encircle them in a giant pincer operation; that was the plan at any rate. TORCH was due to be launched on 10 November.

The Sherwood Rangers were still part of 8th Armoured Brigade and were to be involved in the opening of the attack, through the northern breach in the New Zealand Division's sector and using the southern of the two corridors to be cleared through the minefields. Since this corridor consisted of three narrow channels no wider than a tennis court, this was no easy task – and especially at night, with the fog of war rapidly descending . . .

Friday, 23–Saturday, 24 October 1942

We waited for an hour at Bombay Track where we replenished with petrol. My crew gave me a cup of coffee, which we were able to make from the water we carry in tins by the engine. When the engine runs for any length the water invariably gets heated up, from which we can make excellent coffee. On the way up Sergeant McCann's tank sprang a bad water leak so we had to leave him behind. Also Ronnie Hill had trouble with his sprocket, but he was able to join us later.

We had an hour's wait at Springbok Road, where we met the divisional general, and then got the word to go forward. We proceeded line ahead, with Sam's troop in the lead, followed by Patrick McCraith, who was navigating, followed by me and the other two troops. In all I had nine Crusader tanks in the squadron, made up as follows. Squadron HQ, Basil Ringrose and myself; 2 Troop, Mike Hollingshead, Corporal Truman; 3 Troop, Mike Bilton, Sergeant Hardinge; 4 Troop, Sam Garrett, Corporal Dring and Corporal Hudd.

Just as we were about to enter the passage through the minefield we were held up by the New Zealand Light Cavalry and the 9th Brigade moving south. Urgent messages came up to me from the CO on the air to push on, which I couldn't do.

We passed through our own minefield without incident. The sappers had clearly marked the path with lights and white tape on the ground. Halfway through they had one control point established where I met David Summers from Division. At that point the heads of all three columns were level: ourselves, Staffs and 3rd RTR.

We then started through the enemy minefield. The New Zealand infantry were to have pushed through and formed a bridgehead on the far side of the enemy minefield so that the tanks could debouch from the lane and take up positions on the ridge on the other side.

Then came the enemy minefield. In the distance we could see some enemy solid shot flying about the place, green tracer shot. Halfway through the enemy minefield Sam, who was leading, was again stopped by a control post. I came up to the front and learned we could go no further for 50 minutes as a lane had not been properly cleared. However, a message came through from the divisional commander that we should proceed at all costs, which we did, expecting at any moment to go up on a mine. However, we finally got to the end about an hour before light – at least, we were told by a sapper that we had reached the end – but we came under heavy anti-tank and machine-gun fire from both sides, and we were eager to get out into the open, and so were the people coming along behind us, so I gave the signal. No sooner had we gone about 200 yards than we ran straight into German anti-tank gun positions, and five Crusaders were immediately knocked out in the squadron.

It was quite one of the worst moments in my life. It was dark, I couldn't go forward, and all the heavy tanks were behind me, so I couldn't go back on account of them and the minefield. The infantry had not been able to clear the ridge ahead.

We had to sit there, and then eventually, at the CO's orders, managed to withdraw behind a ridge and onto the minefield, on which we lost some Grants and scout cars.

The ridge they were behind was the Miteirya Ridge, a long, low, narrow rise in the ground of about four miles long. It rises not much more than about 30 feet, but that was enough to shield a tank.

This is what happened to every troop in my squadron.

The idea was to advance three up: 2 Troop on the left, 3 in the centre, and 4 on the right.

2 Troop was under Lieutenant Hollingshead, who had only been with the Regiment a very short time. A 50mm anti-tank shell hit the tank and wounded him and his operator, Wright. The tank was again

hit by a shell, which killed Hollingshead and also Wright. The driver, Gerrard, jumped out and called to Lewis, the gunner, to follow him, but he continued to stand on top of the tank trying to get Wright out, and he received a direct hit from another shell, which killed him outright. Gerrard remained in a slit trench.

The other tank in 2 Troop was commanded by Corporal Truman. His tank received a direct hit, which put it out of action, and as the guns were jammed, he and his crew evacuated the tank and hid all day in a slit trench. They later contacted Gerrard from the other tank and after dark tried to get back to us again. However, they were caught by a German patrol and taken prisoner. They spent the rest of the night in a gun pit, where they found Chadwick, another of our drivers, badly wounded, and being looked after by a New Zealander. The Germans treated them well and gave them chocolate and water. They were astonished at the extreme youth of the Germans, especially the NCOs. The next day was extremely unpleasant on account of our own barrage, but they were eventually rescued by some tanks of the 3rd Hussars and reported back to us.

Mike Bilton was in charge of 3 Troop, the centre troop. His tank received a direct hit, which gave him a nasty wound in the stomach, and which wounded his operator, Wright, and put his tank out of action. Incidentally, his tank was on a minefield.

Sam Garrett was in command of 4 Troop, the right-hand troop. His tank was immediately hit twice, and he gave the order to his crew to evacuate, but not before he took the signal watch from the wireless set. This is the message which he passed back to me: 'Edward. I have been hit twice, tank on fire, am evacuating.' Before I could reply the CO came up on the air and said, 'Get off the bloody air, and your name is King, not Edward.' As his crew left the tank they were machine-gunned. Bingham, the operator, was badly wounded, Corporal Ives, the gunner, slightly wounded. The driver, Wilkinson, made off on his own, but I have since heard that he is in hospital. Sam Garrett led them back and was unwounded himself, but livid at having to leave all his kit on the tank.

As a result of this debouching from the minefield before dawn,

I lost five Crusader tanks from the squadron. The Grant tanks, eager to be free of the minefield before the sun rose, pushed on from behind and had four tanks knocked out, including Mike Laycock's. Having withdrawn behind the ridge for the rest of the day, and still more or less on the minefield, we came in for some very heavy shelling.

Bill Kepner got killed during the morning. He left his tank to assist a wounded man in the minefield and a shell got them both.

My squadron sergeant major, Hutchinson, dashed forward to some of our knocked-out tanks and tried to rescue the crews, but was also wounded and has since been recommended for the MM by the colonel.

Sergeant Grinnell and Lance Corporal Hopewell received a direct hit on their scout car and were both badly wounded.

I met Mike Laycock on the ground after his tank had been knocked out. He got heavily fired on by machine-gun fire and his tin hat saved him. I took him back on my tank to one of his own. He told me that Bill McGowan had gone, but this turned out to be incorrect. It was another of B Squadron's tanks which had gone up, not Bill's.

On my way back behind the ridge I saw Mike Bilton lying on the ground beside his tank. I got out and found that he had been badly wounded in the stomach. At that moment, Jack Tyrrell, our gunner OP, came past in his tank on the outside of which he had about 10 badly wounded gunners. He immediately stopped, heaved Mike on the back of his tank, and took him off.

Until about 16.30 it was impossible to get anything to eat, except biscuits and bully in the tank, but at 16.30 I pulled out from the ridge and we brewed up behind the tank. A cup of hot tea could not have been more acceptable.

At that hour I had only the following tanks left in the squadron: Corporal Dring in a 6-pounder (after Sam had lost his tank he joined Corporal Dring). They had some quite good shooting with their 6-pounder; Ronnie Hill, having broken down on the approach march, had now found me, and finally Corporal Butler, who later during the day received a direct hit on the side of the tank from an HE shell. This put the tank out of action, but fortunately did not damage any of the crew.

At about 17.15 I went to our left flank on the ridge to see what I could see from there, together with Tyrrell, the OP. The Hun started to develop a tank attack with about 20 or 30 tanks. I feel certain that his idea was to destroy our forward knocked-out tanks on the minefield. One Panzer Mk IV special had crept right up a depression and suddenly appeared about 300 yards to our immediate front. When the turret began to travel round in our direction and point at us, I beat a rather hasty retreat behind the ridge, especially in view of the fact that the breech mechanism of our 2-pounder had jammed. So did old Jack Tyrrell in his Honey tank. I then contacted the other tanks on our left and saw Bob Crisp, the squadron leader of their light squadron. I left my tank and got on the back of his to have a word with him. At that moment he and his OP were trying to pick up an 88mm, which was blitzing them. He told me that he had lost two officers that morning, most unnecessarily, as they had left their tanks and wandered about. I took the hint and got back into mine.

On my return, a shell burst just overhead. I had a very lucky escape. All it did was to completely close my left eye, blacken both, give me a violent nosebleed, slight concussion and some splinter wounds round the eyes. I was taken back to the RAP, which belonged to the New Zealanders, slightly nervous about left eye as I thought a splinter might have damaged the sight. I was sent back to hospital in Alex, had the eye examined and passed OK, so returned immediately with Sam Garrett, who had also found his way back.

We returned in time for the next battle and in the meantime very little happened as the Regiment was sent back to re-form. Basil Ringrose took over A Squadron in my absence.

On the evening of the first full day of battle, 24 October, the Sherwood Rangers had pushed on through the gap beyond the Miteirya Ridge, but tanks need support to maintain their advance; as the Regiment's support trucks – 'soft skins' – moved up they were attacked by Stuka dive-bombers and a number were hit and caught fire. Unfortunately, the

flames provided an ideal aiming point for the Axis artillery and soon
after both the Rangers and the 3rd Royal Tank Regiment were forced to
pull back. Captain Bill Kepner, who Stanley mentions was killed, had
joined the Sherwood Rangers in 1939 as an NCO, but was one of the new
breed of officers to have been commissioned from the ranks. He is buried
at the Alamein cemetery.

The following sequence of events took place after I left.

On the night of the 24th, the brigade formed up again to get through what remained of the enemy minefield after a passage had been prepared by the sappers. They moved off at 21.00 hours but Pat McCraith, the navigator, was told by the REs that he could not go further. The CO demanded an explanation for the delay, to which Pat replied that a 'big niner' (that absurd expression supposedly in code, which meant commander) had stopped him. The CO answered that our immediate 'niner' had told him to proceed at all costs. Pat replied that he couldn't go forward against the orders of a 'ninety-nine' and so the argument continued, which Pat won.

The Sherwood Rangers had not yet quite got to grips with using their
radio sets or the prescribed code. The perceived wisdom at the time
was that each squadron had four troops of four tanks plus a squadron
headquarters troop, thus twenty tanks in all. Each squadron was led
by a major with two captains, one who was second-in-command, and
one who was the 'rear link-man'. The idea was that these would
communicate with each other via the B set wireless radio, which had a
range of around 200 yards. The A set had a wider range and was used for
communicating between squadrons and other units. The trouble was
two-fold. First, the Rangers went into battle, for the most part, with their
turret hatches down and using the periscope. At night, and with the
intense dust, this made it next to impossible to see a thing. Second, each
tank was supposed to use strict code with which to communicate, but in
the confusion, this was often forgotten or became muddled. John Semken,
who had been the signals officer at one point, admits it was pretty
chaotic. 'Our wireless procedure,' he says, 'was being constantly changed.'

Keith Douglas noted that the Sherwood Rangers stuck to prescribed code-names as far as possible but code for their actions was based almost entirely on allusions to horses and cricket. 'I shall need a farrier, I've cast a shoe,' meant a track had come undone; 'returning to pavilion,' meant withdrawing. 'It was,' says John Semken, 'bloody silly.' The Rangers certainly maintained their idiosyncratic radio language for much of the North African campaign, but learned that it made sense for tank commanders to operate with hatches open and their heads sticking up for much of the time.

At 22.00 hours our barrage started. The whole brigade was formed up line-ahead when a bomber came over and dropped some bombs on our column. Five more soon returned and bombed our soft-skinned vehicles, which were literally nose to tail. There is a general opinion that the bombers were our own. Part of our echelon was completely destroyed, including our fitters' truck, killing Sergeant Headland, A Squadron fitter sergeant, a grievous loss, as well as Trooper Bence the electrician, and Trooper Long, the driver. Trooper Else, whom I had put in the truck to operate a wireless, which I had installed, was wounded. Trooper Hemingway, another truck driver from A Squadron, was also killed, and Troopers Hall and Whatley wounded. The Regiment lost a good many 3-tonners.

At last the brigade moved off. The leading regiment had not gone far before it turned and came back at a very undignified pace. We covered their retreat and the Staffs were then in the lead and remained there for the night.

Sunday, 25 October

The Regiment found itself on exactly the same ground as the previous day, but the enemy must have suffered heavily from our terrific barrage and bombing, to say nothing of the gunfire from the tanks.

The CO then decided to take the ridge with the Regiment alone and made necessary plans with the gunners, but Brigade refused to allow the CO to carry out his plan.

Ronnie Hill got killed during the morning. He was standing on the outside of John Semken's tank, which received a direct hit from an HE shell and this blew the poor boy to pieces. John Semken was quite unhurt.

Ronnie Hill was in A Squadron with Stanley, but was a good friend of John Semken, who was in C Squadron at the time. Ronnie had always been convinced that nothing would happen to him – that, somehow, he would make it through. But that day he came over to John Semken's tank in his Crusader, climbed out and onto John's turret and was chatting to him. 'Then he was blown to bits all over me,' says John. 'I was drenched in his blood to my navel. So much for being convinced it won't happen to you.'

The Regiment then pulled out and took up position at Point 33, which was NW of their present position.

Monday, 26 October

The Regiment took up a position facing west and almost opposite Tel el Aqqaqir.

Keith Douglas came back from Division, where he had been acting as camouflage officer, and joined the squadron again. At that time A Squadron was very short of officers, so the CO accepted his return with alacrity. He had left them at Division without saying a word to a soul, after having had a row.

Most of the day, enemy snipers in derelict tanks and vehicles sniped at the crew commanders of our tanks whenever they showed their heads above the turret. Keith Douglas captured an infantry position and brought back 30 prisoners. He was followed all the way back by enemy mortar fire.

At 17.00 hours 13 enemy tanks attacked and were driven off by the Regiment. All our tanks opened fire. The visibility was extremely bad. The CO saw a strange and suspicious object in front, and said over the air that unless that funny object in front of the Regiment moved he would open fire. Jack Tyrrell, the OP, as usual well out in front, suddenly became aware that the CO must be referring to him, and beat a hasty retreat.

The Regiment was ordered to retire behind Springbok Road to refit. Our gunners, B Battery, 1 RHA, remained to support the infantry.

Tuesday, 27 October

After the Regiment had withdrawn, Jack Tyrrell had orders to withdraw at 02.00 hours on the morning of the 27th. He found that his tank wouldn't start. He dismounted and conducted a shoot from behind the tank. The enemy tanks had remained in exactly the same position and on to them Jack brought down fire from behind his tank. They must have thought he had been knocked out because they never opened fire. He managed to get the tank started and withdrew under a smokescreen, which he asked his guns to lay down. Before leaving he discovered the Regiment had knocked out five M13 tanks.

Our gunners then came back and rejoined the Brigade just behind Springbok Road for a few days' rest.

The M13 was Italy's main battle tank of the war, and while it was comparable with early German and British tanks, by the Battle of Alamein it was both underarmed and under-armoured and no match for the latest German Panzer IIIs and IVs or Allied Grants and Shermans.

Stanley mentions that after his wound he was back in time for 'the next battle'. This was Operation SUPERCHARGE. The early part of the battle had not provided the decisive breakthrough Montgomery needed, and had ground to something of a halt, although enemy counter-attacks had been crushed, and constant air and artillery continued to grind down Rommel's forces. SUPERCHARGE was much the same as the original plan, with a night-time infantry attack and armour following close behind, but a bit to the north of the initial main strike and on a narrower front, and by now with fewer mines to deal with. It was launched on the night of 2 November.

Monday, 2 November

The second phase of the battle started on this day. At 06.00 hours in the morning we left Bir Mataka, where the Regiment had rested for a few days. We lined up line-ahead, A Squadron leading, and proceeded along the Boomerang Track. The end of this track brought us out on the edge of the enemy minefield, which the sappers were to clear, followed by the New Zealand infantry. 9th Brigade were to go through before us, as were 23rd Motor Brigade. As a result of the terrific barrage put down by the gunners, and all the dust, etc., visibility was extremely bad, and when we eventually arrived at the end of the marked track it was most difficult to find our location and the direction to Tel el Aqqaqir, which was our objective, most especially as we suspected enemy minefields ahead of us. Jack Tyrrell, gunner OP attached to the squadron, was up with me. We met some gunners whom he knew. They couldn't help us with direction but gave us each a most acceptable cup of tea. I could not drink all of mine as the CO arrived on the scene.

We then made off in a NW direction and contacted the Staffordshire Yeomanry. We learned that the 9th Armoured Brigade had had a very sticky time and that the infantry had not secured a bridgehead on the enemy side of the minefield.

Enemy shelling was very unpleasant in our new position. I ordered 1 Troop under John Bethell-Fox to push forward in front of the heavy squadrons. I followed behind with our close support tank. Enemy tanks appeared so Sam Garrett came up on the right and Keith Douglas on the left. John Fox had an excellent shoot with his 6-pounder at the tanks, which were approaching diagonally, and his troop claimed two tanks. Sam got rather separated on the right flank and had an unpleasant time with enemy snipers.

In the afternoon we had to withdraw to operate on another flank. Shelling during refuelling was most unpleasant. Troopers Bell and Jefferies, who were in a Squadron HQ tank, were killed early during the day. They appear to have been looking out of the turret when a shell exploded above their heads and killed them both. It was very sad, as they had only arrived the day before, and Jefferies told me that he was quite capable of commanding a tank in spite of not being an NCO. We formed an open leaguer facing south.

Tuesday, 3 November

At 2 o'clock in the morning we moved out of leaguer and joined the rest of the Brigade, 3rd RTR leading, ourselves on the left and Staffs Yeomanry on the right. We moved off at daylight, in a south-easterly direction. Owing to mechanical troubles I was very short of Crusader tanks. I only had three, John Bethell-Fox, Sergeant Hardinge and Sam Garrett. Mine had broken down so I travelled with Sam and he acted as my gunner. Jack Tyrrell was as usual with the squadron in his Honey tank. The four of us all worked well ahead and it wasn't long before we had spotted an enemy battery, on which he brought down fire and put it out of action. We then spotted another enemy battery straight ahead. By acting as an OP to Bill McGowan in B Squadron he was able to bring indirect fire down with his 75mm gun in his Grant tank. I could do no good with my 2-pounder AP shells.

We were then able to proceed over the next ridge and came upon a battery of five 75mm anti-tank enemy guns, manned by Italians who immediately showed a white flag. We captured all the crews, about 30 in all. John Bethell-Fox then rather rushed the next ridge and immediately had his tank knocked out by another battery behind. Trooper Martin, his driver, was killed, and his gunner, Trooper Davis, and himself were wounded. In the meantime I had been recalled by the CO and did not know that he had been knocked out until Jack Tyrrell came rushing back in his tank, not having been able to get me on the air. I asked him if he could possibly get him out and I would rejoin him after I had seen the CO. Sam and I then dashed back and found that Jack had rescued John Bethell-Fox, his gunner, plus four German prisoners.

Keith Douglas returned with a new tank. I asked him to take charge while Sam and I went out to refuel and took with us John Bethell-Fox, who was wounded in the knee. It was rather a foolish request to Keith to take charge as at that time there was only one other tank besides his own. However, he did get an order from the CO to control the squadron properly and stop them wandering about! While we replenished Sam and I had a quick brew. We handed over our prisoners to the infantry.

One of the features of Eighth Army by this time was its ability to pull broken-down and damaged tanks off the battlefield and get them repaired and back in action again. Mobile RASC repair workshops did much of the work, but depending on how bad the damage was, tanks might be sent further back to workshops in and around Cairo, Alexandria and the Canal Zone. But towing trucks and tractors would have been a feature of the battlefield, scurrying about, especially at night, and dragging broken tanks out of the fray. In addition, each armoured regiment had its own administrative platoon of trucks – B Echelon – which would bring forward ammunition and supplies, while each squadron of four troops would also have an administrative troop of a dozen or more trucks and vehicles. These would bring ammunition and supplies, but also rations. They might take a tank crew back to the rear echelons, several miles back out of the immediate battle zone, where replacement tanks could be picked up.

On our return we found that Jack had spotted two 88mm anti-tank guns on our left flank, which had remained very doggo. He knocked out one, but the other managed to get away behind a lorry.

B Squadron lost four Grant tanks from anti-tank guns during the evening. The Staffs on our left also lost a couple, and by the end of the day we had not been able to reach the line of the Tel el Aqqaqir telegraph wires and withdrew back into leaguer for the night.

My squadron SQMS brought up some rum with the rations, which was greatly appreciated. At 10 o'clock that evening our artillery started a terrific barrage on the telegraph lines, but a good many of the shells landed in our leaguer, one of which seriously wounded Derrick Warwick in the head as he was lying behind his tank, and another got Bill McGowan in the arm. The sight of five burning Grant tanks, glowing in the night, was rather depressing. C Squadron had a couple of their Shermans hit, but no damage was done to the crews and the tanks were recovered. Since Stephen Mitchell has gone back wounded, Michael Gold now commands C Squadron.

As soon as the shelling started, Sam came and woke up me and Jack Tyrrell, who immediately realized from what direction the shells were coming. He and Sam lay down in front of my tank and I spent the rest of the night inside my tank.

Donny Player arrived up from Alexandria where he had been in the LOB camp.

Wednesday, 4 November

Moved out of leaguer at first light and soon discovered that the enemy had evacuated from the line of the track and telegraph poles. I was left with only three Crusaders, those of Sam Garrett, Keith Douglas and Corporal Truman. Mine broke down so I travelled on Jack Tyrrell's tank. This proved a most satisfactory way of working because he was connected both to RHQ on one set and to his Battery HQ on another set, and I could control the squadron on the RHQ link.

We soon surprised a concentration of MET defended by a rear-guard of anti-tank guns. Jack Tyrrell immediately brought down fire on these guns, knocking out one 88mm and making the others shift. Twelve enemy tanks then appeared, which he engaged with HE but left off when Keith Douglas and Corporal Truman engaged with their 6-pounders from the Crusaders. The enemy tanks then withdrew.

The idea of a regimental group, that is a regiment of tanks working with a battery of 25-pounders and a company of infantry, has proved a tremendous success and we have been most fortunate in having the 1st RHA working with us, and most especially Jack Tyrrell, who has been the forward OP working with A Squadron. The speed with which he can pick up enemy gun positions and bring down accurate fire is quite remarkable. His use of ground and sense of direction are absolutely first class. He has fought in France, Greece and the Western Desert and was actually in Tobruk when this regiment was there.

Sam Garrett told me that quite a few 'rockets' from the CO came over the air for me for not answering his calls. But I never heard them.

Geoffrey Brooks, our MO, discovered some Scotch infantry breaking the neck of some bottles, which they had discovered in a case. After discovering the contents to be neither whisky nor beer, they threw the remainder away. On further investigation, the bottles turned out to be Veuve Clicquot Champagne. Needless to say he took charge of the remaining bottles!

At 6 o'clock in the evening we moved south for about eight miles, then halted and bedded down until 01.00 hours. Just before moving off at 6 o'clock that evening, when the whole brigade was formed up ready to move, we were attacked by Stukas. Fortunately, our guns and B Echelon escaped damage.

Earlier during the day, when first Jack and I spotted that concentration of enemy MET, he asked his CO for an 'air blitz' on that area and, after an hour, he got it.

General Ritter von Thoma, captured at the end of the battle.

After going for about six miles due south along the telegraph lines, we halted until 24.00 hours.

Axis cohesion collapsed that day. General von Thoma, commanding the Deutsches Afrika Korps, was captured near the Sherwood Rangers to the north-west of Tel el Aqqaqir, at around 5.30 p.m. Around the same time, Rommel issued the order for his entire Panzer Armee Afrika to withdraw. The Battle of Alamein was over.

Stanley's comments about the close co-operation of armour, artillery and infantry demonstrates just how quickly they were learning – and not just they as an armoured regiment, but Eighth Army as a whole. All-arms combat – that is, the co-ordination of armour, infantry and artillery – was still a relatively new concept within the British Army. By this time, however, not only was the army building strength, it was developing both tactically and operationally too.

Allied close air support was also increasing, and there is no doubt that air power played a crucial role in the battle – even Montgomery, never quick to offer praise of others, acknowledged the vital role the Desert Air Force and RAF Middle East as a whole played in the battle.

11

Pursuit to Tripoli

The coast road littered with debris after the battle.

Thursday, 5 November 1942

WE TRIED A NIGHT march from 01.00 to until 03.00 hours. This was far from being successful as the brigade had not formed up properly before starting. Anyhow, the Regiment was badly out of formation and as a result we got lost for a short while. It was straightened out next morning and we proceeded towards Galal station in a sweep south in order to cut the road.

We went on the right and it wasn't long before the squadron started swanning off in the true sense of the word, picking up prisoners and capturing loot, led, of course, by Jack Tyrrell in his Honey, and very soon I found I was the only tank of A Squadron in front of the main body. The remainder were well away to the right flank.

Sam Garrett captured three lorry-loads of Italian infantry, disarmed them and sent them off on their own. Keith Douglas found a

German officer and 20 men, as well as a good load of compasses, binoculars and revolvers. Basil Ringrose and Jack Tyrrell captured a 50mm anti-tank gun on tow. The crew endeavoured to get the gun into action but Jack was too quick for them and captured the lot. After a great deal of trouble and calling them up on the wireless I managed to get them all back together again.

On his way back to us, Keith Douglas, being rather blind at the best of times and having rather lost direction, approached what he thought was our column. He brought his tank alongside a vehicle and, much to his amazement and to the utter consternation of the vehicle driver, found it was a German column. When the German driver saw a tank alongside his vehicle, utter confusion broke out and the whole column broke up. Keith tried to fire his Besa, which jammed, then turned to his 6-pounder, which was quite useless against vehicles of that type, so finally resorted to his Tommy gun, which also jammed. He ended up by having a first-class row with Davis, his gunner. His wireless also failed to work at the critical moment.

Jack spotted something interesting on our right front so I went off with him, leaving the squadron under the care of Basil.

We saw a column moving in the far distance but it was too far away to do any good. We came across an aerodrome on which there was an M13 Italian tank. We captured the crew and I put the tank out of action with four rounds from the 6-pounder. Being slightly apprehensive about enemy mines, we then rejoined the main body.

We arrived at Galal station and sighted a large enemy column making for the coast road, with some tanks, an English 25-pounder gun and some of our captured 3-tonners. At first it was difficult to determine whether the column was friendly or not, but the tanks soon decided the matter for us. Jack Tyrrell immediately engaged the MET with the artillery and Sam, Corporal Truman and I engaged the tanks, two of which we knocked out, all claiming hits.

Jack Tyrrell made a terrible mess of the enemy transport. Every vehicle was practically knocked out and all the men from the vehicles got hell. The speed with which Jack can get his guns into action is really amazing. The captured 25-pounder was quite undamaged, so

Sam Garrett took it on tow back to the gunners, who were a gun short.

Jack and I then proceeded on across the road up to the sea, where we found an evacuated Italian field hospital, and from which Jack and Sam got a great deal of loot at a later time.

Some remaining enemy transport was still trying to sneak past, using a wadi and creeping along the seashore. One Mk IV Special came up from the sea. Jack yelled at me to look out. At the time, I was standing on the top of the tank looking the other way. All the firing had made me extremely deaf and all I could say was 'What? What?' In the end, he dashed over and warned me of the possible danger. We immediately withdrew to a hull-down position and engaged but the tank got away. It might have been rather awkward as the rest of the Regiment were about two miles behind in the neighbourhood of the station.

In the meantime, 13 or 14 M13 Italian tanks approached Galal station and ran straight into the Regiment, which knocked out every single tank. It's quite a debatable point whether they were coming in to surrender as we found a white flag afterwards, but we made a horrible mess of them and Geoff Brooks was worked to death patching up Italian and German wounded. Sam and I found one poor fellow who was in a terrible state. However, he had had enough strength to tie a tourniquet around his leg, which had been horribly shattered.

It made us think how illogical war was. First of all we do our best to kill these Germans and Italians, shelling them and machine-gunning them, and then afterwards we do all we can to save their lives.

Mike Laycock had his tank shot up and one of his crew killed by one of our own 6-pounder anti-tank guns. He was livid with rage. Accidents will happen, though. He had to be evacuated.

The tanks we shot up were from the 90th Light Division.

While Sam and Jack were looting the evacuated hospital, they found two German Mk IV tanks with their engines still running, but no sign of the crew. They poured petrol inside the tanks and set them on fire.

While on his way back with the recaptured 25-pounder, Sam Garrett ran straight into a tank battle, which gave him a slight shock, especially when his engine stalled.

We formed up in leaguer just west of the station. It was dark when we got in but on our left we saw a column moving fast in a westward direction. We tried to get leave to follow, but the CO wouldn't let us as he didn't want the force to get split. We went a short way on foot with a Tommy gun but didn't see anything further.

Friday, 6 November

Broke leaguer at daybreak and joined the rest of the brigade, which had leaguered further down the railway. As a result of the tremendous pace at which we had been pushing on, and the lack of maintenance, I had exactly one other tank left besides my own with which to start the day. So, again, I had to act as leading point.

The brigade formed up and proceeded westwards along the railway line, 3 RTR up, ourselves left, and Staffs right. After we had gone a short way, we were then held up by two batteries of enemy artillery on the top of an escarpment. Jack Tyrrell soon brought down fire and knocked out one gun. They were well out of range for the tanks. We came under fire from some solid shot, but none of us were hit. Keith Douglas ran onto an isolated mine, which blew off one of his tracks. He changed into another tank.

The CO ordered us to do a right flank movement and cut the road behind and west of the enemy. I went off with two other tanks plus Jack Tyrrell. We had a steep climb to the top of the escarpment and then worked slowly round. B and C Squadrons followed us.

By the time we reached the top, the enemy had gone. We turned right and it was a flat-out race to cut the road. Jack won in his Honey tank. The Grants moved like hell across the extraordinary open and good-going desert. Freddy Cooper, who was in charge of B Squadron, had a bad runner and received continual rockets from the CO for lagging behind. How I laughed. We eventually cut the road at Kilometre Stone 62 by an aerodrome.

Sergeant Wooley, in an RHQ Crusader, who had been lent to me as we were so short, captured four Italian officers. As usual, the Hun had gone and left the Italians. One of these Italians had a slight knowledge of English and from what we could make out he claimed to know the exact position of a food dump. We immediately sent him off with Sergeant Wooley (before handing him over) to see whether we could increase our larder. However, it turned out to be a salvage dump and not a food dump.

We remained in the vicinity for the remainder of the day, each squadron taking up a position of observation. We were continually expecting to come into contact with the remainder of the enemy armour, especially the 21st Panzer Division in the south.

No sooner had we taken up positions when we had a very heavy rain storm, which completely flooded all the lower ground. Jack Tyrrell had taken up his position right next door to a wooden hut on the edge of the aerodrome and inside I found him having a tremendous brew-up: tinned sausages, beans, potatoes and some excellent tea. He immediately asked me to join him and we had a most delicious meal, completely under cover.

Our B Echelon, instead of following the road, which was now clear, followed our course and as a result became completely bogged.

We closed into leaguer in the same area but as the rain continued practically throughout the night we slept in our tanks. Not very comfortable.

Saturday, 7 November

Early in the morning we continued along the road towards Mersa Matruh. This time we were in the lead. It wasn't long before Jack discovered an Italian general's caravan, beautifully fitted up inside. He immediately took it on tow! But later we had to hand it over to Brigade. Keith Douglas wandered too far out to the right flank, broke a track, and had a long walk back to the road to get help. However, he captured an Italian concert party all waiting to give themselves up. Until the LAD arrived to help him, they sang to him and the crew, helped him brew up, and even assisted in replacing the track.

As we got nearer to Mersa, the divisional general, General Gatehouse, came up into the lead in his tank. I had an idea that he wished to be in Mersa first. However, we were informed by a scouting infantry platoon that one of their carriers had been knocked out by an 88mm A/T gun from the outer defences! The general retired behind the Regiment and A Squadron was sent forward to reconnoitre.

We found that the Hun had left behind a rear-guard. C Squadron sent a troop around the right flank, but it soon came under fire and two tanks received hits, which didn't penetrate. Michael Gold was then in command of C Squadron as Stephen Mitchell had not returned from hospital.

At the time, I was extremely short of tanks, owing to mechanical trouble and not being able to get them up fast enough. In fact, mine was the only one left, but nine more were on the way. I managed to creep up pretty near and had a very good shot at a 50mm A/T gun with my 3-inch howitzer. That close support for tanks is most useful. The CO then decided that he would lead a frontal attack with the remainder of B Squadron.

I knew that it was dangerous as I could still see a 50mm pointing directly down the road. However, he went in and received a direct hit from a 50mm, which killed his driver and loader and wounded his gunner, Trooper Sanders, who used to be my groom.

The gunners offered to put down smoke and cover the advance, but he considered that the tanks might be silhouetted as they came through.

One truck, which I believe held air-force personnel, came bumming along the road, straight through our tanks, and towards the outer defences. The occupants had a nasty shock when a mortar bomb fell right beside their truck and small arms opened up at them. They turned about, and returned along that road at a great speed!

A platoon of the Buffs tried an attack, but that failed with heavy casualties. Jack Tyrrell saw some movement in one sector of the wire defences and started to bring down some 25-pounder fire. This alleged enemy turned out to be a cow, and the following message came over the air: 'You are shooting at a cow – I say again, a Charlie Orange William!' We closed into leaguer at too late an hour as there was no moon, so we had some difficulty in getting in.

Basil Ringrose brought up nine tanks, which had been just right, but they all developed trouble again, mostly minor problems, which the LAD and fitters put right early next morning. A donkey wandered into leaguer, which caused some amusement. A BBC van also arrived, which made some recordings. I was very weary.

Eighth Army, and Montgomery in particular, have often been criticized for not pursuing Rommel's forces with greater urgency, but Stanley's diary makes it clear that numerous mechanical problems, hold-ups by enemy rear-guards and time spent mopping up prisoners hindered their rapid progress considerably.

Sunday, 8 November

Mersa Matruh fell and we were the first to enter and drove right down to the sea, where we met the 3rd RTR and the Staffs. We passed the spot where a few months earlier we had handed over our Honey tanks to the 1st RTR – the day before we evacuated the town.

Jack Tyrrell and Sam Garrett looted Navy Stores and found some excellent food. At about 10 o'clock we pushed on west along the road towards Charing Cross, and halted at Kilometre Stone 11, where we spent the night. The first time in pyjamas for a long time.

Monday, 9 November

A day of rest and maintenance. The traffic on the road heading westwards is terrific, the congestion appalling. We sent some of the men down to bathe. Keith Douglas rejoined but without a tank.

Tuesday, 10 November

Sam went off on a scrounging party and brought back an excellent blue tent, which we have made into the officers' mess. A church service in the morning which the brigade attended.

Two new tanks arrived. Bathing in afternoon.

Wednesday, 11 November

A football match in the afternoon against the RHA on a very danger-ous and hard ground. Sam Garrett and Keith Douglas had some drinks on board a torpedo boat in Mersa harbour. They both came back much the worse for wear! I had a squadron photo taken with a captured Italian camera.

We heard that Sergeant Grinnell, reputed at one time to have been killed, was progressing well. There are plenty of rumours about our future, some say Tripoli or Syria, even India, and England seems to be a favourite among many. We heard that all the church bells rang in England in honour of the Eighth Army's victory. Water is very short, and until they get the thing organized we are on ¼ gallon per man per day.

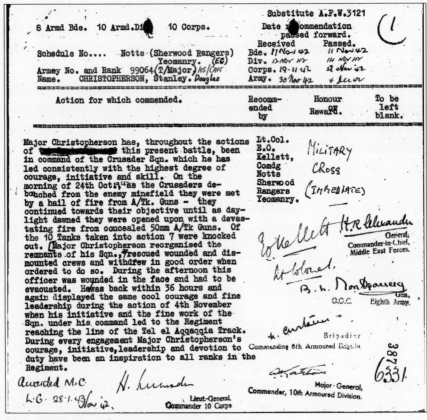

The citation for Stanley's first Military Cross.

Stanley was put forward for a Military Cross on this day, although news did not reach him of the award until 28 January the following year. It was for leadership of the squadron during the Alamein battle, 'which he has led consistently with the highest degree of courage, initiative and skill . . . During every engagement, Major Christopherson's courage, initiative, leadership and devotion to duty have been an inspiration to all ranks in the Regiment.'

Thursday, 12 November

PT before breakfast. Bathing party in the afternoon. At 16.00 hours the brigadier came around each squadron and talked to tank crews. He then addressed all the squadron, congratulating us on helping to win the Battle of Alamein, which he said, combined with the American attack from the west, had finished off the Hun and the Italians in Africa. We had completed our victory in 12 days. He also pointed out the PM had mentioned the part played by the brigade in Parliament. About the future he could tell us nothing definite: we might go forward or back depending on the Germans. But we must keep ourselves fit and the tanks in perfect running order and be prepared for anything – an attack on the south of France, or Italy. The question of going home was not mentioned.

After dinner Basil Ringrose, Sam Garrett and I went and had a drink with B Battery, 1st RHA. The battery commander, Egerton, Jack Tyrrell and a couple of other officers were there. We have been so fortunate in having them to work with us. The co-operation between the armour and the guns, as far as this regiment and especially this squadron is concerned, has been quite perfect, thanks largely to Jack Tyrrell.

I sent back the SQMS with Sergeant Bacon to get some stuff from the NAAFI for the squadron. Basil Ringrose told me tonight that he was going to command B Squadron in the absence of Mike Laycock. It will be good experience for him.

Admiral Darlan has now thrown his hand in with the Americans, after having been captured by them. We heard today that Sergeants

Grinnell, Bingham, Lance Corporal Hopewell and Trooper Else are in hospital after all, having been reported missing or dead. I am especially pleased about Bingham, as he was in my troop when we had horses.

As a result of this battle A Squadron has had 34 casualties: 14 killed, 19 wounded and one missing. This includes two officers killed, one seriously wounded, and three slightly wounded. As far as the Regiment is concerned, out of 22 officers who entered the battle, 16 have been casualties.

Admiral Darlan had been the leader of all military forces in Vichy North Africa, but had clandestinely agreed a deal with the Allies prior to the TORCH landings on 8 November. After half-hearted resistance, Vichy French forces had surrendered three days later and Darlan had been announced as political leader in French North Africa.

Friday, 13 November

Squadron leaders' conference at 09.00 hrs. The men need a rest, but if we are to be left for any length of time we shall have to employ them in some way. Bathing will be a great help. A squadron of the 41st Tank Regiment has been attached to the Regiment. The CO is not too pleased about this, and has decided to have four squadrons instead of mixing the personnel. They will have Sherman tanks and this will not affect this squadron in any way. We heard today that Tobruk has fallen and had been left in flames.

We have been told that we are going to be made up to strength, but our future is still unknown. It rather looks as if the Americans will reach Tripoli first.

I reorganized the squadron into the following troops: Sam Garrett comes to Squadron HQ as 2i/c, Archie Stockton 3 Troop, Keith Douglas 2 Troop, Sergeant Goodridge 4 Troop, and Sergeant Hardinge, 5 Troop.

Saturday, 14 November

Two new tanks arrived for the squadron today, making us 14 in all. All tanks have to be painted with division and squadron signs, etc., and all given a name beginning with A. Keith Douglas submitted 'Apple Pie & Apple Face' for his tanks. I squashed this, as something told me that the CO would not approve!

Bathing party in the afternoon. Still no news about moving or our future. Great speculation. Heard today that Roger Wenlow and Claud Ashton had been killed in a flying accident. Roger's death was a great blow.

Myles Hildyard is now adjutant until Derrick Warwick comes out of hospital. A letter from Patrick McCraith, also in hospital, told the CO that Derrick was very comfortable and sitting up in bed, 'and although still on the danger list was much better than any other blokes in the hospital who had been belted in the head', as Patrick put it.

The SQMS arrived back from the NAAFI with some food. On the strength of it we asked the CO to dinner, sending a formal invitation. He accepted for tomorrow, answering in Latin! Tomorrow we shall send him a reminder in Greek!

Sunday, 15 November

We had a church service parade for the whole Regiment. A detachment of 1st RHA came. The divisional commander and the brigadier also attended. Padre Hales took the service and delivered a sermon. Jack Tyrrell came for the service, but arrived too late, so waited at the squadron office for a glass of beer. We persuaded him to stay for lunch.

The colonel and Myles Hildyard came to dinner. We gave them soup, stew with fresh cabbage and tinned fruit, a bottle of wine, Italian cigars, German cigarettes and a bar of chocolate.

Monday, 16 November

Michael Laycock returned to the unit from hospital. He came with good news about Derrick Warwick, although Stephen Mitchell has been evacuated even further back. Before lunch he and I went on a recce to find a shooting area, but we were unsuccessful. There are too many people about. Like a good many other people my stomach is out of order.

Now that Division HQ (G Branch) have not much to do they suddenly realized that the camouflage officer (Keith Douglas) was missing. Having gone through the battle he had quite made up his mind never to return to Division. Having discovered what had happened, the G1 at Division was somewhat narked that Keith had not consulted him, and complained to the CO somewhat bitterly at his actions. The CO made Keith go and apologize, which he did tonight, but returned with a bottle of rye whisky and also a bottle of lime!

Tuesday, 17 November

We took the tanks out for the first time since we have been here. All the troops have been made up differently and we have many new personnel, so I let each troop go out on its own. Sam Garrett and I went and watched in the 30-cwt. Jack Tyrrell came to lunch. He told us that he had heard that the division was going back to Cairo, but the brigade was going forward to Tobruk to join the New Zealanders, supported by a battery of field artillery, and that the 1st RHA would go back with the division. It would be a great blow to lose the 1st RHA.

A terrific downpour of rain in the afternoon, which literally flooded out B and C Squadrons, who have leaguered in a wadi. I was sitting in C Squadron office at this time and only just had time to remove everything from the floor before the whole place came under water. Even up on the high ground most men had their kit soaked.

Some of C Squadron's Sherman tanks, which were training in the low ground near the sea, became badly bogged and two of them are now submerged up to the turrets! I dined with Stephen Mitchell, who has just returned from hospital. Michael Gold, who has been acting C Squadron leader, arrived very late, having spent a futile four hours trying to get the tanks out, and greeted Stephen with this news! B and C Squadron offices are a mess and some of the Grants almost submarines on land, with only their pennants floating just above the water. It was really most amusing! The last wireless call B Squadron heard from C squadron was 'Come quick, we are sinking fast.' Mike Laycock went out in the CO's tank and decided to drive over an Italian's derelict car, which he did, and as a result took a wing off the tank. The CO, who is ill in bed with neuralgia, is going to write him a strong letter on the subject! Two of my squadron tanks threw tracks today.

Wednesday, 18 November

Some of the gunners from B Battery RHA (Jack Tyrrell's troop) came up and inspected our tanks in the morning. We allocated one to each tank and sent them out for a couple of hours. They expressed their appreciation and said they had enjoyed themselves.

We heard that almost certainly Division HQ will be returning to the Delta area, with the following under command: 9th Armoured Brigade, 1st RHA, 133 Light Motorized infantry. This brigade, the 8th Armoured, will have to be prepared to join the New Zealanders further up the line, together with 90th Field Artillery as their gunners – who are, in fact, the Surrey and Sussex Yeomanry – have never worked with armour. Jack Tyrrell will be a tremendous loss, and I shall hate working with anybody else.

Thursday, 19 November

A miserable cold day, with a foul wind blowing. We were to have had a TEWT with our new gunners, the Sussex Yeomanry, but we hear that when we go forward, we shall take no gunners from here, but take over gunners from 22nd Brigade, who we are to relieve.

The move, so we heard today, will be to an area south-west of Benghazi, and the tanks will go on transporters, which arrive here on the 22nd, and we move on the 23rd. A good many of the squadron are going sick, mostly with stomach trouble. Myself, I feel as if I am about to produce 14 babies and I have been kept running to and from an incredibly draughty 'rear seal' throughout the day and night, but never felt any relief.

On 22 November, Stanley was sent to hospital, and in his absence, Sam Garrett took over temporary command of A Squadron and led them across vast swathes of Libya as they followed the Panzer Armee Afrika back across Cyrenaica. They passed through Benghazi on 29 November, then Eighth Army paused as Rommel withdrew his forces back behind El Agheila, from where he had begun his first offensive 18 months earlier.

Meanwhile, the Anglo-US forces in First Army had entered Tunisia but were being checked at Longstop Hill well to the west of Tunis.

Stanley rejoined A Squadron on 15 December, having made a full recovery from what appears to have been a particularly debilitating attack of dysentery, just in time for Montgomery's renewed assault against Rommel's forces.

Tuesday, 15 December

Enemy withdrew in the night. Pushed on to Agheila. The Buffs entered the town at 09.30 and found it deserted. Major Christopherson rejoined from hospital after having to travel 1200 miles to rejoin unit. Such are our L of C.

Wednesday, 16 December

The brigade moved along the coast road towards Marble Arch, with Notts Yeomanry leading. We met no opposition and found the aerodrome at Marble Arch mined and evacuated. The whole area is stiff with mines and booby traps. Sergeant Nelson's tank struck a mine.

The fitters did excellent work and got it on the road again. B Squadron lost their flying fitters in a '99H', which went over a mine. Both killed.

Thursday, 17 December

At daybreak moved west for another 10 miles. Halted five hours for maintenance. We are outstripping our supplies. Sam Garrett and the OP did a recce over the ground five miles westwards. Moved again at 14.00 for another five miles. When we leaguered we were given to understand that we should be static for a few days, so immediately pitched our squadron tent. We shall have to wait for our supplies to catch us up.

Friday, 18 December

John Harding, divisional commander of the 7th Armoured Division, to which we are attached, visited the Regiment today. We were told that the Regiment might have to join the New Zealanders under Freyberg, now at Nofilia another 10 miles to the west. He had demanded an armoured regiment as extra support. We didn't like this idea much, as the 9th Armoured Brigade served under him in the last of the battle and complained that he made them do a TEWT during the battle – i.e. Terrible Experience Without Tactics!

Major Lawrence Biddle has now become brigade major in place of Ian Holme, who has become 2i/c of the Staffs.

Saturday, 19 December

For the moment we do not go to the NZs – it looks as if we shall be here for Xmas. Maintenance on tanks during the morning. Sports competition in the afternoon against B Squadron between tank crews, which we lost. Events included Digging in, Brewing up, Cumberland wrestling, Cockfighting, and obstacle race. I had to jockey race against Michael.

Sam Garrett went out on a recce for water and brought back a ewe lamb! We are only on ½ gallon per man per day.

Sunday, 20 December

Our new RHA battery – i.e. K Battery, 5th RHA – are a most charming crowd, especially the OP who works with A Squadron and the battery commander Major Stephen St John. I feel quite certain that we shall never get another Jack Tyrrell, but these people, with practice, we feel will combine well with us. They have worked with armour before, but have already said that they have learned more with us in a week than ever before with other armoured regiments where co-operation had not been good.

The padre gave a service at four o'clock, with his usual good sermon. After the service Donny Player congratulated the CO on his DSO and we all gave him three cheers, which he thoroughly deserved. As usual he made a charming reply.

Monday, 21 December

The regimental group moved out for a short exercise during the morning for the purpose of teaching the A/T gunners on formations and tactics. It was most instructive to us all. The 25-pounder battery fired a few rounds on an imaginary target picked up by our leading troop. They got a round down in five minutes, and effective fire within eight.

Orders came round that the brigade is to move to Nofilia.

Tuesday, 22 December

The move was cancelled again and the brigade is at eight hours' notice. Last night we ate the lamb Sam Garrett had brought back. Our squadron cook, Putman, cooked it to a turn. I have not tasted anything so good for months. Rations are improving; bread issued now. Water ration is still very small – only ½ gallon per man per day.

Wednesday, 23 December

Tanks did not go out today. General Montgomery came and presented the awards for the last battle. The Buffs, 3rd RTR and ourselves provided a guard of honour: 10 men from each squadron under command of Sam Garrett. Afterwards, Monty inspected three of our tanks and their crews. One belonged to Freddie Cooper, which he has had since the battle started and which has received at least six hits.

Thursday, 24 December

Orders came out that we move on Boxing Day. We have to clear the enemy out of Saita. At the moment the squadron has 16 Crusader tanks.

At 7 o'clock in the evening the padre arranged some carol singing at RHQ. Tim Toft played his saxophone and it was a great success. Mike Gold is going back to Cairo to collect winter clothing, etc. I don't anticipate he will be back for at least two weeks.

Friday, 25 December, Christmas Day

All the officers in the squadron went to early service at RHQ. Putman cooked us a very good breakfast afterwards: porridge, fried bread, bacon, biscuits and treacle. The CO sent a written Xmas message, one copy for each vehicle, in which he told us that this would be his third and last Christmas as CO. General Montgomery also sent all the troops an excellent Xmas message, copy of which is in the troop book.

At 11.15 we had a regimental church service. At 12.30 we had our squadron Xmas dinner. Michael Gold has somehow procured for the Regiment some turkey, pork, Christmas pudding and cake. Putman cooked this fare in our mobile squadron three-ton fitter! We formed a semi-circle of petrol tins round the back of the lorry, and the men sat on the ground using the tins as tables. The officers did the waiting. Each man had a bottle of beer and 50 cigarettes free. So, considering our location, we all did very well.

The CO visited each squadron during the meal. He wished us a happy Christmas and we gave him three cheers. The officers all had their Xmas dinners at RHQ and, with the help of 3-tonner canvas tops, we managed to erect a tent large enough to hold all. It was an excellent dinner. We each brought our own drink, which consisted of whisky and rum. We all agreed when we had finished that we had not been so full since being in the desert!

It rained hard during the night. Some managed to catch some, which improved the water situation.

Saturday, 26 December, Boxing Day

We were due to move and were at ½ an hour's notice, but the order never came through. In the evening Sam and I had a drink with Major St John and the remainder of K Battery officers. The rest of the day we stood about waiting.

Sunday, 27 December

A and C Squadrons moved across country to Matratia to pick up transporters and from there we went to meet the rest of the regiment at Nofilia. I had a bet with Bert Churchman, our tech adjutant, that on our next move no Crusader tank in the squadron would need a fitter for 10 miles. Wager: two bottles of whisky! Quite unobtainable at the moment. After going 500 yards from camp area Corporal Rush had a petrol leak. We had no more trouble for another 30 miles. How I swore. When we reached Matratia, we found that the transporters had moved on to Nofilia so we had to go all the way on tracks.

Monday, 28 December

There are mines and booby traps everywhere and the sappers have suffered heavy casualties. Moved further west. All bridges on the road are blown, which means making detours. The country looks lovely, full of tiny stocks which give off a heady smell. Spent the night just outside Sirte. Water situation much better.

Thursday, 31 December

Spent the day on maintenance. Scott, Stephen Mitchell and Ronnie Hutton came in the evening to drink in the new year, which we did with rum, whisky and gin. Ronnie told us some excellent tales.

The end of 1942 saw Eighth Army halted at the Wadi Zem Zem, some fifty miles to the west of Sirte, which had fallen on Christmas Day. The same day, Admiral Darlan had been assassinated, and was replaced by General Henri Giraud as leader in French North Africa. Elsewhere in the war, the Japanese were facing defeat by the US on the Pacific island of Guadalcanal, while on the Eastern Front, the Germans had been held on the edge of Moscow and were now facing encirclement at Stalingrad. On almost every front, the tide appeared to have turned against the Axis. Just how the Western Allies were going to go on and win the war was to be the subject of a major Anglo-US conference in January in the French Moroccan city of Casablanca.

Friday, 1 January 1943

New Year's Day! The CO, Patrick McCraith, Stephen Mitchell and I, with Stephen St John, the commander of K Battery RHA, went out on a recce to Wadi Tamet. We have heard that the Germans are holding a line from Gheddalia to the sea. They have about 98 tanks, with a quantity of petrol, and might make an attack. As a result we were duty regiment today on half an hour's notice. We looked at battle positions, with a view to protecting the infantry from a frontal or flank attack, and to prevent a swoop southwards on the part of the enemy. We went in three Jeeps. Had bully and biscuits for lunch. Stephen Mitchell ate all the cheese, which I had brought.

Saturday, 2 January

An officers' shop in the form of a 3-tonner arrived at Brigade HQ. We all went down and bought various articles of clothing. During the morning crew commanders' net on the wireless.

After lunch, Keith Douglas gave the squadron a lecture on camo usage and showed the squadron some photos taken from the air.

Young, our new MO, has been awarded the MC. He is a grand man and most popular.

Sunday, 3 January

A very rough and unpleasant day. Cold, a sand storm and rain.

Sent seven skeleton crews away to Brigade workshops to fetch tanks. We are going to be made fully up to strength, and have three Mk IIIs in reserve to travel with B1 Echelon.

The weather worsened over the next couple of days and badly affected the flow of supplies from Benghazi where the port had only just been cleared and begun to function fully again. With Eighth Army's line of communications tightly stretched, it meant fuel, rations and ammunition to the front would be affected in the coming days before Montgomery's next push towards Tripoli.

Thursday, 7 January

I went to the 4th Light Armoured Brigade HQ at 08.45 and met there a young officer from the KDGs attached to Brigade HQ as navigator. He took us westward to within three miles of the Bir Ngem Road, which is the enemy patrol line. We didn't go further as some tanks and A/T guns were trying to get across the road into an area where a quantity of enemy MET had been reported. After making a detour SE we came back to Brigade HQ. All the 'going' was excellent. Before returning at 14.00 hours we mended a puncture. Arrived back at 18.00 hours and went straight to Brigade and handed in my report to Lawrence Biddle, the brigade major.

The general impression is that the enemy are still going westwards and that all their digging in and blasting positions is bluff. We saw quite a lot of air activity. Regimental conference here in the afternoon about possibility of using Shermans in a recce role, as there is a possibility that Crusaders may not be coming into the country any more.

Friday, 8 January

We are now on a gallon of water per man per day instead of ½ gallon.

Saturday, 9 January

A Company, of the Buffs, brought their NCOs and officers over here, and with the NCOs and officers of this squadron, we discussed the use of their 'floating punch' in conjunction with the Crusaders. The punch consists of two heavy machine-guns on a range of 4000 yards and two Posan carriers. If they could bring fire to bear from a flank onto an A/T gun that is holding us up, it would be most helpful to enable us to push on.

We are gradually being made up with tanks and in a short time we should have 20 in the squadron. Each troop will each have a reserve tank, probably travelling with B1 Echelon.

Sunday, 10 January

A Company Buffs came and did a scheme with the squadron at 10.00 hours. We practised working with their 'floating punch' and worked out a scheme whereby one of the Crusaders carried up the crew of the machine-guns to a position on the flank of an enemy A/T gun. A man called Potts is the commander of the floating punch. He is actually a padre, but chose to become a regimental soldier and won the MC the other day.

During the afternoon he went to a conference at Eighth Army HQ for regimental commanders and above. The army commander, General Montgomery, disclosed his plan for the final phase of the North Africa campaign. I expect that we shall hear about it tomorrow.

Some NAAFI stores arrived today.

Monday, 11 January

A great petrol shortage at the moment so we can't take the tanks out. Spent the day in maintenance in preparation for the coming push.

All officers in the brigade down to squadron leaders attended a conference under the divisional commander, who gave a detailed plan for the coming push. The 8th Armoured is attacking in the centre across the Wadi Zem Zem. The New Zealanders, plus the Greys as their armour, are to be on our left and we'll sweep up from the south. The 22nd Armoured Brigade are to be reserve on our right. The Highland Division plus a battalion of heavy tanks are to work along the coast road to clear it as the main line of supply. The road is heavily mined, so a special detachment of sappers is to be attached. This is to be essentially a 'battle of supply' and all vehicles are to carry 10 days' rations and water on a basis of ½ a gallon per man per day.

Tuesday, 12 January

The brigade started the approach march today towards Wadi Tamet. We travelled 40 miles and the squadron arrived at our destination with 19 tanks.

Wednesday, 13 January

We lay up all day. The CO came round each squadron and told each man the details of the divisional plan. Final squadron leaders' conference at 17.00 hours. Moved off again after dark for another 20 miles, which brought us to within two miles of the Bungem road, which runs north and south and the Wadi Zem Zem.

Thursday, 14 January

The brigade moved forward, ourselves on the left, 3rd RTR in the centre, and Staffs on the right, to attack enemy positions in the wadi. We drew fire almost immediately we had crossed the road. The Germans had 88mm guns and other A/T guns very cleverly concealed in this very dry wadi, which gave them a magnificent field of fire as we came over the horizon. They also had heavy machine-gun posts in many of the sub wadis, which were most difficult to locate and most uncomfortable for crew commanders. My squadron managed to work their way down the wadis, but Keith Douglas's troop had an unpleasant time on the left flank, where the ground was very undulating. He played a game of hide-and-seek with a German tank, which was eventually knocked out by a C Squadron tank.

The enemy had every inch of the ground under fire. Stephen Mitchell took a troop of Shermans on that flank. He had his own tank knocked out and also that of John Semken. Stephen and his crew managed to get out before the tank burst into flames; John Semken also got away with slight burns.

Keith Douglas and White both had their tanks knocked out. They started to walk back to get help for their wounded crew but trod on an S mine and were both injured – White seriously so, but Keith not as bad. Our RHA OP, Stan Burroughs, who was also working on that right flank, had his tank knocked out too. All his crew were machine-gunned as they left the tank and he was very badly wounded in the leg, which he has lost. He is the only survivor of that crew.

From White's tank, Trooper Barrow and Trooper Heal managed to walk back to safety, but Corporal Levy and Trooper Deane were both wounded and stayed out until late that night, when they were picked up by Mike Laycock and Bert Churchman. They had gone out in a scout car after dark to try and find Freddie Cooper, whose tank had been knocked out. Fortunately they found him and brought him in.

I suddenly came across Major Barrie, whose battery was attached to the brigade. His OP had been killed, so he was acting OP. He came forward on my tank to try and shoot some 88mm German guns on the other side of the valley. As we moved forward we came in for a shower of HE and AP and I think he was quite pleased to leave me!

We had moved forward so far that we had become the leading regiment, but it had been a costly day for us. My squadron lost three tanks knocked out, with two officers and three ORs wounded. C Squadron had nine tanks knocked out, and B Squadron, three. Freddie Cooper and Ken Graves were both killed, which was a great blow. Freddie Cooper was such a cheery person.

Mike Laycock with part of his squadron, and also Sam Garrett and 1 Troop from A Squadron, tried to contact the New Zealanders on the left flank. They had to travel four miles to do so. Late in the evening, the Greys came up the wadi with their heavy tanks and a bit of a tank battle ensued, but I don't think we did much damage to the Hun, except that he moved during the night. We formed leaguer late that evening and I had difficulty in finding the leaguer as we had the furthest to come in. We were all very weary. The Staffs Yeomanry, and the 3rd RTR had hardly any casualties. Bill McGowan had his tank knocked out and had to spend most of the night out with a wounded man before he was rescued by the 3rd RTR.

This was a hard day for the Regiment and particularly so for John Semken, in Stanley's A Squadron. John noted in his photo journal that they had been told that 'one good punch' at Wadi Zem Zem and Rommel would not stop again before Tripoli. 'We gave him the punch,' he noted, 'but at what cost! Eleven tanks, many men and Freddie Cooper and, most bitter of all – Ken Graves! For nights afterwards I lay awake and thought of that vile day . . . My tank, in spite of its new Eye of Horus, was this time among the stricken. Frank Hilton, my driver – dead! Mac died from his burns! And Ken – Ken!' Ken Graves had been John's closest friend. He admitted his nerves were beginning to fray.

Saturday, 16 January

The enemy had gone during the night and we pushed on fast towards Sadada. In the afternoon we contacted an enemy column protected by a pretty strong rear guard of A/T guns.

In the evening we bumped up against it again, but they had had time to prepare a position, although they were rather surprised to see us so soon. Some cleverly concealed A/T guns held us up, and also some German and Italian tanks. Mike Laycock was ordered to attack from the left flank, but this was a dangerous operation, as he couldn't see what he was attacking. We were fortunate to have no casualties, but a Stuka attack did some damage to the guns behind, and some of the B Echelon lorries. During the day we travelled 70 miles and the strain is beginning to tell on the Crusaders; we are having a good deal of mechanical trouble. We all miss Jack Tyrrell, who was the gunner attached to the squadron for the Alamein battle.

We knocked out two enemy tanks during the action.

Sunday, 17 January

Moved off again early in the morning. The going is becoming increasingly difficult and we had to find our way down a most difficult escarpment. Travelled another 40 miles. Another Stuka attack.

Monday, 18 January

Before starting we spent two hours on the tanks and this was sorely needed. We had another Stuka raid during the afternoon. We heard that 17 German tanks had been knocked out on another part of the front, which put us in good cheer.

Tuesday, 19 January

Arrived at the town of Tarhuna, which we found held by the enemy.

Spent the day sitting outside and came in for a good deal of shelling. B Squadron lost Godfrey, who had a splinter from a shell right through his brain. We drew back in the evening, and the Staffs took over our part of the front. The country now is becoming more attractive, cultivated, and surrounded by the most fantastic-shaped hills.

Wednesday, 20 January

The Staffs entered Tarhuna, and we pushed on north-westwards, over most difficult ground to start with. We came across a farming settlement, flying white flags from their communal building. One fellow spoke a little English. He said that the Germans had left at 5 o'clock that morning. Today we struck the main Tarhuna–Castel Benito–Tripoli road, coming into Tripoli from the south. This road passes through a range of hills, which will have to be cleared before the tanks can get through.

I moved forward and joined the light squadron of the Staffs who were working along the road from Tarhuna. After a most difficult climb, we came to a point which gave us a magnificent view. Coming up the valley, we saw the 3rd RTR far below us being shelled by enemy guns, which we could see far up the valley in some trees. We had an OP with us and so were able to bring down fire onto the enemy guns. We could also see the road winding through the hills.

In the evening, Donny Player returned to the Regiment. Just after Christmas he went with the Long Range Desert Group to reconnoitre the front for the 7th Armoured Division. He was captured by some German armoured cars with a sergeant and taken to Army HQ where he was interviewed by some German staff officers, who had been educated at Oxford and Cambridge. They treated him exceedingly well and he messed with them. They had most interesting conversations. He has come back with a very high opinion of the discipline, turn-out and efficiency of the Germans, even when they are in retreat. He was eventually handed over to the Italians and taken to Castelvade, from where he escaped having made his Italian guard drunk with

Chianti. With the help of the Arabs, he walked for 200 miles and contacted our advancing forces. A jolly fine effort.

In the morning we killed the fatted calf to celebrate his return, having managed to obtain some Chianti, eggs and cheese from the local farmers. He seems none the worse for his experience.

Thursday, 21 January

Spent the day on maintenance. The country is most picturesque. The squadron fitter staff and the LAD have done wonderful work in keeping our Crusaders on the road.

Friday, 22 January

We moved out at 03.00 hrs. The 131st Infantry Brigade had cleared the road through the hills. It was bitterly cold when we moved. The CO led in his tank, and when we struck the road, we went flat out. Sergeant Bacon's tank broke a track, and almost went over a ravine. The 3rd RTR had been held up outside Castel Benito, which prevented further progress. The Regiment was then sent to watch the left flank against a possible German tank attack. In the evening we pushed on again. Now we are going through orchards in full bloom and cultivated land. Most of the farmers appear to have left their farms. Having to run over olive trees, fruit trees and young grape vines in a tank is rotten. It would be so much better if all wars could be fought out in the desert.

Just as it was getting dark the squadron was sent out to probe the defences of Castel Benito. I am rather glad that darkness prevented us probing too much as the next day we found a most unpleasant and cleverly concealed anti-tank ditch and many pill-boxes. The squadron did not rejoin the Regiment that night, but remained out on its own in an orchard.

Saturday, 23 January

Today Tripoli was entered by our tanks at dawn. The Jocks entered from the east and marched into the town with full pipes!

We stopped the night at a place called Suani Ben Adam. We found an Italian barracks, consisting of a white building into which we all prepared to settle ourselves. I packed my tanks comfortably into an orchard.

12

The Tebaga Gap

Churchill's Parade, Tripoli, 4 February 1943.

Sunday, 24 January 1943

SAM GARRETT AND Ian McKay went off in the Jeep on a scrounging party immediately after breakfast. The CO and squadron leaders went on a recce of the area to form a defence plan. We called in at the Greys, whom we found settled in a farmhouse quite close. On returning we found that orders had come through for an immediate move further west, as the 3rd RTR had met opposition. How we all cursed, especially as most of the tank engines were having a thorough maintenance. We moved through the village of Bianchi, where luckily we met Sam and Ian, who had had a most successful morning, and obtained the following: one lamb (alive), two dead chickens, one turkey, vegetables, cheese, and a huge cask of Chianti. At every house where they had stopped they had been given a flask of wine, so they were in tremendous spirits and Sam was wearing his hat at a most exciting angle!

They were amazed to see us on the move and soon jumped from the Jeep into their tanks. We contacted the XIth who told us that Zaila was held by the enemy with some 88s and 50mm. We had to push forward parallel to the main road through some orchards and very close country. The heavy squadrons remained behind to form a 'firm base' for us!

Sam, Mac and I went forward to do a recce on foot and we were suddenly fired on by a machine-gun, which had us flat on our faces. It was too dark to see from where it came, so we crawled back to our tanks and went back and leaguered with a troop of armoured cars whom we were supporting. We heard today that Brigadier Custance had given up the brigade and was being flown back to England. Roscoe Harvey from the 4th Light Armoured has taken his place and Erskine has got the division in place of John Harding, who has been wounded.

The Casablanca Conference ended on 24 January with the decisions made to invade Sicily following the end of the campaign in North Africa, and that only unconditional surrender by Germany would be accepted. There would be no armistice and no deals.

Monday, 25 January

Rejoined Regiment after much difficulty and pushed westward. The Buffs were attacking along the road. In the afternoon we came in for some shelling.

Tuesday, 26 January

During the night the enemy had evacuated Garman but had held Gabbatha. We had to try and work round the left flank. The going was exceedingly difficult, and the CO and C Squadron became detached from B and A Squadrons who were leading. In the end, I had to go myself to find them. On the way my tank broke down so I had to walk the rest of the way, much to the amusement of Stephen, who was watching me through glasses. The squadron had so many breakdowns that I only had three tanks. Mike Laycock did some useful shelling from the left flank on to enemy gun positions, but they were most difficult to see owing to the very enclosed country.

The CO sent me out with an OP from the 6-pounder plus two Shermans to find the railway and to discover exactly where we were. I discovered from a farmer that the Germans had left that area at 10 o'clock that morning. At 5 o'clock that evening a battalion of the 23rd Armoured Brigade relieved the Regiment and we came back about 10 miles to leaguer.

Wednesday, 27 January

A day of rest and maintenance and cleaning up. We are in quite a pleasant spot among some trees and near a farm.

Thursday, 28 January

The LAD have condemned six out of the remaining nine Crusaders in the squadron so they will be evacuated. Another day of cleaning up.

Friday, 29 January

Our new divisional commander, General Erskine, paid his first visit to the Regiment. Unfortunately, the colonel and Donny were out and they took half an hour to find Stephen. The general was rather annoyed by this time and when Stephen did turn up he got the full blast of the general's rocket, who said there was far too much of a peacetime atmosphere. He reminded us that although we had been relieved we were still in reserve.

All our squadron mess tents have to come down and lean-tos

against 3-tonners put up instead. RHQ have moved into a stable lent by the farmer, who has also lent some furniture and an aspidistra!

Sunday, 31 January

How pleasant this is after the desert. Excellent rations, ample water, trees and fields and sunshine. It's been a most glorious day. Four of my tanks were evacuated to workshops, three more have been condemned and that only leaves me two here.

A conference with Donny Player at midday about the reorganization of squadrons. All B Echelon drivers are to be transferred to HQ Squadron under Roger Nelthorpe. Donny and Mike Gold went out shooting with the Italian farmer. He is a racing motorist and the biggest stiff to look at that you have ever seen, but he has a good heart. He turned up for shooting in a complete white suit of plus-fours.

Monday, 1 February

Steve Mitchell received a parcel from home, marked 'Contents Books and Tonic'. Why his father should have sent him 'Tonic' was quite beyond his comprehension. However, on opening the parcel the mystery was solved, for instead of tonic we found two half-bottles of Veuve Clicquot Champagne! He called on Sam and me to come and share it with him, which we did with alacrity.

Wednesday, 3 February

The CO went into Tripoli to see the rehearsal of the victory ceremonial parade and march-past. From the Regiment, we are sending 10 men. He came back full of enthusiasm and told us that everything was most impressive and beautifully laid on. Most of the Highland Division wore kilts and as each battalion went past the saluting base they played their own march on the pipes. All the streets were lined with tanks shoulder to shoulder. The PM's attendance tomorrow was a greatly guarded secret, and the CO was sworn to secrecy as nobody knew about it. As soon as the CO arrived back here, the Italian who owns the farm came up and asked the colonel whether it was true that Mr Churchill was to attend the parade tomorrow! So much for security.

The CO was telling Myles Hildyard about this when suddenly Randolph Churchill appeared in a Jeep to see the colonel. He could only stay a short time but he was quite interesting. He told us that the Germans had 300,000 men in Tunisia, which gave us rather a shock! The Soviet success had not been exaggerated: two and a half million Germans had been killed by the Russians. He was with his father for the conference with Roosevelt at Casablanca and spoke to some American Army commanders. They had made many mistakes, had lost heavily in tanks but had learned a great deal from their mistakes. They had rather underestimated the German 88mm gun and had suffered accordingly. Their air force was doing extremely well. On one occasion they got a mixed squadron of Honeys, Grants and Shermans bogged completely. All the crews baled out and made rather a quick exit in Jeeps! A British officer who was present accused them of rank cowardice in the face of the enemy as all their tanks were captured by Germans in thin-skinned vehicles! In a strong American accent, an American officer answered, 'These lads are good guys, but I figure they are a little bit frightened that's all!'

He was a little surprised to hear that we had had so many tank casualties, being under the impression that the infantry had borne the brunt of the attack. He finished off by telling us that Eighth Army would probably have to take Tunisia, to which we gave him an appropriate reply.

Saturday, 6 February

Mike Laycock and I took 22 men into Tripoli to play a game of football. Mike and I had a look around the town, which we decided was completely and utterly dead-beat! All the shops are shut and it's quite impossible to buy a single thing. However, Donny Player had told us that you could obtain a meal at one small café called Café Roma. After a long search, we managed to find the place in a dingy square full of Arab buses. But inside it was really quite comfortable and we had quite a good lunch – rice with tomato soup, followed by tinned tuna and lettuce and a little cheese. We each drank a small bottle of Chianti. This cost us 4s each and we paid out with British military money notes, which have just been issued. After lunch we had a look at the cathedral, which was most impressive and not damaged at all. A good many buildings along the sea front have been damaged. There appeared to be a great many troops in Tripoli, mostly Highland Division, but the general standard of turn-out was deplorable. All the men found the place equally dull. It will take some time before they get the place going.

Tuesday, 9 February

The army commander addressed the majority of XXX Corps officers in the main theatre of Tripoli. He spoke of the enemy positions on all fronts, then about Eighth Army and finally about the future. He was full of praise for Eighth Army especially the 7th Armoured Division, and told us how pleased the PM had been and what he had said to him when he visited us here in Tripoli. There was no mention about going home, and it looks as if Eighth Army will help to take Tunisia, where there are the remnants of Rommel's army and the 5th Panzer Army facing the Americans. He told us that the attack on Tunis would be co-ordinated with the other armies coming the other way and that all forces would be under the command of General Eisenhower, much as the air force on both sides would be commanded by an air general who had been specially appointed.

Thursday, 11 February

In the afternoon a rehearsal at the theatre in Tripoli for the demonstration which the 3rd RTR and ourselves are putting on for the army command. It's a grand little theatre; some of the stalls have been taken out, and a sand table made on the floor. We do all the speaking on the stage behind. I gather that some rather important people are going to be there.

Friday, 12 February

At 4 o'clock in the afternoon the corps commander came to see the show and to criticize. At the end he told the CO that he was thrilled with it and gave us to understand that we should have some very important visitors to see the demonstration on the day. I rather expect that Eisenhower and some other Americans from the other end will be there.

We have had continuous rain and gales for the last 24 hours. Last night the tent in which Mike and I are sleeping blew down in the wind. After a great deal of trouble, and getting very wet in the process, we managed to move our things from under the very damp tent into the half-finished hut, which we are building. Sam Garrett was very pleased with himself as he didn't trust the weather and dug himself a hole in the ground and covered it with a ground sheet and kept himself perfectly dry. Rather a disturbed night. No mail for a very long time. Damn it.

Sunday, 14 February

Spent the day in Tripoli at the theatre where we had the dress rehearsal for our demonstration. We brought all our crew commanders to watch the demonstration. They were all very intrigued. We took our lunch with us and had it in the theatre – bully, biscuits, tinned fruit and dates.

Monday, 15 February

An early start today for Tripoli. The army commander addressed all the generals who have come to see our demonstrations on the campaign from Alamein to Tripoli. General Paget, OC Home Forces, and five other generals have come out from England. Six American generals have come from First Army, and a great many other generals from the ME. The army commander was excellent. General Frisby continued after lunch. I had never seen him before. The first part of his lecture was dull but it improved. Frank Bowler of the Greys was sitting next to me. They were attached to the New Zealanders on all their outflanking sweeps. He didn't quite agree with all that Frisby said. He made an amusing observation at the end about the army commander's dress, pointing out that he was wearing New Zealand battledress and a New Zealand sweater. General Monty confirmed this and added that he was even wearing NZ underclothes.

While Montgomery was regrouping his forces at Tripoli, he decided to hold a conference of Allied commanders at which they could share experience and lessons from the recent fighting. It was not a bad idea and reflective of the way in which the Allies were trying constantly to improve their fighting ability. The turn-out at Tripoli was impressive – among the six American generals mentioned by Stanley were Walter Bedell-Smith, chief of staff to General Eisenhower, the American Allied Supreme Commander in the Mediterranean, and George S. Patton, who would shortly take over command of US II Corps in Tunisia. General Alexander and Air Marshal Tedder, C-in-C of all Allied Mediterranean Air Forces, also attended.

Tuesday, 16 February

The Highland Division put on their demonstration during the morning. This was very well done and most interesting. I sat next to Henri Le Grand. Since he left our regiment he has been attached to the 6th RTR and the 10th Hussars and has been right through the battle and has been awarded the DSO and I should think thoroughly deserved. He is a most capable, charming and brave man.

After lunch the 8th Armoured Brigade put on their demonstration and we used the stage. The CO, three squadron leaders and three troop leaders of the Light Squadron went on the stage sitting in dummy tanks. Pete Pitman, CO of the 3rd RTR, conducted the models on the sand table, giving explanations where necessary. Pitman was quite excellent all the way through, especially in his summing up. The CO also made a very good introductory speech. The army commander told Pete that he had never seen a better demonstration and the Americans were very impressed. There is no doubt at all that ours was quite the best and that opinion was quite universal. During the interval one of the American generals came up to Mike Gold who came to watch and said, 'Lee,' and held out his hand, to which Mike replied, 'Gold,' and grasped the outstretched hand and a long conversation followed. These American fellas are most charming and only too willing to converse with even captains and lieutenants. Somehow our generals, especially the ones from England, did not seem to make any effort to talk to the Americans, anyhow during the demonstrations.

After our show they had a period for asking questions. I thought this would be most interesting, but only one question was asked, and that by General Gamble. He pointed out, in a most pompous manner, that he didn't agree with the Armoured Brigade Group organization at all. Monty soon squashed him by saying that he would deal with that in his final summing up! And that was the only question that Monty allowed. He then spoke of the very close co-operation which existed between the air force and the army and then asked Air Vice Marshal Coningham to address us. I was extremely impressed by him as a man and by what he said. He confirmed that the Air HQ and Army HQ should work together in the field and that during this last campaign they had been beyond mere co-operation, but intimate. The army had cleared advanced landing grounds of mines and had helped in every possible way during the advance, and the RAF, among many other things, had flown back to Cairo over 5000 casualties. He stressed the necessity of the air force and the army being two separate bodies, as they were both so technical now, and told the Americans that he did not agree with their organization, which combined both army and air force. He told us that he had just been home, where unfortunately such a happy state of affairs did not exist, and the reason for this was that since the first day of the war the RAF had been at war, while the army had been merely training. How very true. Likewise with First Army, greater co-operation was needed. He is leaving the ME to command our air force with First Army. I was tremendously impressed with him.

'Mary' Coningham had been honing his thoughts about tactical, or close, air support since the previous summer when the Desert Air Force had saved Eighth Army during the retreat from Tobruk. 'The doctrine that we have evolved by trial in war over a period of many months,' he told his audience at Tripoli, 'could, I think, be stated in its simplest form as follows: the Soldier commands the land forces, the Airman commands the air forces; both commanders work together and operate their respective forces in accordance with a combined Army-Air plan, the whole operations being directed by the Army Commander.'

Wednesday, 17 February

Today the REs gave the final demonstration of Eighth Army before the visiting generals. This was held out of doors and showed them the various skills of mine lifting and clearing of booby traps, etc., both by hand and mechanical, i.e., Scorpions, etc. Very well done and impressive. They held it after lunch.

Before leaving, Sam Garrett and I had a talk with a brigadier from First Army (I think the 6th Armoured Division). He showed us a picture of a German Mk VI, with the 88mm gun, which one of his regiments had knocked out. We had a most interesting talk with him, about their equipment and tactics. I wish he could have come and lectured to the squadron.

Eric Sanders and Henri Le Grand came to dinner. They are both at Army HQ. A most interesting conversation with Henri about indirect shooting with AP on the Sherman, by ranging first with HE. He tried it with considerable success while attached to the 10th Hussars during this last battle. Tremendous possibilities.

The Panzer Mk VI Stanley mentions became better known as the Tiger. At nearly 60 tons, it was huge and had very thick armour and the high-velocity 88mm gun. However, it used vast amounts of fuel, was incredibly over-engineered, and only 1347 were ever built. The continued determination of the Sherwood Rangers and Eighth Army as a whole is impressive and perhaps runs counter to popular perception of Allied, and particularly British, troops in the war.

Friday, 19 February

A conference was held under the leadership of Major Player on the formation of the new recce troop. A great deal of discussion ensued as in all probability we shall have to operate in enclosed country. The CO is very keen that Sam Garrett should train and command the new Recce Troop. He himself is very much against this as he fought all the last battle as 2i/c to me, and I can ill afford at the moment to lose him as 2i/c. I hope that Patrick McCraith will get command in the end.

My syndicate proposed that the Recce Troop should be made up entirely of Jeeps, especially for enclosed country. To my mind their mobility and speed outweighs their extreme vulnerability. I understand, however, that each regiment is being equipped with 10 armoured cars to form the basis of a recce troop, and these to my mind in enclosed country where it is impossible to get off a mined road will be useless.

Wednesday, 24 February

The Recce Troop is being formed again under Patrick McCraith, and I am having to give up Sergeant Bartle, Corporal Hindson, Troopers Shewell, Sparham, Bennett and Corporal Stuart, which is making somewhat of a dent in my squadron strength. The squadron has received no reinforcements since the Battle of Alamein and I have made up casualties by using members of the old Recce Troop who for some time past have had no vehicles.

Sergeant Thompson of C Squadron returned to the Regiment

today, having left about a year ago to go to a RAC OCTU in England. He has been posted to B Squadron. Before leaving he called at Michael Laycock's home and brought out for him a large box of cigars (one of which I smoked after dinner, truly excellent) and a large tin of his favourite mixture of tobacco, which is very black in colour and to me smells exactly like high-class Royal Mews.

Thursday, 25 February

Lieutenant Thompson gave a very excellent lecture to both A and B Squadrons about his trip to England, bombing, rations, clothing and amusements, etc. It was all most interesting and he put it over very well.

Sergeant Bacon has put in an application for a commission, which I am sending to the commanding officer. A great many of our best NCOs have left the Regiment to get commissions and they will be difficult to replace. However, one can't stand in the way of promotion.

The days now are becoming extraordinarily warm and we all hope that the Tunisian battle will be finished before the summer begins because another desert fight in the summer is not a very delectable prospect. It will be most interesting to see whether any of us get home after Tunis has fallen.

The army issued an order yesterday that the clocks should be put back one hour, but this only reached the Regiment at midnight last night so we all missed the extra hour in bed.

Being commissioned from the ranks was increasingly common during the war, even though it had been unthinkable in the pre-war Yeomanry. It was recognized that experience was vital, and that this experience often led to the development of authority. The increasingly battle-hardened Sherwood Rangers understood that their officers needed to be the best men they could get, whatever their class and background.

Friday, 26 February

Trooper Rose of B Squadron has just returned from hospital in Tripoli, where he had a German prisoner in the next bed, who told him that our air raids on Berlin had been devastating and that he himself had lost his mother, father and two sisters.

Prepare to move tomorrow.

Air Marshal Harris, commander-in-chief of RAF Bomber Command, had received a new directive agreed at the Casablanca Conference: 'Your prime objective will be the progressive destruction and dislocation of the German military, industrial and economic system, and the undermining of the morale of the German people to a point where their capacity for armed resistance is fatally weakened.' Harris had spent the best part of a year in the job building up his heavy bomber force and improving targeting technology, and now, with the US Eighth Air Force also building strength within the UK, was about to launch his first all-out bombing offensive against Germany at the beginning of March.

Saturday, 27 February

The Regiment moved by RASC lorries to Ben Gardane. There is every sign that Rommel is going to attack Eighth Army and it looks as though we are being rushed up to meet such an attack. I understand that we are going to take over the tanks from the 2nd Armoured Brigade.

We are now stationed in an olive grove quite close to the sea, which is a great contrast to the barren desert country from which we moved.

The Sherwood Rangers were moving up towards the Mareth Line, a defensive position that protected the southern Tunisian border. First Army had not reached Tunis and, rather, had suffered a number of setbacks. The US II Corps had received a bloody nose by a typically swift and dynamic counter-attack by Rommel, while in the north of the

country General von Arnim had arrived with substantial reinforcements
– Hitler was determined to fight on in North Africa for as long as
possible, fully aware that defeat would most probably hasten Italy's exit
from the war and then expose the Reich's southern flanks. Now, with
First Army subdued, Rommel turned back to face Eighth Army and
prepared for a counter-attack at Medenine.

Recognizing that Tunisia had not been going as well for the
Allies as had been hoped, Eisenhower had been made Supreme Allied
Commander in the Mediterranean at the Casablanca Conference,
while Alexander had relinquished his Middle East post and had been
appointed commander of the newly formed 18th Army Group, the first
such combination of Allied armies in the war. After touring the front, one
of his first decisions was to set up battle schools for the inexperienced US
troops, where they could train with live ammunition and learn modern
tactics and techniques. General Patton also took over command of US II
Corps.

Monday, 1 March

Warning order to move came through and this was followed by a
squadron leaders' conference at 10.30 in the morning. At this conference the CO told us he was leaving to become second-in-command to
the 8th Armoured Brigade and that Donny Player would succeed him
as colonel. Michael will become 2 i/c, and Basil Ringrose would take
over B Squadron from Michael Laycock.

It was a compliment to the Yeomanry that a 'Regular' soldier
should not come in to command the Regiment. Although it is not
really surprising as ever since the Battle of Alamein the Yeomanry tank
regiments and ex-cavalry regiments appear to have done so very much
better than the RTR.

We had a mobile cinema in the area, the first we have seen for a
very long time.

The American force approaching Tunis from the south-west have
recovered all the ground which they lost and also claimed to have
knocked out 87 enemy tanks.

Tuesday, 2 March

Today this brigade took over all the tanks from 2nd Armoured Brigade. This is the second time they have had to hand over new tanks to us within a very short time. We have now christened them the Tank Delivery Brigade, who ferry tanks for the Notts Yeomanry.

We moved off at midday on a track across country to Ben Gardane. We ran into some salt marshes and, after getting some transporters thoroughly stuck, we had to turn about and continue the journey on the main road. Sam Garrett and I went off in a Jeep to discover the regimental area at Ben Gardane. The rest of the party did not arrive until 04.00 the next morning and as a result we had very little sleep. The squadron cooks and technical store got hopelessly bogged, with half the echelon, and are still there now.

The Germans had been shelling Ben Gardane, especially the aerodrome, where they did a certain amount of damage with a pretty big gun, which it was reckoned was positioned 17 miles away.

Wednesday, 3 March

We have some new gunners attached to the brigade, the 111th Field Artillery, who have been attached to the 22nd Armoured Brigade. The battery commander is Captain Mark Strutt, with whom I was at Winchester. When they first came out here history relates that, on being ordered to march for 10 miles on a bearing of 60°, they marched for 60 miles on a bearing of 10°.

We hear General Montgomery appreciates that Rommel has been told to prevent Eighth Army reaching Tunis at all costs for the summer and so avoid an invasion of the continent from Africa this summer, and that is why he is expecting an attack here at any time.

Thursday, 4 March

The Regiment took up battle positions facing north-west towards the mountains. We are being held in mobile reserve to move to certain positions in the event of attacks from different directions. Squadron leaders and the attached battery and infantry commanders recced these positions today.

At this time of year the country here is covered with most attractive wild flowers, much more spectacular than most parts of Palestine. They include Michaelmas daisies, aubretias, wild stocks, mignonette and many others to which I cannot give a name. RHQ have placed themselves in a small, very old olive grove surrounded by green banks covered with these wild flowers.

Friday, 5 March

I was coming back with Stephen riding in my tank when the adjutant rang me up on the air and told me that Stephen Mitchell had been awarded the MC. We were all exceedingly pleased to hear about this, which he has so thoroughly deserved, and we hope to get him equally thoroughly tight tonight.

From air reports it appears that the Germans are going to attack from the north. There has been a great deal of air activity and German planes have been much in evidence. Yesterday we brought down four but I am afraid we saw a Spitfire shot down very close to us.

Saturday, 6 March

This morning early the Germans attacked with infantry and with a hundred tanks towards the town of Medenine. We moved off early to take up battle positions and sent out our new gunner OP with Sergeant McCann and his troop as protection. The OP had a most excellent shoot at some infantry advancing over open country and had satisfactory results. Mark Strutt also went out and conducted the troop.

The army commander issued yet another order of the day, which I understand he had written 10 days ago, telling us that the Germans were obliging us by attacking Eighth Army, which is exactly what he wanted.

Sunday, 7 March

At dawn we broke leaguer and I sent out Sam Garrett with half the squadron plus the gunner OP to their positions of yesterday. We found that the Germans had withdrawn into the hills and examined the damage we did yesterday. They got one prisoner, who turned out to be a Pole, but in appearance looked to be the usual blond, well-made, thick-necked German. He was brought back to RHQ where Myles Hildyard, our adjutant, interviewed him. He spoke very freely and told us the following: after Poland had been captured he had been forced to fight for the Germans and that was why he gave himself up to us. Moreover, now he was willing to fight for us. He had disliked the idea of fighting against Eighth Army, and finally that, on the day before the German attack, on a battalion parade they had been told by their commanding officer that unless this attack was successful and that they captured the village of Mettamour and the high ground on which we were actually stationed, the North Africa campaign as far as the Germans are concerned was lost. If this was true it was very interesting. He was then taken off to Brigade for further interrogation. He was certainly very bomb happy and whenever anything fell in the vicinity he would go to ground like a rabbit.

Sam also brought back a black pair of Panzer trousers and a blue pair of Canadian bathing drawers, size 34, I suppose captured from the Americans. The first he gave to the CO and the second to Donny Player. He found also a German textbook on the American Army with some very good illustrations of American tanks and equipment.

As a result of the German tank attack the enemy lost 52 tanks, and all the credit goes to the anti-tank gunners (infantry), who did the greatest part of the damage. He appears to have put in his tank attack without previous recce, and as a result suffered the obvious tank casualties. This only goes to prove once again that the anti-tank gun will always beat the tank, especially in country like this when the gunner can wait until the tank approaches to within 500 to 600 yards. This German attack has certainly cost Rommel a great deal of blood from his nose.

Stanley was absolutely right in his assessment of Rommel's counter-attack at Medenine. Falling into the trap of an anti-tank screen used to be a habit of Eighth Army – and was what had happened to the Rangers in their first tank action at Alam Halfa. The tables were turning. Three days later, on 9 March, Rommel, by now a sick man, flew back to Germany, leaving North Africa for the last time.

Monday, 8 March

The Germans have withdrawn into the hills and appear to be regrouping, according to the BBC, for another attack, but I hardly think it likely and my own appreciation is that we shall do the attacking next.

We moved back to our old area. During the afternoon the CO and the colonel of the gunners and infantry attached to the Regiment, plus squadron leaders, went and had a look at the battlefield. We found four German tanks that had been knocked out by our anti-tank gunners and followed their approach along a wide wadi. Our gunners had let them go past and shot at them broadside. They were all Mk III Specials. We then held a discussion how the Light Squadron would have operated on that piece of ground and against similar opposition. I am perfectly convinced that, in this kind of country, if recce is to be thorough and close a certain amount must be done on foot, with the aid of the Recce Troop or carriers, otherwise the leading tank will be cat's meat every single time.

Wednesday, 10 March

The whole morning was spent on maintenance and, according to the fitters' report, the drivers had worked extraordinarily well.

At 16.15 hours the colonel called a regimental parade in order to say goodbye on relinquishing command of the Regiment to become second-in-command to the brigade. As usual, he made a very well-thought-out speech, pointing out that he handed over command of the Regiment to Major Player, who had seen longer service in the

Yeomanry than anybody else in the Regiment. Donny Player followed with a short speech pointing out that it was entirely due to the tact and initiative of the colonel that we had been one of the first Yeomanry regiments to be made up into an armoured brigade. This was all the more creditable, remembering that at one time the Regiment, while coastal gunners, were operating in four different places, namely Tobruk, Benghazi, Cyprus and Crete. They both pointed out that, in spite of everything, we were recognized universally as one of the best armoured regiments in the British Army, and personally, I do not consider this an exaggeration.

I came on parade with corduroy trousers and none of my officers had belts on, and for this, a slight rocket arrived from our new colonel that evening, with which I quite agreed.

While troops would have been expected to smarten up for parade, attitudes to dress had relaxed considerably, as it was recognized that comfort and pragmatism were more important. In many ways, the change of attitude was led by Montgomery, who made a virtue of wearing corduroys, sweaters and a black beret, only just coming into wider use, rather than the more usual formality expected from senior commanders.

Thursday, 11 March

The squadron went out shooting on the range in preparation for a brigade shooting competition, which we hope to have before the next battle commences. Each regiment will have to produce one heavy and one light group for the competition. It will be extraordinarily difficult to decide as they all shot so well today. The brigade commander and the colonel came and watched the shooting. The colonel was wearing red on his cap for the first time and when Sam Garrett saluted him he concluded by remarking that he was pleased to notice 'that the colonel was wearing pink'. To this came the reply, 'Don't pull my leg, blast you.'

Saturday, 13 March

Brigade shooting competition. C Squadron won the Heavy Tank competition and the Light Squadron of the Staffs Yeomanry won the Crusader competition. The brigadier presented two lambs as prizes.

Sunday, 14 March

We started our movement to join the New Zealanders in 'Left Hook'. A great deal of deception will be needed and this will mean a lot of night travel. The first part of the journey will be done on transporters. At 10.00 hours, Donny Player went through all the formations with models on a sand table with the Buffs and the Gunners who are to be attached to the Regiment for this operation. We left the area at 12 o'clock, travelled 14 miles on tracks and mounted transporters at 14.00 hours, which we met along the main road. Sergeant Harding unfortunately went over a mine, which knocked out his tank. Fortunately, nobody was injured in the tank. We travelled all through the night on transporters and Michael Laycock was in charge of the transporter party.

The 'left hook' that Stanley mentions was an extraordinarily audacious plan to carry out a 250-mile march around the desert flank of the Matmata Hills and then to burst through a gap in the mountains at Tebaga in southern Tunisia. The idea was for a two-fisted attack – one through the Tebaga Gap and the other an assault on the main defences at the Mareth Line.

Monday, 15 March

We halted at 04.15 hours and started again at midday. The going was extremely bad in places and at times we had to offload the tanks and a certain amount of winching was necessary. Our general direction was north.

Tuesday, 16 March

We arrived to a point south of Foum Tataouine at 03.30 hours. For the last few days we have had very little sleep. We stayed in this location all the day.

Wednesday, 17 March

We lay up all during the day and hoped that our presence had not been located by enemy aircraft. At 7 o'clock in the evening we proceeded to the assembly area through the hills along a lighted track. A heavy shower of rain kept the dust down, which otherwise would have made visibility extremely difficult. We arrived at the assembly area at 12 o'clock at night, where we were met by the Recce Troop who had preceded us and who showed us our various areas.

Thursday, 18 March

Donny Player had a conference and explained the plan. Our Left Hook is to coincide with the main attack on the Mareth positions and we hope to be able to put a major portion of the German forces in the bag. Donny Player now has taken over command of the Regiment and Flash Kellett has become second-in-command of the brigade.

Flash Kellett took Sam Garrett and myself to see the New Zealand Gunner brigadier. The squadron may be required to give right flank protection to the New Zealand guns while on the move.

The New Zealanders had a sand table demonstration of the forthcoming operations, but Sam and I did not get there to attend.

Friday, 19 March

We had a lecture from the member of the LRDG who had done a recce of enemy territory around Tunis and Sousse. He gave us an idea of the going we are likely to meet. This was followed by a lecture to the

Regiment from Mark Strutt, who is the battery commander of the gunners attached to the Regiment. We are trying to work out a plan for the leading Crusaders to conduct a shoot with the 25-pounders in the event of the OP not being available.

The brigade moved off at 18.00 hours and travelled for 30 miles. We reached our destination at 22.00 hours with no tank having fallen out through mechanical trouble. It was a beautiful moonlit night.

Saturday, 20 March

Continued the advance at 07.00 hours in a northerly direction, with the brigade moving in formation A. The 3rd RTR on the left, Staffs Yeomanry in the centre and ourselves on the right. We met slight enemy opposition, which we managed to brush aside. The Staffs lost one Crusader, which was giving chase to an enemy lorry, which had a 50mm gun inside and this caused the damage. We covered 50 miles during the day.

Sunday, 21 March

Contacted the main enemy position, which was protected by a wide minefield. It was Donny Player's first day of battle and he commanded the Regiment extremely well. Sergeant Dring was operating on the right flank and did some good work in extricating some carriers belonging to the Buffs that had gone forward to probe the enemy front.

The New Zealanders attacked during the night and cleared a passage through the minefield.

There was later some criticism directed at General Freyberg, the New Zealand Corps commander, for not pushing 8th Armoured Brigade on through that night and securing a quick breakthrough. Some years later, in 1972, Stanley returned to the scene during a staff ride (exercise over past battlefields) with the army, and was asked his opinion on this.

'I pointed out that at the time,' Stanley noted, 'I was just a squadron leader, and the problem was not mine. However, on looking back, General Freyberg must have appreciated that the 8th Armoured Brigade was weary and short of sleep after the "Left Hook" forced march, also that the brigade was not up to full strength and that a night attack by tanks over unknown ground and a possible minefield against unknown enemy strength was a great risk to take. Furthermore, and even more important, at that time he had no other armoured reserve. In my humble opinion, he took the right decision.'

Monday, 22 March

We pushed through the gap in the minefield early in the morning. The enemy had command of the high ground where they had established OPs and the shelling was extremely unpleasant, not only for ourselves but even more for the echelons and the gun positions in the rear. The enemy held wonderful observation posts. As we crossed a certain road, the squadron knocked out a 50mm gun and captured some German and Italian prisoners. We pushed on and took up position on some high ground on the left of our axis. We did a certain amount of stalking on foot as we did not want to expose the tanks. There was, however, an enemy tank on the other side of the ridge whose crew commander must have decided to do a similar stalk. As a result we both came face to face, had a quick look and beat a somewhat hasty and undignified retreat back to our respective tanks. As I rather anticipated, it was a Mk IV Special and as I was only in a Close Support I didn't feel a great deal of enthusiasm to give battle. Sergeant Butler, who was operating on my left, poked the nose of his tank over the ridge and received a direct hit on his gun. Nobody was injured. However, we had to evacuate the tank. Neville Fearn, who was operating on the right, received a direct hit on his tank by a German 88mm AP and almost immediately afterwards he received a direct hit on the back of his tank from a 75mm off one of the tanks of our friends on the right, who mistook him for a German tank. Fortunately none of his crew were injured but the tank had to be evacuated. Corporal Hill, working along the road, came under extremely heavy shellfire and his tank was put out by HE. Unfortunately we couldn't do anything about it and he spent the remainder of the day in the tank under fire.

Much later, Stanley mentioned this episode to his son, David. It seems that he had clambered out of his tank for the 'stalk' that he writes about in the diary, but had forgotten his pistol. When he came face to face with the German tank commander, he reached for his sidearm only to realize with horror what he had done. By great good fortune, the German had apparently done exactly the same.

Colonel Flash Kellett was killed by a shell, which burst very close to his tank. It must have been instantaneous, but it has been a very great blow to us all.

We were shelled during the night in leaguer, but fortunately suffered no casualties. We did not make much progress during the day and we were rather of the opinion that we should have to fight for the positions we held.

It appears Flash Kellett had been killed while shaving in the turret of his tank. Although he was no longer commanding the Sherwood Rangers, his loss was keenly felt. Although originally from the Irish Guards, he had joined the SRY in 1930 and later became Member of Parliament for Aston in Birmingham. Not only was he one of the mainstays of the pre-war Regiment, but had guided it from its deployment overseas, through its time as artillery, its conversion to an armoured regiment and its transition into one of the leading tank units in Eighth Army. He is buried in Sfax War Cemetery.

Tuesday, 23 March

We managed to push forward a little distance in the afternoon. In the evening Stephen Mitchell had to do a left flank attack with his squadron on an enemy position. It was a most unpleasant operation for him as the light was bad and the ground extremely difficult. John

Walters upturned his tank in a wadi and had to leave it there for the night. We did not form leaguer until after dark, and as the Regiment was scattered over a large area, we had the greatest difficulty in getting in. I eventually got down to bed at 1 o'clock, but as we had to get up again at 5, we were all very short of sleep.

Wednesday, 24 March

A very unpleasant day. The 3rd RTR put in a tank attack on the same position as Stephen had attacked last night. We were ready to support them on the left with one heavy squadron. Donny Player then ordered my squadron to go and thicken up their fire power with my 6-pounder tanks. To reach them, I had to cover a large expanse of open ground. I decided to go as fast as the tanks would travel and as a result, thanks to the sandy ground, we kicked up such a dust that we presented a very small target. What with the shellfire and the fading light and the dust spread up by the movement of tanks, visibility was absolutely nil. The 3rd RTR had one tank knocked out, which brewed up.

The co-operation with the air force has been most excellent and we were able to point out to them the exact location of enemy tanks. As a result our Tank Busters knocked out six enemy tanks. We had orders to remain for the night in our present location. One Company of Buffs came to join us and the company commander did a recce in a Jeep and wandered into a German leaguer not more than 500 yards away. His arrival rather disturbed their rest and they opened up on us with machine-guns and mortars. There was very little sleep for us that night.

Thursday, 25 March

We remained in more or less the same position all day without being able to move forward. The New Zealand infantry came up at 4 o'clock and took over the position. We captured one Austrian prisoner but we couldn't get much out of him as he was slightly barmy from lack of sleep and water. The whole brigade moved back in preparation for the attack next day. We understand that the whole brigade would attack in line, preceded by a very heavy barrage and followed by the New Zealand infantry. We don't much like the idea of being used as 'I' tanks, but this position has got to be broken. We have heard that the attack on Mareth has not proved a great success.

Eighth Army's assault on the Mareth Line had begun on 20 March by General Oliver Leese's XXX Corps. It was a strong position, with anti-tank ditches and huge numbers of mines and wire entanglements. Also it had been raining hard so the dried-up riverbeds around it were not quite so dry after all. Leese's attack soon floundered, hindered further by his misuse of his tanks. 'This battle's a mess,' noted General Tuker, commander of the exceptional 4th Indian Division.

Friday, 26 March

So far the squadron has lost four tanks through enemy action, i.e. since we have started on the Left Hook. As regards casualties, we have been very fortunate and have had nobody killed.

Yesterday the whole brigade withdrew and regrouped for the famous Balaclava Charge. The order was that the brigade would advance in line with the heavy tanks leading, preceded by an intense barrage. The Crusaders were to follow close behind and finally the New Zealand infantry would bring up the rear. We operated with the Maori Battalion and actually carried some of the Maori infantry on the backs of our tanks.

At 4 o'clock the brigade formed up along the line of the old Roman wall, which ran almost the whole length of the bottleneck gap through which we were to attack. The Staffs Yeomanry were on the left, the 3rd RTR were in the centre, and we were on the right. A quarter of an hour before zero hour, the RAF made devastating attacks on the enemy positions. At 4 o'clock precisely the whole movement started. It really was most spectacular and remarkable and must have presented a most formidable and frightening spectacle to the Hun. The barrage and the dust made visibility practically nil so that the tanks almost overran the enemy positions before they could be seen.

The opposition on the right was stiff, and the Staffs Yeomanry and 3rd RTR reached their final objective before we did. The final objective was indicated by the creeping barrage firing smoke when it had reached its final destination and the tanks were notified that the objective had been reached in this manner.

I have never looked forward to seeing smoke so much in my life.

Sam Garrett was killed during this attack: he was hit by a piece of shrapnel in the head and never recovered consciousness. It must have been extremely unlucky as I understand from his crew that for most of the time he was using his periscope, and he was wearing his tin hat at all times and never showed his head above the turret. Every tank had orders to fire their Besas and throw hand-grenades at any suspected position. I got rid of all my Besa rounds and hand-grenades. Ian McKay had his tank knocked out, being hit from the right flank by an 88mm gun. All the crew were uninjured except for Calvert, the driver, who was slightly wounded.

Stephen Mitchell suddenly came upon two German Mk IV Specials waiting behind the ridge. He knocked out both with a left and a right. Owing to the hold-up on the right flank the squadron got separated and I found myself with half the squadron and Michael Laycock, with a certain amount of Maori infantry in a deep wadi, held up by anti-tank guns to our front and strong enemy machine-gun positions on a high hill on our right flank. The Maoris had difficulty in capturing that height and only succeeded in doing so after a night attack. My gunner, Randall, had an extremely good shoot with the 3-inch howitzer at various targets at the top of that hill.

The Regiment had great difficulty in re-forming into leaguer after dark, and the area which the colonel eventually chose contained two German Mk IV Special tanks, which had been knocked out. One even had its engine running and was in perfect condition. It appeared the crew commander and other members of the crew had been killed by a direct hit as they had been leaving or entering the tank. The other German tank had brewed up completely.

We eventually joined up with the rest of the Regiment and finally got down to bed at 1 o'clock, all very weary after possibly one of the most spectacular, frightening and successful days of the campaign. There is no doubt that we broke through the positions and destroyed many enemy tanks and guns. Except for Sam and Calvert, this squadron suffered no other casualties, but Robin Taylor in B Squadron and another new officer were killed, and Bill McGowan and Leinster were wounded. The heavy squadrons lost four tanks. The plan was for the 1st Armoured Division to pass on through us after we had captured our objective.

Bert Jenkins, who was a tank driver in B Squadron, reckons that this was his most terrifying day of the war. 'We were all lined up,' he says, 'sixty-odd tanks only a few yards apart.' They set off behind a rolling barrage of artillery. From inside his tank, Bert could see little. 'There was a tiny little piece of glass, about nine inches by three – and that's all you ever saw.' It was also insufferably hot inside. They were carrying New Zealand infantry on their tanks, shells were landing a short distance ahead of them, aircraft were roaring overhead, enemy guns were firing, and although Bert could see almost nothing, 'you could hear it all'.

The loss of Sam Garrett was a huge personal blow to Stanley. 'Not only was he a first-class second-in-command,' noted Stanley, some years later, 'but a great personal friend.' Like Flash Kellett, Sam Garrett is buried in the Commonwealth War Cemetery at Sfax.

Saturday, 27 March

For most of the day we sat on the ground we had captured. The Germans demonstrated with their tanks and infantry and gave us the impression that they might counter-attack, but nothing came of it.

When Bill McGowan and Corporal Sadler in B Squadron were wounded, they managed to bale out of the tank but after dark crawled in what they thought was the right direction only to eventually end up in a wadi that was occupied by a German outpost position.

The German officer in charge gave them both bread and wine and carried them to positions safe from fire by both sides, and left them with a promise that later they would return to collect them. But they never did, and so they remained in no man's land until today, when they were seen and together with a carrier I collected them in my Crusader. It was rather difficult to get them onto the tank as we came under machine-gun fire from the high ground on the flank. Corporal Sadler will be all right and Bill McGowan will have a holiday for six months. He got a compound fracture of the left leg.

Stanley typically downplays his part in the rescue of Captain Bill McGowan. Having personally organized the rescue party, he led the men to McGowan, all the time under shell- and machine-gun fire and 'with complete disregard for his own personal safety'. He was awarded a Bar to his Military Cross for his actions that day and for the leadership of A Squadron in this battle. 'He had shown an utter disregard to danger and his determined leadership,' ran the citation, 'and personal example has had its full effect on those under his command. They will virtually follow him anywhere.'

Sunday, 28 March

The brigade moved forward again at 01.30 hours, all very weary as we were short of sleep. We travelled north-east for 10 miles and then turned east. We were pushing on as hard as we could in order to cut off the Germans who had evacuated the Mareth position. There can be no doubt the Left Hook was entirely responsible for ousting the Germans from the very formidable and cleverly constructed concrete defence positions of the Mareth Line. About midday we bumped an enemy rear-guard consisting of tanks, 88mm guns and 50mm guns. The Regiment claims to have destroyed one 88mm and three 50mm guns, and some of this was done by indirect shooting. The enemy shelling was extremely unpleasant and very accurate, although

Bill Sellar, Vivian Berry and Bill McGowan.

The citation for the Bar to Stanley's MC.

fortunately the Regiment suffered no casualties. Stephen Mitchell and I endeavoured to conduct an indirect AP shoot against an enemy tank 2000 yards away on a hill. Unfortunately they had pin-pointed Stephen Mitchell's position and every shot he fired brought down a shower of counter-battery stuff.

It is interesting how well informed Stanley is about what was happening at Mareth. The Axis had abandoned the Mareth Line that day, realizing that otherwise they would be cut off by the British now sweeping through the Tebaga Gap. The following day, the 51st Highland Division successfully crossed the Mareth Line but by this time the Axis forces had slipped through the Gabes Gap between the coast and the mountains to the north.

Monday, 29 March

We pushed on again at dawn and found that the rear-guard had with-drawn. However, the squadron was ordered to go on and eventually ran into, and captured, one complete Italian company. The Italian officer in charge was really a most pleasant individual who spoke English without any kind of a foreign accent. I commented on this and he informed me that he had lived many years in England and had been educated at Sherborne. He asked me where I had been educated, and when I told him he replied, 'I know many from your school but, of course, they are considerably older than you.' It came to light after-wards that he had looked after Dan Ranfurly and General Neame, who are now POWs in Italy. I sent him back to RHQ on a tank and on leaving he presented me with a magnificent pair of field glasses.

Our object is to close the Gabes Gap before the enemy can get through.

Tuesday, 30 March

We continued the advance over very difficult going. We got three tanks bogged at a certain village but after some difficulty managed to get them out. Late in the evening we were held up by enemy occupying the hills through which it will be necessary to force a gap and clear mines before we can go through.

Wednesday, 31 March

We spend the day sitting opposite the hills being heavily shelled and occasionally doing an indirect shoot on the 'Sugar Loaf', a conical-shaped hill.

I fear I shall never get anybody to replace old Sam. His death was a very grievous loss to the Regiment, the squadron and myself.

13

Victory in North Africa

Tunisia, 27 February 1943. Regimental HQ in an olive grove near the sea. Roger Nelthorpe, Donny Player, Mike Laycock and Micky Gold having lunch.

Thursday, 1 April 1943

WE REMAINED IN the same position the whole day.

The padre held a short and very impressive service in memory of Colonel Flash.

We were exposed to shelling throughout the day. One 110mm German shell landed ten yards from my tank as the squadron was passing after the service. Fortunately, the shell did not explode, which was extremely fortunate for us all. It is interesting to note that a great many of the shells, especially from the German heavy guns, fail to explode.

Friday, 2 April

The brigade handed over the area it was holding to an Indian brigade who, I understand, will put in an attack on the hills, clear the mines and make a passage for the tanks.

In the afternoon the army commander, General Montgomery, informally addressed the 8th Armoured Brigade, congratulating us on what we had done with the New Zealanders and telling us that there was still fighting before us, and hard fighting, before eventually the Germans could be driven out of North Africa.

He spoke to Donny Player after his address and, in answer to a question about the Americans' progress, he told Donny that he was very disappointed with the help he was receiving from the Americans.

In the evening Donny Player, Stephen Mitchell and myself had a bathe. The water was very cold and refreshing.

Montgomery did little to further Anglo-US relations, and his sniping at American performances on the battlefield would continue until the end of the war. It was deeply unhelpful, usually unfair, and often filtered down to the troops in much the way that Stanley describes. The truth is that the US Army had begun the war as the nineteenth largest in the world at just 188,000 strong, and in effect had had to start from scratch, much as the British Army had been forced to do following the defeat at Dunkirk and loss of France in June 1940. However, the Americans had an even smaller pool of experience and were having to learn the hard way. Like the British, they were doing so very quickly and would, in fact, prove generally more adept at learning those lessons and implementing changes than the British.

The scene was now set for the end game in North Africa and in this, the US II Corps, not to mention their contribution to the Allied air forces, would prove invaluable.

Saturday, 3 April

A day of rest and maintenance, and five new tanks arrived for the squadron. At the moment my troop leaders are: Neville Fearn, Ian McKay and Sergeant Hunt. Patrick McCraith has become second-in-command of the squadron.

Monday, 5 April

In the afternoon Donny Player gave out his final orders to squadron leaders and other commanders of the Regimental Group. The infantry are to make an attack at dawn tomorrow and we are to push through the gap.

Tuesday, 6 April

The barrage started at 4 o'clock in the morning and the infantry put in an attack along the whole front. After we had formed up all ready to go through the gap made by the infantry, we were bombed by our own bombers. Lance Corporal Smith, who had joined the squadron yesterday from hospital, was killed by a bomb that fell very close to his tank. Trooper Cook and Trooper Harmsworth were wounded by the same bomb and had to be evacuated. The infantry attack on the left had been successful but the brigade could not get through the hills as the Staffs, which was the leading regiment, were held up by heavy anti-tank fire at the exit to the pass. The Germans counter-attacked and retook some of the ground on our right flank. Three thousand Italian prisoners were taken.

This was the Battle of Wadi Akarit. After a superb outflanking manoeuvre in the mountains by the 4th Indian Division, the gap created in the line was slow to be exploited by X Corps so that, although it was a resounding victory, the opportunity to rout the mostly Italian forces there and then was missed.

Wednesday, 7 April

The Germans pulled out during the night and we followed the Staffs Yeomanry through the gap in the hills onto the plains on the other side. I saw a fox, which I chased in my tank for some considerable distance before it went to ground.

The going was extremely good and we managed to move at quick speed. As a result the squadron captured some enemy transport and some Italian prisoners, including two Italian officers. In the evening the Staffs and ourselves were attacked by approximately 30 enemy tanks consisting of Tigers, Mk IV Specials, and some captured Shermans. We held some very favourable high ground and waited for the Germans to follow up their attack. However, they did not do so and remained in hull-down positions about 2000 yards away. The fire from the Tigers, both HE and AP, was extraordinarily accurate. We had no tanks knocked out but Sergeant Dring received a very close HE shell and he himself was wounded and had to be evacuated. The brigade, less the 3rd RTR, formed up after dark and moved north until 01.00 hours in order to contact 3rd RTR, who had worked forward a good many miles on our left flank. We must have been moving parallel to the German tank force, which had made off in the same direction after dark.

Thursday, 8 April

We contacted the 3rd RTR early in the morning. We saw some enemy transport moving off along a road to our left flank and the squadron was ordered to pursue the transport at maximum speed in order to cut it off. The going was excellent so we were able to travel at the tank's maximum speed.

When the enemy transport saw us coming they split in two directions and as a result I detailed half the squadron to pursue those moving to the right and I took the remainder of the squadron to deal with those making away to the left. I had with me Patrick McCraith, Corporal Levy and Sergeant Charity, who got left behind.

As we topped a rise we came face to face with one 88mm and one 105mm, manned by German crews. It was too late to turn back and my tank was knocked out by the 88mm, not more than 150 yards from the gun. We all managed to bale out but Trooper Bielby, my driver, was wounded and had his leg broken. We managed to get him out of the tank but unfortunately he was killed by a shell from the 88mm, which landed on the far side of the tank. Sergeant Bacon, my operator, was also wounded, in the arm, but Trooper Randall and I were very fortunate and escaped injury. We managed to crawl away from the tank, our movement hidden by the smoke coming out of it.

In the meantime, Corporal Levy had charged the guns but unfortunately had struck a bank behind them and was unable to move. As far as we could see, all three of the crew were uninjured but taken prisoner. However, we did see them fire one round from the 6-pounder and later found out they had put the 105mm out of action.

The ground was extremely flat and Sergeant Bacon, Randall and I had to lie very still in order not to attract the attention of the German gun crew. This was more especially the case when we were sniped from German infantry positions on our left, and when one of the German gunners stalked towards the tank and had a look at Bielby and at the ration box outside the tank. The tank had been burning for some considerable time so there was not much left. Sergeant Bacon could not have been more than 30 yards away from him and I can only assume the German thought he was dead.

After about an hour, during which time we were hoping that the heavy squadrons might come up, the Germans made off with the 88mm, Corporal Levy and his crew.

We were then able to inspect their positions and the 105mm, which had been knocked out. After a short period, Sergeant Nelson appeared in his tank, a doctor and an ambulance from the 1st Armoured Brigade following behind. We buried Bielby and I rejoined the Regiment on the back of Sergeant Nelson's tank.

I learned that the other half of the squadron had shot up some enemy transport, including one German armoured car with a senior German officer, and procured a good deal of booty, mainly American stuff that the Germans had captured. I found Corporal Jackson sitting on the top of his tank, wearing a fur coat, smoking a cigar and swinging a badminton racquet, all American, which they had found on one of the trucks they had shot up.

We were held up by enemy tanks but no battle took place. Patrick commanded the squadron for the rest of the day, and I went back to

George Hales, our padre, to put a cross on Bielby's grave. Another night march until 24.00 hours.

Friday, 9 April

Pushed on towards the landing ground north of Sfax. Slight tank battle in the afternoon and the Staffs Yeomanry knocked out four enemy tanks without loss to themselves.

In the middle of the battle my gunner informed me that 'she had done it again' and placed a chicken's egg in my hand. Apparently, without my knowledge, a hen was travelling in the sub-turret next to the driver and had laid an egg during the tank battle.

As we approached one of the main roads leading into Sfax a German armoured car dashed right across our front and escaped, passing right under our noses, and those of seven of our tanks.

For once we had an early night and did not have a night march.

Saturday, 10 April

The advance continued all day in a north-west direction, towards Sfax. Our next objectives are the airfields south-west of Sfax.

Sunday, 11 April

We were stationary until 15.00 hours, which enabled us to spend a certain amount of time on maintenance, which the tanks sorely needed. At 15.00 hours we moved 30 miles towards Sousse, which late that evening we heard had been evacuated by the enemy. The last part of the journey we did along the main road, flat out most of the way. Stephen Mitchell complained that his tracks were red hot when we eventually pulled into leaguer. It was a glorious evening and the moon lit up all the surrounding country, which is so very fertile. The tanks ran well and we had none of them falling out through mechanical trouble. We finished up that day just south of a village called Msakert.

Monday, 12 April

At dawn we moved on a road parallel to the coast road, leaving Sousse on our right. The going was extremely difficult as the track, although marked well on the map, was very narrow and difficult and the surrounding country covered with orchards, which meant we had to stick to the track. We received a tremendous welcome from all the French people living in these small villages, who had evacuated from Sousse and Sfax and other of the larger towns. We had great difficulty in getting through one village, nor could we find a way round. However, Patrick McCraith found a Frenchman (an extraordinary-looking specimen) who volunteered to guide us round the village. When Patrick introduced me to him he insisted on embracing me in the true French fashion and likewise all the members of my crew. My gunner remarked drily that he hoped he received a similar welcome from the female elements of the town. In spite of the guide we had a most difficult time in getting through this village whose streets were no wider than the usual Arab village street, and the heavy tanks only managed to get through and round some of the very tortuous corners by knocking down some of the corner houses. However, this did not dampen the enthusiasm of the crowd, who cheered and clapped their hands as we passed through. I happened to look round at Patrick McCraith, whose tank was following mine, and there I saw him and Lenton sitting on the top of their tank bowing left and right to the cheering crowds as if they were on their way to a coronation.

We eventually got out of the village and came on the main road to Sidi Ben Ali. Incidentally, on the last lap of our tortuous and eventful journey through the village I ditched my tank in an enormous hole and had to change to another.

The road on which we came was being shelled so Patrick McCraith and I endeavoured to get some information from the local inhabitants. Suddenly round the bend came three girls on bicycles, whom we stopped and proceeded in our best French to ask questions as to when the enemy had left the area. They were all terrified and started to make off so Patrick and I gave chase, which made them all the more frightened. However, after we'd shouted, '*Nous sommes amis*,' they eventually stopped to answer questions. One of them, very young, was one of the most attractive young girls I had seen since leaving England. Their first question was whether we were American or English. A shell then landed about 500 yards away, which scattered them and their bicycles amid shrieks of terror in all directions. We eventually all met again, with other French people at the village post office. They were very helpful and told us that the Germans had left the previous day and were forming a line at Enfidaville. Patrick and I would have liked to stay longer but needless to say urgent calls came over the net asking why we were not pushing on.

Colonel Donny was asked by the brigadier to name a rendezvous for the brigadier and two infantry brigadiers who were following up the brigade. We laughed like hell when he arranged for them to meet at a crossroads in the Arab section of the village, which we had passed and where there were two dead donkeys, one dead dog and one dead camel. Donny pointed out that they ought easily to be able to recognize the place.

Tuesday, 13 April

We arrived in the early morning at Enfidaville and joined up with the rest of the brigade, who had been moving along the coast road.

The New Zealand infantry had entered the village during the night and the enemy had withdrawn into strongholds in the hills. The Regiment moved back behind Sidi Ben Ali and found a most attractive spot for a short rest. The country is really remarkably green and the wild flowers are most attractive. I have never seen so many varieties, not even in the most spectacular spots in Palestine.

Wednesday, 14 April

A day of rest, which we spent on maintenance. Took the opportunity to write some letters. RHQ brought up the mess and the squadron leaders are eating with the colonel.

Stanley took a photograph of them having a meal among the olive groves south of Enfidaville (see page 341). By now the desert had been left behind and the Tunisian landscape had turned decidedly more Mediterranean.

Thursday, 15 April

The Regiment moved north to just south-west of Enfidaville. Colonel Donny and I did a recce on to the main Enfidaville road, where the Staffs are in position. They have had a very sticky time from enemy shelling and John Cunliffe-Lister was hit in the head by a piece of shrapnel and died from wounds.

The area is lousy with partridges so Donny Player took his gun with him on the recce. I only wish the Germans could have seen Donny Player suddenly jump out of the Jeep as we put a brace up, get a left and a right, while enemy shells landed within 500 yards and our Long Toms were firing 800 yards to our rear. We gave one of the partridges to Jim Eadie, colonel of the Staffs.

The mosquitoes at night are quite deplorable and everybody is getting thoroughly bitten, especially as we have no mosquito nets. However, we are told the malaria mosquito does not inhabit this area.

Friday, 16 April

We remained in our new location, which is among the cactus hedges, throughout the day.

Saturday, 17 April

Spent a quiet day, mostly on maintenance, among the cactus hedges. Mosquitoes at night and flies during the day make life hell.

Sunday, 18 April

Some American mechanics visited the Regiment and spent the morning discussing with the fitters of the heavy tanks various mechanical problems which they had met since we were equipped with the American Shermans. I understand they were most helpful and very pleasant personalities. It's a great shame that English mechanics who actually manufacture the Crusader are not available for the same purpose.

An American brigade major came and had lunch with the Regiment. He was very pleasant but appeared to be the usual type of American and gave us all rather the impression that the Americans still have a great deal to learn about soldiering, like we did when we first arrived in the desert.

Monday, 19 April

During the morning, various conferences about the forthcoming attack. The infantry, consisting of the New Zealanders, the Highlanders and the Indians, are to attack along the whole line and capture if possible some of the high ground from which the enemy has such excellent observation. The Regiment is to be in support of and under command of a New Zealand brigade.

During the day we had a look at the ground over which we are to operate, and at 19.00 hours the Regiment moved out into position. The barrage and infantry attack is to start at midnight.

Tuesday, 20 April

During the early hours of last night the infantry called for 1 Troop to support their attack on the right flank, which was hindered by thick cactus bushes. They said they required the tanks to break a way through the bushes. However, as I rather anticipated, my troop of Crusaders, which I put under Patrick McCraith for a short period, were used in the role of an 'I' tank, for which they are thoroughly unsuitable.

Patrick McCraith told me that when the tanks had broken through the cactus they found visibility nil owing to the shellfire, and they came under terrific artillery fire, mortar fire, and sniping from the high ground. Furthermore, after advancing another 100 yards they were immediately engaged by anti-tank guns. They had the greatest difficulty in keeping contact with the advancing infantry who, owing to the intensity of the enemy barrage, were compelled continually to lie flat on the ground.

We were supporting a battalion of New Zealanders who were attacking Takrouna. A portion of this battalion had worked round the right flank of the village and were in grave danger of being cut off or of having a heavy enemy counter-attack made against them before they could get up their supporting arms. In consequence, the New Zealand brigadier ordered the Regiment up to support them. We set out about dawn and I managed to join up with the other two troops, both of whom had rather an unpleasant time.

We came under extremely heavy artillery fire. There were also still enemy machine-gun posts and snipers very well concealed on the high ground where it was quite impossible to take a tank. As a result, we couldn't show even a finger above the turret. Sergeant McCann in the early stages received a bullet through his cheek from an enemy sniper. He was very fortunate and the latest report says he will recover.

Takrouna is an Arab fortress village situated on the topmost peak of the highest hill, which has perpendicular sides. Half the hill has been captured but the further side remains in the hands of the enemy. Practically every spot had been previously registered by the enemy gunners.

The rest of my squadron worked on forward, endeavouring to reach the foremost New Zealand infantry. We tried to use a wadi for cover but when we were travelling along the bottom the shelling seemed to be concentrated on us. Ian McKay received a direct hit with HE on the driver's cab, which completely wrecked his tank, killed his driver, but miraculously did not injure any other member of the crew, who all jumped out and took refuge in a slit trench which had been evacuated by the Germans. Ian ran over to tell me what had happened and as he was talking another shell landed about five yards from my tank, but fortunately he was on the other side to which the shell landed. It completely blew off the ration box on the side of the tank, causing a bag of flour to shoot up in the air and cover the turret and myself with flour.

In the meantime, the heavy tanks were endeavouring to follow us but five ran onto mines and were all put out of action. This could not have happened in a more unfavourable position as the tanks were exposed to every kind of enemy fire. Very fortunately the enemy had no anti-tank guns covering that area. I retraced some of the ground in order to contact the battalion HQ of the New Zealanders and on my way back again I also went up on a mine. My driver, Trooper Barrow, was slightly wounded. I found myself about 50 yards from Stephen Mitchell's tank, also on a minefield. Fortunately I managed to board another tank and rejoined my squadron.

I heard afterwards that today was Stephen Mitchell's birthday, and that his gunner in the middle of the afternoon, after spending about six hours on the minefield under the most unpleasant conditions imaginable, said, 'I believe it is your birthday, sir. Many happy returns of the day,' to which Stephen replied rather irritably, 'What the devil makes you think that I want to spend another day, let alone a birthday, on an enemy minefield?'

On our way up we passed through the Maori Battalion, who, as usual, had done wonderfully well. I saw the most remarkable spectacle of one Maori stalking and capturing a German machine-gun post containing eight men on the side of a small hill. Pat and I had worked round to the back and we were able to bring fire on to the post, but the Germans were well aware of the Maori who was stalking them and we saw one German throw three stick hand-grenades at the stalking Maori, who appeared to be quite unconcerned. It was a grand sight to see eight Germans coming out with their hands up. As a result of the day 200 Germans were captured.

Wednesday, 21 April

The Regiment moved up to support the infantry behind Takrouna. Colonel Donny wanted to find out whether we could work round a narrow valley on the south side of the village, so I took Sergeant Dring and Sergeant Butler with me to see what we could find out. We passed a troop of B Squadron heavy tanks and pushed forward to the next ridge. From there we got an excellent position and view of the far side of Takrouna Hill, which was still in the hands of the enemy. We also picked up a couple of enemy machine-gun posts on the far side of the valley and we conducted a very successful indirect shoot with B Squadron.

On our way up my tank broke down so I changed on to Sergeant Dring's tank.

Just before sunset I saw a Maori stalk down from the top of the Takrouna Hill, fire a couple of shots from his rifle and eventually succeed in weeding out a machine-gun post containing 20 Germans. The whole scene was silhouetted against the skyline and to watch all these Germans coming out of their very well-concealed dugout with arms in the air surrendering to one British Maori was indeed an inspiring and spectacular sight. Sergeant Dring had an excellent shoot with his Besa gun on some Germans whom we had disturbed with the HE fire from the heavy tanks.

We saw two Germans carrying a wounded comrade away on a stretcher and I found it extremely difficult to decide whether or not we should continue to fire on them.

The capture of the Takrouna feature by the Maoris was indeed a remarkable piece and I am afraid cost them many lives. Before they eventually gained control of the whole of the village, six Italians had crept up and thrown a hand-grenade into a room where Maoris had established a first-aid dressing station. As a result of this two Maoris ran amok, managed to capture two of the Italians whom they bayoneted to death, later caught another two to whom they gave the option of being bayoneted or thrown over the precipice of the Takrouna feature. The other two Italians were eventually captured by another Maori company, but they, too, were fetched by the same two Maoris and met with a similar fate.

We drew back into leaguer as it grew dark. The sniping from the high ground on either side of the valley was most unpleasant and they still had OPs, which can bring down accurate shellfire.

The 28th (Maori) Battalion had a deserved reputation for being among the toughest soldiers in Eighth Army. Unlike white New Zealanders, who faced conscription, the Maori were all volunteers, and their companies divided on a largely tribal basis.

Thursday, 22 April

The 3rd RTR took over from us and we were in reserve. However, we came in for rather a lot of shelling.

Friday, 23 April

We moved up in position to support one of the Guards brigades to protect them against any counter-attack by enemy tanks. We hid all day in an olive grove.

Saturday, 24 April

We had orders to withdraw as the country does not warrant any tank action and we were still coming in for a certain amount of shelling. About 5 o'clock in the evening Colonel Donny Player and Myles Hildyard went back in a Jeep to reconnoitre a route through the village of Enfidaville and to our next position.

As they passed through a village a heavy enemy barrage came down on to the village and Donny was mortally wounded. He died in the ambulance on the way to the ADS. Myles, who was with him, fortunately escaped all injuries.

His loss is a very great blow to us all, especially as he was doing so well since he had taken over command of the Regiment, even though it was for such a short time.

In the space of barely a month, the Sherwood Rangers had lost the two men who had most shaped and guided the Regiment during its transition from pre-war Yeomanry outfit to an increasingly skilled and proficient armoured unit – first Flash Kellett, and now Donny Player. He was 40 when he died, and a member of the Player's tobacco family – rich, well-connected and good-looking, and a much-loved officer and commander. He is buried at the Commonwealth War Cemetery at Enfidaville.

Sunday, 25 April

Donny was buried in the little cemetery of Enfidaville in the morning. The padre had a very short memorial service at the graveside, which Michael Laycock, Myles Hildyard, Arthur Leadbetter (Donny's batman), Trooper Rugman (Donny's butler) and I attended.

Donny's grave at Enfidaville.

The cemetery is so very peaceful and there are buried there British, German and Italian soldiers. The whole area of the cemetery is a mass of wild flowers of the most lovely colours and we even found geraniums and two English rose bushes. We planted a geranium bush on Donny's grave and Myles took a photo to send back to his father. The flowers and the grass in the cemetery have for many months been neglected and everything is running wild. However, in spite of shell firing going on outside, in the cemetery it was all so peaceful.

Monday, 26 April

The Regiment is now in an area just off the road about four miles due south of Enfidaville. We spent the day on maintenance.

Thursday, 29 April

Arthur Cranley from the 4th CLY has been posted to command the Regiment. This came as somewhat of a surprise as we knew there might be a possibility that Sandy Cameron might come but no mention had been made of Arthur Cranley. He is an exact counterpart of mine at Winchester, where I knew him well. At one time he had the Light Squadron at the CLY, where he did very well and was extraordinarily popular with his men, and Michael is to be second-in-command of the Regiment.

Saturday, 1–Sunday, 9 May

During this period we have remained in the same area, just south of Enfidaville. Officially we are at two or three hours' notice and ready to move up to support the infantry in the event of enemy counter-attack.

A certain number of new officers have arrived. I was sent down to TGR to collect and select six from a batch of reinforcements. I found there the colonel of the Staffs, the colonel of the 3rd RTR and the colonel of the 22nd Armoured Brigade (the 2 i/c of the brigade). They were all there for the same purpose. We saw approximately 20 officers in all and asked them various questions. We were then asked to make our choices. Of course, we practically all put the same six names down, so the matter had to be decided by drawing out of the hat. I only took three.

As is customary, we held an auction for some of Donny Player's military kit, the proceeds of which will go to the Regimental Welfare Fund. Some of the articles fetched very high prices, thanks to Stephen, who was acting auctioneer. How Donny would have laughed if he could have seen Michael Gold paying £1.10s for a piece of soap. Everybody paid very generously and we raised about £30 for the Regimental Welfare.

On 6 May Keith Douglas rejoined the squadron after being in hospital recovering from a wound he received in the battle at Zem Zem. He will take over 5 Troop but in the meantime he has been sent away to try and collect some NAAFI stores for the Regiment.

I had the greatest difficulty to get Patrick out of bed, his batman having utterly failed to wake him. The previous night he had slightly overindulged and took three hours to get from the mess to the squadron area, which are only about 800 yards apart. When we eventually did manage to get him on the move (it required half a bucket of water to do so), he travelled with me in the front of a Jeep and would keep falling asleep. When going along a piece of road I had to make rather a sharp turn to avoid a bump and he fell out of the side of the Jeep and landed on his face on the hard road, taking all the skin off his nose, giving himself a nasty cut over the left eye and making him bite a bit out of his lip. He is OK but will have a rather painful face. The doctor has completely covered it with bandages and as a result he walks about looking exactly like the Invisible Man.

I am now having to select a fresh crew for my own tank since my driver, Bielby, has been killed, and Sergeant Bacon, the operator, has left to go to an OCTU. My selection has been as follows: the driver – Trooper Bland, who is a Yeoman and one of the original recce troop; gunner – Trooper Randall, who is also a Yeoman and has always been my gunner; operator – Trooper Simons, who joined the Regiment

Brewing up.

Crusaders from Stanley's A Squadron by Keith Douglas.

as a Yeoman and was also at one time a member of Sam's recce troop.

On Saturday, 8 May, we had some wonderfully encouraging news about the progress of Eighth Army on our left, who have linked up with First Army, and the progress of the Americans and the French. We heard that both Tunis and Bizerte have now been occupied by our forces. The air force has been wroughting [*sic* – wreaking] terrific damage and is reputed to have sunk 25 out of 30 Axis ships crammed with troops who have left all their equipment behind.

The line in front of us is still held by the enemy and it remains to be seen whether they will attempt to evacuate. According to a report from a Pole who was captured, the whole area is extremely heavily mined. This Pole is a sapper and gave the whole layout of the enemy minefields.

Lawrence Biddle, the brigade major, came over and visited the Regiment. We had a talk about the present position and about what the future would hold for us after all this had been cleared up. We came to the conclusion that home leave for any of us would be very unlikely, and rather anticipated that First Army would remain, first to clear up this area and then possibly as garrison troops, that Eighth Army and any of First Army who could be spared would go back to the Delta and train for some kind of combined operation. I hope that I may be wrong in my supposition that we get no home leave, especially as regards those who have been out here for three and a half years.

The war in North Africa was now all but over. On 5 May, First Army, having been given X Corps, made their final assault in the Medjerda Valley in a thrust to break through to Tunis. The battle, planned by General Tuker of the 4th Indian Division, not only went almost entirely to plan but was so successful it was all over in a day. Both Tunis and Bizerte fell on 7 May. The last remaining Axis troops were now cornered into the Cap Bon peninsula.

Tuesday, 11 May

We heard today that approximately 11,000 Germans and 9000 Italian infantry remained in North Africa to fight it out. They are supported by approximately 50 tanks from 10th and 21st Panzer Divisions. Those figures come from First Army. According to Eighth Army estimates there are about 30,000 troops facing them. We heard today that the 15th Armoured Division blew up its tanks and surrendered. This division is one of the oldest in North Africa and can claim the honour of getting nearer to the Nile than any other German unit in August 1942, when Rommel made his unsuccessful 'recce in force'. As the New Zealanders say, this unconditional surrender is hardly a suitable conclusion to a career that hitherto has been distinguished and extremely gallant.

We heard today that our padre, George Hales, has to leave the Regiment to go to X Corps with the rank of major. It will mean promotion for him but will be a very great loss to the Regiment, and he is very loath to go, but I am afraid he can't get out of it.

Wednesday, 12 May

The forces opposite Enfidaville on our front are now completely surrounded, as First Army has worked round behind them and captured Bouficha on the coast. It remains to be seen how long they will hold out. A great many more prisoners have been taken. A terrific barrage has been put down all day by our gunners and a tremendous air attack took place this afternoon. We heard today that General von Arnim was captured by elements of 6th Armoured Division (First Army) and is reputed to have stated that he ordered cease fire at 16.00 hours.

General Messe, GOC 90th Light Division, is reputed to have been captured, and I only hope by Eighth Army. They have been the most ancient and formidable division against the 8th Armoured Brigade ever since the Battle of Alamein.

I gather that tonight organized resistance has practically ceased, but we have not yet heard the final figure of prisoners and war matériel.

Thursday, 13 May

The victory in Africa was officially declared completed and the campaign officially ended soon after 8 o'clock last night, Tunisian time. At the moment we have taken 150,000 prisoners and vast quantities of war matériel.

Somehow it is extremely difficult to fully realize that the war out here is finished, and everybody is speculating wildly about the future. I am afraid that home leave appears to be out of the question but, still, one never knows.

General Alexander, C-in-C 18th Army Group, signalled to Churchill at 1.16 p.m. on 13 May, 'Sir, it is my duty to report that the Tunisian campaign is over. All enemy resistance has ceased. We are masters of the North African shores.'

Final numbers of prisoners vary, from 275,000 registered by the Americans to 238,000, according to British figures. At any rate, around a quarter of a million surrendered, along with a huge arsenal of tanks, guns, and aircraft. It was a huge victory, the biggest of the war to date, and one that eclipsed even the German loss at Stalingrad back in early February in terms of numbers.

Friday, 14 May

At 12.30 all senior officers of 8th Armoured Brigade had an informal address from General Freyberg. He first of all told us that he came to bid us farewell as all the New Zealanders were returning to Cairo tomorrow. He pointed out that the New Zealanders had worked with this brigade ever since Alamein, and that it was entirely due to the 8th Armoured Brigade and the New Zealanders that the line at Mareth was broken as a result of our famous Left Hook. He added that all New Zealanders wished to thank us for the close co-operation and the support we had always given them.

In the afternoon Myles Hildyard, Stephen Mitchell and I visited and climbed to the top of that ancient fortress, the Arab village of Takrouna. It really was most interesting, examining some of the infantry positions that the Germans had had on that hill, and I shall never cease to wonder at the superb view of the whole surrounding countryside, which one got from the top. No wonder we were so heavily shelled and machine-gunned as we worked our way round on the morning of the attack, trying to get behind the village and up the valley between the high ground.

I saw the positions where Sergeant Dring and I engaged a machine-gun nest on the far side of the valley, and I saw the machine-gun nest on the side of Takrouna, which was captured single-handed by the Maori. It was certainly most interesting having a look at the ground and the various positions after it is all over.

I shall never cease to wonder and admire the extraordinary feat performed by the New Zealanders and the Maori battalions in capturing that hill. There were a lot of New Zealanders inspecting the battlefield.

The view of Takrouna is largely unchanged since the ferocious battle there. It is quite possible to clamber up to the top of the hill and still see the remains of mortar and machine-gun pits carved into the rock.

Saturday, 15 May

The officers' mess gave a cocktail party, to which they asked various members of regiments from the brigade. We put up four tents and decorated the interior with flowers, of which there was a large and varied assortment, including roses and geraniums, and gave one the impression of an English flower show. The party eventually broke up at about 10 o'clock at night after Michael Laycock and Michael Farquhar from the Staffs had collapsed from the top of the tent into the centre of the room.

Above: D-Day, 6 June 1944. Landing craft line up on Gold Beach amid a clutter of anti-invasion obstacles.

Right: Montgomery's message issued to all the men of the invasion force. Stanley kept his, along with a large number of other written souvenirs.

Below: A knocked-out Jagdpanther near St Pierre in Normandy. German tanks had grown in size since the early days in the Western Desert, but British artillery, air power and the 17-pounder- equipped Sherman Fireflies could all defeat both Panther and Tiger tanks. St Pierre was a terrible battle for the Sherwood Rangers and it was where Stanley was suddenly thrust into command of the Regiment.

21 ARMY GROUP

PERSONAL MESSAGE FROM THE C-in-C

To be read out to all Troops

1. The time has come to deal the enemy a terrific blow in Western Europe.

The blow will be struck by the combined sea, land, and air forces of the Allies—together constituting one great Allied team, under the supreme command of General Eisenhower.

2. On the eve of this great adventure I send my best wishes to every soldier in the Allied team.

To us is given the honour of striking a blow for freedom which will live in history; and in the better days that lie ahead men will speak with pride of our doings. We have a great and a righteous cause.

Let us pray that "The Lord Mighty in Battle" will go forth with our armies, and that His special providence will aid us in the struggle.

3. I want every soldier to know that I have complete confidence in the successful outcome of the operations that we are now about to begin.

With stout hearts, and with enthusiasm for the contest, let us go forward to victory.

4. And, as we enter the battle, let us recall the words of a famous soldier spoken many years ago:—

"He either fears his fate too much,
Or his deserts are small,
Who dare not put it to the touch,
To win or lose it all."

5. Good luck to each one of you. And good hunting on the mainland of Europe.

B. L. Montgomery
General
C.-in-C 21 Army Group.

1944.

Above: 30 Corps commander, General Horrocks, puts us in the picture somewhere in Normandy. Horrocks succeeded General Bucknall.

Below: Sergeant Nelson (*left*) and the crew of the Recce Troop in Normandy.

Above: A knocked-out Panther tank, Normandy.

Below: Stanley had scrawled 'Mk 2 tank, Normandy' on this picture. In fact, it is one of the German much-feared Tiger tanks. At 72 tons, and armed with the 88mm gun, it was a beast, but prone to mechanical failure. This one appears to have been knocked out, however.

Above: Sherwood Ranger Sherman tanks in Beek. This was yet another fierce and bloody battle. As the Regiment grew steadily more and more proficient, so they were increasingly used to accompany the infantry in the vanguard of an assault.

Left: Christmas 1944 at Schinnen, in Holland. Since landing on D-Day, the Regiment had had officer casualties of double its normal compliment. The chances of any tank crew surviving unscathed was slight.

Below: German refugees on the move – an all too common sight.

Above: Sherman tanks camouflaged with white paint in the winter of 1944/45.

Right: Crewmen from C Squadron in Germany, February 1945.

Below: Tank barrage before the attack on the Reichwald (*left*). Dead cows lie bloated in the flooded waters of the Maas near the Reichwald (*right*).

Above: A column of exhausted German prisoners. The end was near, but there was to be no let-up in the ferocity of the fighting and the Sherwood Rangers were never far from the action.

By the KING'S Order the name of
*Lieut: Colonel (actg.) S. D. Christopherson, D.S.O., M.C.,
The Nottinghamshire Yeomanry, Royal Armoured Corps,*
was published in the London Gazette on
22 March 1945,
as mentioned in a Despatch for distinguished service.
I am charged to record
His Majesty's high appreciation.

Secretary of State for War

Left: Stanley's citation for being Mentioned in Despatches. He was also awarded the DSO, the MC and Bar and an American Silver Star.

Below: Preparing to cross the mighty river Rhine.

Right: Trooper Mogford, Stanley's batman in the closing stages of the war.

Far right: Trooper Bull, Stanley's driver.

Below: With the war in Europe finally won, there was a chance for some relaxation and games. Races at Einbeck, (*left*). Corporal Tuft and his band play at the Kellett Kanteen, named after Flash Kellett (*right*).

Below: Stanley relaxes by the pool at B Squadron HQ in Hanover, with his dog "Beek" in the rubber dighy. He had carried an incredible amount of responsibility but managed to remain outwardly cheerful and optimistic to his men.

Above: The Farewell Parade at Einbeck in October 1945 before the Regiment lost its tanks. This one is Stanley's own Sherman – it was a tradition that the Officer Commanding's tank was named *Robin Hood*.

Below: Stanley, seated centre, with his officers in Hanover, January 1946. Soon they would be going home – Stanley to civilian life once more.

Sunday, 16 May

The corps commander (General Horrocks) addressed all squadron leaders and their SSMs at rear Corps HQ in order to explain the last phase of the battle of Tunis. He spoke very well, and what he said was extremely interesting. After the first attack of First Army not being altogether successful he told us that the army commander had decided to break the line here at Enfidaville. He never liked this plan, owing to the extreme difficulty of the country and the well-fortified positions held by the Bosch, and was very well pleased when eventually it was decided that the attack should take place further west in First Army where the whole of the air force out here, with the 7th Armoured Division and the 1st Armoured Division, had been sent to increase the strength of First Army. And as Horrocks admitted, with such an amazingly strong force under his command, if he had failed he would certainly have deserved to be sent home with a bowler hat.

As regards the future, he told us that none of us were going home as the shipping situation would not allow it and that we should have to fight our way home through Europe. We should go back to an area near the sea where we would have a fortnight's relaxation before we started once again to be reinforced, re-equipped and trained flat out.

A mobile cinema visited the regimental area and we saw *Desert Victory*, which was not the same as they showed in England but quite enjoyable and fairly accurate in detail.

Monty and General 'Von Thoma' Thomas of 43 Division, Brunssum,
November 1944.

PART III

D-DAY TO VICTORY
June 1944–May 1945

14

D-Day

Gold Beach, D-Day.

AFTER THE END *of the war in North Africa, the Sherwood Rangers
remained in Tunisia for a few weeks and then were sent to a camp near
Tripoli before finally heading back to Egypt in October. On 17 November,
they sailed from Alexandria – the Mediterranean was open once more
to Allied shipping – and, after a week in Sicily, set sail for England via
Gibraltar, arriving into Greenock on 9 December.*

*Throughout this time, Stanley stopped writing a day-by-day diary.
Instead, and for the rest of the war, he jotted down his experiences
intermittently.*

*Between May 1943 and February 1944, much happened in the wider
war. In July, the Allies invaded Sicily in what was to be – and would
remain – the largest seaborne invasion ever mounted. Later that month,
after it became inevitable that Sicily would fall, Mussolini was overthrown.
The island surrendered on 17 August, but not before some 60,000
German troops escaped across the Strait of Messina to mainland Italy.*

Along the Eastern Front, the Germans counter-attacked the Kursk Salient, but were repulsed and then forced to retreat; that July marked the last time German troops advanced eastwards. Elsewhere, in the Crimea and around Kharkov, the Germans continued to fall back. By January, the Red Army had crossed into Poland. In the strategic air campaign, Allied bombers continued striking at German cities and other targets throughout the Reich; in September, Berlin became the latest to feel the full weight of Allied bombers. At sea, the German battle-cruiser Scharnhorst *was sunk, while the U-boat force was being hammered by Allied navies in the Battle of the Atlantic.*

In the Mediterranean, Italy signed an armistice, announced on 8 September, and the following day the Allies landed at Salerno, to the south of Naples. Bad weather and German determination to fight for every yard ensured there would be no easy march on Rome, however. By February 1944, the Allies were stuck at the Gustav Line, stretching across the leg of Italy and, at its closest, some 60 miles south-east of Rome, and in a small bridgehead at Anzio.

In the Far East, American forces continued to retake one Pacific island after another and were now dominating the skies with the introduction of the new B-29 Superfortress. In Burma, the British recaptured the key port of Maungdaw and Australian troops were winning the battle for New Guinea.

In this now truly global war, the net was inextricably tightening around the Axis. In the coming summer, the Soviet Union would launch Operation BAGRATION along the Eastern Front while the Allies would, at long last, make their cross-Channel invasion of France. This was Operation OVERLORD, and in the forthcoming battle for Normandy, the Sherwood Rangers Yeomanry would have a crucial role to play.

February–6 June 1944

A month's leave, after four years abroad, was indescribably good. I spent all my time with my family in London paying several visits to different parts of the country, which looked so very lovely.

My home in the centre of London was surrounded by bomb damage, but beyond several bruises and holes our building was intact.

During all the bombing – like all other Londoners – the family, all of whom were doing war work, must have had a nerve-racking time, and had spent many nights in the basement. My father had aged, and I found him a sick man. After having worked hard all his life, he found retirement and enforced inactivity unbearable, suffering so acutely from sciatica. He knew that he would not live much longer and his one great wish was to see me again – a wish which was happily granted. He died during my leave.

My mother I found exceedingly well, and looking as young and pretty as when I last saw her four years ago. The loss of my father, after 30 years of married life, was a great blow to her. In spite of 20 years between their ages, they had found great happiness together and enjoyed unique companionship.

My brother, refusing to take a commission, left for Italy soon after my arrival in England, but it was a great joy to see him again even for a short time, and to find that he was the same big-hearted, cheerful but completely irresponsible person I had known four years ago.

My two young female cousins, cared for and brought up by my family since the loss of their parents, had grown from gawky, long-legged flappers into exceedingly attractive young girls. The eldest one had qualified as a VAD, and the younger one was employed at the Foreign Office in some 'hush-hush' capacity. I promptly fell in love with my younger cousin, much to the consternation of the rest of the family, who immediately had visions of barmy grandchildren.

As usual, my leave went far too quickly and at the end of January 1944 I rejoined the Regiment at Chippenham Park, near Newmarket.

I was delighted to hear on my return that I was still to command A Squadron, and gradually the squadron reassembled as the various leave periods were up, and a number of people, including George Harding, returned married. George Jones came back engaged, and Neville Fearn also returned in some kind of matrimonial tangle, the exact nature of which was not very clear.

Following the end of the war in North Africa, the 8th Armoured Brigade, with which the Sherwood Rangers had fought from Alamein to

Enfidaville, was broken up. For the forthcoming invasion, Montgomery
wanted experienced units mixed with those new to battle, so the
Staffordshire Yeomanry and the 3rd Royal Tank Regiment left
the brigade, to be replaced by the 4/7th Royal Dragoon Guards and the
untried 24th Lancers. The Essex Yeomanry were to join them as artillery,
as were the 12th Battalion of the 60th Rifles, as motorized infantry.

The Sherwood Rangers also had a new commanding officer, the sixth
of the war: Lieutenant Colonel J. D'A. Anderson, a regular cavalry
officer, who immediately insisted the Regiment smarten up. Away went
the desert boots and lax attitude to uniform and even discipline. The
Sherwood Rangers were now, after their long apprenticeship in North
Africa and the Middle East, the senior regiment in the brigade. In the
forthcoming battle for north-west Europe, they would be expected to
take the lead. Anderson wanted them to set an example.

Stanley's A Squadron was now re-equipped with American Sherman
tanks and in the re-shuffling of the Regiment, Keith Douglas became
squadron second-in-command.

Chippenham Park was a most delightful country estate surrounded by
a park, and situated about five miles from Newmarket. The whole of
the 8th Armoured Brigade had been stationed in the park, the beauty
of which was somewhat spoilt by the erection of Nissen huts and
concrete tracks for tracked vehicles. However, we were very comfortable, and the owner of the estate, a charming old lady, did all she could
to add to our comfort.

Soon after our arrival at Chippenham we were informed that the
8th Armoured Brigade, consisting of my regiment, the 4/7th Royal
Dragoon Guards and the 24th Lancers, would take part in the initial
assault of the invasion of north-west Europe, and that our time for
training would be limited. This news was received with mixed feelings.
Naturally we had anticipated that we should be used somewhere in
north-west Europe, for which purpose we had been brought back
from the Middle East, but the idea of invading Europe in a tank was
somewhat alarming.

Soon after the reception of this news, reinforcements and

equipment began to arrive, and intensive training started in earnest.

After a short time, our days at Chippenham became extremely hectic, when the individual training of the new reinforcements commenced. This consisted of teaching the driver to drive and maintain his tank; the gunner to fire and look after his guns; the wireless operator to work and understand his set, and to load the 75mm gun, which was one of his duties; the co-driver to be able at any time to take over the duties of any other member of the tank crew; and finally the tank commander to direct the driver by means of internal communication when in action, to spot and direct gunfire on to any target, and, at all times, to be in constant wireless communication with his troop leader, and to be able to work in tactical co-operation with the other two tanks of his troop.

Troop training followed individual training. Each troop of each squadron, under its troop leader, was taught, and practised, to operate together, and to work tactically. Then followed squadron training, regimental training and finally brigade training.

I am convinced that the most important and essential part of our training was the original individual training, especially the gunnery and wireless parts. The success of any tank versus tank battle depended on accurate and quick fire, and it was quite impossible to fight any kind of battle, either on a troop, squadron, regimental or brigade level, unless wireless communication was good, which could only result from thoroughly sound basic training.

By this time, the days of referencing cricket and horses for wireless code were long gone. The Sherwood Rangers were highly experienced with a core of men who understood the value of hard training, discipline and dedicated professionalism. Some of the older members of the Regiment, like Stanley, Stephen Mitchell, John Semken and Michael Gold, might still have given off an air of casual insouciance, but by June 1944, that was all that remained of the old Yeomanry regiment that had gone to war.

All orders were passed forward, and all information was passed back on the wireless, both so vital in any action. It often happened that the whole Regiment, comprising around 60 tanks, each with its own wireless, would operate on the same frequency, which enabled every tank to listen in and pass messages, but only one station could come on the air at one time. A very high standard of wireless operation and procedure was essential both on the part of the operators and the tank commanders to prevent complete confusion on the air, which could be caused by one tank being off-frequency (off-net, as it was called) or by speaking out of turn.

News suddenly came through that B and C Squadrons would proceed to an unknown destination and would undergo some special tank training for the invasion. There appeared to be considerable secrecy and mystery regarding this training, which intrigued us all and caused speculation, mixed with certain apprehension. A Squadron had at first been selected for this training, but Michael Laycock, the regimental second-in-command, told me that in view of the fact that A Squadron had led the Regiment across Africa, it had been decided that B Squadron should replace us. A clear indication was given that this special training might not be too savoury!

B and C Squadrons soon left for their unknown destination, which turned out to be Yarmouth, and not until their arrival were details disclosed regarding their future. They certainly had a startling surprise. They were informed that they would be trained to 'swim' their Shermans to the shore. Having been launched from a tank landing craft up to 4000 yards from the coast, they would then support the first wave of the assaulting infantry – rather an alarming prospect and somewhat disconcerting to the Sherwood Rangers, who somehow could not picture a Sherman tank waddling in the sea like an overgrown duck under heavy shellfire. When we of A Squadron heard about it we were only too pleased that the other squadrons should have been given the privilege!

These were the DD tanks, or Duplex Drive, especially adapted for D-Day. They were adapted with two propellers and given an inflatable canvas screen, which enabled the tank to float. Vision was difficult, the tank became even more claustrophobic than normal, and while it was reasonably reliable, there was much that could go wrong, particularly

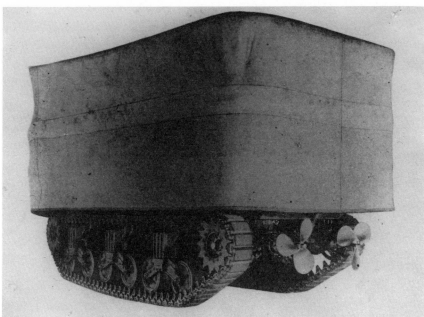

Sherman 'DD' amphibious tank.

when under fire or operating in a rising swell. I was certainly glad A Squadron were not using DD tanks. Each man had to train using the 'Davis Escape Apparatus'. Once wearing this suit, he then descended into a specially constructed cistern filled with water, into which the hull of a Sherman tank had been sunk. He was required to seat himself in the underwater fighting compartment, operate the controls for a specific time and then surface.

Six men flatly refused to do this, in spite of orders, pep-talks and threats. In the end Michael Laycock was summoned to deal with the situation. He addressed them in his usual energetic and sincere way, pointed out the simplicity of the operation, and proceeded to demonstrate. All went well until he had surfaced, when in his eagerness and enthusiasm he removed the Davis Apparatus in the wrong sequence, which was the only part of the whole operation that required care and, if not done correctly, caused a certain amount of coughing and spluttering. The effect of the demonstration was somewhat marred by a fit of choking, spluttering and gasping on Michael's part, from which he took some time to recover, which caused certain silent mirth and apprehension to those present. However, in spite of everything, through his perseverance, good humour and tact, he dispelled all the doubts and fears of those who had refused and nearly all went down. An NCO who had been decorated in the desert was among those who refused flatly to descend into the cistern. Having almost been drowned as a child he presented a psychological case so often encountered not only in war but peacetime. Naturally he lost his stripes, but just prior to D-Day he volunteered to join the crew of a DD tank for the invasion on the condition that he was excused from wearing a Davis Escape Apparatus, which was agreed. He fought and behaved magnificently on D-Day and during the following days and by D+28 he was promoted once again to sergeant.

Bert Jenkins remembers the episode well. 'They were Valentine DD tanks,' he says, 'and they kept sinking.' Bert and the other men in B Squadron knew Mike Laycock as 'Black Mike' – although he was a stalwart of the Regiment, he was known to have a quick temper and was thought of as somewhat over-zealous. 'He gave us this sob story about how we were saving the country and God knows what else,' says Bert, 'and he convinced us it was all going to be all right.'

At the end of April, A and HQ Squadrons were posted from Chippenham to Sway, near the coast in Hampshire. It became very obvious at that time that D-Day was getting close. We spent our time waterproofing and de-waterproofing our tanks, and partaking in various amphibious exercises, working in close co-operation with the navy and infantry. All embarkation leave had been completed, and each time we went on an exercise nobody knew whether we would return to our billets again. One day in the middle of May we left Sway, never to return, and ended up at Hursley Park, near Winchester, which turned out to be our assembly area preparatory to the invasion.

Training had been completed, and all exercises had now finished, and the time had arrived for the final briefing and the endless O Groups that would follow with the various infantry we were to support in the assault. Nobody had been told the actual date of the invasion, or, naturally, the place, but on 20 May all squadron leaders were informed that the invasion would take place on 5 June, and we were given the broad outlines of the army, corps and divisional invasion plan and a most detailed briefing of our brigade plan and objectives that our tanks and the infantry had to capture. The plan of the assault was illustrated on a sand model representing in minute detail the portion of the beach which we had to assault, but all features and villages had codenames, likewise the maps we were given. We were told that not until we had actually left the shores of England would maps be issued with the codenames substituted by the real names, and these would be handed to us by the craft commanders. After one conference at which we had been studying the sand table for a long time, John Bethell-Fox, a troop leader in my squadron, came up and said, 'I lay you 10–1 we shall land in Normandy – I recognize the coastline.' And he was right. His mother was French and he had spent most of his youth in France.

As regards the enemy forces, we were told that in France, Belgium and Holland the Germans had 60 divisions, including 10 panzer and 50 infantry divisions, of which 36 infantry and 6 panzer divisions were located in the general coastal area opposite England. In the Normandy assault area the Germans had concentrated nine infantry divisions and one panzer division.

Our brigade, the 8th Armoured, had been placed under command of the 50th Division (in XXX Corps), and they had been ordered to assault the beach known as Gold and to capture the villages of Asnelles-sur-Mer, Arromanches, Meuvaines and Ryes. The division was to attack on a two-brigade front, 231 Brigade Group on the left and 69 Brigade Group on the right. The Sherwood Rangers were placed in support of 231 Brigade, consisting of the Hampshires, the 1st Dorsets and the 2nd Devons, who had to assault the beach between Le Hamel on the west and La Rivière on the east. B Squadron were to swim in, supporting the 1st Hampshires on the right and C Squadron the 1st Dorsets on the left. These two squadrons were scheduled to land at H Hour minus 5 minutes. A Squadron, my squadron, would land as a reserve squadron, straight from the tank landing craft on to the beach. In the second phase the Regiment would operate in support of 56 Infantry Brigade group.

Although 8th Armoured Brigade was under command of 50th Division for the invasion, they were one of a number of 'independent' brigades, not permanently attached to any division. This meant they could be repeatedly moved about and temporarily attached to different infantry divisions to offer armour support. In other words, wherever the infantry were in action, these independent brigades, like 8th Armoured, and the individual regiments within them, were likely to be fighting too.

The assault would take place at first light and would be preceded by an intensive air attack on all known enemy gun positions on the beach and naval bombardment. Naturally, a very thorough air reconnaissance had been carried out and practically every gun position and gun emplacement had been pin-pointed and photographed. Wireless silence had to be maintained up to H minus 15, except for the DD squadron tanks who could relax wireless silence on the B set, or the short-wave set, to control landing and the swim-in.

All this information, still all with codenames, had to be passed on and discussed, which necessitated endless conferences with the various infantry to be supported in the different phases of the assault.

By the end of May, all briefing and conferences had been completed and we moved from Hursley Park to our final concentration area a few miles outside Southampton. The whole camp was wired in and heavily guarded and once having entered nobody was allowed out under any pretext; all contact with the outside world was completely broken. Our camp, identified as C10, was well organized, well fed, and included a great variety of troops, who were taking part in the invasion, mostly Canadian. At this period various messages were distributed to all units, which had to be read out to all ranks, one from the Supreme Commander Eisenhower, one from Montgomery and one from the divisional commander – for some reason I always hated being wished luck before going into action. While in this camp, I found myself treading on a playing card, which I discovered was the nine of hearts – the luckiest card in the pack. I kept it in my wallet for the rest of the war.

The weather at the beginning of June was extremely cold and unpleasant, and we all kept wondering whether there would be a postponement. Sometimes I hoped that there would be – a kind of urge to put off the evil hour – and at other times I had a longing to get cracking and to get the thing started.

On 1 June we left the various camps for Southampton docks to be loaded on the tank landing craft. As we passed through Southampton the people gave us a wonderful welcome and each time that we halted we were all plied with cups of tea and cakes, much to the consternation of the Military Police escorting the column who had strict orders to prevent any contact between civilian and soldier. I wondered so much how many of those good people realized that we were leaving to assault Europe and not proceeding on yet another exercise. The organization for this complicated journey from camp to craft through Southampton was remarkable as regards the move itself, replenishment and rations – considering the mass of vehicles and the vast number of men all to be embarked in the correct sequence, on the right craft, at the right time. Meanwhile all the DD tanks moved from their secret training camps on specially constructed runways, down out of the cliffs to the beaches, and embarked from there onto the landing craft. As soon as it was announced that A Squadron should be the reserve squadron for the invasion, and that B and C Squadrons should undertake the role of DD tanks supporting the first wave of the assaulting troops, the latter two squadrons had the impudence to christen A Squadron 'The BASE WALLAHS'.

The Regiment was aboard craft belonging to 15 and 43 LCT Flotilla. Each craft with its crew of three or four, commanded by a sub-lieutenant, could take up to six tanks and their crews, and with a full load on board it was practically impossible to move, let alone find a place to sleep on deck at full length.

Each tank from RHQ and A Squadron had to be reversed up the ramp of the craft, which was not very wide, so that when the time came to disembark it could proceed forward from off the craft. As soon as each craft had taken on its load it withdrew and tied up along-side the quayside or another craft. These tank landing craft were flat-bottomed and open to the sky, except for a small but comfortable wardroom in the stern. The commander of our craft was a most delightful youngster, who showed great hospitality and insisted that I should use his wardroom at all times. Once the tanks had been embarked the troops were allowed to wander along the quayside, but naturally were strictly prohibited from leaving the dock area. As I wandered along the water front I gazed with amazement at the tremendous variety of craft of all descriptions, including the vast 'Mulberry', or artificial harbour, which was to be towed across the Channel to the invasion beaches after the assault. Such a conglomeration of shipping presented a magnificent target for aircraft, and I felt extremely grateful to the RAF for having knocked the German Air Force from the skies.

*

The invasion fleet was certainly an impressive sight as it silently sailed down Southampton Water, and I tried to visualize other invasion fleets which had left England over the years, and vaguely wondered whether the invader of bygone days had had the same 'rats in the stomach' feeling, which I had then and always experienced before going in to bat, or ride in a steeplechase. I am quite certain that his invading craft was more comfortable than a landing craft tank.

Almost immediately after we had set sail our craft commander presented each tank commander with a small imitation-leather despatch case, securely wired and sealed, and containing the maps of our invasion area. I immediately set about sorting out my set of maps into the map case and endeavoured to identify from coded maps the various place names and objectives, a somewhat awkward under-taking on a flat-bottomed craft in a choppy sea, and it made me feel decidedly seasick. However, a mug of soup made all the difference. The soup that had been issued to us was contained in an ordinary tin, and when punctured in the base a certain chemical action was set up which heated the soup in five minutes. A most remarkable invention and extremely useful; an excellent piping-hot beverage in an amazingly short time!

We spent an uneventful, but uncomfortable and sleepless night. It was cold and the sea was very choppy and most of us felt sick, in spite of the seasick tablets that had been issued. At dawn, our very young and pleasant craft commander, who was on his first operational command, was most relieved to find that he had kept station through-out the night and had not completely lost himself. He confided to me that navigation was not his strong subject.

As dawn broke we heard the preliminary naval bombardment and bombing, and, as we drew nearer to the French coast, we passed by a great variety of naval craft including battleships, cruisers, destroyers, minesweepers and motor torpedo boats that had played their part, either in escorting the invasion fleet or bombarding the beaches.

At H-hour we switched on the tank wireless sets to find out how B and C Squadrons had fared. Reception was extremely poor and there was continual interference from other stations, which was not surprising considering the tremendous number of frequencies that had to be used on D-Day. I heard the voice of Stephen Mitchell, C Squadron commander, cursing some other station interfering with his 'net'. He certainly appeared to be most irritated, but it was good to hear his voice, which meant that he was safe for the time being.

In all, five DD tanks from C Squadron and three of B Squadron sank, but the rest made it, largely thanks to the good sense of the navy. Realizing the sea was far too rough to release the tanks 7000 yards out, as had originally been the plan, the LCTs had gone in to a few hundred yards from the beach instead. Others reached the beach safely only to be hit from the shore defences. A 77mm gun casement at Le Hamel, the western end of Gold Beach where the Sherwood Rangers were landing, proved particularly troublesome.

Bert Jenkins and his crew had been dropped 700 yards out, reached the beach safely, then had to stop to disengage the propellers. At that moment, the tank was hit, and the canvas screen around them for swimming to the shore went up in flames. Christ, thought Bert, we're going to be fried in here. We're finished. But he, Lieutenant Monty Horley, whom he had served under in North Africa, and one other managed to get out and were crouching behind the tank, wondering how to escape the fray when Monty and the other man were shot and killed. Bert remained there until much later, when the beach was finally cleared. He had no idea what had happened to the fourth and fifth members of his tank – but he was the only survivor. The casement, however, was knocked out by a 25-pounder fired by a member of the Essex Yeomanry – the round went straight through the aperture.

When we were about a mile from land, all crews were mounted and tank engines running in preparation for landing. The craft had to be steered through the numerous underwater obstacles, just visible above the water, but also had to avoid other LCTs struggling with the same difficulty and all converging on the same point; it was a formidable task for the craft commander. We did, however, ram an obstruction –

an iron stake, fortunately not capped with a mine – which prevented further forward movement, but caused no extensive damage. It took a little time to extricate ourselves: we had to reverse and make a complete turn, and as our nose pointed once again towards England I had a sneaking desire to continue in that direction!

At that time, except for spasmodic shelling directed at the ships and the beaches and the odd sniping, B and C Squadrons appeared to have captured their objectives and silenced all the front-line beach defences, consisting of concrete gun emplacements, and strong-points surrounded by barbed wire.

About 100 yards from the shore, the craft commander gave the order 'full speed ahead' and drove his craft at the shore: when the bows touched down, the ramp was released with a crash, down which each tank slowly and painfully made its way through a few feet of water onto the shore.

As I landed I noticed Bill Enderby, wounded in the arm, and in obvious pain, slowly making his way onto a tank landing craft, which was just about to reverse and return to England with other wounded aboard. I waved to him and continued to extricate my way up the beach, which was littered with a variety of army equipment, including knocked-out tanks, and pitted with deep bomb holes, which made progress difficult.

Eventually A Squadron joined up with what remained of B and C Squadrons at the prearranged rendezvous, and then came under command of the 56th Infantry Brigade of the 50th Division. En route we passed through a tiny village called Asnelles where we anticipated some sort of opposition, but the Germans had apparently cleared out, and all we saw were some local inhabitants, who appeared to regard us with disinterest and unfriendly suspicion; I do not blame them, as the invasion had caused untold damage to their countryside and should any of them have lived in the villages situated on the invasion beaches their houses would have been completely wrecked.

Michael Howden, one of my troop leaders, experienced some difficulty in finding the rendezvous. Michael was known as 'Dis-Mike', because he suffered from a slight stammer and somehow always managed to have certain difficulty with his wireless set. So often after trying to contact him on the wireless he would suddenly come on the air and say, 'Sorry, but my m-m-m-mike is d-d-d-dis.' In other words, the microphone of his set was not working. After repeated calls over the wireless, which drew no reply and caused me anxiety for his safety, I was most relieved to hear once again that well-known stammer from Dis-Mike about his dis-mike.

Stan Cox was the gunner in Mike Howden's tank. As they moved inland on D-Day, movement was clearly spotted in a nearby tree. Fearing it was a sniper, about which there had already been many warnings, Howden ordered Stan to give the tree a burst of the Sherman's machine-gun. Having traversed the turret, Stan then fired, by mistake, the main 75mm gun instead, hitting the trunk about halfway up and felling the tree completely. 'B-b-b-bugger, Cox,' exclaimed Howden. 'That was a b-b-b-bit b-b-b-bloody drastic!'

Naturally I was most anxious to learn how B and C Squadrons had fared. Owing to the bad weather and choppy seas, the DD tanks were launched very close to the beaches and only swam for a comparatively short distance. Even so, five C Squadron tanks and three B Squadron tanks were swamped after leaving the landing craft, and sank to the bottom of the sea. Most of the crews were rescued, I was relieved to hear, and were awaiting fresh tanks. The villages of Le Hamel and La Rivière were captured without undue opposition. Snipers, however, proved most unpleasant to all tank commanders, and claimed Colonel Anderson as a casualty. A German 50mm anti-tank gun concealed in a house was causing some trouble, and the colonel decided to do a recce on foot. He was warned both by Sergeant Towers, his signal sergeant, and George Jones, the adjutant, to beware of snipers, to which he replied, 'Don't worry, I shall be wearing my tin hat.' He was immediately hit twice by a sniper, and pinned down in a ditch for an hour before he was rescued and sent back to England. Michael Laycock, the regimental second-in-command took charge of the Regiment. Monty Horley, who commanded a troop in

B Squadron, was killed as he was landing his tank on the beach.

The Sherwood Rangers had been a bit rudderless since the death of
Donny Player. Colonel Ian Spence, who had taken over from Player,
had been brought into the Regiment and had not been especially popular.
He had annoyed some of the officers by playing poker in the mess and
winning not insignificant sums from some of his men. Back in England,
he was promptly given a staff job and replaced by Colonel John D'Arcy
Anderson, who had been second-in-command of 2nd Armoured Brigade
but had no practical experience of leading a regiment in battle. John
Semken, who was now technical adjutant, was certainly unimpressed by
Anderson, who had asked him what the technical adjutant actually did.
'Commander of an armoured bloody regiment who didn't know that!'
Anderson also tended to speak to the driver of his tank on the A set radio,
so that the whole Regiment heard what he was saying, no matter how
trivial. Despite these apparent shortcomings, he went on to become
General Sir John Anderson, GBE, KCB, DSO, and deputy chief of the
Imperial General Staff.

After a short period for de-waterproofing the tanks and maintenance,
the next phase of the battle started and A Squadron supported the
Devons in capturing Ryes [*sic*], which fell without much opposition.
Except for Tunisia this was the first time that we experienced tank fighting through villages and in enclosed country, and it was not altogether
pleasant, as we found once again that a 30-ton tank with a crew of five is
extremely vulnerable to one German infantryman who simply had to
conceal himself in a ditch while the tank went past, and then either fire
a 'bazooka' or throw a sticky bomb on the engine of the tank, which he
would write off most easily and then slip away without being seen.

The Germans did not have American bazookas, but did use two types of
anti-tank projectile: the Panzerfaust *and the rocket-fired* Panzerschreck.
Both could be extremely effective, but were only so at short ranges of no
more than around 150 yards. Using them against oncoming tanks
required nerves of steel.

Further, the tank commander, who cannot control his tank or troop or fight a battle without his head above the turret, was extremely vulnerable to snipers, who caused so many casualties among our best and most experienced tank commanders. We soon learned that in the bocage country, consisting of deep-sunk lanes bordered by high hedges on either side, tanks could not be operated without close infantry support.

After the fall of Reyhs [*sic*], A Squadron fought with the Essex Regiment to capture the high ground outside the old town of Bayeux. I had the greatest difficulty in locating the colonel of the Essex Regiment, who had failed to appear at the prearranged rendezvous, but I was informed by a member of his battalion that he had been seen four miles down the lane. It was most imperative that he should be contacted immediately, so I either had to find him in my tank, as no small vehicles had been landed, which entailed making a most painfully slow and cumbersome journey along a very muddy lane swarming with infantry waiting to take part in the next phase of the attack, or use my feet, which, of course, appeared equally unattractive. However, I found a most happy and ideal solution to my problem, for, much to my amazement, I discovered a fully saddled horse belonging, presumably, to the local policeman, standing patiently outside a house. I immediately mounted and dashed off to locate the commanding officer of the Essex. Never in my wildest dreams did I ever anticipate that D-Day would find me dashing along the lanes of Normandy endeavouring, not very successfully, to control a very frightened horse with one hand, gripping a map case in the other, and wearing a tin hat and black overalls! The Essex colonel was somewhat startled when I eventually found him, and reported that my squadron was all ready to support his battalion in the next phase of the attack.

Bayeux could have been attacked and captured that evening, as patrols reported that the town was very lightly held, but the commanding officer of the Essex preferred to remain on the outskirts for the night.

So ended D-Day. The landing had been successful and objectives had been taken and all units of the 50th Division were in the exact position as planned on the sand table over so many conferences. All of us were weary and maybe suffering from reaction; however, after replenishment of the tanks and various order groups for the battle next day, most of us had about five hours' good sleep.

On the whole, D-Day was a success for the Allies. It came as a surprise to the German defenders who had not been expecting an attack in such weather and who had been caught off-guard with a number of senior officers away – not least Rommel, commander of Army Group B and the Atlantic Wall. The bridgeheads around each of the five invasion beaches were not as large as had been hoped, and opposite Sword Beach, the British failed to secure the key city of Caen, one of the principal D-Day targets, but the landings had not been pushed back into the sea, which had been the planners' greatest fear. Overall, too, casualty figures were only a third of those expected. By the end of D-Day, 132,715 troops had been landed along with some 20,000 vehicles.

The Germans had 10 panzer divisions available in the west: three directly under Rommel's control, three more in the south-west of France, and four under command of Panzer Group West, which fell beyond Rommel's direct command. They now had to bring these divisions up to the front as quickly as possible. It was some of these crack units that the Sherwood Rangers would confront in the following days and weeks.

15

Fighting in Normandy

The first Jagdtiger knocked out by the Sherwood Rangers.

THE NEXT DAY reports came through that the landings on all the beaches had been successful, and that, generally speaking, opposition had been less severe than anticipated, except on Omaha Beach, on our right, where the Americans suffered heavy casualties. At one time their position was very precarious owing to the withering fire on the beach, and they had great difficulty in holding their very limited beach-head.

The Americans on Utah Beach met the least opposition of all: owing to an error in navigation, they landed where there were fewer obstacles and less resistance – apparently the Germans in that area had relied on a flooded countryside as a form of defence.

It was interesting to learn afterwards that the coastal defences had not been destroyed by the bombing and the naval bombardment that preceded the attack, owing to the enormous thickness of the concrete and to the fact that accurate bombing was made difficult by the low cloud. However, it must have had a tremendous effect on the morale of the defenders and produced a most unhealthy Maginot Line complex.

We all had a most wonderful feeling of relief on D-Day+1, knowing that beach-heads had been established all along the invasion coast, resulting from a landing that had been made from high seas which had swamped many landing craft and caused many infantrymen to be swept away as they waded to the beach from the landing craft. At the same time we still appeared to be a long way from Berlin.

In tank warfare there are two distinct types of fighting: the deliberate frontal attack against prepared enemy positions in order to make a hole in the enemy's line, through which an armoured column can pass; and the pursuit battle, which follows the piercing of the enemy's line.

In the deliberate battle, generally speaking, the tank regiment is placed in support of an infantry brigade, and each squadron of the tank regiment supports an infantry battalion, and the attack is preceded by intensive artillery concentrations on known enemy strong-points, during which time the sappers clear lanes through the minefields through which the tanks can pass. The tank colonel works with the infantry brigadier and the tank squadron leader with the infantry battalion commanders.

The pursuit battle is altogether more satisfactory and follows the breaking of the enemy's line. The armoured regiment is sent off on its own, with its company of motorized infantry and battery of guns, and works independently of the brigade to exploit successes and cause havoc in the rear of the enemy; light opposition is brushed aside or, if too strong, bypassed. It is an ideal command where the armoured regiment commander can use initiative, speed and is entirely independent of his brigade commander.

From the Battle of Alamein to the end of the North-west European Campaign, the fighting consisted of a series of deliberate and pursuit battles and as, throughout the war, only a limited number of armoured divisions existed, the 8th Independent Armoured Brigade was continually called upon to support the very numerous infantry divisions who were not in armoured divisions, for a deliberate attack and then again for the pursuit battle.

The most unsatisfactory operational command in the army is that of the brigadier of an armoured brigade. Seldom does he take direct command of his three armoured regiments, which are either fighting under command of an infantry brigade in a deliberate battle or have been sent off independently as a regimental group in a pursuit chase. Not often in Europe did he command his whole brigade operating as one unit in a pursuit battle, although he did so in the desert, which in fact can be considered a somewhat specialized, and certainly more pleasant kind of warfare.

From now on the Regiment fought a continual series of deliberate or pursuit battles until the end of the war, varying in intensity.

Although this section was probably written after the end of the war, the contrast between the authority and experience of his writing here and that of the young captain new to armoured warfare of just a couple of years earlier is particularly striking.

On D-Day+l, 7 June, the Regiment attacked that ancient and historic town of Bayeux. A Squadron attacked with the Essex, and B Squadron came in from the north with the South Wales Borderers; C Squadron remained in reserve with Regimental Headquarters at St Sulpice. We were the first troops into the town and were most relieved to find that, except for isolated strong-points in the town and the odd sniper, no Germans were to be found, which prevented any damage to the beautiful and historic buildings. We were given a most enthusiastic and spontaneous reception by the inhabitants, who appeared genuinely delighted to welcome us and demonstrated their joy by throwing flowers at the tanks and distributing cider and food among the men.

One enemy machine-gun post concealed in a house held out in the south of the town. The building caught fire as a result of our gun-fire. After a very short space the clanging of a bell heralded the arrival of the Bayeux fire brigade, manned by a full team all wearing shiny helmets. Regardless of the machine-gun fire, they held up the battle, entered the house, extinguished the fire and brought out the German machine-gun section.

On 8 June all the regiments of the 8th Armoured Brigade rejoined the brigade and formed a mobile column to move south. The Regiment was ordered to make a small right hook and to occupy some high ground known as Point 103, which overlooked the villages of St Pierre and Fontenay. We encountered en route certain anti-tank guns, which we bypassed, and snipers as usual compelled all tank commanders to keep their heads down, but we arrived at our destination without a casualty, except for Victor Verner, one of my troop commanders, who was hit in the head by a sniper and eventually died from his wound. He had fought with us in North Africa and at all times in battle nothing ever disturbed him: his imperturbability and quiet efficiency inspired confidence from those under his command. His death was a grave loss to the squadron.

On arrival at Point 103, the squadron took up fire positions in the trees overlooking St Pierre, which appeared to be deserted by the civilians and Germans. As no infantry had arrived, John Bethell-Fox, one of my troop commanders, and Keith Douglas, my second-in-command, climbed down the hill into the village, but had the greatest difficulty in making contact with any of the civilians, who had all taken refuge in the cellars. They eventually persuaded an old Frenchman to come out of hiding; he told them that there were Germans in the village and tanks in the vicinity, then, thinking discretion the better part of valour, they beat a retreat back to their tanks, but on turning a corner they came face to face with a German patrol under an officer. Such an unexpected meeting caused alarm and surprise on both sides and they turned about and made for their respective bases. Keith, however, managed to empty his revolver in the direction of the enemy, but did not wait to ascertain the damage.

The Germans in the village were the vanguard of the Panzer Lehr Division, one of the finest armoured units in the German Army.

That evening we were more than pleased at the arrival of some anti-tank gunners, with a company of machine-gunners, as we felt rather naked and lonely on this high ground, especially at night, without infantry protection.

On the morning of 9 June Point 103 became most uncomfortable and appeared to be the main target of German mortar and shellfire. Enemy tanks had also appeared on the scene. Although the trees on Point 103 gave some cover from view, it was quite impossible for the tanks to find a hull-down position, and each time they came forward to engage from the top of the hill they became a sitting target for the German tanks in the village, especially for one which cleverly and continually ran up and down a deep lane in the valley that afforded natural cover and in which alternative fire positions were plentiful. However, after watching his movements very carefully, Sergeant Dring eventually scored five hits with his 17-pounder and blew him up, but not before he had caused us some damage.

Michael Howden (Dis-Mike), Sergeant Rush and Sergeant Houghton all had their tanks knocked out, but they and their crews baled out without injury, except that Dis-Mike's stammer prevented any kind of speech for half an hour and his complexion – which at the best of times is devoid of colour – was even whiter than snow. Peter Pepler from B Squadron was killed by a piece of shrapnel as he was entering his tank and Keith Douglas, my second-in-command, was hit in the head by a piece of mortar shell as he was running along a ditch towards his tank, and was killed instantly.

Keith had joined the Regiment during our early days in Palestine and had been badly wounded at the Battle of Zem Zem in the desert, but had recovered in time to land with us in Normandy. His early youth had been unhappy owing to parental matrimonial trouble, but an adoring and hardworking mother had found sufficient money to educate him and to send him to the university for one term before the war started. When he joined the Regiment he appeared to have a grudge against the world in general and particularly his fellow Yeomanry officers, of whom there were quite a few at that time, who had been with the Regiment before the war and consisted of the wealthy landed gentry: these he regarded as complete snobs and accused of being utterly intolerant of anyone unable to 'talk horses' or who had not been educated at an English public school. He was a complete individualist, intolerant of military convention and discipline, which made life for him and his superior officers difficult. His artistic talents were clearly illustrated by his many drawings and the poetry that he wrote very much in the modern strain, and, had he lived, I am convinced that he would have made a name for himself in the world of art. I recall so many times at various conferences and order groups having to upbraid him for drawing on his map instead of paying attention.

In action he had undaunted courage and always showed initiative and complete disregard for his own personal safety. At times he appeared even to be somewhat foolhardy – maybe on account of his short-sightedness, which compelled him to wear large, thick-lensed glasses. I regret that he was not spared to know that he was mentioned-in-despatches for outstanding service.

At the end of the desert campaign he wrote a book about the Regiment and the fighting in North Africa, which he asked me to read and write a Foreword to, and I readily agreed to this request. He disguised all personalities with fictitious names and described with cynical detail (for the most part with accuracy), various personalities in the Regiment, including some unkind and unjustified allusions to certain officers who had been killed. These I insisted he should omit for the sake of next-of-kin who would certainly hear about and read the book and find such references most hurtful.

In the original text he described my dancing as being 'deplorable', to which I objected, pointing out that he had never seen my efforts on the dance floor and that I considered myself well above the average, and as a result of my protest he agreed to alter the text.

Keith Douglas was as good as his word, and by the time Alamein to Zem Zem *was published, Stanley's dancing had been upgraded to 'competent' in the 'restrained English style'. It says much about Stanley, however, that what he objected to was the description of his dancing when some of the*

*other comments Douglas made about him might, on the face of it, have
seemed more hurtful.*

*Padre Leslie Skinner claimed that Douglas had had premonitions of
his death, although John Semken remembers him talking about wanting
to be part of the invasion so that he could then write about it. 'He wasn't
proposing to write about it hereafter, was he?' says John. Stuart Hills, a
new troop commander in C Squadron who had been befriended by
Douglas, thinks it was inevitable that, after several years of war, those
who had survived until then would harbour fears of approaching death.
Certainly the returning odds pointed towards it. 'I was a little nervous,'
Hills noted, 'but I had the advantage of simply not knowing how awful
war could be.' Whatever Stanley believed were his chances of coming
through, he never noted them down. Perhaps he did not wish to
tempt Fate . . .*

During the afternoon of 9 June the remainder of the brigade moved
up and the 4/7th Dragoon Guards took over our position on Point
103, which we were delighted to hand over, and the Regiment retired
a couple of miles to reorganize. Each day was extremely long, as dawn
broke at approximately 04.30 hours when leaguer had to be broken,
and the tank wireless sets had to be 'netted in' to the control set in the
colonel's tank, and at night, by the time the tank and ration replenishment and various order groups were completed midnight had passed,
which did not leave many hours for sleep.

The whole of Headquarters Squadron, consisting of all the supply
vehicles under command of Roger Sutton-Nelthorpe and the
Reconnaissance Troop under Patrick McCraith, had now been landed
and had come up to within a few miles of the Regiment.

Our respite was not for long, for on the next day, 10 June, the
Regiment moved forward once again on to Point 103. My squadron was
placed on the left flank to support the infantry, who were anticipating a
counter-attack, which our tank fire frustrated, and accounted for
approximately 40 Germans; in the meantime the 24th Lancers attacked
and captured St Pierre, supporting the infantry. B Squadron was detailed
to spend the night in the village as the 24th Lancers were withdrawn,

while A and C Squadrons spent a sleepless night in the outskirts anticipating a counter-attack, which I am glad to say never eventuated.

June 11 I shall long remember and proved a very sad day for the
Regiment and especially for myself. The position round Point 103 – St
Pierre and Fontenay – was still fluid and unhealthy, the country was
extremely difficult and unpleasant for tanks, and the enemy,
reinforced with tanks and men, started infiltrating back. A Squadron
went once again up to Point 103 to keep observation on the main
Juvigny–Fontenay road, while C Squadron under Stephen Mitchell
moved south to attack the high ground south of the village. B
Squadron remained in reserve with Regimental Headquarters in the
village.

At midday, in answer to an urgent call on the air from John
Hanson-Lawson, I returned to Regimental Headquarters and was told
by John that 'Robin Hood', the CO's tank, had received a direct hit
from a heavy shell, which had instantly killed Major Michael Laycock
(who had been acting colonel since Colonel Anderson had been
wounded on D-Day), Captain George Jones, the adjutant, and
Lieutenant Laurence Head, the intelligence officer, and that Patrick
McCraith, the Recce Troop leader and Sergeant Towers, the signal
sergeant, had both been wounded. Three senior officers killed and one
officer and one sergeant wounded by the same shell, and all from
Regimental Headquarters. This was indeed a shattering blow.

Michael Laycock had joined the Regiment as a Yeomanry officer
soon after leaving Eton and so often he had told me that his great
ambition was to command the Regiment in which his father, Sir
Joseph Laycock, had served both in the Boer and the 1914–18 wars. No
doubt his ambition would have been fulfilled had he lived. Having
served with him since I joined the Regiment in 1939, I can claim to
have been one of his best friends in the Regiment. His manner was
abrupt and sometimes rude, and his temper, which he often lost, was
fiendish, and this, with his dark and swarthy complexion, caused him
to be nicknamed 'Black Michael' by men in the Regiment. But beneath
this superficial exterior, he had a great, kind heart and a simple,
serious and most lovable nature. He had the courage of a lion and

would never issue an unpleasant order in battle that he himself would not be prepared to carry out. His family, knowing our friendship and my great regard for Michael, kindly sent me his wrist-watch, which I wear today and shall treasure always.

The army career of George Jones had been quite remarkable – in fact he was an outstanding personality. The younger son of the head woodsman at Wiseton, the Laycock estate in Nottinghamshire, he had joined the Yeomanry as a trooper a few years prior to the war. When war started he was troop corporal to 2 Troop, C Squadron, under Michael Gold, when the Regiment was a horse cavalry unit. A few weeks before the Regiment embarked from England for the Middle East at the end of 1939, he was sent on a course, from which he returned with such an excellent report that he was immediately pro-moted to sergeant, and soon after became C Squadron sergeant major. During our early days in the Middle East he attended a cadet course in Cairo, which gave him a commission, and he returned to the Regiment at our request to command a troop as a second lieutenant. He fought with us throughout the desert as an officer and died at St Pierre on 11 June 1944, holding the rank of captain and adjutant to Michael Laycock, younger son of the owner of the Wiseton estate. His pleasing appearance, courteous manner and delightful nature endeared him to his brother officers, and after having been commissioned he immediately won and retained the admiration and respect of all those with whom he had served as an OR – other rank – a most difficult attainment. In spite of only having had a village-school education he was quick to learn and possessed great intelligence and a faculty for teaching others what he knew. In battle he was completely imperturbable. Out of battle he was unobtrusively efficient – he was, in fact, if I may use the phrase, 'one of the World's Great Englishmen'. Michael and George were buried beside each other in the orchard at St Pierre.

At 5 o'clock that afternoon the enemy counter-attacked St Pierre and Point 103, and endeavoured to work around the flank and, as a result of this movement, a nasty threat developed to the echelons (i.e. the brigade supply vehicles); with Brigade Headquarters they experienced some very unpleasant shelling, which created something of a flap, and most of the soft-skinned vehicles had to make a hasty retreat. However Roger Sutton-Nelthorpe, Headquarters Squadron leader, decided not to move our regimental echelon, and no vehicle was hit. Our brigadier, Craycroft, was wounded by this shelling and had to be evacuated. He took command of the 8th Armoured on our return from the Middle East. Lawrence Biddle, his brigade major, was also put out of action. Lawrence and I had been commissioned together from the Inns of Court to the Regiment in October 1939; Brigade Headquarters had claimed his services in the desert. It was not surprising as he had a brilliant legal brain – and a lovely sense of humour.

The counter-attack against St Pierre had been checked and the whole Regiment had concentrated in and around the village supporting the Durham Light Infantry. Being the senior squadron leader I took control of the Regiment, feeling utterly dejected and shocked by the deaths of Michael, George, Keith and Lawrence Head – furthermore extremely worried about Stephen Mitchell, commander of C Squadron, whose tank had been brewed up earlier in the day, and of whom nothing had been heard since.

One incident brought us some comic relief. John Hanson-Lawson, Peter Seleri, second-in-command of B Squadron, and I were having a discussion on the back of my tank regarding the reorganization of Regimental Headquarters, with half a bottle of whisky beside us. A very sudden and sharp spell of enemy 'stonking' put an end to all discussion, and I suggested that we should adjourn to our tanks until I recalled them when things were quieter. Soon afterwards, in between mortar-bursts, I distinctly heard the noise of somebody stealthily climbing up onto the back of my tank and immediately jumped to the conclusion that a German sniper had infiltrated through our lines and was in the act of throwing a grenade into the turret of my tank. I seized my revolver and looked over the top of my turret and, to my astonishment, I saw Peter Seleri halfway up the side of the tank, with his arm outstretched, surreptitiously straining for the whisky bottle, which, in my haste to take cover, I had left on the back of the tank. When he saw me he quickly withdrew the tell-tale arm and, covered with confusion, having been caught in the act, said, 'Did I leave my map case on the back of your tank?'

'I don't think so, Peter,' I replied, 'but do take the bottle of whisky.'

'Thanks a lot.' Grabbing the bottle by the neck, he scrambled off the tank and beetled back to his own, dodging the mortar shells that were falling in the orchard.

He reminded me so much of Mr Pickwick, with his portly figure, protruding blue eyes and bristling fair moustache.

All squadrons spent that night in St Pierre in a very tight and compact circle with what remained of the infantry, anticipating a night attack. After midnight, much to our great delight, Stephen Mitchell with his crew walked into leaguer. They had all managed to bale out without injury from the 'brewed-up' tank and had taken shelter in an old barn. Practically surrounded by German Infantry, they were compelled to wait until dark before they could rejoin the Regiment. None of them appeared worse for their experience. Nobody slept that night, but no attack came. Padre Skinner, our Methodist minister, carried out sterling work during those days, burying the dead and extricating the wounded and dead from 'brewed-up' tanks, sometimes a most difficult and sordid job. The padre was a short, dark man with a very pronounced North Country accent, which advertised his Yorkshire descent of which he was extremely proud, and he always exuded energy and humour.

I shall always remember the opening words of the first service which he found time to conduct after landing in Normandy. He said, 'There are no atheists in a slit trench.' He continued by telling us that the day before he was compelled to dive very smartly into a slit trench during an unpleasant spell of shelling and found himself with four others, all endeavouring to make themselves extremely small. Some of the shells fell uncomfortably close and when he looked for the reaction on the part of his companions he saw only too clearly that each one was praying silently and fervently to some god, obviously for deliverance from their temporary and exceedingly unhealthy predicament. He compared this occasion to his visit one Sunday evening before the invasion to the NAAFI crammed with singing and beer-

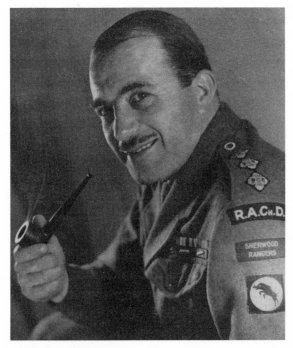

Padre Leslie Skinner.

laden men, where he listened to a couple of men swapping stories, the brunt of which ridiculed the religion to which we all turn when frightened or near to death. There is a great deal in what he said.

The next day, 12 June, we were given a 'holding role' for our immediate front; at the same time we protected the left flank of the 7th Armoured Division, which had recently landed as a 'follow-up' division and was to attack Tilly-sur-Seulles. A Squadron again operated in the neighbourhood of Point 103, with which we had all become so very familiar. We received a nasty shock in finding that some German Tiger and Panther tanks had, during the night, worked their way through a gap in our lines into the thickly wooded area around Point 102. It was extremely difficult to engage and after a game of hide-and-seek in the woods they slipped away down a sunken lane, but Squadron Sergeant Major Hutchinson had his 17-pounder tank knocked out at very short range; fortunately he himself escaped injury.

That evening the whole Regiment drew back to the Bayeux area to replenish and re-equip, and during the days of 13 and 14 June we were given time to reorganize and rest, which we sorely needed. Since landing on D-Day we had been continually in action and were very short of sleep. Even so the Regiment was placed at an hour's notice to move to support the 7th Armoured Division, if needed, which attacked Villers-Bocage on the 14th. Their attack misfired and the Regimental Headquarters and leading squadron of the Armoured Regiment – the County of London Yeomanry – were cut off and captured when the enemy counter-attacked with tanks and infantry. I am glad to say that we were not called upon.

Villers-Bocage has become one of the most mythologized episodes of the Normandy campaign. The British were desperate to try to envelop and then isolate the key town of Caen and, on 13 June, pushed forward to the south-west of the city to the village of Villers-Bocage and, due to the urgency of pressing on, arrived there without the normal reconnaissance. Unknown to the County of London Yeomanry, who had received a rapturous reception from the inhabitants, they had been spotted by Tiger tanks of the 101st SS Heavy Tank Battalion, commanded by the tank ace Michael Wittmann. In a matter of minutes Wittmann personally knocked out around 13 tanks of varying kinds and a similar number of other vehicles. However, his tank was disabled and later, as the Germans counter-attacked, they lost much the same number of men and tanks. The Battle of Villers-Bocage was hardly the British disgrace it has often been painted, but as the German defence was hardening, it marked the last chance for a quick dash to take Caen. The Germans, like the British, understood the importance of this key city in Normandy and were determined to defend it until the last.

On 15 June the brigade commander told me that I had been appointed to command the Regiment, which gave me a great thrill and was indeed a great honour. The casualties among the commanding officers of the Regiment since the Battle of Alamein had been high. We had lost Flash Kellett, Donny Player and Michael Laycock, killed, and D'Arcy Anderson wounded.

Stephen Mitchell left C Squadron to become my second-in-command and I appointed Terry Leinster my adjutant. He was a pre-war member of the Yeomanry who had returned to the Regiment with a commission. My squadron leaders were John Semken, A Squadron, John Hanson-Lawson, B Squadron, and Peter Seleri, C Squadron, and of course Roger Sutton-Nelthorpe remained Headquarters Squadron leader commanding the echelons. Since Patrick McCraith had been wounded at St Pierre, Ian McKay had taken command of the Recce Troop.

Strictly speaking, Stephen Mitchell was the most senior officer after Michael Laycock, and on this basis should have taken command. It appears he was reluctant to do so, however, although very happy to be second-in-command under Stanley, his great friend. 'Those two were like Flanagan and Allen,' says John Semken. 'Always chipping each other along, always laughing.'

The following day, 16 June, the Regiment moved to Aurailles to assist 69 Brigade, and B Squadron had a difficult day supporting the 7th Green Howards; as so often happened, they experienced the greatest difficulty in maintaining contact with the attacking infantry in the extremely enclosed country. This problem was never satisfactorily solved: when the infantry went to ground during an attack all contact between tanks and infantry was lost. The solution must be found in some shape of wireless communication between the tank troop commander and the infantry company commander. Certain experiments were tried but never developed.

Between the 17th and the 20th the brigade was placed under command of the 49th Division, which had recently arrived, and we supported 147 Brigade of that Division. Some very unpleasant fighting took place around Cristot, Chouain and particularly on the high ground covered by the beautiful woods of Le Parc de Boislonde, which A Squadron was instrumental in capturing and which was subjected to very heavy mortaring and shelling. The Duke of Wellingtons, with whom we were holding this high ground, took a bad hammering and retreated without orders, leaving its anti-tank guns and equipment, some of which were captured in a counter-attack. For a day the Regiment felt very naked in this thickly wooded country without infantry protection. During this period Denis Elmore, a very young troop leader who had just arrived with the Regiment, John Bethell-Fox and Sergeants Rush and Harding, all of A Squadron, were wounded, John for the third time. Sergeant Bill Bartle, the Recce Troop sergeant, carried out a recce on foot and positioned himself at the edge of the wood with a pea-lead (i.e. communication line) back to his tank. No trace of him has ever been found, in spite of an intensive search when the battle moved forward. I presume that he must have been caught by a direct hit from a heavy shell. Sergeant Bartle had been with the Regiment since the beginning of the war. We called him 'Old Bill Bartle' because of his striking similarity to the caricature of 'Old Bill' of the 1914–18 war. He invariably clutched a foul-smelling pipe between his teeth, he wore a heavy dark moustache and the edge of his tin hat balanced on the bridge of his nose. Nothing ever ruffled him and he was loved by all.

All the fighting up to this date had taken place in a limited area on an immediate front, progress had been slow and we had not been able to break out. Owing to the continual bad weather the build-up of troops and sappers from England had fallen behind schedule, and at one time the supply position looked serious. The country around Point 103 and Le Parc de Boislonde we traversed continually and knew every inch of the ground. In one of the narrow rides through the Boislonde, continually used by our tanks, a German private had been killed and his body protruded over the edge of the ride. Every time that a tank passed along this ride his arm was crushed by the tracks until nothing remained except a congealed mass of blood and bone. Never shall I be able to obliterate this picture from my mind.

I paid a visit to the headquarters of 29th Armoured Division, having heard that Major Henri Le Grand was most anxious to come back to the Regiment. Henri was a Belgian regular army officer who had escaped from occupied Belgium to England from where he had been sent to the desert to learn about tank fighting; he was posted to my regiment with a view to forming a Belgian Armoured Brigade. He was a most delightful man with an expert knowledge of gunnery and in fact taught us all a great deal about gunnery while he fought with the Regiment in North Africa. My visit, however, was unsuccessful after a cordial interview with Brigadier Roscoe Harvey. I also made an effort to get Michael Gold back to the Regiment. He had gone to the 23rd Hussars, and I received a promise that, provided his commanding officer agreed and that the casualties among their senior officers were not serious, Division would recommend his transfer back to the Sherwood Rangers. I had a few words with Michael, who threatened that he would desert and return to the Regiment if Division did not agree.

Between 19 and 23 June the Regiment remained in the line supporting various infantry units in a non-aggressive role and I had to attend various conferences in preparation for the attack on Fontenay and Rauray. The attack had been delayed owing to bad weather, which had held up the build-up of reserves and supplies from England. We were told, however, that the general picture was satisfactory in that since D-Day we had destroyed six German divisions and had depleted two more to half their original strength, and that all along the front we outnumbered the Hun by two to one.

The bad weather Stanley refers to was in fact a massive storm that wrecked one of the two artificial harbours established along the coast and made a huge impact on the build-up of troops. By 22 June, Montgomery was three divisions short of what had been planned but he still needed to launch his next offensive to take Caen as soon as possible before yet more German reinforcements arrived – II SS Panzer Corps, for example, had now left Poland for Normandy and 1st SS Panzer Division had left Belgium on 17 June. The two-to-one advantage Stanley mentions was not enough: a tenet of military thinking was that an attack should not be launched without an advantage of at least three to one and preferably a higher ratio than that.

Operation EPSOM, as the new offensive was codenamed, would push one armoured and two infantry divisions as well as two

independent armoured brigades across the Odon valley south-west
of Caen. Opposite them were the Panzer Lehr and 12th SS Panzer
Divisions, both among the best the Germans had, but already battered
by the fighting of the past fortnight.

Six new officers joined the Regiment during this period, but with very
limited experience of the Sherman tank and little knowledge of
gunners and troop control.

On 25 June the offensive started at daybreak. The Regiment
supported 147 Infantry Brigade in capturing Fontenay, Rauray, and
finally in occupying the Venres-Tessel Bretteville-Rauray road. Three
days of most unpleasant fighting followed in most appalling misty and
wet weather, which at times reduced visibility to nil. B Squadron
started off by supporting the Royal Scots Fusiliers on the right and C
Squadron the Duke of Wellingtons on the left; A Squadron remained
in reserve. The fighting in Fontenay was most confused, and after the
first day the Germans still held the southern end of the village, which
was finally cleared on the following morning, 26 June – but not before
John Semken, on turning a corner in the centre of the village, came
face to face with a German Tiger tank trundling along the road.
Fortunately he had an armour-piercing shell in the breech of his
75mm gun, which he released at 30 yards' range and then followed up
with another six shells in quick succession, which brewed up the Tiger.
I happened to be following, talking to Brigade Headquarters on the
wireless – in fact, John had just passed me, which was indeed most
fortunate, otherwise the Tiger and I would have met and the result
might have been very different.

The attack on Rauray commenced in the late afternoon of 26 June
when C Squadron led for the first 800 yards, after which A Squadron
passed through it and met very strong opposition on the outskirts;
however, the squadron had a most successful shoot and knocked out
approximately 13 enemy tanks, of which Sergeant Dring bagged four.
A Squadron completed the last part of the attack without infantry
support over very open ground, and finally found itself on the outskirts of the village among a platoon of German infantry, well dug in

and refusing to surrender. Ronnie Grellis, whose troop was in the lead, endeavoured to eliminate it by throwing hand-grenades from his tank, which had no effect, and eventually dismounted from his tank and made it surrender at the point of his revolver. In his excitement he forgot, as so often happened, to switch his wireless from the regimental external frequency to his tank internal communication, both of which work off the same set. As a result the whole Regiment heard the most thrilling and enthralling conversation between him and his crew and appreciated the shouts of encouragement from his crew as he dealt with the German infantry.

The Rangers' bag of 13 enemy tanks compares well with the number of British tanks knocked out at Villers-Bocage.

On the morning of 27 June, B Squadron sent out two troops to investigate the position in Rauray, but unfortunately the Germans had brought up some tanks during the night, which were cleverly concealed in the trees at the edge of the village, and all the tanks of Ray Scott's troop were knocked out. Sergeants Biddell and Green were both killed during the morning. By midday the village was eventually cleared and in it we found eight or nine German tanks, including Panthers, Tigers and Mark 4s, some brewed up and others damaged in some degree. One Tiger tank, hidden among some very thick scrub, appeared completely undamaged and we immediately tested it and found it in perfect running order. We soon found a crew from those dismounted who had lost their tanks in action, painted the Fox's Mask, the brigade's sign, most conspicuously on the front and rear, and attached it to Regimental Headquarters. Unfortunately, Corps Headquarters demanded our Tiger for despatch to England, as it was the first Tiger ever to be captured in Normandy.

John Hanson-Lawson, B Squadron commander, tried to stalk a German tank that appeared to be 'dead'; however a Mark 4 shooting from the flank brewed him up. John and Sergeant Crooks, his signal sergeant, were both wounded, but all the crew managed to bale out from the burning tank, and, thanks to Bill Wharton who dashed out on foot to help, the whole crew, including the wounded, were brought back to safety in an old farmhouse at which I had established Regimental Headquarters. Sergeant Crooks was in a bad condition, but when I spoke to him he smiled and told me that he suffered no pain; he died very shortly afterwards from shock and loss of blood. Crooks was another of the original Yeomen who had fought with the Regiment throughout. He was my troop farrier when I joined in October 1939, and commanded 3 Troop, C Squadron, and after we were mechanized, he made himself one of the most efficient signal NCOs in the Regiment. John Hanson-Lawson had to be evacuated, suffering from a nasty wound and shock. John had been at the university with my cousin Malcolm, and I knew him well before the war; it was through me that he joined the Inns of Court. When war broke out he went to Camberley with the mechanized squadrons while I went to Edinburgh with the mounted squadron, and we were both commissioned to different Regiments. We didn't meet again until he joined us at Newmarket, when he and Michael Gold swapped regiments.

The capture of Rauray and Fontenay had proved most costly. B Squadron could now only muster two officers and only seven out of their 16 tanks.

One evening outside Rauray a very small black rabbit suddenly started up from under my feet and disappeared into the hedge. Thinking that we needed a regimental mascot I gave chase and plunged through the hedge in pursuit of the rabbit. Similar to so many Normandy hedges, this one was thick, strong and full of thorns of no mean size. With great difficulty I eventually caught the rabbit and emerged on the other side of the hedge perspiring profusely and in a somewhat tattered condition. Unfortunately I stumbled over a private from the Durham Light Infantry, slumbering in the ditch on the far side of the hedge, who awoke with an expression of sudden alarm, which soon turned to astonishment when he saw a very dishevelled lieutenant colonel grasping a struggling little black rabbit. He said nothing, but I am quite convinced that he thought the rabbit would be eaten. I walked away trying – without any success – to appear

Men of C Squadron, July 1944.

completely unconcerned and as dignified as the circumstances would permit. As I went back to the Regimental Headquarters tanks I passed through C Squadron tanks and, on enquiring for the squadron leader, Peter Seleri, was informed that he was asleep in his squadron scout car. I approached the scout car and on opening up the sliding roof I found Peter stretched at full length and fast asleep. (Incidentally, if the driver's seat is removed a scout car is the most comfortable of all vehicles for sleep.) Obviously he was dog-tired and, fascinated, I listened to the usual whistling which emanates from the open mouth of a deep sleeper, and vaguely wondered what he was dreaming about. I then suddenly decided that I would have my revenge for the very recent rabbit episode, so I gently lowered the rabbit onto his chest. For quite a while the rabbit gazed with unflinching eyes at Peter, who must have gradually become conscious of the weight on his chest, for he suddenly opened his eyes and found himself regarding a little black rabbit within six inches of his nose. He received a horrid shock, and his first reaction was to rub his eyes vigorously as if to obliterate a most unreal and unpleasant vision. When the vision remained he made a frantic effort to grab the rabbit, which beat a hasty retreat to the end of the scout car. I then made my presence known to a somewhat embarrassed and very sleepy-eyed Peter, who made a valiant effort to salute and extricate his large body from the scout car all at the same time. I gently pushed him back again and told him to resume his sleep, which I had so rudely disturbed. In 15 seconds he was once again unconscious.

On 3 July the Regiment was relieved by the County of London Yeomanry (part of the 4th Armoured Brigade), commanded by Sandy Cameron, a very great pre-war friend of mine and an ex-colleague in the Inns of Court. He had fought in the desert and collected a DSO and two MCs. It was good to see him again, but after showing him our dispositions and introducing him to the infantry commander I was extremely happy to hand the 'Rauray front' over to him. Before we withdrew, C Squadron took part in an attack with a company of the 10th DLI, to capture Quedeville, approximately 1000 yards south of Loury, which place was held by a party of fanatical Germans. One DLI platoon was cut off and was eventually extricated by the recce troop, which lost two tanks. Sergeant Nelson did some sterling work in bringing the two crews back under heavy mortar and machine-gun fire.

EPSOM ended in stalemate. The British had not achieved the decisive breakthrough to Caen that they had hoped but, on the other hand, the German counter-attack launched on 29 June had been mauled. Although their line had held, it had cost the enemy precious reserves and had meant sacrificing the chance of any significant future counter-offensive.

On 4 July the Regiment moved all squadrons to a most delightful orchard in the area of Chouain, and for the first time since we landed the whole Regiment, with all the B vehicles (i.e. supply vehicles) was assembled together. The knowledge that we should have a few days' uninterrupted rest and time for sleep, maintenance and reorganization in pleasant surroundings brought us immense relief.

Michael Gold rejoined the Regiment on 6 July and took command of B Squadron. He was delighted to be back again and we were equally pleased to see him. I am afraid that he found a very depleted squadron. He wrote these words after he had been around the whole squadron and asked me to include them in my personal war diary:

When I resumed command of my old squadron in the Sherwood Rangers I found that many of my old friends had become casualties. I miss them all, and in particular I would like to pay tribute to the memory of four sergeants, three of whom were killed in action in June 1944 and one who died of wounds received on the beaches. They are Sergeants G. Green, L. Biddell, W. Crooks and W. Digby. The four of them were all great friends and were largely instrumental in creating within the squadron an exceptional spirit of friendship and loyalty. They were as proud of their squadron as we were of them. To say that they did their duty is an understatement. They were leaders and a magnificent example to us all. We were all close friends, a friendship proven by daily companionship, dangers shared and difficulties over-come. As friends we mourn them who cannot easily, if ever, be replaced but we shall for ever retain their memory and be eternally grateful for the 'tradition' which they left with the Regiment, and, if I may say so, particularly in B Squadron. We cannot measure what they did for England; we cannot add up the destruction they wrought on the enemy. Sufficient to say that throughout the desert campaign until the fall of Tunis and from D-Day in Europe until their death they were continually in the lead. May there never be wanting in this realm a succession of men of like spirit and discipline, imagination and valour, humble and unafraid.

On the same day Myles Hildyard, who left the Regiment to join the staff of the 7th Armoured Division, paid us a visit. He told us that the higher command was very satisfied with the general position and that Monty had forecast that we should be in Paris by the end of the month.

We were shocked to hear that Henri Le Grand had been killed while fighting with the 23rd Hussars. Apparently he had sought permission, which was granted, to borrow a troop to eliminate an anti-tank gun; as he was leading the troop his tank was brewed up and he was instantly killed. I heard afterwards that he had made a very great reputation for himself during the time that he had spent with the British Army. He was a most unassuming man with a cheerful and lovely disposition.

Geoffrey Makins, a young major from the Royals, joined the Regiment and took command of A Squadron.

On the first evening of our rest period I had dined with B Squadron officers, under a tent they carried in one of the echelon vehicles. We had most sumptuous fare, thanks to the local inhabitants, who were only too willing to barter their local farm produce for bully beef. The Camembert cheese and local cider were delicious.

The usual conferences and order groups at Brigade Headquarters started again immediately for the next attack – known as Maoriz – and on the afternoon of 10 July the Regiment moved to a concentration area in Folliot. From the 11th to the 13th all three squadrons were involved in very heavy fighting in the usual thickly enclosed country, supporting 70 Brigade and 231 Brigade of the 50th Division, which we had not encountered since the invasion. Both these brigades expressed their delight at being with us again, and stated quite firmly that the 8th Armoured Brigade and especially the Sherwood Rangers had given them better support than other armour with which they had fought. This operation was part of a full-scale attack along the whole front to make a break-out and our immediate objective was the line of the Juvigny–Hottot–Landes road and the high ground 400 yards due south.

The objectives were eventually taken, but with the usual casualties, the fighting in Hottot proving exceptionally unpleasant.

This action had cost the Regiment six crew commanders – Sergeant Baker, Corporal Footit and Geoffrey Makins (his first action with the Regiment) killed, and Michael Howden, Corporal Deane and Corporal Read wounded. Since we landed, 40 tank commanders from the Regiment had been either killed or wounded.

The casualties were horrendous. In an armoured regiment there were just under 700 men, of which about 210 made up the three main squadrons of around 50 tanks in all, each with their own commander. In other words, by mid-July, just six weeks after landing, the Sherwood Rangers had lost 80 per cent of their tank commanders. The trouble was that the tank commanders had to be in the turret and for much of the time had to stick their heads above the parapet, where they were very vulnerable to snipers and shellfire. Replacing them effectively was proving increasingly difficult.

The infantry had also suffered heavy casualties during this action and was badly shaken. The commanding officer of the Hampshires was killed and the commanding officer of the Devons wounded.

On 14 July we pulled out of the line again and I tried to organize a cadre class for junior NCOs to train prospective crew commanders. Tony Gauntley undertook to do this and carried out an intensive training, but only for a very limited period as on the 17th we moved into the line again.

During these few days of rest we had an exceptional piece of bad luck. The enemy was trying to shell some guns close to our leaguer area and a stray shell landed among B Squadron tanks, mortally wounding Sergeant Hardy, another experienced tank commander.

16

Normandy Break-out

The 'Big Three', Normandy, July 1944: General
Graham of 50 Division, General Horrocks, XXX Corps
Commander, and General Thomas of 43 Division.

*SLOWLY BUT SURELY the bitter and attritional battle for Normandy was
swinging the Allies' way. On 27 June, the garrison at Cherbourg had surrendered, as did, three days later, the last of the German troops in the
Cotentin peninsula. On 8 July, Montgomery began his latest drive for
Caen, which was preceded by the carpet-bombing of the city – 90 per
cent of the old medieval town was destroyed. Two days later, what
remained of the city was finally in Allied hands. Montgomery now
prepared for his latest offensive, Operation GOODWOOD, a thrust south
and south-east of Caen, while the Americans prepared for Operation
COBRA, their attempt to break out of the bridgehead to the west.*

*On the 17th, Field Marshal Rommel was badly wounded in his car
by an Allied air attack and was replaced by Field Marshal von Kluge, one
of a number of senior commanders brought into the Normandy battle
since the invasion.*

On 17 July the Regiment took up a position in the Caumont area, relieving the 67th American Armoured Battalion commanded by a Colonel Wynn. When I met him he immediately recognized the Sherwood Rangers' green shoulder flash, and told me that he had instructed the Regiment in the American Honey tank when we were first mechanized in Palestine. He appeared most efficient and showed me very clearly the front line lay-out. I had time to visit the CCS to see some of our wounded, including Geoffrey Makin and Colonel Neville of the Devons; both were still on the danger list, and Geoffrey looked extremely ill. In spite of the doctor telling me that he had a fair chance of pulling through, Geoffrey died shortly afterwards.

In our new sector we supported in a defensive capacity the Recce Regiment, which had recently been dismounted and turned into infantry. The most important feature on our front was an extremely thick wood called Le Bois de Buissard, on the edge of which our infantry was dug in. I had a request from the infantry to send a squadron of tanks to give it moral support, as it felt somewhat lonely in the wood, to which I had to agree. Michael Gold lost the toss, so B Squadron had to go. Michael was furious as he had found a most comfortable farmhouse as a squadron headquarters a very short distance behind the front line.

Caumont was at the western end of the British sector so the Sherwood Rangers were not directly involved in GOODWOOD.

Certain major changes took place within the brigade at this time. Much to our surprise, the 24th Lancers were broken up in order to provide reinforcements for existing armoured units. They had only been formed during the war and had joined the brigade prior to the invasion, but their commanding officer, Lieutenant Colonel Anderson, was bitterly disappointed. Their place was taken by the 13/18th Hussars, a regular mechanized cavalry unit. Brigadier Craycroft had to relinquish command of the brigade owing to his wound and he was succeeded by Brigadier Errol Prior-Palmer, whose appointment caused us certain apprehension, as he was reputed to be a typical regular cavalry soldier, with no previous experience of the Yeomanry. He turned out to be a great stickler for smartness and saluting, which of course was right. At the same time we soon found him to be an excellent commander with great drive and initiative.

A letter arrived from Lawrence Biddle informing me that he had decided upon matrimony, which came as a great surprise. He wrote, 'In order to fill up time during my sick leave, I intend to get married to a girl called Bacchus, whom I met just before D-Day.' His security was masterly as none of his colleagues on the brigade staff, on which he had served, had had any inkling of the romance. His proposal would have been interesting to behold.

A 1000-lb bomb was dropped and exploded in the area occupied by the Essex Yeomanry, the brigade gunners, in fact only a few yards from a slit-trench occupied by Arthur Phayre, their commanding officer, who was most indignant. Three French civilians, who were working in the orchard when the bomb exploded, were wounded. The Normandy farmers in this area, in spite of being almost in the front line, continued their farming activities when things were quiet and took cover when the shelling started.

It was all a matter of luck in Normandy, or in any other European country, whether or not the local inhabitants had their houses or home towns completely demolished, depending on whether they happened to be situated in the line of advance, or where the Germans decided to make a stand. Some were fortunate and others suffered desperate hardships, returning to their shattered homes after the battle had passed on. So often during this campaign, after having passed through a completely desolated and ruined village, I felt so relieved that these battles were not being fought on English soil and in English villages.

About this time we met for the first time the 43rd British Infantry Division, consisting of 214, 129 and 130 Brigades, whom we continually supported in various battles until VE-Day. This division, known as the Wyvern Division, was commanded by General Thomas, nicknamed 'Von Thoma', after the German general. He was a wiry little man with piercing little eyes, a long nose, which protected a bristling moustache, devoid of any sense of humour and a hard and unrelenting driver, but a good soldier whom I am convinced enjoyed his fighting and discomfort.

The end was now approaching in Normandy, as the Reich faced renewed attacks on all fronts. Operation COBRA had been launched on 25 July, and three days earlier, the massive Soviet offensive, Operation BAGRATION, had begun across Byelorussia as the Red Army advanced into Poland.

On 1 August a general advance started along the whole front. A Squadron was involved with 214 Brigade in capturing some high ground south of Le Bois du Homme. They advanced steadily during the day, meeting moderate opposition, and reached their objective that evening. During the advance they met a Jaguar for the first time, the heaviest of all German tanks. It was immobilized at 30 yards' range, three shots were fired, none of which penetrated, but the track was damaged and the crew baled out.

The 'Jaguar' Stanley mentions was the 'Jagdtiger' – or 'Hunting Tiger'. It was a huge beast: nearly 72 tonnes, with almost 10 inches of armour and a 128mm anti-tank gun that could outrange and outgun any Allied tank. They were formidable opponents, to say the least, although, like many German tanks, they were massively over-engineered and plagued by fuel shortages and mechanical problems. Fewer than 90 were ever built, so it was quite a coup for the Sherwood Rangers to disable one in the fighting around Le Bois du Homme.

While doing a quick reconnaissance Sergeant Dring spotted a couple of Tiger tanks. He directed his tank into a fire position from the flank and brewed one up. The German crew from the other Tiger must have deserted their tank, which on arrival was found to be bogged down, but complete with kit and rations, which immediately requisitioned by the members of A Squadron.

That evening I received orders for Operation BLUECOAT, the

object of which was the capture of Jurques and Ondefontaine, under the command of 130 Infantry Brigade. This operation was intended to be a bold thrust to obtain the maximum advantage from the enemy's present difficulties, following the American and British advance on the right.

On 3 August the attack went in with C Squadron supporting the 5th Dorsets, and the village of La Bigne was captured after some sticky fighting; the squadron lost Lieutenant Campbell and two of his crew. Progress was slow owing to the numerous mines that had been recently laid and the REs attached to C Squadron did some magnificent work in clearing them. After the fall of the village C Squadron advanced 300 yards south and, having consolidated, A Squadron passed through it with the 5th Dorsets to capture Ondefontaine, which the enemy intended to hold, as soon became evident. A Squadron had to proceed along the one and only road, which was narrow and bordered by a high hedge on either side, and along the whole length of which the high ground to the right flank, containing Le Bois de Buron, commanded an ideal view. In this wood the Germans had placed their gunner OPs and tanks. This made A Squadron advance very slowly and prevented the capture of Ondefontaine the same evening. The following morning, after a very heavy artillery stonking, C Squadron again took the lead and, with the infantry, captured the village.

Peter Seleri told me afterwards that he was wounded by a mortar bomb, while in the midst of a conference with the infantry commander, the gunner FOO, and Jack Holman. All the party were hit except Jack, the smallest target. Peter swears that he hid his small frame behind his own bulk. His driver, Trooper Howie, who had left the tank was killed by the same shell. A somewhat taciturn sort with a quietish sense of humour, he was one of the bravest. To drive a tank in action was a most unenviable and thankless occupation as one was quite unable to see anything, but was fully aware of the explosions from within and without. He carried out his orders from the tank commander on the intercom, either 'Driver advance full speed!' 'Driver halt', 'Driver right or left' or 'Driver reverse', and had so much time to brood over his worries and dangers. In reply to Peter's letter of condolence on the death of his son, the driver's father wrote, 'He has gone with a Grand Company', a remark so very true.

Two complete troops, consisting of three tanks each, arrived from the 24th Lancers, which had recently been broken up, under Lieutenants Cameron and Cowan. These I posted to B Squadron. Jack Holman took command of C Squadron, since Peter Seleri had been wounded. Nothing ever got Peter down. In battle he knew no fear, or at least he never showed it, and proved a most able squadron leader whom we all missed when he was evacuated. He was inclined to be somewhat pedantic in speech, and was prone to using long and ponderous words, even when reporting over the wireless: instead of saying, 'In the wood to my left front, three enemy tanks moving left to right. Am engaging,' he would monopolize the air by reporting 'I can without question discern three moving objects in yonder wood, which give me an unquestionable impression of resembling three Tigers, which appear to portray hostile inclinations. It is my intention to offer immediate engagement', much to the frantic impatience of the other tank stations with important messages for transmission over the regimental frequency.

The brigade joined up into a strong mobile column on 6 August to capture Condé, advancing on two axes, the Sherwood Rangers on the right, followed by 214 Brigade and the 4/7th on the left. However, after proceeding for a short while, the higher command decided that until Mont Pinçon and Le Plessis Grimoult had been cleaned of enemy it would not be advisable to endeavour to capture Condé and, much to our delight, we heard that the Regiment would pull back for three days' rest. We heard afterwards that three divisions were employed to take Condé. Before the Regiment retired, a troop of B Squadron was ordered to support elements of 130 Brigade to clean a pocket of resisting enemy east of Ondefontaine.

On 7 August the Regiment withdrew to a most pleasant apple orchard five miles behind the lines, where it was joined by Roger Sutton-Nelthorpe and Headquarters Squadron.

In this latest round of fighting, the Sherwood Rangers had destroyed
three Panthers, one Tiger and, of course, the Jagdtiger, but had also lost
six tanks themselves and had suffered 24 casualties, including a further
eight crew commanders. Casualties among tank commanders had now
reached almost 100 per cent since D-Day.

On a more positive note, four of the six knocked-out tanks were
recovered and made workable again – a recovery of hardware that was
almost entirely denied to the Germans.

General Horrocks, XXX Corps commander, paid us a visit and
addressed all officers and NCOs. He made some most complimentary
remarks about the Regiment, which I am sure were sincere and not
mere pep-talk, and reminded us that we first fought under his
command as far back as August 1942 at Bare Ridge. From then we had
continually served under him. He displayed a large map, which gave
all our dispositions and described the fighting along the whole front.

The welfare arrangements laid on by XXX Corps were excellent
and in a very short time mobile baths and cinemas appeared, and on
the second day an ENSA party arrived in the regimental lines.

Before the evening show each squadron entertained some of the
ENSA party for dinner; naturally there were no officers' messes, so
the meals had to be eaten sitting on the ground or on empty petrol
tins around the tanks. At Regimental Headquarters we entertained
three members of the cast, including a lively and amusing 'Blonde
Bombshell'. They all appreciated our efforts to produce a good meal,
especially the blonde, who slightly exaggerated her enthusiasm by
describing as 'delicious cider' the most delectable bottle of French
wine, which had been procured from the local inhabitants in exchange
for tinned meat.

One day Michael Gold and I, after visiting Corps Headquarters,
decided to have a look once again at Bayeux. Michael explained that,
en route through the town, he had managed to befriend a delightful
family who had been extremely kind to him. I vaguely wondered how
he had managed to do this while his regiment passed through the
town, but remembered that he had the most amazing faculty for

making life-long friends with every type of human being in a very short time, and generally under most unusual conditions. However, I felt convinced that certain female influences contributed to his enthusiasm that we should revisit his new-found friends in Bayeux.

To my enquiry as to how he made these friends, he explained that, in passing through the town from the beaches to the front (at which time he was still with the 23rd Hussars and had not rejoined the Regiment), his squadron had stopped in the town for a midday meal and, by good fortune, his tank had come to rest outside the house of a French leather-maker and his wife, who had most graciously offered to cook his rations on their kitchen fire and he had taken advantage of their kindness.

On arrival at Bayeux we soon found the house of the leather-maker and, in answer to Michael's bold knock, the front door was opened by a truly delightfully pretty young French girl, who, on beholding Michael, gave a shriek of delight and shouted, '*Maman, Papa, Marie, venez-ici, toute de suite, Michel est ici, vite, vite.*'

Thereupon the rest of the family came rushing down the passage in great excitement – Papa, an enormously fat man with no collar, bedroom slippers and an old pair of trousers secured only by the top button, Mama almost as large, covered with a brightly coloured apron, gripping a ladle, and Marie, a brunette, equally as attractive as her sister Angèle.

They surrounded Michael, each talking voluble French at top speed. Regarding this extraordinary scene, I really considered for a moment that Michael must have known this family before the war, for surely such a reception could only be for a son, brother, husband, lover or very old friend of the family returning after a long absence at war, and could not be merely for an acquaintance of one fleeting meeting, but then concluded that there could be no alternative, and I was, of course, right.

I was duly introduced to each member of the family and made most welcome, and we were ushered into a small but comfortable sitting room. They insisted that we should stay for lunch. We protested in view of the food shortage, but they would not listen and declared that they had a full larder and, leaving us to talk to Father, the three women departed to the kitchen to prepare lunch.

We sat down to a magnificent meal, omelette, lamb, fried potatoes, apple tart and cream, washed down with cider, which we both thoroughly enjoyed.

Michael, speaking French fluently, was in great form and kept the whole family in fits of laughter. Both the daughters were uncommonly good-looking, with attractive figures and, like all French girls, beautifully dressed, in spite of coming from such a small, unpretentious, but clean and comfortable home.

After lunch Michael decided that he wanted to go shopping in the town, and in spite of being informed that locally made women's straw hats were the only articles that could be purchased, he immediately displayed an earnest desire to buy these straw hats. So Angèle, Marie, Michael and I set forth on a shopping expedition. We spent half an hour in the hat shop waiting for Michael to make a choice from the large variety of locally made straw hats for ladies. He tried every hat on each member of the party, including the two girl shop assistants, much to their delight, and in the end bought four, which he sent to England.

We took the girls back to their home and, after bidding the whole family *au revoir* and many thank-yous, we drove back to the Regiment after a most pleasant and amusing few hours with a delightful family.

Our greatly enjoyed rest terminated on 12 August when, once again, we moved up into the line for the next attack, supporting 130 Brigade – A Squadron with the 5th Dorsets to capture Proussy, B Squadron with the 7th Hants to capture St Denis de Méré, and C Squadron to remain in reserve for the start of the operation, which started at dawn on 13 August.

Brigadier Leslie, the commander of 130 Brigade, was somewhat slow in crossing the start-line, and was then held up by opposition, about which he did nothing as he was under the impression that the brigade on his left would deal with it. 'Von Thoma', the divisional commander, appeared in his armoured car and promptly sacked Leslie in the field. I felt sorry for him, as the original orders were not clear, and I felt somewhat apprehensive myself as the Sherwood Rangers were supporting Leslie's brigade. Furthermore, he had sacked one of his battalion commanders, who did not know if his anti-tank guns had been brought up, and the colonel of the 12/60th, which was in our brigade.

The senior battalion colonel of 130 Brigade was summoned to command the brigade – a man called B. A. Coad, affectionately known as 'Daddy Coad', as he was like a father to all. I have never seen a man in such a dither, as at the time the battle was not going well. All the brigade and battalion commanders in 43 Division were somewhat fearful of Von Thoma, who at the same time infuriated them as he insisted on 'fighting their battles' and would not leave them alone after the final operational orders had been issued.

One of the most difficult skills of any commander was to delegate properly, and few instinctively understood that with promotion came a new job description. General Thomas was not alone in over-involving himself in the minutiae of battle or of being over-controlling: the same allegation was often cast at Montgomery. It tended to stifle initiative and sap the morale of immediate subordinates.

After the capture of Proussy and St Denis de Méré the river Noireau had to be crossed and the village of Berjou captured, situated on the high ground on the far side of the river and commanding a dominating view of the river and the whole countryside. As usual the enclosed country made tank fighting extremely difficult and unpleasant, and conditions were not improved by continuous rain, which lasted for two days.

Sergeant Cribben of the Recce Troop did some exceptionally good work in reconnoitring the narrow road that led up to the bridge which crosses the river. He found the bridge blown, which necessitated a night attack by the infantry. He managed to shoot up and destroy a German 50mm anti-tank gun which was the last to be drawn across the river before the bridge was blown. He was continually under mortar fire and had to avoid the usual sniper.

From 12 until 17 August, when Berjou was eventually captured, the Regiment was continually involved, sometimes supporting three brigades a day. A brigade would advance to an objective and another would pass through the next objective, until the village was finally reached. The steep climb to Berjou on the other side of the river caused great trouble and heavy tank commander casualties, especially in C Squadron.

This was a frenetic time along the front, as the Americans began to sweep out of their bridgehead to the west and the Germans were almost encircled in what became known as the Falaise Pocket. Hitler, who had recently survived an assassination attempt on 20 July, then demanded a decisive counter-attack. On 7 August, they launched an assault against the American flank through Mortain. Initially helped by poor weather, which restricted Allied flying, they made some ground, but the Americans quickly recovered and so did the skies and the Germans were doomed. Canadian and British troops were still pushing southwards towards Falaise from Caen and it seemed the Germans in Normandy might be completely trapped. Fearing American and British troops might end up clashing as the encirclement was completed, General Omar Bradley, commanding US 12th Army Group, halted his troops, which offered von Kluge the chance to allow his forces to withdraw – but not before many were caught by Allied ground-attack aircraft.

Lieutenant Stanley Perry's tank was the first to cross the hastily con-structed bridge over the Noireau and led the advance up the hill through the small bridgehead which the infantry had made during the night. Frank Gavin was killed when an anti-tank gun brewed up his tank, Sergeant Sleep was killed by a sniper and Sergeant Guy Saunders was killed when trying to rescue his great friend Corporal Brooks, who had been wounded by shellfire while doing a recce on foot – he was killed by the same shell – all of them first-class tank commanders with great battle experience during their years with the Regiment and, more important, greatly loved and respected by us all as fellow men. After the capture of Berjou, except for Stuart Hills, no officer troop leader remained in C Squadron. Stuart, I am afraid, was terribly distressed about the loss of his fellow tank commanders. He had relied on them so much and they were real friends who had shared so many discomforts and dangers since D-Day. In his diary he wrote this about them: 'They died with clear and very brave consciences, and there were never more deserving cases for peaceful sleep.'

On the evening of 17 August, after Berjou had been captured, I walked to the end of the village and looked down onto the Noireau river. From there I had a wonderful view of the surrounding country and could fully appreciate why the mortar and shellfire had been so accurate. The Germans could see every movement that we made.

The whole Regiment moved on a few miles to Sainte-Honorine-la-Chardonne, a picturesque village, which I am pleased to say had not suffered severe war damage. Civilians were beginning to return to their homes; in spite of the hardships they had suffered they showed great cheerfulness, and were obviously delighted to be returning home with a few belongings stacked in some kind of rickety log cart. Most of them, if they had the opportunity, asked anxiously for news about

A devastated Normandy village.

their homes and villages, so many of which had been irretrievably damaged. It was difficult to tell them the truth.

With the capture of Berjou on our immediate front, the German line had been cracked and he had withdrawn many miles. So ended, for a time, three months of continuous deliberate battles in the difficult bocage country of Normandy.

17

The Pursuit through France and Belgium

Message from Brigade: 'Crack on – we are through the ring!'

WE ALL WOKE UP to the chime of church bells on Sunday, 17 August, which was most refreshing. A service for the Roman Catholics was held in the village church and the padre held a voluntary church service at Regimental Headquarters, which the whole Regiment attended. As usual he gave a simple but inspiring address. I read the lesson and chose the hymns.

I received the following most appreciative letter from Brigadier Esme, thanking the Regiment for the support given to his brigade when it crossed the river Noireau, with a letter from our own brigadier:

Headquarters,
214 Infantry Brigade,
B.L.A.

Dear Prior-Palmer,

I have now had an opportunity of getting a first line account of the operations of the Sherwood Rangers around Berjou, in support of this Brigade. No Brigade ever received better co-operation. Will you please accept the thanks and admiration of all men in the Brigade.

If you decide to put Holman in for a decoration I feel you would be 100% justified.

Gold also did grand work and also the Squadron Leader of the 7th Somersets.

Thank you,
Yours very sincerely,
(Sgd) H. Esme

From our own brigadier:

Headquarters,
8th Armoured Brigade.
20th August.

Dear Christopherson,

I thought you might like to read the enclosed.

Let me have it back sometime.

Your chaps really did do a super-human job up that ruddy mountain and I am sure some decorations were well deserved.

Yours sincerely,
(Sgd) Errol Prior-Palmer

During the morning, while walking around the Regimental Headquarters tanks, I suddenly perceived a small and tubby figure frantically struggling to extricate himself from the middle of a barbed-wire fence, which securely held him by the seat of the pants. After I had rendered assistance, he saluted smartly and introduced himself as Major Leigh and informed me that he had been posted to the Sherwood Rangers as our second-in-command. Previously he had commanded the Gloucestershire Yeomanry, which was stationed in England. Thoroughly bored with inactivity, he had applied to join a regiment in the field and had been posted to the Sherwood Rangers. Major the Lord Leigh was small, inclined to be fat with a very red face, and was immediately christened 'The Baron'. He spoke very little, but possessed a subtle wit, which he showed on many occasions, and when something amused him he displayed his mirth with a most delightful giggle that shook the whole of his frame. He adored his comforts and his pipe. When Robin Leigh took over, Stephen Mitchell once again returned to command C Squadron, but only for a short time, for much to our sorrow he was claimed for service in England and I was forced to release him.

During the day I had to attend a conference for Operation KIT-TEN, an eastward movement of the whole brigade to l'Aigle; as no opposition was anticipated, this was considered a 'Peace Move', with 1st Armoured Division in the lead followed by 50th Division and 8th Armoured Brigade.

At 06.50 on 23 August the chase started in earnest, and we galloped through France at a great rate, passing through Courteilles, Habloville, Occagnes and Bailleul. After leaving Chambois we travelled along a road on which a large German column, consisting of tanks, guns, infantry and transport, largely horse-drawn, had been squarely caught by our rocket-firing air force. Never in all my life have I witnessed such utter destruction and complete desolation. Both sides of the road were littered with burned-out vehicles, dead Germans, dead horses, dead cows and, alas, a few civilians, including children, who had been caught in the strafing. Owing to rain and continuous use the road was a sea of mud. The dead, both men and beasts, had been lying there for a few days and as a result had swelled to twice their normal size. The stench was unbearable. Unfortunately the Regiment halted for maintenance right in the midst of this carnage. Robin Leigh, whose tank was behind mine, dismounted and came across to talk. This was his first experience of a battlefield and proved to be the only time that I ever saw him without an extremely red and ruddy complexion. He had gone completely yellow, and made a gallant attempt to conceal his great desire to vomit by puffing vigorously at his pipe.

'A bit of a mess,' he said, as he approached.

'Yes, the air force got them fair and square,' I replied, puffing equally vigorously at my pipe and praying that Robin didn't realize that his commanding officer was as near vomiting as his new second-in-command.

'Is it generally as bad as this?' he enquired.

'I have not seen much worse than this,' I replied, and moved away, as slowly as I could, from a dead horse, which had been blown to bits, lying a few yards from my tank and giving off a fearful stench. Robin told me at the end of the war how impressed he was on this occasion by my apparent imperturbability, but I had to admit that I was just as revolted as he was.

When we eventually arrived at l'Aigle, 19 tanks were off the road suffering from 'bogey wheel' trouble caused through travelling fast on tarmac roads. Laille we found a most attractive village surrounded by small farms, on one of which each squadron selected to leaguer. The local farmers were sincerely pleased to welcome us and generous with their gifts of eggs and milk. The countryside was most picturesque; at last real summer weather had arrived. Regimental Headquarters came to rest in a typical 'English' pear orchard.

The announcement that the Regiment would withdraw from the line and be out of action for a few days produced a feeling of indescribable relief. On arrival at the pre-selected leaguer area, it was wonderful to pass the order on the intercom to Corporal Bland, who had driven my tank in the desert and through Europe, 'Switch off, dismount, we're here for three days,' then send out to all tanks on the wireless, 'Close down until 10.30 hours tomorrow. Niners to report.' All stations would reply, 'OK – out.' In wireless procedure for security reasons the word 'niner' represented 'commander', but a very little intelligence was required on the part of a German station to connect the words.

After replenishment everyone would retire to bed, undressing for the first time, probably, for many nights, with the delightful antici-pation of a full and undisturbed night's sleep and a long lie-in next morning – the roar of tank engines warming up would not disturb the dawn, nor the voice of the wireless operator 'netting' his set to control.

Next morning each tank crew would cook their own late break-fast, consisting of rations and food bartered from the civilians, which had been accumulated and reserved for such an occasion. The quality of the breakfast would depend upon the resourcefulness of the member of the crew who had been appointed as cook.

After breakfast a couple of hours would be spent on maintenance. The gunner would strip and clean his guns and await the arrival of the regimental armourer for final inspection. The operator would over-haul his set and report any defects to Signal Section from the Royal Corps of Signals, which had been with the Regiment since before Alamein. Squadron fitters would visit each tank in their squadron under the supervision of the technical adjutant and make any necessary engine adjustment. Any major repairs would be carried out by the LAD (Light Aid Detachment), which had been with the Regiment, with our signal section, since before the Battle of Alamein. The efficiency and speed of their work were quite remarkable and we all considered them part of the Regiment. The orderly room (a 3-ton truck) would arrive with Sergeants Holland, Payne and Corporal Brocklehurst, with each squadron office, consisting of a 15-cwt truck and, most welcome of all, the quarter master with the mail and possible NAAFI ration.

The rest of the day would be spent in washing from head to foot in a dixie, a cut-down petrol tin, and sitting in the sun reading, writing letters, talking and sleeping and thoroughly appreciating the peace.

For squadron leaders, the adjutant and myself there was always a certain amount of administrative work to be done – reorganization of squadron and troops, returns to be completed, the war diary to be written up and letters of sympathy to the next-of-kin of those who had been killed in action. But during those peaceful days out of battle, somehow, one learned the importance of the natural and simple things that life can give.

We spent a very enjoyable time in this area, and even found time to play cricket matches on the bumpy but interesting pitch, which we improvised in the orchard – thanks to Roger Nelthorpe, who had had the foresight to pack two pairs of pads, a bat and a cricket ball in one of his B3 vehicles. The officers challenged the rest and won. The following day we played Brigade Headquarters at football in the same orchard and scored another victory.

Every morning and evening two milkmaids appeared from the farmhouse at the end of the orchard, and proceeded through the orchard to milk the cows. Only once they were alone and unsupported in their work. Finally there were three Sherwood Rangers carrying each pail, three to each, and two on the flank of each maid as an independent escort, and finally each cow had three Sherwood Rangers struggling with an udder, some displaying more proficiency than others.

On the second day I carried out, with Robin Leigh, an informal inspection of the squadrons in each squadron area, arriving last in B Squadron area, which was the furthest away. I found Michael Gold chatting with the farmer in whose orchard his tanks were leaguered. Robin and I were immediately introduced and the farmer insisted that we should enter his house and share a glass of wine. I intimated to Michael that I would prefer to carry out a short inspection of his tanks first, but the farmer informed us that in half an hour he had to attend the funeral of a friend who had been killed by a mine, so in order not to be discourteous I agreed and we entered his house. Formal introductions took place to the whole of his family and the various refugee families who were living at the farm, and we were all given a large glass of very excellent, but potent, cider, followed by some local wine. One of the lady refugees was great with child and just about to give birth, much to the consternation of all the household, as the local doctor had left the village. The farmer pleaded that our regimental doctor should be made available when the happy event occurred. I told him that I should consult our MO, but warned him that we should almost certainly be gone in a couple of days. We had such a merry time that the farmer clean forgot about the funeral until his wife reminded him. He gulped the remainder of his wine and fetched his Sunday suit, into which we all helped him to climb, and with unsteady step ran down the steps into the orchard, closely followed by his wife, grasping the bowler hat her husband had forgotten.

By that time no inspection of B Squadron tanks was possible, and I returned to Regimental Headquarters and told Hylda Young about the pregnant lady. He was not at all thrilled with this idea, but volunteered to take action should the necessity arise.

Hylda joined the Regiment in the desert after Geoffrey Brooks was wounded. I never quite understood why he was called Hylda, but he joined us with that name – maybe it had something to do with his highly coloured complexion. In peacetime he had a practice in Somerset and, in order to join up, he had deducted a considerable number of years from his age. He looked much younger than he was and should his correct age have been known he would have been sent back to his country practice. He was with us, I am glad to say, until the end of the war. He had a very happy disposition and was invariably cheerful and would roar with laughter at various jokes of his own, of which he would be the only one to see the point. He would not tolerate personal comfort, and should ever an opportunity of spending a night under a roof occur, he would prefer to lie on a stretcher in the open. He was the most conscientious and hardworking man I have ever met – nothing was ever too much trouble. In battle I continually had the greatest trouble in preventing him from dashing up to brewed-up tanks and attending the wounded instead of waiting for them to be brought back to the regimental aid post.

August had been a good month for the Allies. Across the other side of the world, the Americans had continued to push back the Japanese on both land and sea, while in Burma the British were also clawing their way back, capturing Myitkyina on 3 August. On 15 August, the Allies launched Operation DRAGOON, a major landing in southern France, while after the collapse of the German forces in Normandy, Paris fell on the 25th. This marked the start of the pursuit across France and into the Low Countries, and after their brief pause, it was time for the Sherwood Rangers to join the dash through northern France and into Belgium.

On 27 August Michael Gold sought permission to go on a reconnaissance in order to visit his old regiment, the 23rd Hussars, which I granted in view of the fact that the Regiment was at 24 hours' notice to move. Away he went in his Jeep, with his squadron sergeant major and his squadron clerk. After lunch, resulting from a very sudden change of plans, I received an order from Brigade to prepare the Regiment to move within an hour. Within 70 minutes from the receipt of this order the Regimental Headquarters tanks moved out of our delightful orchard with great reluctance to join the leading squadron on an axis of advance to Vernon. We travelled fast, passing through Rugles, la Neuve-Lyre, Conches, Evreux, Caillouet and some very lovely country.

Michael Gold we were forced to leave behind. I don't quite know whether he had conceived the idea before he started on his so-called recce, or whether he suddenly saw a signpost to Paris, but to Paris he went, with his squadron sergeant major and his squadron clerk. He drove straight to the Ritz, outside which a Tiger tank had been brewed up and was mobbed by a crowd of hysterical Frenchmen, who led the whole party into the hotel and plied them with champagne for the rest of the day and night. I think they can claim to have been the first British soldiers from a fighting unit to enter Paris, which had so recently been liberated. When he eventually in the very early hours of the morning tore himself away and returned to his squadron area, he received a rude shock to find that nothing remained, except the deep track marks made by his 16 tanks as they rolled out of the orchard, and his squadron pay clerk, sitting mournfully on an empty petrol tin, who had given up hope of ever seeing his squadron leader again, or of rejoining the Regiment.

They rejoined the Regiment on the following afternoon, and when Michael reported to me he still appeared to be reliving his hectic hours in Paris and was in no mood to attend an order group. His only excuse was that elements of B Squadron had raised the prestige of the Regiment and the whole British force, by having been the first British fighting soldiers in Paris since the occupation.

On 28 August we crossed the river Seine in order to support the 7th Somersets and DCLI to enlarge the bridgehead that had already been made. A Squadron had a particularly heavy time having to operate in dense forest. That day we covered 28 miles.

The next day, 29 August, the advance continued to Amiens. The 13/18th Hussars, who were in the lead, were held up at Gasny by a blown bridge. I was ordered to bypass the bridge and travel across country, rejoining the axis of advance at St Rémy. We had now moved into open and rolling country and were able once again to adopt the old desert formation, one squadron in open formation in the lead, Regimental Headquarters following close behind and a squadron on either flank. We worked now as an armoured regimental group, being supported by our battery of guns from the Essex Yeomanry under Chris Sidgewick and a company of motorized infantry from the 12/60th under Derek Colls. Both these commanders travelled with me in Regimental Headquarters group. It was an ideal formation and proved a first-class team, as both our batteries and companies were highly trained and so well known to us, besides all being most delightful companions. We found the village of Ecos held by an enemy rear-guard, but it was captured with St Rémy by B Squadron and the 12/60th.

The use of armoured regimental groups marked another development of the British Army in the war. This was an entirely mechanized all-arms combination that was able to function with both speed and co-ordination, and mirrored the often much-vaunted German 'Kampfgruppe' – or battle group – system. One of the virtues of the Kampfgruppe *was its versatility and flexibility; these virtues were being reflected in the speed with which the armoured regimental group had been set up.*

To travel at full speed across hard open country on a lovely morning with the knowledge that the Germans were on the run was most exhilarating, and everybody was in the highest spirits.

We had to wait an hour at St Rémy for the 13/18th Hussars to come up; once again it took the lead and we followed on its tail. We covered 30 miles on that day and leaguered for the night on the road between Dangu and les Thaillers.

On 30 August the chase continued at full speed. At one o'clock in the morning I received orders to clear the les Thaillers–Dangu road, which spoiled a complete night's rest for myself and B Squadron, which I detailed for this operation.

Again I was ordered to travel across country, and cut the main axis (called Heart) 10 miles further north at Flavacourt, towards which C Squadron headed at full speed. The Regiment followed, passing through Berneville, St Denis le Ferment and crossing the river Eate.

At Flavacourt orders came over the wireless from the brigadier to continue north across country to Espaubourg, then to swing east and cut the axis once again north of Beauvais.

For some of the way we were compelled to use the roads, and passed through the villages of Lachappelle-aux-Pots, Savignies, Fougers and Tres Serfuy, where we had great difficulty in finding a crossing over the river; we finally did get across, but A Squadron bogged six of its tanks, which were eventually hauled by the ARV from our Light Aid Detachment.

We met slight opposition, which we either brushed aside or bypassed. That day we covered 54 miles, and leaguered at Juvignes, five miles north of Beauvais.

The chase through France continued on 31 August. No organized resistance appeared to exist, but German columns of various sizes were still making their way back to Germany and some villages were held by rear-guards, sometimes consisting of fanatical young Nazis, who, being short of ammunition and petrol and realizing that the Führer's regime was lost, chose to fight on to the last rather than to return to a Germany without their beloved Hitler.

Our role now was to clear the axis to enable the corps commander to move north and establish his headquarters near the Somme. That evening we spent the night at Sauflieu, after passing through Francastel, Viefvilliers, Fontaine-Bonneleau and Fleury, covering 27 miles.

When we leaguered we met an American fighter pilot who had been shot down over Caen and taken prisoner. He had eventually escaped from a POW camp and, sheltered by the local inhabitants, had actively operated with the local Maquis.

B Squadron led the brigade across the Somme on 1 September, crossing without meeting opposition until we arrived at Flesselles, where a German Mark 4 tank concealed in the railway station knocked out a Recce Troop tank killing Sergeant Cribben, who had carried out such sterling work at the crossing of the river Noireau, a very brave man whom I had recommended for a DCM. The Mark 4 was eventually knocked out by B Squadron and our company of the 12/60th dealt with the German infantry holding the village.

At the next village, Naours, we again had to eliminate a considerable force of German infantry, but fortunately not supported by either anti-tank guns or tanks. The last battle of the day was at Doullens, which was strongly held, and for the capture of which we had to call up some infantry to help our motor company of the 12/60th.

Two troops of A Squadron knocked out two German tanks after some very clever manoeuvring around the back streets of the town. By late afternoon we had captured 200 German prisoners, knocked out three anti-tank guns and three tanks, most of the damage being done by A Squadron, who must have the credit for capturing the town.

Doullens proved to be the site of flying bombs, which we inspected before continuing to Sus-Saint-Léger, where we leaguered for the evening.

The Regiment achieved much on this day. We led the brigade for 50 miles, crossing the Somme and capturing three towns with a large number of prisoners.

Again we leaguered in desert fashion with the guns, motor company and our B1 echelons surrounded by the tanks.

September 2 we spent at Sus-Saint-Léger, maintaining the tanks, which badly needed attention, and receiving great hospitality from the local inhabitants.

Our Sherman tanks had stood up to the chase remarkably well, and we experienced very little engine trouble, which is a great credit to their mechanical performance. But owing to so much fast travelling along tarmac roads the bogeys had continually to be changed by virtue of the rubber on the tracks rapidly wearing away.

On 3 September the regimental group moved to Lille passing through large industrial areas where there appeared to be extensive slums and considerable poverty; however, our reception was even greater and wherever we stopped outside a house we were plied with food and wine. We covered 65 miles and were fortunate in the evening to find an open space in this dingy, well-populated industrial area, in which the regimental group could leaguer together.

The next day, 4 September, we were again in the lead on a north-eastern axis. Early during the morning we were ordered to halt, and I was recalled to Brigade Headquarters and given orders to the effect that the regimental group had to protect the left flank of the corps axis and prevent any interference by the large bodies of Germans who were travelling north, between the sea and the corps axis, and that the 61st Recce Regiment would be placed under my command.

18

The Capture of the St Pierre Garrison and Liberation of Brussels

Men of the Essex Yeomanry, the artillery with which the Sherwood Rangers worked very closely.

LATER DURING THE DAY, after passing through Chéreng and Baisieux, we crossed the border into Belgium at Tournai. The country appeared highly cultivated and prosperous and the villages clean and picturesque. The Belgian countryfolk gave us a sincere and warm welcome as we passed through their villages, but maybe a little more reserved and less demonstrative than the French.

In order to carry out our task squadrons had to cover a considerable distance, and by the end of the day they were well split. I made the following dispositions – A Squadron to Oudenarde, B Squadron to Kerkhove, both to watch the river crossings and C Squadron to Renaix, the most northern limit of our zone of protection, together with Regimental Headquarters. I established my headquarters outside the dye works at Renaix, the manager of which insisted that we should drink some wine with him to celebrate our arrival, and Stephen Mitchell, Chris Sidgewick and I readily accepted his invitation.

Renaix was a delightful town, completely unscathed by war, and we were the only troops there, the first to arrive. From the windows of every house fluttered a Belgian flag and a large number displayed Union Jacks and the Stars and Stripes. Certain houses, belonging to 'collaborateurs', had been burned to the ground.

Chris Sidgewick, Derek Colls and I visited the château of the town belonging to a Belgian count, who entertained us with champagne and cigars. The count was a most distinguished-looking old gentleman who had spent some time in prison for his anti-Nazi activities.

We were still in wireless contact with Brigade but they were 40 miles away, which was pleasant.

The next day I moved Regimental Headquarters to the high ground at the north end of the town in order to improve wireless reception. C Squadron operated north of the town and reached the outskirts of Ghent, 25 miles away, and there engaged a German column, which unfortunately escaped. One of B Squadron's patrols working south-east of the town was informed by members of the local Maquis that the village of St Pierre was firmly held by approximately 1200 Germans who had no intention of surrendering and that certain members of the Maquis had been captured by this garrison, of whom some had been shot. Bill Wharton, who commanded the B Squadron patrol, set off forthwith to St Pierre, but was immediately engaged by an anti-tank gun. He contacted the local priest of the neighbouring village, and together they entered St Pierre under a white flag of truce and demanded the surrender of the garrison from the commander, a German colonel, who bluntly told Bill that in view of the size of his force and supporting arms he had no intention, as an honourable German officer, of surrendering his garrison, and in any case he would only consider negotiating with an officer of equal rank.

This situation was communicated to me over the wireless, and with Stephen Mitchell, who claimed to be able to speak German, and Chris Sidgewick, I proceeded to the scene of action.

I found Bill Wharton talking to numbers of the local Maquis who had definite proof that the garrison had shot four of their members and demanded that I should hand over two Germans for every Maquis who had been shot. In the meantime they had produced a very old open Renault car, which they placed at my disposal for entering the village, warning me that the Germans would shoot up any military vehicle. I accepted their offer and mounted the car, with Stephen Mitchell and Bill Wharton, and the enormously fat priest took up a position on the bonnet, grasping a huge white flag. Not surprisingly, it took a long time to get the car started, but after being pushed for half a mile by shouting and excited members of the local inhabitants, the old car, with a mighty back-fire, was suddenly galvanized into action. It shot forward with a great lurch, which almost unseated the priest, and we roared down the street in a cloud of dust to St Pierre. Somewhat naturally, it stopped again after 200 yards, and the process of starting had to be repeated, each pusher trying to give advice to the driver. We soon got going again and this time the driver took no chances, keeping his foot right down on the accelerator, and, gathering speed as we went, we charged into St Pierre and eventually came to rest beside a very surprised and startled German infantry posted on the main approach to the village.

I shall never forget the most remarkable spectacle of the worthy priest balancing, with great difficulty, his fat bottom on the bonnet of the car, vigorously waving the huge white flag, which was a sheet fixed to a pole, and clutching his large black straw hat.

After dismounting, Stephen, Bill and I were escorted by a couple of German soldiers to the garrison headquarters, situated in the village inn.

I demanded to see the colonel, and was informed by an orderly that he and his officers were having a conference in one of the upstairs rooms. I told the orderly to lead the way and we followed. He pointed to the room and I gave an imperious knock on the door, which I opened without waiting for a reply. We found the colonel addressing approximately 20 officers who all turned and looked at us with the greatest disdain. Drawing myself up to my full height, but feeling slightly apprehensive, having seen at least six anti-tank guns as we walked to the headquarters, I said, in what I hoped to be a most impressive and haughty manner: 'I am Colonel Christopherson. I presume you are the commander of this garrison. If so, kindly clear the room so that we can discuss terms of surrender.'

I was rather proud of these opening words, which caused all the Germans to stand up, but was somewhat irritated by Stephen, who would shuffle his feet, fiddle with his moustache and not stand straight.

The German colonel, a dapper, stout little man with a bull neck, who I noticed was wearing an Iron Cross, first class, bowed slightly, introduced himself and said: 'I should be obliged if you would allow me five more minutes with my officers, alone, then I should be pleased to hear what you have to say.'

'I shall return in five minutes,' I replied, and we left the room and retired downstairs, Stephen still tugging at his moustache.

We entered a room where, much to our surprise, we found a Belgian major who had been captured by the Germans and was guarded by a German private, who was so surprised at our unexpected entry that he almost shot at sight. The Belgian major was delighted to see us. He told us that, as far as he knew, the garrison was strong in numbers and equipment, and consisting of a certain number of officers who had pledged themselves to fight to the last man and the last round, which was most disconcerting news. He also informed us that they held four members of a British tank crew as prisoners, which we subsequently found to be correct: the men belonged to the 4th RTR.

After ten minutes we again ascended the stairs and entered the conference room. I found time to tell Stephen to remember his German and to stop tweaking his moustache, as it was undignified and might give the impression of nervousness. Stephen scowled and murmured something about me being irritated at not having a moustache to pull to conceal my own nervousness.

When we entered the room the conference was breaking up and finally Stephen, Bill and I were left alone in the room with the colonel and his adjutant. I noticed that an armed guard had been placed outside the room. He introduced his adjutant, who was a tall and good-looking young German with a scarred face, wearing black uniform and black boots. He reminded me so much of Raymond Massey. In return I introduced Stephen and Bill.

All our conversation took place in German, translated into English by Stephen, and to start with I was most impressed with his German. The following conversation ensued.

I said, 'No organized German resistance now remains in France or Belgium. My regiment, consisting of tanks, infantry and guns is outside this village waiting to attack. I can summon air support within half an hour,' not strictly true, 'you are completely cut off and without contact with your higher formation. I demand the surrender of this garrison.'

'I realize,' he replied, 'that the German Army has withdrawn from France, but I have under my command a garrison strong in men, guns and ammunition. It is my wish, and the wish of my officers, to fight and to delay your advance. It would be dishonourable for me as a German officer to surrender so large a garrison without fighting.'

Such a speech was most disconcerting and caused Stephen to forget all the German that he had ever learned, to such an extent that I attempted to talk in French, much to the delight of the German adjutant who spoke French fluently and Stephen's French was much better than his German. Again I addressed the German colonel, who was gazing out of the window in a most stubborn manner.

'While I appreciate that as a German soldier you must consider your honour, it is my duty to tell you that should you choose to fight, many unnecessary casualties will be inflicted on German soldiers, and more families in Germany will suffer in consequence. Any further resistance would be useless and the subsequent casualties would be your direct responsibility. Under these circumstances I consider that it is your duty to make an honourable surrender.'

Those words appeared to have some effect on the old colonel, as he had a rapid conversation in German with his adjutant, and I winked at Stephen to indicate to him how pleased I was with my last address. I was most anxious for a surrender, whether honourable or dishonourable, and I had no wish to attack the place, which would result in unnecessary casualties to our company of the 12/60th and to the Regiment, which at that time was well dispersed. Neither did I wish to call for more support from Brigade, which was all actively employed elsewhere. Furthermore, the village still contained civilians, and would have suffered damage should we be compelled to attack.

The German colonel still continued to worry about his honour and it took a full hour to persuade him that neither Wehrmacht, the German people, nor Hitler would consider that he had failed in his duty or that to surrender would be dishonourable. Eventually, much to our relief, he said: 'I agree to surrender, but should like to be allowed these considerations. I should be allowed to march out at the head of my troops, with their arms, and formally surrender at a pre-arranged rendezvous. I should like a sworn, written statement from you that no German soldier will be handed over to the Maquis. I should like medical attention for my wounded.'

I agreed to his requests, signed a statement, written both in German and in English, guaranteeing protection for him and his troops from the Maquis, and arranged to meet him at 6 o'clock that evening outside the village at the place where the road and railway crossed. I promised also to send in our regimental medical officer to attend his wounded.

We all bowed formally and left somewhat relieved, and were escorted back to the priest who was sitting in the car most worried at our lengthy absence.

Derek Colls, Chris Sidgewick and Ian McKay were even more worried, and had made up their minds that we had either been bumped off or kept prisoners; they were discussing a plan of action. Ian had suggested sending a tank with its guns traversed to the rear, indicating a temporary truce, in order to ascertain our whereabouts.

I told them all exactly what had happened and we discussed arrangements about the formal surrender and wondered if, in view of the fact that we had agreed that they should march with their arms, we should provide some kind of a guard of honour. I seemed to recall something similar when the Duke of Aosta surrendered his garrison. However, we decided that Derek Colls and I should be at the rendezvous at 6 o'clock to receive their formal surrender, but we took the precaution of having B Squadron tanks at close call, with Derek's company of infantry and Chris Sidgewick's guns.

At 6.30 in the evening there was still no sign of the German colonel or his men, and when suddenly we heard Spandau fire, I became instantly alarmed that the garrison was attempting a break-out. At that moment Hylda Young, our medical officer, appeared with his ambulance and was just about to enter the village to collect the wounded. I signalled him to stop and asked him to ascertain what was happening in the village. When he arrived at the headquarters he met the German adjutant and asked him the reason for the shooting, but the adjutant professed complete ignorance. Hylda then suggested he should return to me in the ambulance, while he remained at the head-quarters. This was agreed and the adjutant entered the ambulance, and Hylda proceeded into the headquarters. Suddenly the shooting increased in intensity and was combined with mortar fire and, as a result, the adjutant leaped from the ambulance and started running in the direction of the firing. Thereupon Hylda raced back to the ambulance and drove full speed back to me. He told me he had seen no signs of any Germans in the village, except for the adjutant, and that there appeared to be a small battle taking place at the far side of the village.

I forthwith called for Bill Wharton's troop and we entered the village, expecting to be shot up at any moment, but instead we were greeted by a frantically excited and gesticulating German adjutant, from whom we learned that the colonel and his men had been fired on as they were leaving the village on the far side and they had been compelled to return the fire.

We all rushed through the village to find the Germans taking cover in the ditches on the side of the road from the odd mortar shell that was falling. We raced up the road and through the German column and eventually met a patrol belonging to the Green Howards via which we sent an urgent message to cease firing. We eventually dis-covered that the Green Howards, moving north on a parallel axis 20 miles away, had received information about the Pierre garrison from the locals and had despatched a company to obtain information; they had suddenly come face to face with a large German column marching down the road, carrying its arms, led by a colonel on a white horse and had opened fire. I was most relieved to hear that only one German had been wounded.

I found the German colonel, a very worried man, and explained the mistake but asked him why he was marching out of the north end of the town instead of to the prearranged rendezvous. After consulting the map we discovered that the railway crossed the road in two separate places outside the village, which his adjutant had confused, and they were marching to the wrong crossing.

In the meantime the whole column had re-formed on some open ground and I asked the colonel to explain this unfortunate situation to his men, which he readily agreed to do. In return, he requested that his men should be allowed to break their arms before being marched off, which, in view of what had happened, I allowed.

The German RSM called the men to attention and the colonel addressed them for about a quarter of an hour, explaining what had happened, telling them that he had made an honourable surrender, and bidding them farewell. When he had finished he nodded to the RSM, who gave the order to break their arms, by crashing the butts of their rifles on the ground, after which each man raised his right hand and roared, '*Sieg Heil*,' three times. I was most impressed with their discipline.

The colonel then turned to me, handed over his revolver and signalled to his orderly to hand over his white charger. So ended the surrender of the St Pierre garrison.

Most reluctantly I gave the white charger, a beautiful animal, to one of the local farmers, who was a prominent member of the Maquis, and the revolver to the owner of the house in Renaix where B Squadron had established its headquarters. He was most thrilled, as he was a gunsmith by trade and promised to display the revolver, with a suitably engraved plaque, in his shop window.

The leader of the Maquis came to see me that evening and demanded that I should hand over eight Germans, including the

Postcard photograph of a shop in Renaix.

colonel and his adjutant, for those of their number whom the Germans had shot. I explained that such a request could not be granted, but agreed to write a full report, including statements, signed by themselves, a copy of which they retained, which would be available for investigation after the war.

We left the town of Renaix on the following day, 7 September, after a most pleasant but short stay and the whole town turned out to say farewell. I think they were sorry to see us go. We travelled 60 miles, passing through Voorde, Ninove and finally Brussels, which had very recently been liberated.

I did not relish the idea of leading a whole armoured regimental group, with all the supply vehicles, through Brussels and on to the Louvain road, so I despatched Michael Gold on ahead to recce the way through and arranged to meet him on the outskirts of the city. I chose him because of his knowledge of French, but in the haste of the moment forgot his amazing capacity for making friends, and his fatal charm to members of the opposite sex. As soon as we arrived on the outskirts of Brussels we found that the city people were celebrating to the utmost of their capacity. Never have I seen such a fantastic and sincere demonstration of complete joy. Our progress through the streets was, somewhat naturally, excessively slow, as each tank and vehicle was swarming with civilians, and, somewhat naturally also, there was no sign of Michael Gold. Stephen and I led the column in a Jeep swamped with flowers, fruit, food and wine, thrown in by the delirious Belgians, and, after selecting a guide from the numerous civilian volunteers, we gradually made our way through the city to the Louvain road. That day we travelled 60 miles and spent the night at Aarschot a few miles north of Brussels. Michael Gold turned up the next morning full of apologies at having lost his way.

We spent 8 and 9 September on maintenance, which the tanks badly needed. We still had some of the original tanks we had landed on D-Day, some of which registered over 2000 miles on the mileometer.

Michael suggested that we should pay a visit to Brussels and have some dinner there, but I pointed out that as none of us had any Belgian currency, in fact no money at all, I did not quite see how we should get anything to eat. I was told not to worry and that he would guarantee food, so he, Arthur Warburton and I set off in the Jeep.

Michael drove straight up to the Carlton restaurant and parked outside. He led the way to the door and I kept wondering how on earth we should eat without money. As we entered Michael stood aside to allow two very lovely Belgian girls to pass, followed by their escorts. As they entered he gave each of them in turn a slight bow and a winning smile. That, of course, provided us with a most excellent dinner. The food was superb, the wine excellent, and we had a most delightful evening.

After the meal they insisted that we should return to their homes, where we drank more champagne. We finally left at two o'clock next morning, after being kept waiting by Arthur, who, just as we were about to leave, returned to the house on the excuse that he had left his gloves in the drawing room. It took him 20 minutes to find his gloves, assisted by one of our beautiful hostesses.

19

Gheel and MARKET GARDEN

The citation for Stanley's Distinguished Service Order.

THE FOLLOWING THREE DAYS, 10, 11 and 12 September, the Regiment experienced some of the bitterest fighting of the whole war, which cost us very heavy casualties.

I received orders early in the morning of the 10th via a liaison officer from 50th Division to support 231 Brigade, which was passing through a bridgehead over the Albert Canal made by 151 Brigade. On reaching the canal we discovered that the bridgehead was far from secure and that 151 Brigade was being heavily counter-attacked with tanks and infantry, so the Regiment was immediately ordered into the bridgehead with 151 Brigade. The brigadier had crossed the canal and established his headquarters within the small perimeter, and was even so optimistic as to have brought his caravan. Before bringing the Regiment up I was discussing a plan of action with him when his intelligence officer approached and said, 'I think I should tell you, sir, that there are two enemy tanks in a sunken lane 300 yards to our left flank. If you watch carefully you can see them and it is quite easy to hear them.'

'For God's sake,' exclaimed the brigadier, 'bring your tanks up quickly.'

A certain confusion ensued as the brigadier's caravan and other elements of his headquarters went hurtling back over the canal, followed by machine-gun bullets from the tanks.

C Squadron arrived first in the bridgehead and, supporting the 6th DLI, temporarily restored the situation and extended the bridgehead by capturing the village of Gheel. B Squadron pushed forward to the north-west corner of the bridgehead with the 9th DLI, and was violently counter-attacked during the afternoon, but withstood the attack. Michael Gold was wounded in the head as he was travelling in his scout car. He was fortunate not to be killed when the bullet grazed his eye, which I am afraid he lost. The ammunition position became rather serious for the tanks in Gheel, which for a considerable time were cut off, as the Germans had cut the road. However, Sergeant Stanton made a bold dash in the ARV and relieved the situation.

The opposing Germans were youthful fanatics and when night fell we plainly heard them shouting in English, 'We are prepared to die for Hitler, we intend to die for Hitler.' At night they made a clever counter-attack. Their infantry infiltrated our lines and let off flares, which completely illuminated our tanks, making them an easy target for their tanks, which had crept up. We spent a most uncomfortable night.

The following day the reserve company of the infantry was attacked by a whole German company, which had been able to infiltrate during the night, owing to our infantry being so thin on the ground. John Mann, captain in B Squadron, was shot dead by a sniper as he was sitting in his tank at a crossroads and his tank was brewed up. The rest of the squadron tanks supporting the reserve company caught the attacking infantry in the open and broke up the attack. The whole bridgehead consisted of a mass of sunken lanes and thick orchards, which made infiltration comparatively easy.

Colin Thompson, B Squadron second-in-command, was shot up by an enemy tank and received a nasty wound in the leg.

During the afternoon of the 11th, a corporal from a machine-gun section, which was close to my tank, came across and said, 'I should just like to confirm, sir, that that there tank is one of yours.'

I walked across to where he was standing and saw, somewhat to my consternation, a German Panther very slowly creeping down a lane 300 yards to our immediate front.

Fortunately the gun was pointing over its rear and the commander was looking backwards, anticipating trouble from behind. I couldn't engage from where Robin Hood (my tank) was positioned, and I didn't want to disclose our position by starting up the tank's engine, so I rushed across to Dick Holman and Sergeant Charity, whose tank was close at hand, and was relieved to find that from where they were they could possibly engage. Their tank was also in a sunken lane and from their position it was possible to obtain a comparatively clear view of a short distance of lane along which the Panther was bound to pass should it continue in the same direction. I stood on the back of his tank while Sergeant Charity traversed his gun to cover the lane, and we waited breathlessly for the Panther, which we could hear quite plainly, to appear, praying that its gun still pointed to the rear. We suddenly saw it and Sergeant Charity let fly with his first shot, which was high and missed. The Panther immediately halted, and I saw the gun traverse quickly around towards us. Sergeant Charity fired again and once more he was too high; by this time the gun of the Panther appeared to be pointing directly at me. I offered up a silent prayer that the Lord God would improve the accuracy of Sergeant Charity's gunner, and that we shouldn't have a misfire. I heard his repeat order: 'Reload, drop fifty.'

'On,' said the gunner.

'Fire,' shouted Sergeant Charity.

I put my fingers in my ears to avoid the explosion, which rocked the tank forward, and gave a shout of delight when I saw that the armour-piercing shell had struck and entered the turret of the Panther.

He followed with three more shots in quick succession, all of which found their mark and the last of which set the Panther on fire.

Some of the German crew baled out and were immediately engaged by the tank machine-gun and the infantry machine-gun corporal, who had originally spotted the Panther.

Those three days' fighting had cost the Regiment 46 casualties, 50 per cent of which were fatal. At that time I suppose each squadron averaged 10 tanks, making a total of 32 tanks in the Regiment manned by 160 men. A large proportion of the casualties consisted of tank commanders and officers, including Captain John Mann and Lieutenant Cooke killed and Michael Gold, Colin Thompson and Jimmy McWilliam wounded. The Regiment had 11 tanks knocked out and two damaged, which was the heaviest number of tank casualties in one battle that the Regiment had suffered since the Battle of Wadi Zem Zem in the desert. Sergeant Nesling fought magnificently throughout and was afterwards awarded the DCM for his outstanding gallantry.

With the number of men in tanks below 200, the loss of 46 represented almost a third of the Regiment's fighting power. As Stuart Hills pointed out, almost every tank suffered a direct hit at some point – and whether any of the crew managed to clamber out alive was largely a matter of luck. 'It was crazy, really,' says John Semken, whose nerves were beginning to suffer by this time. 'I always used to say we were living on borrowed time.'

The fighting at Gheel was followed by three pleasant days' rest at Bourg-Léopold, where once again we met our old friends, the Staffordshire Yeomanry, who were part of the 8th Armoured Brigade in North Africa. Michael Farquhar commanded the Regiment and Lawrence Biddle was his second-in-command. Michael commanded the Crusader Squadron of the Staffordshire Yeomanry when I commanded the Sherwood Rangers' Crusader Squadron. On D-Day plus 10 they had returned to England to be trained for DD tanks for the crossing of the Rhine. We had a most pleasant party at Brigade Headquarters and consumed some delicious wine, which the brigadier had had presented to him.

I received a letter from Michael Gold, written in hospital in Brussels. He was very cheerful in spite of having had his eye removed and told me that our Belgian friends who had entertained us had shown him great kindness bringing so much champagne to the hospital that a continuous stream of wine kept flowing from his empty eye socket.

I was notified by Brigade that at long last certain decorations had come through, including MCs for John Semken, A Squadron commander, Ian Greenaway, who lost a leg in Normandy, John Mann, who was killed a few days previously at the Battle of Gheel and MMs for Sergeant Dring (a bar), Sergeant Saunders, Sergeant Nelson and Sergeant Birch. All so thoroughly deserved.

I had to attend a conference at Corps Headquarters where General Horrocks, the corps commander, gave us the present dispositions and future plans. He paid a great deal of tribute to 43rd Division and 50th Division and a certain amount to 11th Armoured and Guards Armoured, but I think he might have made mention of the 8th Armoured Brigade, without whom neither 43rd nor 50th Divisions would have got so far. The next operation, he told us, was to make a break-out through the bridgehead over the Escault Canal and drive north to link up in Holland with the American and British airborne divisions, which were dropping at Arnhem and Nijmegen. By doing this it was hoped to cut off all the German forces west of the axis and to prevent supplies being sent from Germany to the flying-bomb sites situated on the coast. The Guards Armoured Brigade was to lead, followed by two infantry divisions and the 8th Armoured Brigade. The Regiment was to be detached from the remainder of the brigade and to operate in a picketing role, with one squadron of Royals, a detachment of RASC and light ack-ack and Field Ambulance, with our usual company of 12/60th and battery of Essex Yeomanry under command. I liked the idea of this independent command. According to how the operation went, we should then pass under command of the 82nd American Airborne Division.

This was Operation MARKET GARDEN, hastily first devised when 21st Army Group was still in rapid pursuit and it was felt that the enemy was

all but finished. The idea was to capture key bridges at Eindhoven,
Nijmegen and Arnhem using airborne forces, who would then be
hurriedly reinforced by XXX Corps driving a 60-mile corridor to join
them. This would offer a back-door route across the Rhine and into
Germany. The three bridges had to be taken intact and XXX Corps'
drive north to stick to a very, very tight schedule before the airborne forces
ran out of ammunition and supplies. If any single part of the plan went
awry, the whole operation was doomed to failure. D-Day had been
months in the planning, yet MARKET GARDEN, despite involving an
entire armoured corps, three airborne divisions and a further airborne
brigade, as well as a vast air armada, took just seven days from being
given the go-ahead to its launch.

As we found practically the whole way across Holland, tanks were
forced to keep to the road owing to the highly cultivated lands and
irrigation schemes throughout the country. As a result the Guards had
the first eight of their tanks knocked out, as they could not leave the
road, which was covered by two battalions of SS, who fought
desperately and made their progress extremely slow, but they
contacted the American parachutists the following day at Eindhoven,
six miles north of the bridgehead.

On the 18th news came through that at Grave the American
parachutists had captured the all-important bridge and I was advised
to contact them as soon as possible. We also heard that the bridge at
Son had been blown, but was in our hands. Bridges at Vegel, Nijmegen
and Arnhem were intact but in enemy hands.

We started up the main axis on the 20th and reached Grave the
same evening after travelling 72 miles. We met no opposition, except
at Son where a pocket of enemy had infiltrated back and attempted to
blow the bridge. However, B Squadron rushed the bridge and got
across before any damage could be done.

On arrival I contacted General Gavin, the commander of the
American 82nd Airborne Division, which had recently landed and was
holding a large area, dominated by the high ground around
Dekkerswald and Groesbeek, a line running through Nijmegen,

Ubbergen, Beek, and Grafwegen and in some places they were actually over the German border, about 2000 yards from the enormous Reichwald, a forest of no mean size.

I moved the Regiment to Dekkerswald where we spent the night. All the attached units were withdrawn, including our Essex Yeomanry gunners and company of 12/60th.

The next morning, 1 October, I attended a conference at the American headquarters; the general, whom I liked, did not appear to quite appreciate the capabilities of a tank and immediately asked me to clear a section of the Reichwald, which was held by the enemy, without offering any infantry support. I pointed out that should we operate in this dense forest without infantry it was more than likely that we should have most of the tanks knocked out without ever seeing a German. He appreciated my point of view and we discussed plans for the attack next day.

Although the Americans had captured Nijmegen and the bridge over the river Maas, the British Airborne at Arnhem on the other side of the river had not been successful and was having a very rough time. The American Airborne troops were continually either being counter-attacked or endeavouring to extend their bridgehead, so during the time that the Regiment spent in this section each squadron had a most active time; however we unanimously agreed that these American Airborne troops, especially the 82nd Division, were among the best, if not the best, infantry we had yet supported. They were tough, brave and cheerful, and when the attack started seldom went to ground, even under formidable shelling. Maybe on some occasions they were too tough, especially in the treatment of their prisoners, whom they seldom took. I shall never forget seeing a Jeep full of American paratroopers driving along with the head of a German pierced with an iron stake and tied to the front. This spectacle haunts me still.

What is incredible about MARKET GARDEN is not that it failed but that it very nearly succeeded. In fact, success or failure was a matter of a few hours as the Guards Armoured Brigade managed to get within 11 miles of Arnhem. There was so much that could have gone wrong and did go wrong, yet despite this, it remains a classic battle of extraordinary bravery and derring-do – actions that so very nearly brought what would have been one of the most astonishing and unlikely victories of the entire war.

Stanley rightly praised the fighting capabilities of the 82nd Airborne, who were highly trained and motivated troops, and whose crossing of the river Waal was one of the outstanding actions of the entire campaign in north-west Europe. General Gavin, with whom Stanley struck up an immediate rapport, was also very highly regarded. Extreme savagery and atrocities were not, however, the preserve of fanatical Nazis, as Stanley records.

The fighting from 1 to 6 October mostly took place on the Holland– German border, near a place called Beek, where the recce troops under Ian McKay first crossed into Germany and claimed to be the first British troops to fight in Germany; as a result of this the Regiment had a good write-up in the British press.

Frank Gillard, a reporter for the BBC, recorded in one of his despatches, 'The most cheerful troops that I have encountered were those on the Reich border. They were the men of a County Yeomanry Regiment, the first troops back from the Middle East to land on D-Day. And they are now the first British troops to enter Germany.'

I received the following letters regarding our being the first British troops to fight in Germany:

1st Dorset Regt.,

BLA
30 Sep 44

My dear Christopherson,
I must congratulate you and your Regiment on being the first British troops into Hunland – we are all delighted it should have

been you and not someone else who has arrived on the scene only recently. The only pity was that we were not there with you as on D-Day.

Also thank you very much for helping my Carrier Officer, Walsh, to get over the border. Unfortunately except for a Nazi armband he brought nothing back and the Bde Comd is very anxious to have some memento. So I would be grateful if you could allow him (Walsh) into your piece of Hunland again for a few minutes.

I hear your chaps dealt with a counter-attack very successfully yesterday and murdered a large number of Huns – good show.

We may be seeing more of you in the not too far distant future – I hope so.

> Yours Sincerely
> (Sgd) A.C. Breedon

The Officer Commanding,
Sherwood Rangers Yeomanry, BLA

From Brigadier Sir Alexander Stanier,
HQ 231 Infantry Brigade, BLA

30 Sep 44

My dear Christopherson,
First of all I do want to send you my and my Brigade's heartiest congratulations on your Regiment being the first British troops into Germany.

Secondly for helping my patrol, from the Dorsets, to go over the border yesterday. We hope we can now say we are the first or nearly the first Infantry to cross. It is all the more a pleasure for us that your Regiment should have this honour as perhaps you will remember 231 Brigade's motto on D-Day was that we

> *would follow the DD tanks with Dash and Determination and you have certainly kept it up all the way.*
>
> *I am sending another patrol this afternoon as I am most anxious to get some mementoes of their visit to the Reich. But if it means any unnecessary risk we can certainly wait for another day.*
>
> *We send you and all your Regiment our very best wishes and good hunting in the days to come. We hope we may once again work with you.*
>
> *Yours ever,*
> *(Sgd) Alex Stanier*

On 2 October C Squadron supported the 1st and 3rd Battalions of 325 Regiment to capture an objective line from Riethorst, Katerbosch, Heikant and Middelaar.

Before the attack I contacted Colonel Billingslea, who commanded the operation, to discuss plans at his forward OP at 05.30 in the morning. As soon as it was light this OP, which commanded a wonderful view, came in for some very heavy shelling and mortaring so we decided to move forward down the hill, but still the shelling followed us. We soon, however, discovered the reason for their accurate aim when we found some German telephone cable and headphones under a tree; these obviously had been very recently and hastily abandoned when we approached. This German must have run out a cable into our lines at night and established himself in a tree from which he could observe every movement that we made.

The attack was only partially successful and in the evening the reserve battalion and A Squadron had to repeat the operation and eventually succeeded in taking their objective.

Just before the attack started, two officers from the Guards Armoured Brigade visited me at Colonel Billingslea's headquarters. They told me that we should be relieved by them in a couple of days. I introduced them to the American colonel and his staff and then gave the lie of the land, and details of past and intended operations. We moved forward in order to obtain a better view of the land, and although we crawled through the trees we must have come under observation of a German OP for shelling started immediately. When the shelling died down and we rose from cover, we found that the American adjutant had been killed and that one Guards officer was missing. Later during the evening the other Guards officer returned and told me that no trace had been found of his colleague, who was the regimental intelligence officer. So once again we visited the place where we had been so badly shelled. We could find no trace of him at all until I found a compass on the ground, which was identified as belonging to the missing man. On closer inspection I discovered that the compass had been lying on the edge of the remains of a slit trench, which had obviously received a direct hit from a very large shell. We dug down and from what we found, which in fact was practically nothing, it was obvious that the Guards' IO must have jumped into this slit trench when the shelling started. I never quite realized that a direct hit from a large shell could remove practically all evidence of a human body. I was badly shaken, as I had been speaking to him just before the shelling. He told me that he had joined the Regiment that day and that he was 21.

During those few days I spent many hours with the American Colonel Billingslea, most of the time in my scout car or on the ground. We both had more than our share of luck for the whole of his headquarters staff were either killed or wounded through shelling and sniping during the time I was with him. On one occasion he established his headquarters in a house situated on a crossroads, just south of Mook, not a prudent decision. We had just arrived back at his headquarters when the mortaring started. He dived for a slit trench and I jumped back into my scout car, which was armour plated. When all was quiet we found that all our party had been wounded except for Billingslea and myself. As I was sheltering in the scout car I recalled having seen a young German private terribly badly wounded lying on a stretcher beside the wall of a house. I felt that I should get out and move him into the house for cover, but decided that I would wait until the shelling had abated in intensity. When I did look I found that he had been hit by a small piece of shell, which had killed him. He was a very young lad. He could not have been more than 17, with thick glasses, obviously a student who should have been continuing his studies instead of fighting a war. I was told afterwards that he had been very badly wounded and in any case he would have had a very slender chance of living. All the same, I shall always have the feeling that I might have given him that chance.

C Squadron did some excellent work and won unqualified praise from the Americans for the support given to them, particularly by Stuart Hills and his troop. In the Beek area his troop had to attack over open country along three parallel lanes, which it could not leave owing to the flooded country. Eventually Stuart's tank slipped off the lane into a ditch and was firmly bogged and he was quite unable to fire his guns. He remained in his tank passing back messages over the wireless, in spite of being engaged by a 20mm anti-tank gun, which did not penetrate the tank but made life rather uncomfortable. His tank was eventually brewed up by a German with a bazooka, who stalked along the ditch on the other side of the road. All the tank crew managed to bale out without injury.

John Holmes, a new subaltern who had recently joined the Regiment, knocked out three tanks during his first action.

In the Mook area 30 Americans were trapped in the north-eastern corner of Den Heuvel woods. Stuart Hills led his three tanks up a ride at full speed to the American position, placed himself at one corner and Sergeant Collis at another and while Sergeant Robinson took the wounded on the back of his tank they blazed away with their 75mm and machine-guns at the woods in front of them and remained there while the Americans withdrew.

I am quite convinced that such an aggressive use of their fire-power prevented any solid shot from being directed at them, although the shelling was extremely heavy.

I am glad to say that Jack Holman was decorated by the Americans. Stuart Hills, I know, was recommended for a decoration, which most unfortunately never materialized. His whole troop thoroughly deserved recognition.

Stuart had commanded a troop continuously since D-Day and had had numerous tanks knocked out, so I decided to make him regimental intelligence officer for a time, and I allowed him to bring his gunner, Cousins, as his scout-car driver, who was ironically wounded the first night that he spent at Regimental Headquarters.

On 6 October the Regiment was relieved by the 4th Coldstreams from the Guards Armoured Division, and bade farewell to the 82nd Airborne Division, which was most appreciative and complimentary about the support we had given it. It had fought extremely well and it was interesting to learn that the whole division consisted of volunteers. We gave the division a 75mm shell case, which the LAD polished up and on the side of which was inserted the Regimental cap badge, with a suitable inscription in memory of the time we spent with it and appreciation of its fighting abilities. The division was most thrilled with this gesture.

Before leaving the Americans, I received the following letter from Major General James M. Gavin, who commanded the 82nd US Airborne Division:

APO 469, In the Field

8 November 1944

Dear Colonel Christopherson,

On behalf of the members of the 82nd Airborne Division I want to thank you and the Sherwood Rangers Yeomanry for the most attractive cup that we have recently received.

I do not know of anything that could be more pleasing to the Division, nor of anything that would contribute more to binding our two peoples together after the war, than this very nice act on your part.

It is an attractive cup and has been the subject of admiration of everybody who has visited the Division since its arrival, but what we treasure above all else is the sentimental attach-

ment and special significance that it will have for us. We will always remember the Sherwood Rangers Yeomanry for its splendid fighting qualities.

> *Sincerely,*
> *(Sgd) James M. Gavin,*
> *Major General, US Army,*
> *Commanding*

Lt. Col. S.D. Christopherson,
Commanding Sherwood Rangers Yeomanry.
VIA OFFICER COURIER

I also received a most appreciative letter from Lieutenant General F. A. M. Browning, who commanded the British Airborne Division, who wrote:

> *From Lieut.-Gen. F.A.M. Browning, C.B., D.S.O.,*
> *Headquarters British Airborne Corps, BLA*
> *26 September 1944*
>
> *Dear Christopherson,*
>
> *You have now been working with 82 American Airborne Division for a week. You have had a lot of scrappy fighting, which inevitably entails very close co-operation with rather small parties, Tanks and infantry on the troop-company level.*
>
> *I think I ought to let you know that the American Airborne Division has expressed unstinted praise and admiration for the way in which your people have operated. I am happy to say that, when I met your Brigadier yesterday evening, he informed me that you have the same opinion of the American Airborne Troops.*
>
> *Thank you very much indeed for this very satisfactory*

exchange of compliments, which is entirely due to the co-operation and fighting abilities of your Regiment.

Yours sincerely,
(Sgd) F. A. M. Browning

Personal
Lieut,-Col. S.D. Christopherson, M.C.,
Sherwood Rangers Yeomanry

Finally the following letter arrived from Colonel Billingslea, with whom the Regiment had fought so much:

Headquarters 325th Glider Infantry
APO 469 U.S. Army.
16 Oct 44

SUBJECT: Letter of Commendation.

TO: Officer Commanding, The Nottinghamshire Yeomanry (Sherwood Rangers) via A.D.L.S. (Br.)

1. It is desired to express to you on behalf of this Regiment our appreciation for the fine support given by your organization throughout the period that it was with us. Particularly I wish to mention the extremely excellent work done by your unit during the attack across the flats near Mook.
2. Your entire command demonstrated a splendid spirit of co-operation in all its relations with this organization.
3. The Regiment wishes you and all members of your unit the best of luck and the greatest success in all your future undertakings.

(Sgd) C. Billingslea,
Lt. Col., 325 Glider Infantry, Commanding

20

Attacking the Siegfried Line

Bridge at Nijmegen.

UNTIL THE BEGINNING of November the Regiment operated in a static defence role, supporting either 43rd Division or the Americans in the Nijmegen area. Two squadrons were in the line practically the whole time, but we took part in no deliberate attacks.

Robin Leigh, my second-in-command, returned from Brussels with seven new officers who served with him in the Royal Gloucester Hussars, for whom we had applied to England. They were Houghton, Charles, Langford, Reed, Hall, Hyde and Scudamore, and were all most welcome, especially as Robin knew them personally. Cagney and Crosbie also arrived, complete with troops from a regiment that had been broken up to support reinforcements.

Frenchie Houghton had been Robin's adjutant when he commanded the RGH, so I made him my adjutant and Terry Leinster returned to a sabre squadron.

Before the war Frenchie was in the legal profession; he was half

French, hence his name, and had a quick brain and a delightful sense of humour. He was dark, small of stature and appeared quite incapable of looking tidy, much, I think, to the irritation of the brigadier. As an adjutant he was excellent, except that his writing was quite appalling.

Robin Leigh was now second-in-command because Stephen Mitchell had stepped down and taken over C Squadron once more.

A leave camp was established by the brigade at Louvain, near Brussels, for other ranks in the brigade. I never went there myself, but it was comfortable and the food was good and enabled the men to have a complete rest and change.

On 12 October Frenchie found a pub near Mook where he established Regimental Headquarters.

The wife of the innkeeper was a one-time opera singer and one evening offered to entertain Regimental Headquarters officers with some singing. Not wishing to be discourteous I accepted the invitation and ordered all the very reluctant officers who were not on duty to assemble in their private sitting room after dinner. Her rendering was fascinating and formidable and the small room, filled with smoke, echoed with the notes of various operas, in spite of which I saw the Baron, who was sitting next to me, gradually lower his head onto his chest and soon her singing was accompanied by gentle wheezing emanating from the sleeping Baron's open mouth. Halfway through the performance the accompanist suddenly struck up with great vehemence a tune that resembled very closely the Dutch National Anthem; the chords must have penetrated into the baron's sleeping brain, for all of a sudden he leaped to his feet with great alacrity and stood smartly to attention, much to the amazement of all present. When he discovered that he was the only one standing he subsided back into his chair covered with confusion. I saw to it that he remained awake for the remainder of the performance, which lasted two and a half hours in all.

On another occasion I had my headquarters for two days in the house of the local village policeman and his wife, a most delightful and hospitable couple. They had two little boys, whom they confided they had adopted, being unable to have children. As apparently it is not possible to find children for adoption in Holland, they had brought these two kids from Croydon in England. They told me that nobody in the neighbourhood knew that they were not their own children and they had decided never to tell the boys themselves.

As a parting gift they gave me a tiny puppy, called a Pinscher, which I gather is a breed of dog peculiar to Holland. It was brown and smooth-haired and when full grown only reached 10 inches. I called the dog Beek, after the neighbouring village where the Regiment crossed into Germany for the first time and were the first British soldiers to do so.

I became most attached to this little dog and I think the affection was mutual because he never left me and was my constant companion, ever in my tank, remaining with me until I was demobilized. He was most intelligent and I trained him to sit and not move until I whistled. He was not popular with Regimental Headquarters officers, especially Frenchie, my adjutant, on account of his shrill and high-pitched bark, with which all were greeted on approaching me, and his occasional habit of snapping if he considered anybody should not be well disposed towards me.

I so well remember on one occasion, later on during the campaign in Germany, when I suddenly discovered, much to my consternation, that Beek was missing and I had the alarming thought that he had been left behind at the place where we had spent the night and which we had left very suddenly. I immediately instigated a search, during which I heard Frenchie say to the IO, 'With any luck the colonel told that blasted dog to sit and forgot to whistle.' I suppose that there might have been certain justification for their dislike.

During the middle of the month Brigade called for applications for NCOs with battle experience for instructors in England, to be drawn from those who had been continuously in action. I sent in the names of SSM Biddle, Sergeants Charity and Evans and Corporal Lacey, and at the same time Bill Wharton and Corporal Newton proceeded on a wireless course in England, much to their delight. Peter

Seleri returned to the Regiment, having recovered from his wound, and took command of B Squadron.

During the month a 'Mechanical and Gunnery Circus' consisting of experts, visited the Regiment in order to give advice on any D&M or gunnery problems that we might have discovered. The gunnery side of it proved most useful.

On the last day of the month news came through that Michael Gold, Jack Holman and Stuart Hills had all been awarded the MC, about which we were all thoroughly delighted.

On several occasions the squadrons of the Regiment had to relieve the 13/18th to support the Americans on what was known as the 'island', a piece of land situated on the river, and connected by bridge with the Nijmegen side. One day I visited B Squadron and found the reserve troop cooking a black rabbit, which they had caught for the pot, and which abounded on the island. As I was leaving I heard a GI say to his comrade, 'I guess that in some ways we may be uncivilized, but we don't have to eat black cats, like those bloody Tommies.'

The brigadier arranged a dance for officers in Nijmegen in the town hall – fortunately undamaged – which proved a great success. The Dutch girls were thrilled and in spite of not having danced for four years they soon learned. It was really rather astonishing as the Germans were only four miles away on the other side of the river, and the periodic shelling was plainly audible. The brigadier tried to get 50 girls up from Brussels, but failed owing to security reasons. At the start of the dance I found myself talking to Peter Seleri, Neville Fearn and two young Dutch girls, one extremely attractive and the other equally plain. Neville, on my arrival, immediately took the floor with the beauty and left Peter and me with the other girl. Anticipating that Peter might beat a hasty retreat and that I should be left alone with rather a large, spotty-faced, but very charming Dutch girl, who spoke no English, I said to Peter: 'I think you should dance with this charming girl.'

'Sorry, Colonel, but I can't dance,' replied Peter.

'I am afraid that I shall have to order you to take a lesson from our charming friend.'

'I am sorry, sir, in that case I shall have to disobey an unlawful command,' he replied.

'If you dance with her, I will give you the next Jeep which is allocated to the Regiment,' I offered, Jeeps being extremely short at that time.

'Make it a Jeep and two first-class wireless operators for my squadron, and I will dance.'

'All right,' I agreed, 'but it's pure blackmail', and away he went at great speed, and not too steady on his feet, to the tune of a very rapid Dutch quickstep, firmly grasping his large fair-haired Nijmegen partner.

During the evening Nervo and Knox, who were working for ENSA, gave us an excellent cabaret show.

I attended a good many conferences during this time on the Siegfried Line, and discussions on the ways and means of breaking through and dealing with the pill-boxes, concrete emplacements and outer defences of this very formidable line. This was to be the next operation working in conjunction with tank flame-throwers, who gave us a most impressive demonstration of their capabilities. It was first decided that we should attack through the Reichwald forest, but the plan was cancelled.

On 2 November I moved Regimental Headquarters to the small village of Winssen, at which time the brigadier was having a great drive on the training in the use of rifle, pistol and Bren gun for all B3 echelons, truck drivers and administrative personnel. He visited Headquarters Squadron and asked three men, who happened to be the orderly room corporal, the regimental sanitary corporal and the technical store clerk, when they had last fired a gun or pistol in practice or anger. None of them had done so since landing in Europe, much to the wrath of Brigadier Prior-Palmer, who gave Roger Nelthorpe a first-class rocket for not training all members of his squadron, regardless of their occupation. With a great deal of grumbling and moaning Roger immediately instigated an intensive training programme for all his drivers during their off-duty periods.

Some Americans from the 101st Division carried out a most

creditable recce patrol onto the other side of the river, where 10 Americans crossed under cover of darkness. They were directed by their own artillery and found out some most useful information regarding the strength of the enemy on the other side of the river. Behind the German lines, they held up a captured American Jeep being driven by some Germans, which they recaptured with the occupants. Soon afterwards they met a lorry carrying 15 Germans, which they also captured and drove back towards the river, taking their disarmed captives with them. Just before reaching the river they dismounted their captives, formed them up in the road and ordered them to march towards the river in a soldierly and smart manner. The Americans fell in at the rear of the column, marching equally smartly, but covered the rear German files with their rifles, having threatened to shoot the last German files should anyone attempt to escape. The German outpost platoon on the bank of the river mistook the column for a relief force, and forthwith were captured. The Americans made all the Germans swim back across the river, while they covered them with their rifles from the boat, and returned to their lines with 30 Germans. They had, however, to leave the Jeep and the lorry, which they most thoroughly immobilized. It really was a most remarkable effort.

About the same time the Germans carried out an almost equally spectacular feat, when seven 'frogmen' swam 10 miles down the river and destroyed the Nijmegen bridge by setting a time charge underneath one of the main structural supports.

On 8 November news came through that the attack on the Siegfried Line would take place further south, and at very short notice the Regiment was loaded onto tank transporters and we moved south to Sittard. I travelled with Frenchie Houghton, the adjutant, in a Jeep and we had an extremely cold journey. Two days later, I learned the corps commander, General Horrocks, had selected the Regiment to support the 84th US Infantry Division in attacking the Siegfried Line. He had made this choice because this division had not yet been into battle, and on account of our previous actions with the Americans. We both immediately proceeded to the American Divisional Headquarters at Gulpen for a conference, while the Regiment had congregated in the coal-mining town of Paulenberg, a most desolate place that had been devastated from shellfire and was swimming in mud from the recent rains and continual streams of tanks and army vehicles.

Except for two troops of A Squadron, which were attached to 333rd Regiment, we had to operate with 334th Regiment, commanded by Colonel Rossond, a pleasant individual, but completely incapable of making a plan or a decision. After the first conference, which lasted an hour, nothing had been decided. When I remarked on this he said, 'I like the Boys to have their say, because the Boys have to do the job!' I managed tactfully to persuade him that it would save much time if he and I could decide upon a plan, orders for which could be given out at the conference, after which he could ask for comments and not wait for his battalion commanders to make a plan for him! I decided to live at his headquarters and detailed each squadron leader to take up residence at the battalion headquarters with which they were to operate.

This operation consisted of an offensive push by the 2nd US Armoured Division in a north-eastern direction on our right, co-ordinated with a frontal attack northwards of the 84th US Division against the Siegfried Line defences. The 333rd Regiment was to capture Geilenkirchen on the left advancing along the main Palenburg–Geilenkirchen road, supported by two troops of A Squadron and the 334th Regiment on the left, fighting with B and C Squadrons and A Squadron less two troops, to make a frontal attack against the defences.

Much time and energy was devoted to planning and preparation. Not only had this American division never worked with tanks before, but it had not yet fought a battle and, in addition, in order to breach these Siegfried Line defences, we had to operate with crocodiles (tank flame-throwers), flails (a Sherman tank with a revolving spindle in front to which are attached heavy headed chains, which beat the ground as the spindle rotates before the advancing tank in order to set off the mines) and AVREs (an armoured vehicle carrying powerful charges for the demolition of concrete defences).

On the 17th, all the armour carried out a full dress rehearsal of the breaching part of the operation, which was greatly hindered by the continuous rain, which made the area a sea of mud resulting in most of the tanks becoming bogged. Colonel Delamore of the Lothian and Border Horse, which had been converted to flails, was to command the breaching forces; their first duty consisted of making two gaps for the tanks over the railway, an anti-tank obstacle, which was heavily mined, after which I took command of all the armour, which, with the attached troops, amounted to a dual regimental command.

At the final conference before the attack, our brigadier informed us that we should be fighting throughout the winter and that the possibility of home leave would be out of the question owing to the shortage of manpower and shipping difficulties, which was somewhat depressing before an operation that had every sign of being thoroughly unpleasant.

The pull on British manpower was immense. British men were not only fighting in the Far East, but also in Italy as well as north-west Europe and, in addition, manning numerous outposts throughout the Empire, stretching from Gibraltar through to the Pacific. In addition, manpower was used to build the vast numbers of aircraft and ships and other war matériel produced in Britain. On top of that, there was Home Defence and the formation of the Pacific Fleet in August. It was no wonder after five long years of war that manpower in north-west Europe was becoming short, but it was both extremely hard and demoralizing for those still slogging their way into Germany. Even the United States was forced to blood new divisions such as the 84th, who were, almost to a man, inexperienced and new to war. The best American units were, by this time, among the finest in the world, but the green divisions often faced a terrible baptism of fire as they came up against fanatical German troops determined to fight for every yard. For Stanley and the Sherwood Rangers, who had been fighting almost continually since D-Day, nursing these rookie troops was no easy task, and especially when there was no common doctrine between British and American troops.

There had been a time when it had seemed likely the war would be

over by Christmas, but while the end was now within touching
distance, both Nazi Germany and Imperial Japan seemed determined
to fight on.

From 18 until 24 November the Regiment fought a continual slogging
battle against the carefully prepared and well-thought-out concrete
defence positions, which, except for D-Day, was a new experience for
us. These defences consisted of numerous concrete pill-boxes
surrounded by wire and mines. The walls were so thick that not even
the tank 17-pounder gun could penetrate.

During the night preceding the attack we had very little sleep.
Artillery concentration started at 03.30 on the morning of the 18th,
and at 05.00 suddenly the whole area was lit by 'artificial moonlight',
produced by a battery of searchlights situated behind our lines, which
proved most effective, and the attack commenced.

One gap through the minefields and over the railway was not
completed in time, so both A Squadron less two troops and B
Squadron, which was supporting the leading battalions, used the same
gap. B Squadron's objective was the high ground north-east of
Gelsenkirchen, and A Squadron's the village of Prummern. By midday
these two squadrons had knocked out, or caused to surrender, six pill-
boxes and had captured 350 POWs, and the Regiment can claim to
have been the first British troops to have broken through the Siegfried
Line.

By the end of the day both squadrons with the American
battalions had taken their objectives, but B Squadron lost Lieutenant
Crosbie who was killed when his tank was knocked out by an anti-
tank gun. John Semken, A Squadron commander, drove his tank over
a cluster of four mines, which exploded simultaneously. The tank was
completely written off; fortunately the crew suffered no injury, but
were all rather shaken up. John Scudamore was shot in the leg when
his tank was hit by an anti-tank gun, and Sergeant Dring of A
Squadron received a nasty wound in the hand when he was doing a
recce on foot. He came across a Panther, which he thought had been
knocked out, but when he approached the tank it was very much alive

and engaged him with high explosive. He was fortunate as a shell landed right beside him.

Without any doubt he was one of the Regiment's most experienced tank commanders and troop leaders. He appeared to be gifted with a sixth sense and always spotted an enemy tank long before anybody else, or before he was seen. He was an expert gunner; deadly accurate and quick with his tank 75mm. He and his gunner knocked out more German tanks than any other member of the Regiment. I recall so vividly a conversation that came over the air between him and another A Squadron tank commander, somewhere in Normandy.

'Nutts 1. (Sergeant Dring talking.) Enemy tank concealed 800 yards to left front, stop where you are.'

'Nutts 1. Never seen a turret with horns, am engaging the cow.'

A German Mark 4 tank was forthwith brewed up by an anti-tank shell from Sergeant Dring.

His wound gave him subsequent trouble, which prevented him returning to the Regiment. However, for his sake I was extremely pleased, for he had fought among the leading tanks of the Regiment from El Alamein to the Siegfried Line, and he was one of the very few NCO tank commanders of a sabre squadron who had survived so much action.

On the 19th, B Squadron, supporting the same battalion, was ordered to capture the high ground south of the village of Wurm, an advance of 1500 yards. This proved most difficult owing to the open ground and the very cleverly concealed pill-boxes. The squadron commander, Peter Seleri, had his tank destroyed and was wounded for the second time. C Squadron spent the day clearing the north end of Prummern and the orchards to the east and knocked out three German tanks. Second Lieutenant Holmes of that squadron was instantly killed when a high-explosive shell landed on his tank. Among the other casualties Corporal Whitfield, an A Squadron fitter, and Corporal Hewitt of B Echelon were killed and Mechanist Quarter Master Sergeant Scott and Sergeant Collis wounded, Sergeant Collis for the third time. Technical Adjutant Bridgford and Mechanist Quarter Master Sergeant Scott carried out most sterling work in attending to various damaged tanks, because even after the battle had gone forward the shelling still continued and they had to work under most difficult conditions.

A Squadron had a comparatively quiet day, except for 1 Troop under David Alderson, which continued to support the 333rd Regiment in capturing Gelsenkirchen and won the sincere praise of the Americans for the support they gave them.

November 20 proved a continuation of the previous day's operation. Progress was painfully slow, as the pill-boxes had to be eliminated one by one and each one was supported by fire from another. A Squadron, still fighting with 333rd Regiment, cleared the high ground north-west of Gelsenkirchen, but owing to the enclosed country, it had to stick to one road, which made progress extremely difficult.

I spent most of the day with B Squadron in the Prummern area and was present when Hubert Beddington, who had recently joined the Regiment, suddenly saw a white flag being waved from a slit trench. Hubert jumped from his tank and advanced with revolver drawn to make a capture, and was somewhat taken aback when one German, almost seven feet tall, clambered with his hands up from the trench. Hubert, who is only five foot four, marched him back to his tank, but had to stand on it in order to search the German for arms, which presented a truly remarkable spectacle! Hubert, unfortunately, was wounded on the following day, together with Alderson, who had done so well with 333 Regiment.

The 21st was yet another slogging day. A Squadron with 333 Regiment was given the job of attacking Wurm, and B Squadron, with 2nd Battalion 334, the village of Beek, not to be confused with the Nijmegen Beek, and C Squadron with the 3rd Battalion 335, the high ground north of Beek. No progress was made and we suffered heavy casualties. A German anti-tank gun from one pill-box knocked out three tank flame-throwers, which were supporting us, in three consecutive shots.

The attack against Beek and Wurm continued throughout the 22nd and 23rd. It was decided not to attack Beek from Prummern,

CITATION FOR SILVER STAR

T/Lieutenant Colonel Stanley Douglas Christopherson 99064, Sherwood Rangers (British Army), for gallantry in action against the enemy in Germany 18 - 20 November 1944, and outstanding leadership in the organization and direction of plans for mechanized support of Combat Team 334th Infantry. T/Lieutenant Colonel Christopherson, from a position exposed to enemy fire and in the face of great danger, did with undaunted courage direct the action of his tanks. With meticulous care and foresight, he gave all possible assistance to the Infantry and cooperated to the greatest extent with Commanding Officers of the Combat Team in the attack on prepared enemy positions. Much of the credit for the success of the Combat Team in attaining its objective was due to the efforts and cooperation of T/Lieutenant Colonel Christopherson and his Sherwood Rangers. His gallantry in action and devotion to duty reflect highest credit on himself, the Sherwood Rangers, and the entire British Armed Forces.

Stanley's citation for the US Silver Star.

Terry Leinster.

which had already proved so costly to the Americans and ourselves, but to launch the attack from a village called Apweiler, which lay due south of Beek. A composite squadron from B and C Squadrons, formed under Terry Leinster, went in, supporting the 405 Combat team, under a barrage and smokescreen. It reached the outskirts, but did not succeed in penetrating into the centre of the village. During this action Sergeant Butler from A Squadron was killed when an anti-tank shot from a German self-propelled gun brewed up his tank. He was one of my most reliable and experienced NCO tank commanders when I commanded A Squadron with Crusaders in the desert, and I felt his loss most keenly. A hunt servant before the war, he joined the Yeomanry and showed himself quite capable of speedily learning the art of gunnery during the time we were gunners in Tobruk, proving himself an outstanding tank commander when the Regiment became mechanized.

By the evening of the 23rd Terry Leinster's composite squadron had dwindled to eight tanks, and since the action of the Siegfried Line had started 10 tanks from the Regiment had been completely brewed up, five damaged through enemy action and five badly bogged.

The officers from the Royal Gloucester Hussars, who had recently joined the Regiment, saw action for the first time and deserved the highest praise for the way they fought, particularly Dick Coleman during the attack on Beek, when he led his troop with great determination through the smokescreen into the orchards on the outskirts of the village, which were strongly held by anti-tank guns. Also to John Hyde and John Scudamore, who showed equal dash and determination. The Americans told me that they had put some of our men in for American decorations, but none came through. So many outstanding things were done during this war, which so thoroughly deserved an award, but were never witnessed.

I was most thankful to receive orders on the evening of 23 November that the Regiment was to be relieved by a battalion of American tanks and would be placed in Corps Reserve, to proceed to the pleasant Dutch village of Schinnen, six miles from the front. So ended six days of most unpleasant and costly battles, fought in continuous rain and mud, against a very determined enemy.

During the six days of battle, B Squadron alone suffered 30 casualties. Twenty-five tanks were used in all, of which 16 (after being repaired) were eventually used again. For all four troop leaders, it was their first battle and a considerable baptism of fire. The violence, the cold and constant rain, the lack of regular hot meals and other discomforts ensured that both squadron and Regiment were both more than ready for a rest.

The Regiment had already spent a few nights in Schinnen en route to the Siegfried Line, so the squadrons returned to their same billets. The local inhabitants gave us a most sincere and affectionate welcome, and turned out in full force when we arrived, and there was genuine distress and even tears among those of the inhabitants who had housed those who had been killed since our previous visit, which was most touching.

Regimental Headquarters once again established itself at the local pub and the Baron and I each had a comfortable room and shared a bathroom. He confided to me that each bath cost three bars of chocolate, but it was well worth it.

We soon discovered that our rest would not be so complete as anticipated: two troops had to be at four hours' notice, one squadron at 12 hours' notice, and the remainder of the Regiment at 24 hours' notice, and furthermore I had to take command of a corps mobile force, known as Fox Force, consisting of the Sherwood Rangers, the 43rd Recce Regiment, 1 Squadron of Horse Guards, armoured cars, and one battery of A/T gunners.

On the second night after our arrival at Schinnen the Regiment received an invitation from the Burgomaster to attend a concert in the village hall, given by the local brass band, which we accepted, and I invited the brigadier to dine and attend with us. The band had not played for five years, but they turned out in full uniform and gave us some stirring music. We all sat in the front row, only a few feet away from the players, who all demonstrated the greatest enthusiasm, each appearing quite determined to make more noise than his neighbour, and in consequence we were almost blown out of our seats. During the interval the Burgomaster made a speech in Dutch and I replied in English, and both speeches were interpreted by a Dutchman who spoke both languages fluently.

After the concert was over and the brigadier had departed, Chris Sidgewick, our battery commander, insisted that we should celebrate and gave a variety of reasons, which appeared adequate, so we returned to the mess and drank. On his way home, in a hilarious mood, he visited A Squadron, which was listening to a piano duet rendered by the daughters of the house in which the officers were bil-leted, while the parents and the third daughter, with A Squadron officers, sat in dignified silence, attentively listening to the music. The place was suddenly disturbed by Chris bursting into the room, seizing the old mother around the waist and doing an old-fashioned waltz at double speed around the room. On completing two circles he released his most astonished partner, and left the room as quickly as he had entered it. The recital continued, but the next morning Chris denied all knowledge of the incident.

The corps commander, General Horrocks, addressed the Regiment and congratulated us on our recent actions with the Americans. He told us again that he had selected us for this operation as he considered that we were the most experienced armoured regiment under his command. I suppose corps commanders must say nice things to troops just out of action, but I do feel that he was sincere in what he said.

The following officers arrived to join the Regiment: Gaiger, Whalen and Smith from Brigade Headquarters, and Cameron from the 4/7th. The brigadier asked me whether I would take Cameron as he was not at all happy with the 4/7th, which I think was somewhat prejudiced owing to the fact that he had risen from the ranks. I found him somewhat awkward in manner, but very brave in battle.

On the last day of November, with Stuart Hills, John Semken, Jack Holman and Sergeant Nelson, I attended an investiture held by Montgomery at Brunssum, at which he announced the great news that home leave would be permitted to all those who had been in the theatre of war for six months. This came as a most pleasant surprise, especially after the pessimism of our own brigadier. He also told us the details of the scheme called Python, which was to come into operation. This meant compulsory repatriation for all those who had been abroad continuously and who had had less than six months in England. This would have been serious for the Regiment as it involved approximately 100 men, all of whom had been with the Regiment for a long time and held key positions, if an alternative of a month's leave had not been granted. I was glad when most of those who were eligible for the Python scheme chose the month's leave. Should they have chosen repatriation they would have been posted to another unit in England with the possibility of being sent to another theatre of war.

On 1 December General Montgomery paid a visit to Brigade Headquarters for the purpose of meeting some of the older members of the brigade. The following from the Regiment were introduced to him: Sergeant Pick, my signal sergeant, Sergeants Jones and Lanes and Corporal McDonald. Before his arrival the brigadier expressed his displeasure at the very low standard of saluting and smartness, which he complained was very evident at the investiture. During his address the brigade major rushed in and announced Monty's arrival 15 minutes before schedule. All the commanding officers had to make a very hurried exit through the kitchen, which caused the brigadier's pep-talk to be somewhat less impressive.

On 3 December Colonel Phayre and I left for Brussels to visit 21st Army Group for a discussion about reinforcements. I saw Tim Redman, who used to command the Greys. On the following day I had lunch with Derrick Warwick, who had been doing staff work since he received a head wound in the desert. He told me that he hoped to rejoin the Regiment after his next medical board. The two days' break in Brussels was most welcome. As usual Arthur Phayre found himself some female company, and insisted that I should dine with him and his ladyfriend. I was somewhat apprehensive about his girlfriend, whom he told me was a chance acquaintance, and I had certain qualms when she insisted on bringing a partner for me. This was nothing compared with the shock I received when they both appeared at dinner time: I almost bolted when I saw the 'blonde number' who was to be paired off with me. I spent a most uncomfortable evening and my dinner was completely spoiled, dreading that some of the brigade or regimental officers on leave in Brussels might dine at the same restaurant.

On my return to the Regiment I found the Baron in a flat spin. He was trying to organize a demonstration tank shoot for the benefit of the 52 Lowland Division, which had not operated with ranks before, carry out Operation DUTCHMAN for the local defence of the area, necessitated by the dropping of German parachutists, and to plan Operation SHEARS, in which the Regiment was to take part in co-operation with 43rd Division for the capture of Heinsberg, and to push the Germans the other side of the Ruhr. Much to our delight, Operation SHEARS was eventually cancelled, owing to the bad weather, which had made the ground quite impassable for tanks.

About the 18th of the month news arrived that the Germans had made a major breakthrough in the Ardennes and that they were driving towards Liège, and as a result the corps plan for an attack on the Reichwald, the extensive forest to the east of Nijmegen, was cancelled. This very offensive thrust, which caused certain panic, especially among the Americans, proved to be a final desperate attempt to split the British and American armies. Frenchie Houghton had gone to Paris to see some of his relations and returned to the Regiment with great speed, anticipating that we should be in action, but as it turned out the Ardennes offensive did not involve the Regiment.

Christmas the Regiment spent in the village of Schinnen and we had a very pleasant time. The day started with Christmas service, at which we sang numerous carols, and received a most stirring address from Padre Skinner and at lunchtime each squadron had its Christmas dinner, consisting of fresh pork, tinned turkey, vegetables, plum pudding and a bottle of beer for the men. With the RSM I visited each squadron and wished them a happy Christmas. Corporal Sam Kirkman of C Squadron had somehow managed to dispose of six bottles of beer and came stumbling to meet me when I arrived at C Squadron. During static periods he always caused trouble, and was a grouser of great magnitude, but he ended as C Squadron signal sergeant; Jack Holman declared him as being one of the finest wireless operators in the Regiment and on whom he relied so much in battle.

On Christmas afternoon the Regiment entertained the children of Schinnen with a party and a Christmas tree. Neville Fearn dressed up as Father Christmas, and George Culley, the OP from our Essex Yeomanry battery, as a clown and these two rode on a sleigh drawn by a Honey tank through the streets to the village school, followed by the delighted children, who all tried to scramble on the sleigh. It was a typical Christmas, as the ground was white with frost and snow. Every man had saved his sweet and chocolate rations to enable each child to have a present from the tree distributed by Arthur and George, who worked like Trojans throughout the afternoon.

George Culley then entertained the children with a display of acrobatics at which he excelled. He was short in stature, very thin, and always wore a thick moustache of great length, of which he was extremely proud. He possessed a delightful sense of humour and a lovely nature. In battle he excelled as a gunner and observation officer.

The officers' Christmas dinner was held on Christmas night, and, for the first time since we left England, all the Regiment sat down together to a meal. Derrick Warwick came up from Brussels and spent Christmas with the Regiment. Every officer received a present from a small Christmas tree, and I was presented with a packet of army biscuits. So ended my sixth and last wartime Christmas: I had spent two in England, two in the desert, one in Palestine and one in Holland.

What Stanley does not mention, with typical modesty, is that at this investiture, Montgomery presented him with an immediate Distinguished Service Order, awarded for his exceptional leadership during the battle for Gheel. 'The enemy counter-attacked with great ferocity on numerous occasions and were successful in cutting off a part of the force in Gheel and the area immediately south of the village. During the night, enemy infantry infiltrated among the tanks and the situation became very confused. Lieutenant Colonel Christopherson remained completely undismayed in spite of extremely critical circumstances and, by his courageous example, was successful in restoring the situation. The bold and determined action of this officer was largely instrumental in the maintenance of this all-important bridgehead.'

Before Christmas, Stephen Mitchell was posted home, which was entirely deserved after such a long time away on active service. It was, however, a personal blow to Stanley: he and Stephen had been best friends throughout the war, and among the endless new faces in the Regiment, Stephen was not only a link to what had gone before, but also his confidant and someone with whom he could share the burdens of command, which were many. 'The only shoulder he could now weep on,' says John Semken, 'was either the doctor's or the padre's.'

21

Approach to the Rhine

Germany: moving out for attack.

THE OPENING DAYS of 1945 found the Allies recovering from the last major German offensive of the war. In what became known as the Battle of the Bulge, the Americans at first gave way, then held, and finally clawed back the ground they had lost. It had been a setback for the Allies.

On 2 January the Regiment relieved the 13/18th, which was supporting the 52nd Lowland Division in the line. A Squadron took up a position in a village called Gangelt with a troop under David Render in the hamlet of Hastenrath, and another troop under Cameron in Vintelen. C Squadron was situated in Starl occupying good fire positions. Regimental Headquarters went to Schinveld, with B Squadron in reserve. All these villages were within a few miles of each other; although at that time we did not expect much opposition from the Germans on our immediate front, our infantry was very thin on the ground.

Vintelen had been attacked on the night of 28 December 1944, and the forward infantry platoon captured; the two attacking German companies had bypassed the village and entered from the south, much to the alarm of the A Squadron tanks, which had been positioned in the centre of the village. I understand that Trooper Lait, a driver of one of the tanks, had been the first to discover the presence of the Germans. While sitting in the driver's seat he heard somebody clambering onto the tank and then, to his great astonishment, heard a guttural voice say, '*Ich denke das ist ein Tschermann*.' Both Lait and his co-driver held their breath, anticipating the arrival of a hand-grenade, but apparently the Germans must have thought the tank was deserted. Sergeant Lanes, the tank commander, who had walked across to another tank around the corner, suddenly appeared and opened fire on the Germans who leaped from the tank and retreated. The Germans attacked the tanks, which had formed a close circle, with hand-grenades and bazookas, but they held them off until the arrival of the infantry from the north end of the village and together they wiped out the two German companies. Cameron was wounded in the head and both Sergeant Lanes and Corporal Redferne did extraordinarily well, according to the infantry OP, who was present during this action. The hamlet of Kievelberg was counter-attacked by David Render and a company of infantry and recaptured, with 30 POWs.

The Germans attacked Tripsrath, employing the same tactics and advancing from the south, having circled the village under cover of dark, which they were able to do owing to our lack of infantry. At one time they held the southern part of the village and we held the north end. Thanks to David Phethean, who commanded a C Squadron troop, the situation was restored. The divisional commander, Hakewill-Smith, told me that he was delighted with the way in which the Regiment had supported his division and asked me to pass on his appreciation to all concerned.

On Old Year's Night, all the Regiment was in the line, but each squadron managed to drink the old year out and the new year in. When I visited A Squadron, I found Neville Fearn and George Culley sitting in a cellar drinking champagne, which they had discovered in the house, from large and ornate German beer mugs, one of which they presented to me.

The weather at this time was intensely cold, owing to the continual snow and frost.

On 1 January the Regiment was relieved by the 4/7th and we moved back to Schimmert and were placed on four hours' notice to operate in the event of a counter-attack. Frenchie Houghton found a regimental headquarters in a convent, which proved comfortable but not quite as pleasant as Schinnen. We remained in this location until 18 January, preparing for the next operation, which was called BLACKCOCK, in which we were to support the 156th Infantry Brigade of the 52nd Mountain Division. During this time John Bethell-Fox, who had been wounded three times since he joined, returned to the Regiment with Denis Elmore and Lieutenant Howard, all of whom had been wounded on D-Day.

The Baron organized the transfer to the Regiment of the following NCOs who had been under his command in the Royal Gloucester Hussars: Sergeants Kean, Maslim, Humphreys, Isham, Pothecary, Marke, and Corporals Edwards and Taylor. They replaced personnel who had chosen repatriation through the Python scheme, and although they had not been in action, they were all first class.

I organized a tank commanders' course within the Regiment immediately.

We had the opportunity to visit the battlefield around Geilenkirchen, Prummern and Beek, inspect the enemy's defences, and we had a look at the ground from their point of view, which was most interesting and made us all realize the difficulty of our approach. We inspected the German tanks we had knocked out and those of ours which had been brewed up and fought the battle all over again. While we were walking along a deserted street in Prummern, a goat suddenly appeared with a pair of women's pants over its hindquarters and a straw hat perched on its head. The animal immediately attached itself to little George Culley and, in spite of threats, shouts and entreaties, refused to be shaken off and followed him for the rest of the morning. How the goat became so attired we never discovered. Myles Hildyard, one of our original Yeoman officers, spent two days with the Regiment. After his return from Crete he joined 7th Armoured Divisional Staff as intelligence officer and remained in that capacity until hostilities ceased. He brought with him a German count who had been educated in England. Myles discovered him when he interrogated him as a POW, and immediately seconded him to his staff. Wherever Myles went he was followed by his German count and I gather that he even had meals with him in the divisional officers' mess, and except for a few caustic comments from the divisional general, nobody appeared to worry about him.

For the Regiment, Operation BLACKCOCK commenced on 18 January, in snowy weather, and with all our tanks white. Two troops from C Squadron reinforced with AVREs and flails, supporting the 4/5th RSF from 156 Brigade attempted to form a bridgehead over the stream running east and west in front of the villages of Lind, Sind and Havert. Unfortunately, owing to excessively wet ground on the banks of the stream, it was quite impossible to lay a bridge for the tanks to cross and the infantry had to attack without tank support. The 4/5th RSF secured a bridgehead through which the 5th HLI passed, and captured the villages of Lind, Sind and Havert. Until 24 January the Regiment captured a series of small villages, all within a very short distance of each other. Some of these were held lightly by a few infantry and others contained infantry and tanks or self-propelled guns.

Boket was taken by A Squadron, carrying the infantry on the back of the tanks. Honton proved difficult and three tanks were destroyed before the village was captured eventually by A Squadron. Selston was captured by B Squadron and the 6th HLI, Laffeld by A Squadron and the 5th HLI and Schandorf, Locken, Ospenan by B Squadron and the 1st Gordon Highlanders.

On 24 January, the whole Regiment attacked Heinsberg, which was for us the major attack of the whole operation. We were again supported by a troop of flails, crocodiles and AVREs. The tie-up before the attack was somewhat complicated, as each sub-unit was widely separated, and only a limited number of roads was available, owing to mines. However, each unit succeeded in appearing at the right time and place, and we crossed the start line at dawn. Eight hundred yards of dead flat ground had to be crossed before it was possible to enter the town, which was heavily protected by self-propelled guns, and we lost three tanks as we advanced through the smokescreen. Sergeant Lanes's troop was the first to get into the town, and it was thanks to this troop that the remainder of our tanks found their way in, with the infantry on their backs. When Heinsberg eventually fell we found that every house had been damaged, and very few remained standing. All the German civilians appeared to have been issued with rifles, which we found in the cellars, but they made no attempt to use them. This operation cost us five officer casualties, including Wharton, Cagney, Perry, Walsh and Langford, none fatal I am glad to say, and 20 other ranks.

After a couple of days out of the line, the Regiment moved once again to Nijmegen, the Assembly area for the next operation, codenamed VERITABLE.

Before leaving we entertained at dinner some old friends from the Staffordshire Yeomanry, including Lawrence Biddle, the Staffs' doctor and Chris Sidgewick, Arthur Warburton and George Culley from the Essex Yeomanry. After dinner Chris, who was delightfully mellow with wine, suddenly remembered that he had to attend a conference with his own commanding officer and other regimental battery commanders. Haughtily disregarding all offers to direct him on the journey he left the room, making a gallant effort to appear steady on his feet, and drove away in his Jeep without waiting for his driver. He reached his regimental orderly room, but from there was quite unable in the dark to locate the regimental tactical headquarters where the colonel was holding the conference, which was only 500 yards away. In the end he gave up, returned to the orderly room and rang up the colonel, having to admit that in spite of desperate efforts he had failed to locate Tactical Headquarters, much to the amusement of all present, who appreciated his condition and had heard the Jeep pass and re-pass the headquarters, travelling at great speed along the very slippery and muddy road.

On 3 February 'Von Thoma', the commander of 43rd Division, explained to regimental commanders the details of the forthcoming operation. Five divisions, including the Canadians, were to break through the Reichwald on to a line from Kleve in the north to the south-eastern corner of the Reichwald. The 43rd Division, supported by the 8th Armoured Brigade, was given the task of breaking through this bridgehead. The Regiment was detailed to operate with 129th Brigade. The first stage of the operation was called PEPPERPOT, during which the tanks of the Regiment were to be used as artillery, which was wrong in principle, in order to augment the existing artillery on the Canadian division front. Each tank in the Regiment was allocated 220 rounds of high explosive.

On 7 February each tank in each squadron, with the aid of the OP lent by the Canadians, registered its targets, and at 05.00 hours on 8 February started firing according to a scheduled programme until 10.30 hours. On a 7000-yard front there must have been at least 1500

Operation PEPPERPOT.

guns firing, including tanks, Bofors and field artillery. When all the allocated ammunition had been fired I ordered the whole Regiment to reload with one round of high explosive, elevate the guns to extreme range, then gave the order to fire simultaneously, in the hope that certain destruction might be caused to a German headquarters situated well behind the front line.

Ronnie Hutton, who since D-Day had commanded Bl Echelon, applied to me for a transfer to a fighting squadron. I was most reluctant to grant his request because he had proved such a reliable echelon commander. Never once had he failed to turn up at the end of a day's fighting with supplies of petrol and ammunition, however late it might have been, or whatever distance we had travelled. He invariably found the Regiment, even without the aid of wireless communications. He had the knack of suddenly appearing when he was most needed. In a battle, when tanks appeared to be running out of petrol and arms, Ronnie would suddenly turn up in his scout car, ready to lead any tank back to his lorries. However, he was insistent and I placed him in A Squadron, much to the indignation of Roger Sutton-Nelthorpe, Headquarters Squadron leader, who was most reluctant to lose his second-in-command; Michael Howden (Dis-Mike) took his place as Bl Echelon commander. Ronnie joined the Regiment in Palestine, having been commissioned from the North Irish Horse. He was tall, short of hair, and spoke with a gentle Irish brogue; a delightful companion at all times, with an unparalleled subtle and quick humour.

The four-divisional assault started at dawn on 9 February and the same evening the Regiment moved forward carrying the infantry on the back of the tanks to Kleve, which had been reported clear, in order to take our first objective, the high ground to the north-east of the town, passing en route through Beek (yet another), Kranenburg and Nütterden. We soon discovered that the information about the position in Kleve was entirely inaccurate; none of our troops had entered the town, and Ray Gaiger, who was the leading troop leader, suddenly reported a roadblock covered by fire, which he broke through, and led the column to the centre of the town. We soon found that the town contained SP guns, as well as a considerable number of infantry, which immediately counter-attacked the compact square into which we had formed ourselves in the centre. German snipers hiding in the buildings overlooking the streets in which we had taken up positions added to our discomfort. A German SP gun attacked up the street where the infantry brigadier had established his head-quarters, and knocked out his scout car, killing his G3 and wounding his brigade major who, however, disposed of three German infantry-men with his revolver before passing out.

One impudent German sniper had the nerve to draw a bead on the head of the worthy Baron who, however, spotted the window from which he fired. He immediately returned the fire with AP and high explosive shot that caused the corner wall of the house to collapse, thus revealing, much to the consternation of the Baron, a German SP gun, which had been hiding behind the house. The Baron and his gunner, Corporal Newton, engaged with much ferocity, but without accuracy, and the SP moved away. He was, however, most indignant that he had received no support from the adjutant, whose tank was positioned just behind him on the other side of the street, and so called him on the air.

'Couldn't you see that I have been engaging a bloody SP gun? You might have given me some support – out.'

'Can't you see that a bloody SP gun is just about to emerge from the street to your right rear, for whom your bottom will be a perfect target, when he does appear? Off.'

The Baron's indignation soon evaporated, and he hastily changed the position of his tank to deal with this new threat.

For a week we fought in the Kleve area, until finally all opposition had been wiped out. The supply position became serious, because at one period there was only one road between Kleve and Nijmegen, and when the Germans flooded the southern bank of the Rhine this road became impassable to all vehicles. However, the situation was saved by the use of 150 Ducks, which were amphibious troop-carrying vehicles.

The final objective, a village called Louisendorf, which included a mental hospital, was captured by A Squadron and the 4th Wilts.

Ronnie Hutton passed back a message on the air that he had captured three doctors, 30 nurses and 1300 lunatics. I replied that he could retain the doctors and the lunatics, but he could send back the nurses to Regimental Headquarters.

In this village I found a snowdrop, the first I had seen for such a long time.

During this week of fighting we suffered 31 casualties. Lieutenant Thomas, a new officer, had been killed, and Whalen, Howard, Coleman and Knapp all wounded, which again made us short of officers. Among the other rank casualties, Sergeant Geddis, one of our very best REME NCOs was wounded and 14 of our tanks had been destroyed. Much to his wrath little George Culley, our OP from the Essex Yeomanry, received a shell fragment in his right buttock and when, with trousers down, he was being examined by Hylda, two German *Fraus* walked into the RAP for medical attention, he made a desperate effort to escape, but was firmly detained by Hylda, who removed his trousers outside, much to his furious indignation.

A very weary Regiment returned to Kleve in which practically no building remained standing. However, we made ourselves comfortable in the cellars, which were well stocked with coal and jars of preserved fruit, and remained out of the line until the end of the month. Most of the German inhabitants had been evacuated, but a few, including old women, had flatly refused to leave their homes and now pathetically existed in the cellars of the ruined houses.

We enjoyed our few days' respite in Kleve, but immediately I had to organize the usual cadre classes to train the new NCOs. Naturally they came to the Regiment with certain basic training but it was imperative, whenever possible, to teach them certain things regarding tactics, gunner and wireless procedure, which were peculiar to the Regiment.

Bill Enderby returned after having been wounded on D-Day. He had a permanent injury to his arm and had been medically downgraded, but somehow he fooled the Medical Board and returned once again to the Regiment and took command of A Squadron.

At Kleve, Stuart Hills returned to the Regiment, having completed his course in England, and I gave him command of the reconnaissance

At Cleve, Germany, February 1945. *Left to right (standing)*: Bob Dare-Smith (Brigade Major), Ronnie Hutton (A Squadron Leader). *Left to right (sitting)*: Derek Colls (Company Commando 12/60), Neville Fearn, Bill Enderby, Chris Sidgewick (Commander, Essex Yeomanry), SDC and Beek (dog).

troop, as Ian McKay had taken over A Squadron. Basil Ringrose applied to come back. He had seen many years' service with the Regiment before the war. In Palestine as a result of a quarrel with Flash Kellett, who was then commanding, he accepted a position in Abyssinia working with Haile Selassie, where he did extremely well, rejoining just before the Battle of Alamein as my second-in-command in A Squadron. After the desert he assumed some kind of staff duties, and now once again wished to start regimental soldiering. Such applications always created certain ill-feeling among those who had fought continuously in the Regiment. Although he had been with the Regiment before the war, his return would block promotion. However, I decided to agree to his return, as at that stage it appeared that the end of the war in Europe was in sight and that Robin Leigh, my second-in-command, would wish to rejoin the RGH.

On 1 March the Regiment once again went into action supporting the 12th Brigade of the 53rd Welsh Division, to capture the village of Weele. From this stage until the crossing of the Rhine we fought against German rear-guards, consisting largely of German parachute troops, who fought fanatically, covering the German withdrawal to the Rhine.

A week's action followed, during which all squadrons were involved each day. A composite force under Basil Ringrose was formed, known as Robin Force (named after Robin Hood, my tank), consisting of C Squadron, 43rd Division, Recce Regiment and a company of 12/60th. It was ordered to work southwards through the woods to capture the bridge south of Weele, while the 4/7th drove along the road leading south of Weele. The thick woods made progress slow, but the bridge was eventually taken with the loss of two tanks. A and B Squadrons, operating in the same woods and each supported by a platoon of the 12/60th, drove south towards the river. The company from the 12/60th proved, as usual, immensely valuable to the tanks operating through those woods. They had worked with us since D-Day and each man in the company appreciated the danger that woods held for tanks. B Squadron, under Ian McKay, encountered several farms containing pockets of Germans who fought to the last man. In one particular farmhouse a German parachute company actually counter-attacked with rifles and bazookas as the squadron attacked, shouting that they preferred death to capture. One tank of B Squadron, which became detached from the rest of the squadron, was knocked out by a German bazooka team. The crew baled out, including Corporal Turner, the tank commander, who was severely wounded in the leg, and found themselves in the midst of a German infantry platoon. The crew, except for Corporal Turner, managed to extricate itself, but he was captured and taken to the German headquarters in a farmhouse. We learned afterwards from the farmer that he had been well cared for, and that the German medical orderly had amputated the shattered leg, but he did not survive and he was buried by the padre when we found him.

On 4 March all squadrons once again formed up in a regimental group, with a battalion of the Oxford and Bucks Infantry Regiment in

'Kangaroos', which were armoured tracked troop-carrying vehicles. I received orders to proceed and capture the town of Issum with all speed. We moved off at 09.30 in the morning, with an advance guard consisting of C Squadron, a platoon of 12/60th, preceded by a section of the recce troop. Just before reaching Issum the leading squadron reported that it was engaging some armoured cars to the right flank. These turned out to be elements of an American armoured-car regiment coming up from the south with orders to keep contact with the British advance. We all met up in the centre of Issum, and apologized for our mistake. Fortunately our shooting had not been accurate.

The American troop commander was most impressed with the issued tank suits, which we were all wearing, and asked whether we could give him a couple. In view of our shooting error, I readily agreed to his request and sent a wireless message back to the quarter master asking for two suits to be sent up immediately.

Issum contained no Germans, but was under shellfire. No progress was possible as all the bridges over the river outside Issum

The ruined German village of Issum, February 1945.

had been blown, and it was quite impossible for tanks to cross. Patrols of the 12/60th reported that Germans dug in had been contacted two miles down the road on the far side of the river. I called up the Regiment's armoured bulldozer, a converted Sherman, which was driven by Corporal Evans, and he did excellent work by filling in a shallow part of the river to make a firm foundation on the bank for a tank bridge. In order to achieve his object he had to knock down a house situated near the bank of the river to obtain more rubble. By midnight a 'scissors' bridge, with the help of a detachment of engineers, had been thrown across the river. This kind of bridge, a clever invention, is carried on a specially constructed Crusader tank, which can lower it across a moderately wide river.

Naturally the engineers required some protection while they worked, and I felt rather mean having to call upon the Recce Troop, when the rest of the Regiment had a full night's sleep under cover in comfortable billets. Stuart Hills and Corporal Morris reported to Headquarters for orders, Stuart complaining that he did not mind having to do the job, but resented the gleeful relish on the part of Frenchie Houghton, who woke him up, after an hour's sleep, at about two o'clock in the morning.

After an hour's work the engineers suddenly had the impression that they were being counter-attacked, and retreated with the maximum speed back to the town. This was entirely imagination on their part. Unfortunately, the brigadier arrived at Regimental Headquarters when the engineer officer, very white in the face, was telling me about the alleged counter-attack, at the same time that Stuart was reporting on the wireless that the engineers had vanished into thin air for no apparent reason. Prior-Palmer became extremely angry and recalled Stuart forthwith, and on his arrival said, 'Stuart, you will take these engineers, under this officer, up to the bridge again and you will be in command, and the bridge will be ready by first light even if you are counter-attacked by 50 Panzer Divisions.' At this stage Chris Sidgewick, our battery commander, having been fast asleep in the next room, and awakened by the irate and raised voice of the brigadier, entered the room carrying a map case. 'What have you to report?' the brigadier shot at him.

'Nothing, sir, all is quiet,' replied Chris, giving a most convincing impression that he had just returned from a most difficult and dangerous reconnaissance.

'I thought as much,' replied the brigadier, and left the room.

Chris returned to the Land of Dreams.

At dawn the next day B Squadron crossed the newly constructed bridge, and in the afternoon A Squadron, in support of 158th Brigade, attacked across the second river obstacle to capture the woods on the other side. Owing to the nature of the ground, the tanks had to use the only road, but the infantry infiltrated forward through the woods. Thanks to James Cagney and Dick Langford, who rushed their troops up the road with the help of a smokescreen put down by A Squadron, the infantry had tank support in the woods as soon as they reached their objective. 1 Troop actually reached the objective well in advance of the infantry, and when the smokescreen cleared they found themselves in the middle of a German infantry position. They spent a very hectic half-hour protecting themselves against the German bazooka teams, and their discomfort was increased when our infantry requested that there should be a repeat of the artillery barrage on the objective for the last stage of the attack. The German company commander who was captured told me that he was extremely impressed with the way that British tanks fought in the midst of their own artillery barrage. I did not disillusion him.

In this area all the local population, obviously having been subjected to propaganda, were extremely scared that they would be exterminated; when Bill Enderby, after spending the night in the house of an old man, shook him by the hand when saying goodbye, he burst into tears.

22

From the Rhine to Victory

The Rhine Crossing.

MOST OF THE GERMANS had now retreated across the Rhine and it became very obvious that the next operation would be the crossing of the river, and this was very soon confirmed by the corps commander, who told me that the Regiment would take part and that the operation was to be called PLUNDER.

By the second week of March, the area to the west of the Rhine had been cleared of German resistance in 21st Army Group's sector. Some 50,000 troops had been taken prisoner in recent weeks; almost as many again had been killed or wounded. The last big obstacle facing the Allies was the giant river Rhine, the guardian of the Reich, and now brought up on the far side was the Panzer Lehr, the Sherwood Rangers' old enemy from the bitter battles around Tilly and Point 102 in Normandy. Crossing the

Rhine was a huge undertaking as it was 400 to 500 yards wide and
had currents of some three and a half knots. There was also the resistance
on the far side to consider. Even so, the planning for PLUNDER was
excessive, although with the war so nearly over, caution was creeping in
at every level. Further south the Americans had already crossed the Rhine
at Remagen and had established a bridgehead, which had drawn off
German troops; intelligence suggested that the defence opposite the 21st
Army Group assault would be weak. In all, PLUNDER involved 32,000
vehicles and the bringing up of some 118,000 tons of stores. Overhead,
10,000 aircraft were supporting the operation, while to assist with
bridging and enemy obstacles, no less than 8000 engineers had been
assembled. As if that was not enough, the crossings themselves were
supported by 3500 artillery guns (there had been fewer than 900 at
Alamein).

I was relieved to hear that the Staffordshire Yeomanry had been
selected to swim the river in their DD tanks and that we would cross
after the engineers had constructed a pontoon bridge. The
Staffordshire Yeomanry for this operation once again joined the 8th
Armoured Brigade.

On 26 March the Regiment crossed the Rhine as a reserve
armoured regiment, supporting the 51st Highland Division. The
Staffordshire Yeomanry swam the river in its tanks, but encountered
considerable difficulty owing to the steepness of the mud banks on the
far side, but it did well to get so many tanks across.

The Staffordshire Yeomanry had become something of a specialist
DD tank regiment, as they had used these tanks to make a seven-mile
crossing of the river Scheldt estuary in Holland on 26 October. Incredibly,
this was not only the longest 'swim' ever attempted by tanks, it was also
without a single loss. The greatest difficulty had been getting ashore
through the mud: 14 became completely bogged down and in the end
only four were available for action. They were in action again during
PLUNDER, and DD tanks were also used by two American armoured
battalions in the same operation. This time they were given special mats

to help them clamber up the banks on the far side and, broadly speaking, it was pretty successful.

On the far side B Squadron went into action first with the 1st Black Watch to capture a small village south of Isselburg, and then transferred to the 2nd Seaforths to take Isselburg. For a week the Regiment fought with various battalions of the 51st Highland Division centring mostly around Isselburg and Dinxperlo. Our object was to break a hole in the enemy line to enable the Guards Armoured Division to 'swan' through and exploit the success of our attack. Somehow it always appeared that the 8th Armoured Brigade was detailed for the hole-making and the Guards Armoured for the more pleasant swanning part of the operation.

Stanley's gripe was not entirely misplaced: 8th Armoured Brigade had a reputation that was second to none and the Sherwood Rangers had already gained more battle honours than any other single armoured unit since the D-Day landings. There was no question that, as an independent brigade, they were used for fire-fighting and were given a greater share of the action than had they been part of an armoured division. The trouble was they were, in many ways, victims of their own success, highly adept at operating with infantry and, to some extent, nursing less experienced units too. It was all too easy for General Horrocks, the XXX Corps commander, to call upon them time and again because their record was so proven. Every general wanted the task before them completed as quickly and successfully as possible; 8th Armoured Brigade and the Sherwood Rangers had earned the reputation to be the ones to deliver that.

I recall so well, after the fall of Dinxperlo, hearing one Sherwood Ranger Tank commander shout to a very dignified Guards officer sitting in the turret of his tank, 'Mind your paint, sir, as you go through,' in reply to which he received a very cold stare. A Squadron and the 5th Seaforths eventually captured the latter place after very stiff fighting on the outskirts. Before they finally entered, the infantry insisted on a very heavy artillery concentration on the town itself, which I knew from my patrol reports had been evacuated by the Germans, and this caused unnecessarily extensive damage to a Dutch town, which could have been avoided.

Since the war in the desert, the Allies had come increasingly to use and rely upon their superiority in fire-power. Both British and American commanders were deeply conscious of the need to preserve the lives of their men as far as possible. If there was ever a choice between risking the lives of their men or destroying a building, village or town, they would invariably opt to save the former. Sometimes, such as in the bombing of Caen, or at Dinxperlo, there was an over-dependence on fire-power and a willingness to see it as some kind of cure-all. In this case, it seems over-caution had taken root; at this stage of the war, with the end very much in sight and with casualties continuing to rise, it is perhaps understandable, however misplaced.

The Autobahn running at right angles to the axis was allocated to A Squadron as an objective, and which it captured without undue difficulty. The whole area was littered with mines, and great credit must go to Dick Holman, who dismounted from his tank and lifted the mines himself as no engineers were available. During the early morning of the 28th, the whole Regiment, and in particular A Squadron, suffered a severe blow when Sergeant Major Hutchinson, A Squadron sergeant major, was killed when a tank, behind which he was walking, blew up on a mine. During the whole time that I commanded A Squadron he was my squadron sergeant major, to which rank he had worked up from a trooper. In civilian life, a yeoman farmer, he was a true representative of the English yeoman stock, which throughout history made England so great. I knew only too well that I had lost a very sincere friend, with whom I had shared so much through the years of war. Neville Fearn was also wounded when the mine exploded and he had to be evacuated.

On 1 April once again the pursuit battle started and we proceeded north as a regimental group with our battery guns from the Essex Yeomanry under Chris Sidgewick and our company of infantry from the 12/60th under Derek Colls. I also had under command a squadron of Kangaroos (armoured infantry carriers) with a company of the 4th Wilts. We reached Ruurlo without opposition, except for two 88mm mobile guns, which fired at the column from the right flank. Both were knocked out by Sergeant Lanes. Beyond Ruurlo, the Recce Troop discovered a viaduct held by a rear-guard. A Squadron and the 4th Wilts went into action and eliminated the trouble. Unfortunately Sergeant O'Pray and all his crew were killed when his tank was hit at very close range by a bazooka. At this stage, the Germans appeared to lack anti-tank guns and tanks, but most of the German infantry were armed with bazookas, which could do just as much damage to a tank as an anti-tank gun.

On 2 April quite a formidable battle developed before Enschede was captured. Three battalions of infantry had to be used, but fortunately casualties were extremely light.

The Regiment spent a few days in a delightful Dutch town called Hengelo. We all lived in various houses in the town and received the greatest hospitality from the people. Jack Holman set himself up in a large house that belonged to a collaborator, who had been imprisoned by the Dutch partisans. He had an extremely attractive daughter, which may have been the reason for Jack having selected that particular house. One morning the partisans called and took her away. They returned after a few hours with her head completely shaved, which frequently happened to girls who had shown favours to the Germans during the occupation. I think Jack was rather upset as he told me that she had such lovely hair.

Stuart Hills celebrated his 21st birthday while we were at Hengelo with a party given by Regimental Headquarters officers. He was presented with a rocket which had been made by the fitters in recognition of the numerous ones that he had received from the adjutant, and a cheque for £10 collected by the officers of the Regiment.

I stayed in the house of an architect and his wife, who made me most comfortable and presented me with a picture of the whole family when we left.

Peter Kent joined the Regiment, and I appointed him IO in place of Denis EImore, who returned to a sabre squadron as a troop leader. Peter was a German with Jewish parentage on one side of his family and, as a result, his family suffered brutalities from the Germans before the war. I think that his father had been shot by the SS, which made Peter leave Germany and find work in England, and become naturalized under a changed name. He was actually interned in England at the beginning of the war before his naturalization papers came through, but eventually went to Sandhurst and was commissioned. Naturally he spoke English and German fluently, and proved himself most useful as an intelligence officer. Although the war was approaching an end, I always had a dread that he might be captured, which I think he shared.

Leslie Raeder also joined the Regiment at this time. He was an American who had spent most of his time in England. He had been captured in Crete while fighting with the RTR, escaped into Switzerland, where he spent a sumptuous three months, and eventually found his way back to England and applied to come to the Sherwood Rangers. He was something of a linguist, a versatile musician, a magnificent scrounger and possessed 'Taurocorprology' to a great degree.

On 9 April, the Regiment moved from Hengelo with many regrets, and I am convinced that the kindly people of that town were sad when we bade them farewell; in memory of our stay the main street of the town was renamed after the Regiment.

It was bitterly cold in the early morning as we passed through Oldenzall, Denekamp and Nordhorn. Progress was slow owing to the extensive demolitions. Strangely enough we suddenly found a B Squadron tank, which had been captured by the Germans in Goch. The turret had been taken off and it had been converted into a command vehicle. We spent the night of the 9th at Lingen where I found a most picturesque old farmhouse, which I made my headquarters.

Arthur Phayre came to say goodbye as he was giving up command of the Essex Yeomanry to become CRA of the 11th Armoured Division. He felt sad at leaving the Essex Yeomanry, having commanded it since D-Day, but the appointment meant promotion, which for him as a regular soldier was important. When he arrived I was wearing a new black beret, which had just arrived from Herbert Johnson's in London, and he had the impudence to tell me that I looked like the Bishop of Southwark!

On 11 April, the advance continued northwards, supporting 130 Brigade. Soon after passing through Haselünne which had been captured by another brigade, B Squadron bumped a roadblock. Hubert Beddington, whose troop was in the lead, dismounted to examine the obstacle, immediately came under shellfire and was wounded, with three members of his crew. Lieutenant Hunt, who joined the Regiment during the previous week, was killed when his tank was knocked out. Roger Gilliet, who commanded the carrier platoon of our company of 12/60th, extricated the crew from the burning tank with complete disregard for his own personal safety. He certainly saved their lives.

Lastrup, the next village through which we passed, was reported clear of enemy, so Corporal Morgan swanked through to the centre of the village and had a rude shock when he was fired on. It was quite impossible to reverse, so he gave the order 'Full speed ahead' to his driver, and his tank thundered down the street, and after taking a right-angled corner at approximately 35 m.p.h., he completed a circle and rejoined A Squadron on the outskirts, having run a gauntlet of fire throughout his journey.

He was most fortunate not to have been hit. Sergeant Budner's tank was hit when the village was attacked and unfortunately he was killed – another highly trained and excellent tank commander.

While A Squadron attacked, Regimental Headquarters and C Squadron plus a company of the 12/60th undertook a left hook in order to cut the road north of Lastrup. The going was excellent owing to the flat country and hard ground, and once again desert formation was used. At this stage the maps that had been issued were not very accurate, and this was not surprising in view of our rapid advance, which had exceeded all expectations. On this left hook we lost ourselves completely, and on the wireless there were continual arguments regarding the presence of thick woods and features that were not marked on the map. We all kept referring to Chris Sidgewick on the assumption that as a gunner he should possess a greater knowledge of map-reading. Chris became somewhat irritated about these continued demands on his intelligence, and being equally unaware about our location abruptly ended the wireless conversation with the words: 'For all I know we may be in Burma.' Eventually we struck the main road and, after a short wait, we were rejoined by A Squadron, and the advance continued.

A scout car with Infantry Brigade markings suddenly dashed up the road and passed A Squadron's leading tank. By shouting and waving an attempt was made to stop it, but without success, and it was last seen travelling at great speed into country not yet cleared of enemy. Ronnie Hutton in the leading squadron made one of his classic remarks on the wireless, when he reported with a strong Irish accent, 'Brigade scout car has now passed my leading tank heading into enemy country – all sorts of good luck to him.'

On 13 April the regimental group advanced on the town of Cloppenburg; progress was slow owing to the hastily constructed roadblocks, consisting mostly of trees felled across the road, which were covered by infantry making their removal difficult and tedious. On reaching the town, the 12/60th sent in a patrol, which discovered that the place was lightly held on the southern part of the river but strongly held in the northern sector.

Stanley's diaries include a report about the capture of Cloppenburg written by Terry Leinster of B Squadron. 'On the 13th B Squadron attacked Cloppenburg with a battalion of infantry. This was defended by paratroops who had destroyed the bridges over the stream running through the town and had also blown large craters in the streets. Cpl McGregor, in command of the regimental armoured bulldozer, did good work in filling in these holes after a false start, in which he optimistically tried to push in front of him a building the size of a town hall: this showed great confidence in his equipment. One of the bridges was not entirely destroyed and Lt Reed was able to take his troop over, along with a company of infantry. On the far bank Sgt Maslin, Sgt Wheeler, Cpl

MacDonald and himself had a lengthy, trying, but eminently successful struggle against obstinate opposition of a type very difficult to deal with. Cpl McDonald, from Hull, relieved the strain when he announced to the world in general over the wireless, "Every time I put my loaf out for a shufti some blanker draws a bead on me. I'm getting reet fed up with it." For the sake of the conscientious German listener-in who is still trying to decode this, we can say that translated it means, "Every time I put my head out for a look round, someone shoots at me."'

The difficulties of town fighting for tanks were well illustrated when Lieutenant Reed, after a hazardous foot journey to find a platoon commander, called on the air to Corporal McDonald to tell him that our infantry were in the 'third house from the left' but were held up by Germans in the 'fourth house from the left', and wanted this 'fourth house' knocked down. Could Corporal McDonald from his present position do it with his big gun? Corporal McDonald put his 'loaf' out for another 'shufti' and replied that he could see the 'third house' but the 'fourth house' seemed to be round the corner from him. Should he try a shoot? Next followed some cross-talk as to which was the 'third house' and where you started to count from anyway, and the dozens of listeners on the regimental wireless net began to feel some concern for the immediate future of our infantry in the 'third house'.

There were under our command some special tanks, which threw a huge bomb called a 'Flying Dustbin', capable of demolishing several houses at once, and their commander, a most enthusiastic dustbin-hurler, now came on the air to suggest he might try a shoot. A shudder ran through the entire regimental group among listeners far back to the rear echelons, as pained imaginations pictured this enthusiast destroying a score or two of houses on the principle that one would be the 'fourth house from the left'.

All this worry was quite unnecessary as Lieutenant Reed had the situation well in hand, the 'fourth house' was duly demolished and the grateful infantry emerged smartly from the 'third house' to continue their advance.

In the evening Lieutenant Hyde's troop had a very dirty hour in the eastern end of the town, and some gallant men were lost in trying to rescue comrades. We were all saddened as we pulled back to a farm to rest and refit.

Sergeant Sage, one of the Regiment's oldest and best tank commanders, was killed during the Battle of Cloppenburg.

From 14 to 18 April the Regiment enjoyed a short and much-needed respite as everybody was short of sleep. Further awards came through: mentioned in despatches, Padre Skinner; Dr Hylda Young, Roger Nelthorpe, Bill Mason the quarter master, Bill Wharton, Keith Douglas, Sergeant Holland, TQMS Montague, AQMS North, and *le Croix de Guerre*, Terry Leinster and Sergeant Needham.

Chris Sidgewick was most annoyed – and justifiably – when, after one day of rest he was ordered to take his battery of guns to support the 3rd British Division in a minor attack.

I paid a visit to the Guards Armoured Brigade to inspect some of its tanks to which it had attached Typhoon rockets as an experiment. I was most agreeably surprised to find that Jimmy Priestley was the squadron leader. I knew him from school, and had seen him so frequently during the pre-war days. He told me that his squadron had used the rockets in anger on several occasions, and that the alarming noise they made when released produced a most demoralizing effect, and that the explosion on impact wrought devastating damage. The problem of aiming had not been overcome at that stage, and as the rockets were fixed on the turret of the tank without any means of elevation or traverse, the only method of aiming was simply to point the tank towards the target, which of course produced no degree of accuracy. Jimmy promised to send me the results of their further experiments.

The English press now began to speak freely about the war in Europe being almost at an end, which was somewhat irritating in view of the continued casualties the Regiment was suffering.

Continually we came across slave workers or displaced personnel of all nationalities, who were now wandering aimlessly around, and it became most obvious that their repatriation would present a grave problem.

*

On the 18th the next operation commenced with the 9th Brigade of the 3rd British Division, which entailed advancing on Bremen, capturing certain objectives en route, and clearing certain of the southern suburbs. Fighting with the 3rd British Division meant that we had supported every British infantry division in the Second Army, and in addition three American divisions. Chris Sidgewick rejoined the Regiment with his battery of guns in time for the battle. He told me that he had had a trying time in that the battalion commander, to whom he had been attached, insisted on establishing his headquarters in an open field instead of in any one of the numerous farmhouses. Such action he considered thoroughly perverse.

Until the 21st we fought in an area a few thousand yards south of Bremen, taking several villages, including Karlshoffen.

Denis Elmore was killed during this fighting when he took the lead through a village, after his leading tank had been damaged. This was his first battle as a troop leader once again, after spending some considerable time as regimental intelligence officer. After joining the Regiment at a very young age, previous to D-Day, he was wounded during the fighting in Normandy, but rejoined after he had recovered. Denis was a delightful boy with rather a reserved nature and a most reliable troop leader. He was our last officer casualty of the war. After having worked as my IO before the arrival of Peter Kent I came to know him so well. His very great friend Stuart Hills – they had joined the Regiment together and previously had been exact contemporaries at Tonbridge – was naturally most distressed about his death. They were inseparable. I could appreciate his feeling so well.

Stuart Hills was in a state of shock and extreme grief and spent hours wandering about and weeping copiously. He was only just 21 and had managed to keep going through all the fighting and losses of friends and comrades. 'But this loss was much more difficult to cope with,' he wrote later, 'because it was so unexpected and so unfairly near to the end of hostilities.'

On some occasions the opposition still remained fanatical, but generally we found that the Germans were only too ready to surrender when we came to close quarters. Mines in the roads and booby traps in the houses were most prevalent. Even sea mines were used under the roads, which were generally set with a time fuse, resulting in the mine exploding after several vehicles had passed over. Never shall I forget a 'Kangaroo', an armoured troop-carrying vehicle with tracks, travelling in front of my tank, blowing up on a sea mine placed under a bridge and completely disintegrating. Nothing, absolutely nothing, remained of the vehicle and not a trace of a man was ever found. Fortunately, Robin Hood – my tank – was not travelling immediately on the tail of the Kangaroo when the explosion occurred, the blast of which almost knocked me unconscious.

German gunboats in the Bremen harbour shelled us periodically without inflicting any casualties.

On 26 April the Regiment attacked the northern sector of Bremen, supporting 130th Brigade of 43rd Division. A Squadron was with the 5th Wilts and B Squadron the 4th Wilts, while the 32nd Lowland Division attacked the southern section of the city. Later C Squadron joined in by passing through A Squadron with the 7th Somersets. Some rather unpleasant street fighting took place, which during the evening became rather confused when A and C Squadrons exchanged a few shots. Both blamed the other, but fortunately no damage was done. The city eventually fell on the 27th and John Talbot actually captured General Becker, the German commander of the Bremen garrison. Ian McKay, B Squadron leader, who was present at the time, took possession of his car, revolver and binoculars, but was extremely irritated when the general broke the glass of his binoculars before handing them over. Ian had a most fortunate escape in Bremen while holding a conference with the infantry company commander, standing at a crossroads. The whole party was fired on by a machine-gun at very close range. Three of the party were killed, including the company commander, but Ian managed to dive into a ditch and crawl to safety.

The dock area of Bremen was completely demolished, but in the suburbs, where the rich lived, we found some beautiful mansions, a number of which were completely undamaged. In several of the houses we discovered that entire families had committed suicide, including the mayor, his wife and three children. The Russian slave workers in the dock area soon ran amok and killed a considerable number of Germans.

On the evening of the 28th, after Bremen had fallen, Chris Sidgewick attended a party given by the sergeants of his battery, and somewhat naturally after having been most liberally entertained with food and wine he was quite unable to locate Regimental Headquarters. He therefore drove up to the largest house and demanded shelter from rather an astonished German house-frau [*sic*], and after having given instructions that he should be woken at 6 o'clock, retired to bed. The next morning, much to his surprise, he found himself in a sumptuous and vast golden double bed, and not having a very clear picture regarding his activities on the previous evening it took him some considerable time to adjust himself to his exotic surroundings.

On 29 April the Regiment advanced north again with 130th Brigade, passing through Osterholz, Bassen and north-west to Quelhorn and Bucholz, where we once again met opposition. Sergeant Webb's tank was hit by a bazooka, but fortunately the reinforced plating in the front saved it and prevented any damage to the crew. The shot was fired by a German officer, who was exterminated with the rest of the section by Sergeant Webb.

In Bucholz, the civilians told us that a German officer had shot nine of his soldiers for wishing to surrender. The civilians had tried to lynch the officer, but he had escaped.

On the following day we passed through Harpstedt, Tarmstedt, Bedhamm and Hanstedt, which we captured practically without opposition, except for the occasional sniper, slight shelling and numerous mines. A Squadron captured Rhade on the following day, when Sergeant Markham, the senior fitter in the squadron was wounded in the foot during a bout of shelling. Being a chauffeur to Lord Yarborough, he naturally joined the Yeomanry, and when the

Regiment was mechanized became a fitter to A Squadron. While I commanded A Squadron, well can I remember his amazing capacity for keeping tanks on the road.

On 2 May, the Regiment suffered the last casualty of the war, unfortunately fatal. Trooper Carter of Al Echelon directed a Military Policeman to a small hamlet, which he had discovered in the wood, containing a few armed Germans. A sniper killed them both.

Progress was extremely slow owing to the extensive demolitions and craters in the road and five Bailey bridges were required to span one crater.

The brigade was the first to liberate the Sandbostel concentration camp, which was situated in the neighbourhood. Our light field ambulance did some magnificent work for the inmates. The brigadier took photographs of this camp, which clearly illustrate that the reports on German horror camps were not exaggerated. The brigade sent off six lorries from each regiment with food and clothing. Most of the inmates appeared to be political prisoners, a large percentage of whom could never survive owing to their pitiable condition. On 4 May the Regiment, led by B Squadron, crossed the Hamme Canal, and Regimental Headquarters moved to Karlshoffen and we established ourselves in a most picturesque old farmhouse, which had been spared damage.

Soon after arrival our old friend 'Von Thoma' – commander of 43rd Division – paid us an unexpected visit and gave me details regarding the next operation, which was to be the capture of Bremerhaven. He told me that once again we should be supporting his division.

That evening I was summoned to Robin Hood, my tank, where I was told that an important message from Brigade awaited me. Sergeant Pick handed me a piece of paper and said, 'This message has just come over the air from Brigade Headquarters.' I noticed that his face was slightly flushed, and that he had difficulty in controlling his excitement.

The message had been taken down on a piece of scrap paper torn from a German exercise book, which the operator had been using to take down rough messages and the text had not been transferred onto an official message form, which slightly irritated me because I had difficulty in reading the scrawl of my rear-link operator. However, I appreciated the reason after I had grasped the full significance of the message:

No advance beyond present positions Stop No further harassing fire Stop No further tactical move unless ordered Stop BBC News Flash confirmed Stop German Army on 21 Army Group Front surrenders WEF 08.00 hrs 5 May 1945 Stop Details as to procedure later Stop

It meant that the war in Europe was over. For the last few weeks we had known that the end must be near, but the receipt of this signal at a time when I was planning my orders for the attack on Bremerhaven, and after having been in action on the previous day, came as a complete surprise. My first reaction was a feeling of profound relief, followed by indescribable exhilaration, and finally a sorrowful longing for those special friends, no longer with us, with whom I wished to share this moment.

The confirmation of the message arrived an hour later by DR from Brigadier Coad, whose brigade we had been supporting for the last fortnight, and he concluded: 'The Brigade Commander wishes to say that 130 Brigade has led 43 Division for the last 14 days and considers that we have done our stuff to contribute to this victory.'

That evening the British Army went mad. Multi-coloured Verey lights and rockets were fired into the air and the sweeping beams from the artificial moonlight illuminated the sky throughout the night.

I immediately sent a signal to Brigadier Coad requesting his company for a drink. After an hour a 'very happy' IO arrived from 130 Brigade Headquarters and informed me that his brigadier was missing but that a search party had been instigated to look under every table, and that with the help of the brigade staff, he had every hope that Daddy Coad would be found provided that they looked under a sufficient number of tables; in the meantime on behalf of his brigadier and himself he would like to drink the health of my regiment and his brigade.

Thanks to the 51st Highland Division, we had a large stock of champagne in the mess truck, which was immediately brought up by Sergeant Marshall. At Regimental Headquarters we joined in a sing-song, which was led by Ward with his accordion and Sergeant Jacques, who conducted the singing. I retired to bed at a comparatively early hour, finding it difficult to fully realize that the war in Europe had been won.

The following day we remained in the same location and we had a constant stream of visitors from Brigade Headquarters, the Essex Yeomanry and the 12/60th, who all came to celebrate. That evening I dined at the headquarters of the 12/60th. After dinner, having found an ancient golf club and one golf ball, we made up a couple of teams, and played a game of golf. The holes consisted of hitting trees, dropping into a water tower, chipping into a bucket and finally hitting the mess sergeant's left leg.

The following day 6 May, Von Thoma held a conference of all COs in the division. As usual he chose the middle of the field in preference to a house, where he pitched his tent which had no side screens, and owing to the rain we all got very wet. He told us first of all the German troops on our immediate front had to be disarmed and the SS had to be segregated from the Wehrmacht, and this would be followed by the gradual demobilization of the German Army, after which proper occupational duties would commence.

It appeared that the brigade would be split up so that each division would have an armoured regiment, which would mean that the Essex Yeomanry and 12/60th would once again operate as a complete unit and that Chris Sidgewick and Derek Colls would leave the Regiment. Such a thought was most disconcerting and depressing as, having fought so long with us, they had become part of the Regiment.

The prime minister made a most impressive speech to the nation over the wireless, which we picked up on the tank sets and in which he nominated the 8 May as VE Day. Monty sent his final message, which had to be read out to all ranks. I had so often wondered during the war when I read all his messages, which he invariably issued before or at the end of a major battle, when and where he would issue his final message of the war. At last it had arrived.

Postscript

James Holland

AFTER THE INITIAL celebrations and a victory parade before General Horrocks through Bremenhaven, the Sherwood Rangers were posted to Hannover. Their task there was to guard the many displaced-persons camps, still full of former slave labourers who had been working in the city's war factories. When the Sherwood Rangers arrived, there had been much looting, killing and raping of Germans by the mostly Polish and Russian DPs. Stanley set himself up in a comfortable house in a village just outside the city, then organized the Regiment so that each squadron was responsible for two or three camps. 'Roger Nelthorpe,' Stanley noted, 'discovered that as well as three DP camps he had a nudist camp in his area. He asked for instructions, to which I replied that the matter rested entirely with his discretion, but I forbade any Sherwood Ranger to join the camp!'

In June, the Regiment moved again, this time to Magdeburg. Soon after their arrival, a new bridge over the Elbe was completed, called the Bridge of Friendship; the far side was the Russian zone, so an elaborate ceremony was arranged for the opening. One squadron of the Sherwood Rangers took their place in the British Guard of Honour, which was immaculately turned out and performed its task to the letter. The same could not be said of the Russians. This was the first time Stanley had come into contact with the Soviet allies, and he was appalled. The Russian Guard of Honour was three-quarters of an hour late, and had 'no march discipline, no uniformity in their arms or uniforms – they were ill-assorted and uneducated humans'. Stanley asked his German interpreter, who had seen action on the Eastern Front, how Germany had lost to 'this rabble'.

'Because our lines of communication were too long,' he told Stanley, 'and because, in spite of our killing thousands until we ran out of ammunition, they still came in hordes.'

During their time in Magdeburg, Stanley and Basil Ringrose also visited Belsen, to the north of Berlin:

All the wooden huts, which had originally housed the inmates, mostly political prisoners [he wrote] had been burned down and they were now living in the SS barracks, which had been converted into a hospital, receiving proper medical attention and regular food supplies. We toured the various wards filled with patients riddled with typhus. Bones and skeletons without an ounce of flesh were all that remained of a once normally healthy person. It appeared inconceivable that a human being so wasted away could survive even for a day. At that time 200 were dying a day, and twice a week they buried the dead in communal graves, containing up to 30 bodies. No names appeared over the graves, just a simple wooden cross with such words as 'Here lie 20 Poles.' We arrived at the conclusion of one of these mass burials, and never have I witnessed such a pitiful and distressing sight.

We were conducted around by a young German Jewess, an inmate of Belsen, good-looking, intelligent and speaking perfect English. With her family she had been interned for publishing subversive literature. Her parents had been killed and she had been moved to Belsen, a camp she described as meaning slow but certain extermination. To my question how it was that she appeared so healthy in comparison to the other inmates, she replied that, being a musician, she had managed to join the Belsen orchestra, which entertained the German guards, and as a result extra food was allowed. 'Music,' she said, 'has saved my life by enabling me to keep my self-respect. In Belsen the loss of self-respect hastens the loss of your life.'

Towards the end of June, Stanley also visited Berlin with Derrick Warwick and spent a couple of nights with Myles Hildyard, who was now on the staff of 7th Armoured Division and gave them a tour of the ruins of the German capital. They visited Hitler's bunker, the remains of the Reich Chancellory (where Stanley managed to smuggle a silver vase past the Russian guards), and also the Air Ministry. Here Stanley picked up a number of photographs of Göring and other prominent Nazis – souvenirs that have survived.

In July, the Regiment moved to Einbeck and provided guard duty to General Horrocks; it was considered a notable honour. Yet while they were there Stanley received the news that the Regiment was to lose its tanks. Thus, at the end of September, they returned to Hannover as a dismounted regiment. The break-up of the Regiment was to follow soon after: on 2 February 1946, Field Marshal Montgomery wrote personally to Stanley to tell him the Sherwood Rangers were to be 'dispersed'. This took place on 1 March 1946.

Stanley's career with the Regiment was finally over. The Sherwood Rangers had left England in 1939 with their horses, sabres and little idea about modern soldiering, and had finished the war as one of the finest armoured units in the British Army. It was quite a journey for a local yeomanry outfit; there cannot have been many regiments that saw more action than they did throughout the whole of the war or were engaged in so many major battles. They were the first to enter Bayeux after D-Day, the first British troops into Germany, and during their time in north-west Europe they supported every single British infantry division and three American divisions, and were often specifically asked for by other formations. Between 1939 and 1945, the Sherwood Rangers amassed an astonishing 30 battle honours, 16 under Stanley's command, more than any other single unit in the entire British Army. And he was in the thick of it for all 30, collecting a Distinguished Service Order, two Military Crosses and a Silver Star, as well as being Mentioned in Despatches four times.

So ended my six years' soldiering with the Nottinghamshire (Sherwood Rangers) Yeomanry [noted Stanley], comprising

*Top left and right and bottom
left:* Pictures of Göring 'liberated'
from Hitler's Chancellery.
Bottom right: Einbeck, July 1945.

many moments of unforgettable thrills, intense fright and utter boredom. Six years is a considerable slice from a man's life and much valuable time had been wasted, but I have seen more of the world, I have made and lost many friends and I have discovered that there can be no greater comradeship, sincere unselfishness and spontaneous humour than that created through sharing danger and discomfort, thrills and happiness.

On one memorable day during the war, while I was endeavouring to make myself very small in a slit trench during a particularly unpleasant spell of shelling, feeling very wet, cold and frightened, I made three resolutions, which I determined to keep after the war – should I survive. First, never to be bored; second, never to be frightened again; and third, when slowly submerging into a steaming hot bath to say, 'Thank God for this Hot Bath – Amen.'

With the war finally over and the Sherwood Rangers disbanded, Stanley left the army and returned to South Africa, taking Stuart Hills with him; following in his father's footsteps, he worked for Consolidated Goldfields. Having had the best part of ten years out there, in which he worked and played hard, and established the Staggerers Cricket Club, he returned to England and took a job with stockbrokers Hoare & Co.

It was during this time that he met Cynthia Smith-Dorrien, already twice married and widowed once; she was worldly, glamorous and spoke four languages. They married in 1959, not in the smarter part of London where they had spent much time but at Stockwell in south London, at the church of Stanley's former padre, Leslie Skinner. Not long after, they bought a large house near Wye, in Kent, called Spring Grove, once owned by Joseph Conrad. In 1960, their daughter, Sara Jane, was born, followed by a son, David, two years later.

It seems that stockbroking never really suited Stanley. After a life of war, adventure and life as an expatriate, the commute from Kent every day to his City job must have seemed somewhat mundane, although he appears to have embraced it with his usual optimism. In the sixties, Hoare merged into Hoare Govett and Stanley left. A new venture beckoned: in 1965, David's pre-preparatory school closed and it occurred to the Christophersons that their large family home could offer a new business opportunity. While they lived in one half, the other became a new pre-preparatory school.

For the rest of his life, Stanley lived and worked at home, became a pillar of the local church and community, travelled and raised his children. He was greatly liked by all who knew him. 'He was so positive,' says his daughter, Sara Jane, 'that I never had the impression he found life mundane although you might expect him to have done so. He was naturally such an optimist that you felt, with him, that every day was a day to be enjoyed.' He died, as charming and affable as ever, in 1990, but with Sara Jane and David knowing, or understanding, little about his remarkable wartime career. Like so many of his generation, it was something he mentioned only very rarely and even then it was usually to recount some amusing mishap.

Sara Jane and David knew more about their mother's war: that she had joined the ATS, had gone out to the Middle East and driven ambulances on the front line in the desert before being sent back to Cairo and becoming a driver for the general staff. There she had met Peter Smith-Dorrien, later blown up in the attack on the King David's Hotel in 1946.

The terrible things Stanley had witnessed, the appalling losses, the huge responsibilities he had borne, were never mentioned.

At Stanley's memorial service, the church at Wye was full to bursting – people had come from far and wide to pay their respects. 'That, for me,' says Sara Jane, 'was really the first time I became aware of what an extraordinary hero he was to the men who knew him and served with him. There was an incredible atmosphere among the congregation – they were really saying goodbye to a hero.'

Neither had the children ever been shown his large collection of photographs and film reels from the war. It was only some years later, when David began reading through his father's diaries, letters and papers that he learned the extent of Stanley's life with the Sherwood

Rangers. He began going to veterans' gatherings and even to the dedication of a Sherman tank at Gheel. 'I was always treated with a certain regard,' says David, 'yet I felt something of a bystander, looking on a world in which my father had been so involved.' As far as David had been concerned, his father was a man who was great fun, to whom he was very close, and with whom he laughed a great deal; a man who was always far more interested in other people than himself and who never lost his modesty or understated way of life. At the end of his life, he was driving around in an old Mini and still smoking his beloved pipe with Player's Three Nuns tobacco.

To David and Sara Jane, he was a father, not a soldier or war hero. 'I've met a part of Daddy through his diaries,' says David, 'that I never knew during his lifetime and it's such a juxtaposition with the man I knew and loved.'

There were, though, dark periods, when Stanley would retreat. At the time, Sara Jane and David had little understanding of why. It makes a lot more sense now. Of all those officers in the Sherwood Rangers Yeomanry who had headed off to war with their chargers back in 1939, only two were still with the Regiment on VE Day. One was Roger Sutton-Nelthorpe, and the other was Stanley. Every single other officer had either been killed, wounded or moved on or, like John Semken, had finally cracked under the strain in the final months of the war. Few today appreciate the huge casualties among those fighting at the front: while it is true that there were fewer British troops at the sharp end in the Second World War compared with the First, the rate of casualties was as high and often even worse. For tank crews, the chance of not being hit was almost nil; survival was usually down to luck.

There are few wartime veterans of the Sherwood Rangers left. Of those I spoke to, two had been officers and two other ranks, but it was striking how all four had nothing but praise for Stanley, as a person and as a commander. 'Stanley was a very, very wonderful man,' said John Semken, almost the moment we sat down to speak. 'How that man wrote all those letters of condolence without tearing his heart out, I just don't know, because he was a very sensitive man. Every commander does feel the casualties – you did suffer very deeply. The Regiment had a very, very rough passage.'

One of the Sherwood Rangers' misfortunes was be part of an independent brigade. This mattered less in North Africa, but by the time of the Normandy invasion, when manpower was becoming such an issue for the British, it mattered a great deal more. 'The curse of it was,' says John Semken, 'that the Regiment was used as an armoured brigade, usually in support of the infantry. This was why Stanley worked such a lot, because every battle that XXX Corps fought, we were sent off to support the infantry. We were simply never at rest.' The result, John Semken points out, was that Stanley was hardly running his own regiment but, rather, acting as a temporary supply agent in which he was always outranked by the brigadier or general to whom the Regiment was attached.

John says that at one point during the Normandy campaign, the doctor told the brigadier the Regiment was suffering from exhaustion and was no longer fit to fight. They were stood down for a day, then went straight back into action. 'I was called into conference with Stanley, who was as bright as a button and said, "Well, chaps, we've just got to do another Balaclava charge and then we'll pull out."' After the attack, they pulled into a field beside a medium artillery regiment and slept the rest of the night and the following day. 'We heard not a thing from all the guns firing repeatedly.'

There is no doubt that Stanley depended on all his friends in the Regiment and when any died he took the loss personally. His closest friend was unquestionably Stephen Mitchell, with whom he had been together since joining the Regiment in 1939. After taking command, it was to Stephen that Stanley turned for solace and comfort; new officers were coming into the Regiment so rapidly by this stage that it was hard to get to know any of them really well. When Stephen left the Regiment at the end of 1944, it must have been a big blow. Thereafter, says John Semken, 'he lived through this, completely isolated, coping with all these bloody infantry generals and brigadiers' on his own. His task was to keep the Regiment going in the face of horrendous losses, despite demands on it that were beyond what should reasonably have

Stanley, 1946.

been expected. Somehow, he managed to continue to lead by example, to appear unceasingly cheerful and optimistic, and still write far too many letters of condolence to grieving wives, parents and families. The only real shoulder he had to lean on was that of the padre, Leslie Skinner – they would drink and write the letters together – and his faith, which was deep and a great source of comfort.

When Stanley died in 1990, Cynthia and the family were inundated with letters from his former wartime friends and colleagues. Reading them now, it is notable how highly he was regarded. Most mention his kindness, his leadership, his cheerfulness, even in times of great strain and difficulty. Dick Coleman wrote of his 'infectious good cheer', Mike Howden of his 'thoughtfulness and steady cheerfulness at all times'. To Basil Ringrose, he was 'a truly remarkable man and will always be remembered by the Regiment'. 'I know from experience,' wrote Derrick Warwick, 'how much the Regiment owes to his courage and leadership as squadron leader and as CO.' Julius Neave, an adjutant in 8th Armoured Brigade, said simply, 'He was a hero to us all.'

A short while after, in March that year, a memorial service was held at Nijmegen for General James Gavin, former commander of the 82nd Airborne, who had also recently died, and for Stanley. David Render, one of Stanley's troop leaders, wrote to Cynthia afterwards: 'Although initially it was set up for Gen. Gavin, I can assure you that more than half of it was for that No. 1 Sherwood Ranger, dear Stanley Christopherson.'

Glossary

2 i/c	second-in-command
AA	anti-aircraft
ack ack	slang for anti-aircraft
ADC	aide-de-camp
A/T	anti-tank
AP	armour piercing
AQMS	assistant quarter master sergeant
AVRE	armoured vehicle, Royal Engineers
Beaufort	a twin-engine torpedo bomber designed and built by the Bristol company. They saw extensive service in the Middle East.
Besa	Czech designed, British-built machine-gun used primarily in tanks and armoured vehicles
BOP	battery observation post
bully beef	tinned corned beef – a staple of British rations
CCS	casualty clearing station
CRA	commander, Royal Artillery
D&M	driving and maintenance
DAQMG	deputy assistant quarter master general
DCLI	Duke of Cornwall's Light Infantry
DCM	Distinguished Conduct Medal
DLI	Durham Light Infantry
doggo	slang, meaning 'lying low'
DR	dead reckoning
Echelon	vehicles supporting the fighting troops, and providing supplies, maintenance equipment, ammunition and food

ENSA ······· Entertainments National Service Association

FOO ········ forward observation officer

FOP ········ forward observation post

G3 ·········· or GSO 3: general staff officer; Grade 3 was the most junior staff officer

GOC ······· General Officer Commanding

HE ········· high explosive

HQ ········· headquarters

IC ·········· intercom

IO ··········· intelligence officer

'I' tank ······ infantry tank, directly supporting the infantry

KDG ······· King's Dragoon Guards

KRRC ······ King's Royal Rifle Corps

LCT ········ landing craft tank

LOB ········ left out of battle; always around 10 per cent of any single regiment or battalion

L of C ······· lines of communication

LRDG ······ Long Range Desert Group

MC ········· Military Cross

ME ········· Middle East

MET ········ mechanized transport

MEWTS ···· Middle East Weapon Training School

MM ········ Military Medal

M/T ········ motor transport

NAAFI ······ Navy, Army and Air Force Institutes

NCO ······· non-commissioned officer

NZ ········· New Zealand

OCTU ······ Officer Cadet Training Unit

OP ········· observation post

OR ·········· other rank, i.e., not an officer

OTC ········ officer training cadets

PMC ······· president of the mess committee

RAC · · · · · · · · Royal Armoured Corps

RAMC · · · · · · Royal Army Medical Corps

RAOC · · · · · · Royal Army Ordnance Corps

RAP · · · · · · · · regimental aid post

RASC · · · · · · · Royal Army Service Corps

RE · · · · · · · · · Royal Engineers

REME · · · · · · Royal Electrical and Mechanical Engineers

RGH · · · · · · · · Royal Gloucestershire Hussars

RHA · · · · · · · · Royal Horse Artillery

RHQ · · · · · · · regimental headquarters

RRO · · · · · · · · regimental ratting officer

RSM · · · · · · · · regimental sergeant major

RTO · · · · · · · · rail traffic officer

RTR · · · · · · · · Royal Tank Regiment

SC · · · · · · · · · · staff captain

SNOIC · · · · · · senior naval officer in charge

SP · · · · · · · · · · self-propelled

SQMS · · · · · · squadron quarter master sergeant

SRY · · · · · · · · Sherwood Rangers Yeomanry

SSM · · · · · · · · squadron sergeant major

TEWT · · · · · · tactical exercise without troops

TGR · · · · · · · · Tank Group Reinforcement

TJFF · · · · · · · · TransJordan Frontier Force

TQMS · · · · · · technical quarter master sergeant

U/S · · · · · · · · · unserviceable

WO · · · · · · · · War Office or warrant officer

YH · · · · · · · · · Yorkshire Hussars

Personalities

Ione Barclay · · · · · · · · · · · family friend

Malc Christopherson · · · · Stanley's cousin

Tony Farquhar · · · · · · · · · close friend from Winchester College

John Hanson-Lawson · · · · friend from Inns of Court

Freddie Luck · · · · · · · · · · · friend

Sydney Morse · · · · · · · · · · Regimental Adjutant

Clive Priday · · · · · · · · · · · Stanley's best friend from Winchester College

John Rowell · · · · · · · · · · · a friend from the Inns of Court, killed 27 May 1940 while with the Xth Hussars

David Steele

John Stormonth-Darling · friend

Derrick Christopherson · · Stanley's older brother

Bridget Christopherson · · Stanley's cousin

Pat Christopherson · · · · · · Stanley's cousin

Diana Pelham · · · · · · · · · · friend

Structure of the Sherwood Rangers Yeomanry on 6 June 1944

Regimental Headquarters, consisting of four tanks

Lieutenant Colonel J. D'A. Anderson · · commanding officer

Major Michael Laycock · · · · · · · · · · · · second-in-command

Captain George Jones · · · · · · · · · · · · · · adjutant

A Squadron, consisting of four HQ tanks and four troops each of three tanks

Major S. D. Christopherson · · · · · · · · · · squadron leader

Captain Keith Douglas · · · · · · · · · · · · · second-in-command

B Squadron, consisting of four HQ tanks and four troops each of three tanks

Major Michael Gold · · · · · · · · · · · · · · · squadron leader

Captain Peter Seleri · · · · · · · · · · · · · · · second-in-command

C Squadron, consisting of four HQ tanks and four troops each of three tanks

Major Stephen Mitchell · · · · · · · · · · · · squadron leader

Captain William Enderby · · · · · · · · · · · second-in-command

Reconnaissance Troop, consisting of two HQ light tanks, and three troops each of three tanks

Captain Patrick McCraith · · · · · · · · · · · troop leader

Captain Ian McKay · · · · · · · · · · · · · · · · second-in-command

Headquarters Squadron, consisting of all supply and repair vehicles

Major Roger Sutton-Nelthorpe ········ squadron leader

Captain Tony Gauntley ·············· second-in-command

APPENDIX II

A Note on Formations

To those unfamiliar with military terminology, the complexities of structure and organization can be confusing. In the Second World War, most troops, regardless of nationality, were divided into armies, corps, divisions, brigades, regiments and battalions. A force could be designated an 'army' if it consisted of two or more corps, whose number is always written in Roman numerals, e.g. XXX Corps, for 30 Corps. A corps had no great significance but was a contained force within an army, usually comprising at least two divisions, i.e., no less than 30,000 men.

Next down the scale was the division, made up from around 15,000 men. This was still a major tactical and administrative unit of the army, and within its structure contained all the various forms of arms and services necessary for sustained combat. Different divisions had different emphases, however. The fighting core of the infantry division was the infantry brigade, while the same for an armoured division was the armoured brigade.

An infantry brigade would also have attached service troops plus artillery and engineers, but at its heart would be three infantry battalions, consisting of four companies of 122 men plus a battalion headquarters. A full-strength infantry battalion would be 845 men.

An armoured brigade operated on the same basis, but there were a number of independent brigades, such as 8th Armoured, which came under direct control of the corps, rather than being attached to a particular division.

Structure of a Typical Armoured Regiment, like the Sherwood Rangers Yeomanry, in the Summer of 1944

Officers: 37
Other ranks: 655
Commanding officer: lieutenant colonel
Squadron: major
Troop: lieutenant or second lieutenant

Regimental Headquarters

Signal Troop (3 × 15-cwt trucks, 1 × 3-ton truck)
Light Aid Detachment REME (3 × 15-cwt trucks, 1 × half-track, 2 × 3-ton trucks, 2 × tractors)

HQ Squadron
 Administrative Troop (8 × motorbikes, 6 × Jeeps, 3 × 15-cwt trucks, 1 × 15-cwt water tanker, 3 × ambulance half-tracks, 2 × workshop half-tracks, 16 × 3-ton lorries)

 Recce Troop (11 × Stuart light tanks)

 Intercom. Troop (9 × Scout cars)

 Anti-aircraft Troop (8 × Crusader anti-aircraft tanks)

A Squadron
 Headquarters (1 × Jeep, 2 × Sherman tank, 1 × Sherman recovery, 1 × close-support Sherman)
 Administrative Troop (3 × half-tracks, 1 × 15-cwt water tanker, 1 × 15-cwt general service lorry, 12 × 3-ton lorries)
 Troops × 4 (3 × 75mm Sherman tanks, 1 × 17-pounder Sherman Firefly tank)

B Squadron

C Squadron

Acknowledgements

Editing Stanley Christopherson's wartime diaries has been a great privilege, but the task has been made considerably easier by the enormous help, support and enthusiasm shown by the Sherwood Rangers Yeomanry fraternity. I am indebted to Jonathan Hunt, Michael Brown, Murray Colville and especially Michael Elliott, who went through the manuscript with such painstaking attention to detail.

I am also very grateful to the surviving veterans who allowed me and Stanley's son, David, to visit them and hear their memories. David Render, Stan Cox and Bert Jenkins all provided fascinating insights into Stanley's leadership and to life in the Sherwood Rangers during the war. Especially helpful, however, was John Semken, who not only spoke to us at great length but also showed me a copy of his illustrated diary/photo album. His recollections and observations were both profound and deeply moving.

My thanks, as ever, go to all the team at Bantam Press, but especially to Bill Scott-Kerr, Phil Lord and Vivien Thompson. I would also like to especially thank Hazel Orme, for her outstanding work copy-editing the manuscript, which, with the vast number of names, both place and person, was no small task. Thanks, too, go to Fran Curtis at Black Sun for her help with the photographs and copying of various of Stanley's papers. I am also, as ever, hugely grateful to Patrick Walsh at Conville & Walsh, for all his help.

Finally, and most importantly, I would like to thank Stanley's son and daughter, David Christopherson and Sara Jane Grace. Both have been hugely supportive of this project from the outset, and David, particularly, has worked with me every step of the way. It has been an honour to spend so much time with their father, albeit his writings only. He was clearly an exceptional man, and my only regret is that I never had the chance to meet him myself.

Index

About the Authors

Stanley Christopherson was born in 1912 and trained to be a lawyer before joining the Sherwood Rangers in the autumn of 1939. Apart from two weeks in hospital, he experienced the Second World War on the Western Front in its entirety and watched as the very nature of war changed and evolved. In the North African campaign, he engaged in the Battles of Alam Halfa and El Alamein and the fall of Tunis. On D-Day he landed on the Gold Beach, before moving across France and Belgium and on to Holland where his regiment endured the terrible fighting in the aftermath of Operation MARKET GARDEN.

James Holland was born in Salisbury, Wiltshire, and studied history at Durham University. The author of the best-selling *Fortress Malta*, *Battle of Britain* and *Dam Busters*, he has also written nine works of historical fiction, five of which feature the heroic Jack Tanner, a soldier of the Second World War. He regularly appears on television and radio, and has written and presented a number of acclaimed documentaries for the BBC. He is Co-Founder and Programme Director of the Chalke Valley History Festival, has his own collection at the Imperial War Museum, and is a Fellow of the Royal Historical Society.